4th EDITION

Commercial Property

COMMERCIAL LINES COVERAGE GUIDE

Bruce J. Hillman, J.D.

Edited by Susan Massmann

The
**National
Underwriter**
Company

This publication is designed to provide accurate and authoritative information in regard to the subject matter covered. It is sold with the understanding that the publisher is not engaged in rendering legal, accounting, or other professional service. If legal advice or other expert assistance is required, the services of a competent professional person should be sought.— from a Declaration of Principles jointly adopted by a Committee of the American Bar Association and a Committee of Publishers and Associations.

International Standard Book Number: 978-0-87218-836-5
Library of Congress Control Number: 2009936503

Printed in the United States of America

Table of Contents

Introduction: The Building and Personal Property Coverage Form CP 00 10 1

Property Coverage Forms 2
ISO Rules 3
Underwriting 5
The National Underwriter Company Coverage Guides 6

Chapter 1: The Insuring Agreement; Covered and Not Covered Property 7

Section A. Coverage 7
Section A.1. Covered Property 9
Section A.2. Property Not Covered 26

Chapter 2: Additional Coverages, Coverage Extensions, and Optional Coverages 35

Section 4. Additional Coverages 36
Section 5. Coverage Extensions 43
Optional Coverages 50

Chapter 3: Covered Causes of Loss— Named Perils Forms.....57

CP 10 10—Causes of Loss—Basic Form 58
CP 10 20—Broad Form Causes of Loss 69
Exclusions that Apply to Both Named Perils
     Causes of Loss Forms 72
Subsection B.2. Exclusions...80
Special Exclusions 81
Additional Coverages 81

Chapter 4: Special Covered Causes of Loss Form (CP 10 30)..85

Similarities to Named Perils Forms.....................................86
Open Perils Exclusions—Section B.2. 87
Losses That Happen over Time—Section 2.d.(1) to (7) 88
Other Exclusions...93
Concurrent Causation Exclusions.......................................97
Special Exclusions 99
Limitations 100
Property Limited to Specified Causes of Loss 102
Additional Coverages and Limitation.................................104
Additional Coverage Extensions 104

Chapter 5: Conditions 107

Commercial Property General Conditions 107
Cancellation 107
Changes..108
Examination of Your Books and Records 108
Inspection and Surveys 108
Premiums 109
Transfer of Rights and Duties under This Policy 109
Commercial Property Policy Conditions 110
Concealment, Misrepresentation, or Fraud.........................110
Control of Property 111
Insurance under Two or More Coverages 112
Legal Action against Us 112
Liberalization 112
No Benefit to Bailee 112
Other Insurance..113
Policy Period, Coverage Territory.....................................113
Transfer of Rights of Recovery against Others to Us 113
Other Relevant Provisions of the Commercial
    Property Policy 114
Limits of Insurance 114
Deductible 114
Loss Conditions 117
Abandonment and Appraisal 117
The Insured's Duties in the Event of Loss 119
Loss Payment...121
Actual Cash Value Defined 122
Valuing Business Personal Property...................................123

Recovered Property...124
Vacancy...124
Valuation...125
Additional Conditions..127
Coinsurance..127
Mortgageholders 128

Chapter 6: Builders Risk 131

ISO Eligibility and Rules...132
Covered Property 134
Property Not Covered 135
Covered Causes of Loss 136
Additional Coverages 136
Coverage Extensions..136
Trees, Shrubs, and Plants...137
Limits of Insurance 137
Deductible 137
Loss Conditions 137
Additional Conditions..138
Builders Risk Coverage Options 140
Building Renovations 140
Builders' Risk Reporting Form 140
Separate or Subcontractors Interest 141
Collapse during Construction 141
Theft of Building Materials, Fixtures,
     Machinery, Equipment 141
Building Materials and Supplies of Others 142

Chapter 7: Business Income Coverage Forms.........................145

Coverage for Business Income 146
When Coverage Applies 147
Extra Expense 148
Extended Loss after Operations Resume...............................148
Blanket Coverage..149
ISO Simplified Business Income Program..............................149
Extra Expense 153
Covered Causes of Loss 153
Exclusions and Limitations..154
Additional Limitation 156
Additional Coverages 157

Civil Authority 157
Alterations and New Buildings.................................160
Extended Business Income 161
Interruption of Computer Operations 161
Expense to Reduce Loss 162
Coverage Extension 163
Limits of Insurance 164
Loss Conditions 164
Loss Determination..166
Other Loss Conditions 167
Coinsurance...168
Optional Coverages..169
Maximum Period of Indemnity 169
Monthly Limit of Indemnity..................................169
Agreed Value 170
Extended Period of Indemnity................................171
Extra Expense Insurance..172
Insured May Need Both...173
Extra Expense Coverage Form, CP 00 50 173
Causes of Loss 175
Additional Limitation—Interruption of
    Computer Operations 175
Coverage Extension and Additions 175
Limits 177
Other Insurance..178
Other Exposures..178
Ingress and Egress 178
Flood 179
Absence of Profits..179

Chapter 8: Other Coverage Forms 183

Leasehold Interest Coverage Form, CP 00 60.......183
Mortgageholders Errors and Omissions
    Coverage Form, CP 00 70 189
Tobacco Sales Warehouses Coverage Form, CP 00 80 203
Condominium Associations Coverage Form, CP 00 17 206
Commercial Condominium Unit-Owners
    Coverage Form, CP 00 18...................................210
Legal Liability Coverage Form, CP 00 40 211
Additional Conditions..219

Chapter 9: Commercial Property Endorsements

Chapter 9: Commercial Property Endorsements....................221

Additional Building Property, CP 14 15 221
Additional Covered Property, CP 14 10................................221
Additional Exclusions, CP 10 50......................................222
Additional Insured and Loss Payee
    (Building Owner) CP 12 18 and CP 12 19 222
Additional Locations Special
    Coinsurance Provisions, CP 13 20.................................222
Additional Property Not Covered, CP 14 20........................223
Agricultural Products Storage, CP 13 30 225
Alcoholic Beverage Tax Exclusion, CP 99 10.....................226
Blanket Insurance–Margin Clause Option, CP 12 32 226
Brands and Labels, CP 04 01 227
Broken or Cracked Glass Exclusion Form, CP 10 52..........227
Building Glass Under Tenant's Policy, CP 14 70.................227
Business Income Changes–
    Beginning of the Period of Restoration, CP 15 56 228
Business Income–Discretionary Payroll Expense, CP 15 04 228
Business Income–Landlord as Additional Insured
    (Rental Value), CP 15 03 229
Business Income–Ordinary Payroll
    Limitation or Exclusion, CP 15 10................................229
Burglary and Robbery Protective Safeguards, CP 12 11 229
Cap on Losses from Certified
    Acts Of Terrorism, IL 09 52 230
Changes – Electronic Data, CP 01 70 231
Changes – Fungus, Wet Rot,
    Dry Rot and Bacteria, CP 01 71...................................231
Civil Authority Change(s), CP 15 32 232
Condominium Commercial Unit Owners
    Optional Coverages, CP 04 18.....................................232
Contributing Insurance, CP 99 20 233
Debris Removal Additional Insurance, CP 04 15 233
Deductible Limitation, CP 03 10......................................233
Dependent Properties, CP 15 08......................................233
Disclosure Pursuant to Terrorism
    Risk Insurance Act, IL 09 85 234
Distilled Spirits and Wines Market Value, CP 99 05...........234
Earthquake and Volcanic Eruption
    Endorsement Form, CP 10 40 235

Earthquake Inception Extension, CP 10 41 236
Electrical Apparatus, CP 04 10 236
Electronic Commerce (E-Commerce), CP 04 30 237
Flood Coverage Endorsement, CP 10 65 239
Functional Building Valuation, CP 04 38 240
Functional Personal Property Valuation
    Other Than Stock, CP 04 39 242
Grain Properties—Explosion Limitation, CP 10 51.............243
Household Personal Property Coverage, CP 99 92...............243
Leased Property, CP 14 60 244
Legal Liability Coverage Schedule, CP DS 05 244
Loss Payable Provisions, CP 12 18 244
Manufacturers Consequential Loss Assumption, CP 99 02..245
Manufacturer's Selling Price
    (Finished Stock Only), CP 99 30 246
Market Value Stock, CP 99 31 246
Molten Material, CP 10 60 246
Multiple Deductible, CP 03 20 246
Multiple Location/Premium and Dispersion
    Credit Application, CP 13 70 247
Newly Acquired/Constructed Property-
    Increased Limit, CP 04 25..247
Off-Premises Services - Direct Damage, CP 04 17 247
Ordinance or Law Coverage, CP 04 05................................248
Outdoor Trees, Shrubs and Plants, CP 14 30 249
Outside Signs, CP 14 40...250
Peak Season Limit of Insurance, CP 12 30 250
Pier and Wharf Additional Covered
    Causes of Loss, CP 10 70..251
Pollutant Cleanup & Removal Additional Aggregate
    Limit of Insurance, CP 04 07 251
Protective Safeguards, IL 04 15 252
Radio or Television Antennas, CP 14 50 253
Radioactive Contamination, CP 10 37 253
Report of Values, CP 13 60, and Supplemental
    Report of Values, CP 13 61 254
Spoilage Coverage, CP 04 40..254
Sprinkler Leakage Exclusion, CP 10 56...............................255
Sprinkler Leakage-Earthquake Extension, CP 10 39 256
Storage or Repairs Limited Liability, CP 99 42...................256
Tentative Rates, CP 99 93 256

Terrorism Endorsements...257
Theft Exclusion, CP 10 33..257
Utility Services–Direct Damage, CP 04 17.........................257
Vacancy Changes, CP 04 60 257
Vacancy Permit, CP 04 50...258
Value Reporting Form, CP 13 10 258
Vandalism Exclusion, CP 10 55 259
Water Exclusion, CP 10 32 259
Watercraft Exclusion, CP 10 35 260
Windstorm or Hail Percentage Deductible, CP 03 21..........260
Windstorm or Hail Exclusion - Direct Damage, CP 10 53 ...260
Windstorm or Hail Exclusion, CP 10 54 261
Your Business Personal Property
    Separation of Coverage, CP 19 10 261

Chapter 10: The Commercial Properties Program of American Association of Insurance Services (AAIS)

Chapter 10: The Commercial Properties Program of American Association of Insurance Services (AAIS)...............................263

Building and Personal Property Coverage Part...................264
Supplemental Coverages...267
Special Causes of Loss Form 274
Other Coverage Parts...277
Endorsements..278

Chapter 11: E-issues under the Commercial Property Policy

Chapter 11: E-issues under the Commercial Property Policy 283

Intangible Property 283
Insuring Intangible Assets 285
The Meaning of *Property* 287
E-Property Policies 288
Newly Developed Policies 287

Chapter 12: Miscellaneous Commercial Property Coverage Issues

Chapter 12: Miscellaneous Commercial Property Coverage Issues 291

ISO Interline Terrorism Endorsements..............................291
Catastrophic Weather Loss Claims Issues.........................296
Wind, Water, and Wind-Driven Water................................297
Wind Percentage Deductible 299
Chinese Drywall 303
Emerging "Green" Coverage Issues 304

Specimen Forms...307

    Building and Personal Property
       Coverage Form CP 00 10 06 07.......................................309
    Condominium Association
       Coverage Form CP 00 17 06 07.......................................325
    Condominium Commercial Unit-Owners
       Coverage Form CP 00 18 06 07.......................................339
    Builders Risk Coverage Form CP 00 20 06 07.......................351
    Business Income (and Extra Expense)
       Coverage Form CP 00 30 06 07.......................................359
    Legal Liability Coverage Form CP 00 40 06 07.....................369
    Leasehold Interest Coverage Form CP 00 60 06 95 373
    Mortgageholders Errors and Omissions
       Coverage Form CP 00 70 06 07.......................................377
    Tobacco Sales Warehouses
       Coverage Form CP 00 80 06 07.......................................389
    Commercial Property Conditions CP 00 90 07 88.................395
    Causes of Loss — Basic Form CP 10 10 06 07.....................397
    Causes of Loss — Broad Form CP 10 20 06 07....................403
    Causes of Loss — Special Form CP 10 30 06 07.................411
    Common Policy Conditions IL 00 17 11 98 421

Index...423

Introduction

The Building and Personal Property Coverage Form, CP 00 10

A business—from the one person office or store to the highly complex global manufacturing or industrial giant—has property exposures that need to be addressed from the overall risk management perspective. These exposures include owned or leased real property, business equipment, processed or unprocessed inventory, property of others such as commercial bailments or employees' and customers' property, and the stream of income generated by the business. These exposures must be analyzed and appropriately protected through various risk management and loss mitigation techniques.

The foundation of a solid risk management program for these items is a property insurance program that transfers the economic consequence of loss or damage to an insurance company. Smaller commercial businesses usually arrange coverage on a businessowners policy, a packaged set of insurance coverages for the insured's liability, property, and auto exposures. This set of coverages is the topic of *Businessowners Coverage Guide*, another National Underwriter Company title in the Coverage Guides series. Larger concerns will use separate general liability, commercial property, business auto policies, and other specialized coverages such as directors and officers (D&O) and employment practices liability (EPL), tailored to work together.

ISO Building and Personal Property Coverage Form, CP 00 10

The standard contract for insuring building and personal property exposures of commercial insureds is the Insurance Services Office (ISO) Building and Personal Property Coverage Form, CP 00 10, generally known as the commercial property policy. Introduced by ISO in 1985 as part of the development of simplified language insurance policies, the form has undergone several revisions. To date, there have been eight editions (also sometimes referred to as versions) of the building and personal property coverage form. The form edition date is the last two sets of digits in the form number. For example, the first edition of the policy was issued as the CP 00 10 07 88 edition, meaning it was released for use in July 1988. It currently exists—where approved—as the CP 00 10 06 07 version; it is this edition of the form that is the basis of this book. A historical tracing of the edition dates is relevant because insurance litigation frequently involves loss under previous forms. The following is a listing of all editions released since 1988:

- CP 00 10 07 88

- CP 00 10 10 90

- CP 00 10 10 91

- CP 00 10 06 95

- CP 00 10 02 00

- CP 00 10 10 00

- CP 00 10 04 02

- CP 00 10 06 07

Not all insurance companies employ the standard ISO commercial property policy. Some insurers use ISO forms; others add, delete, or modify policy provisions for competitive or other business reasons. The American Association of Insurance Services (AAIS) offers its own commercial property policy, which is similar to the ISO policy but varies in several respects. This form's differences from the ISO policy are discussed in Chapter 10.

This book's analysis puts the policy into context with the rest of the ISO commercial property program and all its basic forms and permutations. In addition to the CP coverage form, this work treats the commercial property program's three causes of loss forms (basic, broad, and special), optional coverages, builders risk and business income coverage forms and options, and the other coverage forms comprising the ISO commercial property program.

The building and personal property coverage form is one building block in the ISO commercial property program. Also, the commercial property program is one part of the protection available for commercial insureds. Property coverage usually must be combined with general liability, crime, fidelity, inland marine, workers compensation, and automobile coverages in order to adequately protect the interests of commercial insureds.

Property Coverage Forms

Virtually all types of commercial businesses are eligible for the building and personal property coverage form. Specialized versions of property coverage forms exist for use with condominium and builders risk exposures. Other coverages, such as legal liability, value reporting, mortgageholders errors and omissions, tobacco sales warehouses, and leasehold interest are available through separate forms. The policy's basic coverage may be modified in many ways through the use of various endorsements that add, remove, or change in some way the terms of the unendorsed policy.

The commercial property policy is not self-contained; it is part of ISO's modular format for a seamless combination with a policy declarations form, an appropriate causes of loss form (basic, broad, or special), two conditions forms (commercial property and common policy), and any appropriate endorsements to form a *coverage part*. A commercial property coverage part may be used as a monoline policy covering property only or combined with other commercial lines coverages (e.g., general liability and commercial auto) to form a commercial package policy.

ISO Rules

The rules for the commercial property policy are in the ISO Commercial Lines Manual (CLM) at Division Five—Fire and Allied Lines. A review of some of the basic rules is helpful in putting the form's use into context. These are the ISO rules, which are often supplemented by the underwriting manuals or guidelines of individual insurance companies.

ISO rules allow policies to be written for a specific term, up to three years—for one year, two years, or three years—or on a continuous basis. A policy may be renewed by renewal certificate or by use of the commercial property coverage part renewal endorsement, CP DS 02. When a renewal certificate is used, it must conform in every aspect to current rules, rates, and forms at the time of renewal.

The common policy conditions form, IL 00 17, is used with all policies. This form contains six conditions that must be incorporated into any policy written and that apply to all the policy's coverages. Most of these common policy conditions are restatements of provisions of the standard fire policy, which meet the statutory requirements of the states for writing property insurance. The conditions included in IL 00 17 are cancellation, changes, examination of your books and records, inspections and surveys, premiums, and transfer of rights and duties.

Commercial property conditions form CP 00 90 is also attached to all policies, except when mortgage holder's errors and omissions coverage form CP 00 70 is the only form applicable to commercial property coverage. CP 00 90 contains the following provisions: concealment, misrepresentation, or fraud; control of property; more than one coverage applying to loss; legal action against the company; liberalization; no benefit to bailee; other insurance; policy period; coverage territory; and subrogation.

Interstate accounts may be written on the same policy. One policy may be written to cover locations in more than one state. The coverage may be property or business income and may cover on either a specific or blanket basis. Such a policy is subject to the rules of the state in which the insured's largest-valued location or headquarters is located or where the insurance is negotiated.

Where contributing insurance is an issue—coverage is divided between two or more insurers on a percentage basis—contributing insurance endorsement CP 99 20 may be attached. This endorsement provides that the insurance company's liability on any loss will not exceed its percentage of total coverage. Simply stated, this means that if there are two policies covering a piece of property, one with a limit of $70,000 and the other with a limit of $30,000 ($100,000 total coverage), the first insurer would be liable for only 70 percent of the total of any loss.

ISO rules also call for protective services or devices to be required. Where this is the case, the policy must be endorsed to require that the company be notified if the devices or services are discontinued or out of service using the protective safeguards endorsement, IL 04 15. The endorsement can include automatic sprinkler systems, automatic fire alarms, security services, and security contracts. The burglary and robbery protective systems endorsement, CP 12 11, may also be required.

Underwriting Property Risks

Insurance practitioners use a mnemonic to express the four major areas evaluated when underwriting a risk: COPE. This refers to type of *construction* (what the building is made of), *occupancy* (how the insured uses the building), *protection* (fire protection, such as sprinklers or proximity to fire department service), and *exposure* (such as construction of nearby buildings and how those buildings are used). Together, these indicate the acceptance or nonacceptance of a building risk.

ISO defines seven different types of construction: frame, joisted masonry, noncombustible, masonry noncombustible, modified fire resistive, fire resistive, and mixed. In addition to the construction of the building itself, the underwriter also looks at the floors, roofs, and partitions. The area of the building and any unprotected openings are also considered.

The use of firewalls between portions of a building can greatly reduce the rate for property insurance. The area between firewalls is a fire division. Fire divisions prevent the spread of fire from one section of a building to another. The lacking of fire walls can have an adverse effect on the rate charged. For example, a shopping mall had been a one-story structure with two-story anchor stores at each of the corners. The one-story portion was divided by firewalls into several fire divisions, in effect creating several small exposure units. A remodeling project added a second story over the one-story section. The firewalls were not extended up and through the new second story. The mall went from being several small fire divisions to being one big fire division. Even though the mall was equipped with a sprinkler system and was masonry noncombustible construction, the rate for property insurance increased substantially.

Occupancy refers to the use of the structure. A building that houses fireworks will pay a higher rate for property insurance than the office building next door.

Protection refers to the kind and quality of protection, both public and private, available to a structure. Private protection ranges from fire extinguishers and sprinkler systems to a private fire department. Only the biggest of companies (such as huge manufacturers) have their own fire departments.

Towns and cities receive a protection class code based upon several factors: the firefighting equipment, the training of the firefighters, the mix of full-time and volunteer firefighters, and the local water supply. Class codes range from one to ten, with one being the best and ten being a risk with no responding fire department within five miles. No city in America has a class one rating. Classes two through five require all full-time firefighters. Classes six, seven, and eight can be a mix of full-time and volunteer. Class nine is typically all volunteer, and class ten may or may not have any fire department at all. One issue that many older cities are facing is the downgrading of their fire protection classes, due mainly to the aging of their infrastructure, specifically the water supply apparatus. As the cities get older, many are experiencing a drop in water pressure. Combine the lower water pressure with more and taller buildings, and a problem arises in the efficacy of the fire fighting.

Exposure refers to external exposure of the building. In other words, what is next to the insured structure? In the previous example, the office building next to the fireworks warehouse may pay a higher rate than a comparable office building in an office park elsewhere in the same city. The office building faces a greater chance of loss from fire at the fireworks warehouse.

COPE is further examined in The National Underwriter Company e-Learning Course, *Insurance Principles.*

The National Underwriter Company Coverage Guides

This work is one of a number of books published by The National Underwriter Company reviewing and analyzing individual insurance forms. Other titles in the Coverage Guide series include *Personal Auto, Homeowners, Personal Umbrella, CGL, Business Auto, Businessowners, Directors and Officers Liability, Employment Practices Liability, Workers Compensation,* and *Cyber Liability.* Although business income, also referred to as time element coverage, is discussed as a part of the commercial property program in this book in Chapter 7, a more comprehensive treatment of this critical coverage can be found in *The Business Interruption Book,* The National Underwriter Co. (2004). Additional forms and issues are treated in the *FC&S Bulletins.*

Chapter 1

The Insuring Agreement: Covered and Not Covered Property

Section A. Coverage

It is the insuring agreement that is analyzed first when determining coverage under an insurance policy. It is a solidly established legal precedent in insurance contract interpretation that insuring agreements are construed broadly to find coverage and that exclusions are construed narrowly to deny insurance recovery.

The classic example of this principle is the former use of the phrase "all risks," which was once found in insuring agreements but no longer is. Policies may have read, "This insurance applies to all risks of loss or damage not otherwise excluded in the Exclusions section of this policy." As the rule developed in various court decisions, by employing the phrase "all risks" in the coverage grant, the policy could not be interpreted to contain any restriction of coverage regardless of the policy's exclusions. "All risks" language evolved into "coverage applies to risks of direct physical loss or damage, except as otherwise modified, limited, or excluded elsewhere in the policy" in order to maintain the intended clause equilibrium.

The modern commercial property policy's insuring agreement contains the pledge of indemnification, which is for direct loss—contrasted to consequential loss, the subject of analysis elsewhere—of or damage

7

to, property and includes various clauses describing what is and what is not *covered property*. The insuring agreement states the insurer will pay for "direct physical loss of or damage to covered property at the premises described in the Declarations caused by or resulting from any Covered Cause of Loss." Levels of coverage are arranged by use of one of three (basic, broad, or special) causes of loss forms.

What Is "Direct Physical Loss or Damage"?

The contractual obligation to pay for direct physical loss or damage means that the policy responds to damage that is directly caused by an insured peril. "Directly caused" means there is a causal relationship between the event immediately responsible for the loss (an insured event such as fire, vandalism, or windstorm) and the damage done to property that is included within the policy meaning of "covered property" (building, structure, or business personal property). For example, high winds in a thunderstorm blow shingles off a roof—that damage is directly caused. Contrast that to the same storm knocking out power to the building, allowing refrigerated chemicals to spoil. That damage—to the chemicals—is *consequential*. The cause of loss was not the wind but the heating of the chemicals. If damage is not direct, then it is consequential and it is the distinction between the two that dictates whether damage to property is covered. (There are endorsements and coverages for some consequential losses—*see* Chapter 9, Commercial Property Endorsements.)

Another principle of coverage interpretation is that the standard meanings of words and terms dictate, not specialized or secondary meanings. The *Merriam-Webster Dictionary* definitions of *direct* and *consequential* are therefore helpful in understanding the direct physical loss meaning of the insuring agreement. *Direct* is "stemming immediately from a source," and "proceeding from one point to another in time or space without deviation or interruption." For damage to be directly caused, the insured event (i.e., the peril insured against) must be immediately responsible for the damage.

Consequential is "of the nature of a secondary result. Indirect." Consequential losses arise as a consequence of a direct loss. For example, a restaurant has a small fire that damages the electric box, cutting power to a freezer. Before electricity can be restored, food in the freezer thaws and spoils. The damage to the building by the fire is direct but the food thawing is indirect. It resulted as a consequence of the fire. The electricity was cut by fire consuming the electrical box—the damage to the electrical box is by fire. The food was not burned in the fire; it thawed and spoiled because there was no electric to run the freezer. The policy covers the damage to the electrical box but not the thawed food.

Frequently cited examples of consequential damage are loss from depreciation, delay, deterioration, or loss of market. Some of these consequential losses may be covered by endorsement, but no coverage is available under the unendorsed commercial property policy.

Equipment Damaged by a Covered Peril —Spoilage Loss Consequential

A building and its contents are covered under the commercial property policy with the special causes of loss form. Lightning struck a utility pole located off premises, damaging a compressor attached to a walk-in refrigerator. Food stored in the refrigerator spoiled. The insurer pays for the damage to the compressor but denies coverage for the spoilage, claiming that it is a consequential loss. The insured argues that the spoilage is covered because lightning, a covered cause of loss, was the proximate cause of the entire loss.

The correct coverage analysis is that the spoilage loss is appropriately denied. Due to the lapse in time between the lightning damage and the spoilage, it is common to rule out coverage under the commercial property policy. Lightning is the direct cause of the damage to the equipment but is a remote cause of the food spoilage. Change in temperature caused the spoilage, not lightning striking the compressor. There are consequential loss coverages available for this type of exposure.

Section A.1. Covered Property

The commercial property policy covers an insured's property exposures; there is no liability coverage under the commercial property policy. Even what appears to be a type of liability coverage—coverage for the property of others in the insured's possession—is first-party property coverage. It is not the insured's liability for damage to property of others that is covered under the policy, but property coverage for a specific class of property—property of others on the insured premises. This excludes any coverage for loss of use claims arising out of loss or damage to property of customers, employees, or invitees.

Three types of property are included under the commercial property policy coverage: buildings, the insured's business personal property, and personal property of others in certain circumstances. Coverage must be selected on the policy declarations page. A limit must also be shown in the declarations for that type of property to be covered; for example, the insured may carry $1,000,000 in building limits, $200,000 in business personal property limits, and $20,000 for property of others. The commercial property policy can be written to cover only buildings or only contents (business personal property); property of others coverage also must be separately stated on the declarations.

This section of the policy (A. Coverage) contains a provision (A.1) that describes covered property and another section (A.2) that describes property not covered. In policy terms, "covered property" means the type of property described in Section A.1., and limited in A.2., Property Not Covered, if a limit of insurance is shown in the declarations for that type of property.

Section A.1.a. Building Coverage

The commercial property policy covers the buildings and structures shown in the declarations. For that reason, careful underwriting requires more than a street address to describe an insured's premises. An appropriate statement might be "The premises at 500 Main St., the principle building, two maintenance sheds, a processing pool (pools are structures), and a garage."

A tenet of insurance contract interpretation is that words and phrases in insurance policies are governed by their common dictionary definition unless otherwise specifically defined within the policy. The commercial property policy contains only three defined terms, *fungus*, *stock*, and *pollutants*. Therefore, these terms have the meaning that is specifically given to them in the form; all other terms will be given a common usage meaning. In the absence of a policy definition, if there is a common usage meaning that is more favorable to the insured than the meaning put forth by the insurer, the insured will be allowed the more favorable definition.

Building means the building or structure described in the declarations. As neither term is further defined in the policy, a common meaning will be implied. Inasmuch as the building or structure must be described in the declarations, not much argument can arise regarding what is a building or structure in terms of policy interpretation. The building or structure described in the declarations is the covered item of property. The issue is when there might be multiple buildings at one address; all need to be described separately in the declarations.

However, the term *structure* is broader than the term *building,* and some items that might not readily suggest themselves as buildings could be named in the declarations, thereby affording coverage. These items might include, among others, swimming pools, garages, or semi-permanent items such as a wooden stage floor covered by a tent that is used for events at a private club. The important point is that such items be listed in the declarations. Failure to list all structures for which coverage is desired will result in no insurance recovery on loss to undeclared structures.

Nonfunctioning Water Tower as Covered Property?

An insured had an extensive fire at his hotel. On top of the hotel was a nonfunctional water tower valued at about $40,000. The insurance company adjuster believes the cost of the water tower should not be included in the insurance settlement because it was not functional and therefore had no value. The agent believes that the insurer should pay the $40,000 cost to replace it because (1) there could have been an alternate use for the tower; (2) the tower was a part of the building and did have a value even though at the time it was nonfunctional (and could have been considered decorative); and (3) when a company insures a structure, it insures the complete structure whether a portion of it is functional or not. The issue is how the tower should be adjusted.

The commercial property policy does not refer anywhere to functional or nonfunctional property. It refers only to covered and not covered property. Covered property includes the building. The water tower, being attached to the building as either a fixture or permanently attached machinery and equipment, qualifies as covered property. If a coinsurance requirement is shown in the policy declarations, and if the insured has met the coinsurance requirement for insuring to value, the building, including the water tower, is covered to the full limit of the policy. If the insured has not met the coinsurance requirement, the penalty will apply, lowering the amount available to cover the loss and capping recovery.

An attempt to deny coverage for the tower due to its present nonfunctional state is analogous to denying coverage for an unused second story of a building. It would not be correct to reduce the value of a building due to the nonuse of a portion of that building. It is just as incorrect to reduce coverage for the loss due to whether or not the building structure is functional. The tower should be included in the insurance recovery. How to value the water tower in the event of loss should have been determined at the time of underwriting the account.

The use of the singular (building or structure) rather than the plural (building*s* or structure*s*) does not mean that the policy cannot be used to cover more than one building or structure. Using the singular construction avoids confusion after policy inception in the event the insured builds additional buildings or structures that were not on the premises at the time of the original policy. The phrase "buildings or structures" might be interpreted (or misinterpreted) by insureds (and courts) as implying that *all* buildings and structures on the insured premises are covered, regardless of the qualifying language, "described in the Declarations."

The commercial property policy provides coverage for five other types of property under the building portion:

1. **Completed additions.** The commercial property policy automatically covers the new portion if the insured has added onto the described building. This coverage provides automatic coverage for new additions during the term of the policy; however, it can also raise a coinsurance issue if the overall amount of insurance is not adjusted to account for the increased values. The insured should be counseled to report additions to buildings that affect the value.

2. **Fixtures, including outdoor fixtures.** The commercial property policy also covers fixtures under the building limit. *Merriam-Webster's Dictionary* defines *fixtures* as "something that is fixed or attached (as to a building) as a permanent appendage or as a structural part <a plumbing *fixture*>." *Merriam-Webster's* also provides another meaning: "an item of movable property so incorporated into real property that it may be regarded as legally a part of it." For example, a light mounted into a brick wall on a patio is a fixture; a table lamp on a pool side table attached to the wall only by its electric cord is not a fixture. A hot tub built into a hotel suite such that its removal would destroy the bathroom is a fixture.

Lawn Tent as a Fixture?

A country club has a tent that it uses for outdoor events such as receptions and dances. This tent has permanent solid flooring to which the tent is attached. The tent is dismantled each year during the winter and stored.

> The tent was damaged by fire, a covered cause of loss. The insurance agent maintains it is a fixture, and as such is covered under the commercial property policy's building coverage. The adjuster sees it otherwise, arguing that the tent is business personal property, and, as such covered under the contents coverage.
>
> The tent is not a fixture. It is a structure. Not all structures are fixtures. It is not affixed to the building or to the realty and therefore is not covered under the building coverage of the commercial property policy unless it is listed in the policy declarations as a covered structure. The tent is business personal property and is covered under the contents section.

3. **Permanently installed machinery and equipment.** The commercial property policy's building coverage also applies to permanently installed machinery and equipment. This could include drive-on scales, pulleys, hydraulic lift systems, and similar property. The policy does not define "permanently installed," but *install* commonly means "to set up for use or service," and *permanently* means "continuing or enduring without fundamental or marked change; stable."

    An item does not have to become a part of the structure of the building for it to be considered permanently installed. This may become important when contents coverage limits have been depleted or exhausted, but building coverage limits have not. For example, a refrigerated locker is permanently installed if it is set up for use in the insured's building with the intent that it should remain there as long as the insured is in business at that location. Under the same logic, a telephone system might be covered as building property.

    The insured must be careful in declaring values for limit-setting purposes. If the insured makes a claim for permanently installed machinery and equipment, all permanently installed machinery and equipment must then be considered for coinsurance purposes. Carrying an adequate limit on the building but not on business personal property might lead to serious coinsurance penalties in the event of a loss.

4. **Personal property used to maintain the building.** Personal property that the insured owns and uses to service or maintain the

building or structure or its premises is covered under the building coverage section. Because of the use of the word *including* in the lead-in to the section, the policy contains a nonexclusive list, by way of example, of such equipment: fire extinguishing equipment; outdoor furniture; floor coverings; and appliances used for refrigerating, ventilating, cooking, dishwashing, or laundering. This category might include many other types of personal property, such as a golf cart used to carry items around the premises, lawn mowers, or snow blowers. The list is illustrative, not comprehensive.

5.   **Additions under construction or alteration and repairs to the building or structure.** In-progress construction, alteration, and repairs are covered if no other insurance covers the property, such as a builder's risk form. These items, as well as materials, equipment, supplies, and temporary structures within 100 feet of the described premises used for making additions, alterations, or repairs to the building or structure are also covered under the building section of the policy. This section would provide coverage for building supplies, tools, and the like involved in the project.

The commercial property policy's other insurance provision provides for a pro rata or excess payment of loss if other insurance exists. Other insurance cooperation does not apply to additions, alterations, or repairs in progress. Other insurance in this special case rules out coverage of this property entirely under this form. This points out the distinction between the commercial property policy's incidental coverage for smaller repairs or new construction projects and the more appropriate builder's risk insurance for new building and major construction.

While the commercial property policy does not state that materials, supplies, and equipment must be owned by the insured, the insured must have an insurable interest in order for these items to be covered under the insured's commercial property policy. If a contractor working for the insured leaves a backhoe on the premises with the keys in the ignition and it is stolen, the insured's commercial property policy will not respond, as the insured has no insurable interest in the property. If, however, the backhoe was leased to the insured and the insured was legally liable for it, the insured would have an insurable interest and coverage applies.

Section A.1.b. Your Business Personal Property

In addition to building property the commercial property policy also covers the insured's business personal property. Business personal property is enumerated in seven clauses and, in addition to these specified types of property, includes "all other personal property owned by you and used in your business." This broad characterization of property allows for a wide interpretation of what is covered under the contents portion of the commercial property policy.

The commercial property policy covers business personal property that is located in or on the building described in the declarations or in the open (or in a vehicle) within 100 feet of the described premises. "In the open" includes property in bales or otherwise stored in the open, as well as that stored in open sheds.

Meaning of *Premises*

The commercial property policy covers business personal property including property in the open within 100 feet of the premises. *Premises* is not restricted to the building, but includes the grounds, parking lot, and so on that are part of the property on which the building is located, extending to the perimeters of the property.

Thus, coverage applies to property temporarily stored within 100 feet of the premises on, for instance, an adjoining vacant lot awaiting movement onto the insured's property. In the absence of a more restrictive definition in the policy itself, the dictionary definition of *premises* is "a tract of land with the buildings thereon" or "a building or part of a building, usually with its appurtenances (as grounds)," applies. But grounds should not be thought of so broadly as to include any amount of acreage on which a building might be situated. The grounds are those that pertain to the service of the building.

Inasmuch as the term *premises* is a broader term than *building*, coverage for property off the insured's premises is provided as long as the property is located within 100 feet of the premises. For example, the insured's business personal property in a car parked across the street from the insured's business is covered as long as the car is parked within 100 feet of the insured's premises.

Types of Covered Business Personal Property

The classes of business personal property covered by the commercial property policy are further outlined in seven clauses.

1. **Furniture and fixtures.** Coverage for fixtures appears both under the building and business personal property sections of the commercial property policy. If the insured has purchased both coverages, fixtures are covered under either. The insured is free to call for coverage under whichever of the two coverages—building or property—yields the greater advantage under the following circumstances:

   a. if the business personal property is not insured for the same causes of loss as the building;

   b. if the business personal property is subject to a different coinsurance requirement; or

   c. if the limits under one or the other coverages are exhausted.

   Fixtures that are tenants' improvements and betterments (meaning affixed to the realty and considered the landlord's property) are not included in this item in the tenant's policy. Rather, the tenant's use interest is covered under item number 6.

Modular Office System as Fixture

An insured business that carried only building coverage (not contents) suffered a loss due to a hurricane. The business had a modular office system that was custom designed and installed. The agent argues that those panels that were mounted on the building's walls are fixtures and therefore covered under the commercial property building coverage. The adjuster counters that they can be removed and relocated to other areas as they are furniture and are not covered.

The panels require a wall-mounting kit. In order to move the wall-mounted panels, the insured would have to call an installer because the insured could not move the panels himself.

The issue is whether these panels can be covered as building items or whether the insured would have to have contents coverage in order to recover for their damage.

The panels are fixtures. The term *fixture* is not further defined in the commercial property policy, leaving its interpretation to common lay meaning. A common usage dictionary defines *fixture* as "something that is fixed or attached (as to a building) as a permanent appendage or as a structural part." The term is further defined as "an item of movable property so incorporated into real property that it may be regarded as legally a part of it." *Permanent* does not mean that the item has to be so attached to the property that it can never be removed. It means "continuing or enduring" and "stable." The issue must be decided on whether the insured business could take the panels if the building sold. If the panels can be removed, they are not covered; if not, they are. Free-standing panels, not installed in any way into the building, are not fixtures and could only be covered under contents coverage.

2.   **Machinery and equipment**. Building coverage includes permanently installed machinery and equipment; business personal property coverage protects any machinery or equipment of the insured regardless of the state of installment. Permanently installed machinery or equipment could be covered under business personal property or building coverage, whichever is more favorable to the insured.

3.   **Stock.** The commercial property policy covers the insured business's stock. *Stock* is one of three defined terms in the policy, so any meaning the term may otherwise have is replaced by this specific definition. The policy's definition of *stock* is "merchandise held in storage or for sale, raw materials and in-process or finished goods, including supplies used in their packing or shipping."

One of the property not covered provisions (clause q) contains a list of certain property that is not covered while outside of buildings. The list includes trees, shrubs, and plants. A coverage extension provides limited coverage for trees, shrubs, and plants (*see* Chapter 2). Provision q excepts stock of trees, shrubs, and plants from the property not covered list. Therefore, an insured's stock of outdoor trees, shrubs, and plants is treated as any other stock and is not subject to the coverage limitations imposed by the outdoor property coverage extension. The limited coverage for trees and shrubs provided under the coverage extensions does not apply to trees and shrubs as stock—full business personal property limits are available.

The issue of whether goods sold but not delivered are treated as the insured's business personal property or as the property of others is determined by the bill of sale provisions and the Uniform Commercial Code. After ownership is established, the amount of coverage available and the value of the property must be determined. If treated as the insured's business personal property, the commercial property policy's valuation provision states that stock sold but not delivered is valued at the selling price less discounts and expenses the insured otherwise would have incurred. For example, ABC Widget normally sells its product for $5 each. In a contract with XYZ for 10,000 widgets, ABC offers such a large quantity at $4 each. If a fire destroys those widgets while still at ABC, ABC's insurance policy will value them at $4 each—the normal selling price less the offered discount.

If considered the property of others, the limit for property of others is available. If this coverage has not been purchased, $2,500 of coverage is available under a coverage extension if a coinsurance provision of at least 80 percent or a value reporting symbol is shown in the declarations (see Chapter 2, Coverage Extensions).

4. **All other personal property owned by you and used in your business.** This broad statement means that personal property—of any kind—is covered property under the commercial property policy, subject to the requirements that it be owned by the insured and used in the insured's business. There is no requirement that the property be used exclusively in the insured's business. For example, a portable CD player used in both the insured's home and office would be covered as personal property used in the insured's business.

5. **Labor, materials, or services furnished or arranged by the insured on personal property of others.** This represents the value of the insured's business processes or operations where loss involves property of others that the insured has performed

service or processes upon. For example, the insured business is a television repair shop. A fire occurs and damages a customer's set that was in for repairs. The business's commercial property policy will cover the cost of the TV set plus the value of the materials and labor he put into it prior to the fire. If the business receives $30 an hour for labor and has expended $50 in parts and two hours labor to repair that set, the commercial property policy will pay $110. The commercial property policy will also make payment to the customer for the value of the TV.

6. **Use interest as tenant in improvements and betterments.** When a tenant makes a permanent addition to a leased building, the improvements usually become part of the building and the property of the landlord. A new store front, installed by the tenant with the expectation of attracting more customers, is a good example. The tenant, of course, has the right to use the improvement for the term of the lease but cannot undo the improvement and betterment upon moving out.

Where there is insured damage to the improvements before the lease expires, the insured/tenant has lost no property that belongs to him; the improvements belong to the landlord. What the tenant has lost is the use of the property, and it is the right of use for the term of the lease that creates the tenant's insurable interest in the improvements. It is the possible loss of use of the improvements in which the tenant has invested that represents the tenant's exposure.

Improvements and Betterments
—Coverage Dependent on Term of Lease?

A building suffered lightning damage to a central air conditioning unit. The insured is a tenant and not the building owner. The insured paid for the air conditioning unit five years ago.

The insured carries contents insurance, which includes the use interest in improvements and betterments. The insurance company initially declined the claim, stating that the units were part of the building and, as there was no building coverage, there could be no recovery. The agent argued that the unit was an improvement and betterment. The company agreed with this, and also agreed that the cause of loss was a covered cause of loss.

The claim was then denied on the basis that the tenant had no insurable interest in the improvement and betterment because the lease is an annual renewable lease. Nothing in the lease addresses ownership of improvements and betterments. The lease was first executed a decade ago and renews automatically unless one party notifies the other within a certain time prior to the end of the annual period. The insurance company based its position on the fact that when any lease renews, all improvements and betterments belong to the building owner, and a tenant has only an insurable interest for the period of the lease, in this case one year.

Improvements and betterments coverage would be severely impinged upon under this interpretation. It would limit coverage for improvements and betterments made by the tenant to a one year lease term, when in actuality, the building in question has been continuously leased for ten years.

It is the insured's use interest in improvements and betterments that is covered; further, an improvement and betterment is specifically stated to be a fixture made a part of the building the insured occupies but does not own and that was acquired or made at the insured's expense but cannot be legally removed. The definition of "improvements and betterments" does not tie coverage to the lease term. If there is a fixture that qualifies as an improvement and betterment and the insured's use interest is damaged, there is coverage. In this case, the insured acquired a fixture at his expense that was made a part of the building the insured occupies but does not own and that he cannot legally remove. His use interest in that fixture is damaged and therefore coverage applies.

The phrase "improvements and betterments" implies a substantial alteration, addition, or change to real property that enhances its value. The commercial property policy states "improvements and betterments" are "fixtures, alterations, installations, or additions: (a) made a part of the building or structure occupied but not owned by the named insured, and (b) that the named insured acquired or made at his expense but cannot legally remove." Coverage is automatic if the insured has an improvements and betterments exposure since business personal property is said to consist of, among other things, the named insured's use interest as tenant in improvements and betterments.

Questions have arisen as to whether under given circumstances particular work paid for by the tenant falls within its meaning. An example is the issue of whether repairs made on the building by the tenant constitute improvements and betterments. A court ruled "no" in *Modern Music Shop v. Concordia Fire Ins. Co.*, 226 N.Y.S. 630 (1928). The case provides some guidance, though it involved an older form that referred simply to "the insured's interest in improvements and betterments." The court said, "These words imply and mean a substantial or fairly substantial alteration, addition, or change to the premises used and occupied by the insured, rising above and beyond and amounting to something more than a simple or minor repair."

In *U.S. Fire Ins. Co. v. Martin*, 282 S.E.2d 2 (Va. 1981), the Virginia Supreme Court decided that air conditioners the insured tenant had repaired but not installed were not within the meaning of improvements and betterments. The court reasoned that the tenant had not made the original expenditures for the air conditioners, that the expenditures were not later acquired by the tenant, and the expenses put out by the tenant were for repair only; therefore, there was no coverage under the terms of the policy.

The current policy provision and the decisions in these two cases demonstrate that an improvement must substantially alter the building. A maintenance or repair task, such as painting the building or installing new locks on doors, is not an improvement in the insurance meaning of the word. Tenants often agree to maintain the building or to undertake repairs via lease provision or do these things voluntarily. Such expense should not be viewed as an improvement and betterment.

There is a distinction between *improvements* and *trade fixtures*. The latter are installed by the tenant, often in such a way that they become a part of the building, but—either by express provision in the lease or by established custom—the vacating tenant removes them. Trade fixtures retain the character of personal property. Taking a store as an example, a new front installed by the tenant is an improvement, but counters, no matter how firmly attached to the building, are usually trade fixtures.

The commercial property policy sets out three methods (under section E.7.e Loss Conditions, Valuation; *see* Chapter 5) for determining recovery when improvements are damaged by an insured peril:

(1)   If the insured makes the repairs at his expense and is not reimbursed by the landlord, the commercial property policy covers the improvements at actual cash value just as though the insured owned them. The policy requires that repairs be made promptly but does not define *promptly*.

A court has held that the amount recoverable by the tenant for improvements is reduced by any amount that the tenant is reimbursed by the owner for the cost of the improvements. In *Atlanta Eye Care, Inc. v. Aetna Casualty and Surety Co.,* 364 S.E.2d 634 (Ga. App. 1988), the insured was covered under a businessowners policy for improvements and betterments. The insured made improvements costing $19,000 to the leased property. The lease agreement, however, provided that the owner would reimburse the tenant $8,000, and this was done. After the property suffered a loss, the insurer paid all but $8,000 of the tenant's claim for improvements and betterments. Ruling in the insurer's favor, the court found that the coverage was correctly limited to those improvements for which the tenant had not been reimbursed.

(2)   If someone else (usually the landlord) repairs the improvements at his expense for the insured's use, the commercial property policy owes nothing. In this situation, the insured has suffered no loss. Where the insured has suffered temporary loss of business because of the damage to the improvements, the loss should be covered by business income coverage if the insured has arranged such protection.

(3)   If the improvements are not repaired or replaced promptly, the insured tenant recovers a proportion of the original cost of the damaged improvements. The insurer determines the proportionate value by multiplying the original cost of the improvements by the number of days from the loss or damage to the expiration of the lease. Then this amount is divided by the number of days from the installation of improvements to the expiration of the lease. If the insured's lease contains a renewal option, the expiration of the

renewal option period becomes the expiration date for use in determining the amount recoverable. The lease option provision does not require that the tenant give notice to the owner, either verbally or in writing, of intent to exercise the option.

The third situation is the one that most often presents difficulties. If neither the insured nor the landlord repairs or replaces the improvements promptly—and there is no definition of the word *promptly*—the policy pays an amount generally referred to as the unamortized portion of the investment. An example of recovery under this situation is a tenant who has invested $10,000 in improvements at the beginning of a ten year lease. In effect, the tenant has bought the use of these improvements for ten years for $10,000. A fire destroys the improvements after five years, and the tenant loses half of the investment. If the improvements are not replaced, the third provision sets up the machinery for recovery of that lost half. Of course, when this third provision takes effect is open to question due to the lack of a time schedule. Does promptly mean sixty days, ninety days, six months, or more probably, depending on the particular circumstances surrounding the loss and its aftermath? If the damaged property is not repaired, there is nothing against which to measure promptly. The insured's loss of use is measured from time of loss.

When the insured or the landlord does not promptly repair or replace the damaged improvements, the basis for recovery under the policy is the original cost of the improvements. Depreciation makes no difference. Neither does whether those improvements would cost more or less to replace at the time of loss than they actually cost to install matter. Actual cost of installation is the insured's investment and that investment is what was lost— wholly or partially—if the improvements are destroyed and not restored.

Suppose an insured spent $10,000 on improvements at the beginning of November 2007 under a lease running to the end of 2021. At the beginning of February 2008, the improvements are destroyed and not replaced. Under the formula for recovery in CP 00 10, the $10,000 is multiplied by 167 months, as that is the amount of time from the loss to the expiration of the lease. The resulting amount, $1,670,000, is divided by 170 or the amount of time from the installation of the improvements to the expiration of the lease. The recovery is $9,823.53.

The original cost may be greater than the actual cash value of the improvements. If the insured must tear out a portion of the building in making the alterations or improvements, the original investment is the cost of the improvements plus the amount spent getting ready for them. An example is that the insured tenant spends $10,000 for improvements. But before these improvements could be made the tenant had to spend an additional $4,000 to remove the building front and inside wall. The total investment in improvements is $14,000. A fire totally destroys the improvements. If the tenant chooses to replace the improvements, she will not have to redo the demolition work. The commercial property policy thus ignores the $4,000 that she originally spent, and her recovery is the actual cash value of the improvements—replacement cost less depreciation, which might be more or less than $10,000. On the other hand, if the tenant does not replace the improvements, the commercial property policy bases recovery on the total original cost—$14,000, the cost of the demolition work plus the original cost of the improvements. The policy still bases recovery on the provisions as set forth in the form in the event of a month-to-month lease. However, the tenant has very little enforceable time of tenancy. If the tenant replaces the improvements, she will recover their actual cash value just as if under a lease with a long time to run. But if she does not replace them, her recovery will be very little since the fraction arrived at by the procedure for the third situation will reflect only a small portion of the cost of the improvements.

Such was the situation presented to the New Hampshire Supreme Court in *Magulas v. Travelers Ins. Co.,* 327 A.2d 608 (N.H. 1974). The insured had a two-year verbal lease, but he knew that as a tenant-at-will his legally enforceable tenancy was limited to thirty days. The owner told him that the building, which he leased to use as a restaurant, might be demolished but that it would not be demolished for at least two years. The insured relied on the likelihood of staying in the building for two years and made improvements of $20,000. Two months after the restaurant opened it suffered a fire loss, and the owner refused to rebuild. The insurer argued that the insured's interest in the improvements and betterments was limited to his legally enforceable right to have thirty days notice before tenancy could be terminated. The court found that the insured's insurable interest in the improvements and betterments was not so limited, stating: "[The insured] expected to use the improvements for two years and should recover on the basis of that expectation despite the fact that his legally enforceable rental term was limited to thirty days."

However, if the insured has an option to purchase, his insurable interest in improvements and betterments is still bound by the unexpired term of the lease. Once the option to purchase is exercised, the improvements and betterments are transformed into building property in which the insured has an absolute interest, not merely a use interest.

7. **Leased personal property for which the insured has a contractual responsibility to insure.** One important point to note about leased equipment coverage is that the form provides coverage for leased equipment the insured has an obligation to insure. This provision allows the insured some flexibility by covering unplanned, short-term equipment leases under business personal property. However, the lease terms and agreements must carefully be reviewed. For example, the insured has a commercial property policy and leases some equipment for sixty days. This equipment was damaged while in the insured's possession. The lease imposes legal liability for the equipment. Since the lease does not contain an express requirement to provide insurance, the policy provides no coverage.

A.1.c. Personal Property of Others

The final category of covered property in the commercial property policy is bailments—property of others in the insured's care, custody, or control. The same conditions as to location of such property apply here as to the insured's own business personal property: the property must be on, in, or within 100 feet of the premises.

Contrast coverage for property in the insured's care, custody, or control under the commercial property policy and the commercial general liability (CGL) policy. The CGL policy contains an exclusion of property that is in the insured's care, custody or control. In order for coverage to attach for property of others under the commercial property policy, property must be in the insured's care, custody, or control. This illustrates a difference in the nature of the policies. The CGL policy does not cover property, per se. It covers the insured's legal liability for damage. The commercial property policy covers direct property damage to covered property, including property of others in the insured's care, regardless of legal liability.

The commercial property policy automatically provides $2,500 of additional insurance for the property of others by means of a coverage extension (*see* Chapter 2). The purchase of additional and specific personal property of others coverage is appropriate when the insured needs coverage of values in excess of $2,500. For example, the insured has charge of $10,000 worth of personal property of others at his business. The policy provides coverage for the first $2,500 as an extension of business personal property (assuming 80 percent coinsurance is listed on the declarations). The insured should purchase an additional $7,500 of coverage under personal property of others. The commercial property policy provides no coverage for the property of others, other than the $2,500 extension, unless the agent activates the coverage by the appropriate entry on the declarations page.

Any loss to property of others is adjusted for the account of the owner of the property.

Section A.2 Property Not Covered

The commercial property policy lists seventeen categories of property as property not covered. Any economic loss involving these items is not covered at all.

a.   **Accounts, bills, currency, food stamps, or other evidences of debt, money, notes, or securities.** In previous versions of the policy, deeds were included on this list but have been dropped; therefore the cost of reproducing a deed lost by covered event is recoverable. The policy specifically includes coverage for lottery tickets held for sale (stock) by stating that lottery tickets held for sale are not securities.

b.   **Animals.** However, the policy *does* cover animals belonging to others that the insured boards. It also covers the insured's own animals if they are held as stock if owned by the insured and while inside a building.

c.   **Automobiles held for sale.**

d.   **Bridges, roadways, walks, patios, or other paved surfaces.**

e.   **Contraband, or property in the course of illegal transportation or trade.**

f.   **Cost of excavations, grading, backfilling, or filling.** This provision has caused disputes between insureds and insurers, as seen in the following examples:

May the Exclusion of Excavation Costs Be Applied to Debris Removal?

An insured suffered a total fire loss to his business insured on the commercial property form. The debris from the destroyed building fell into the foundation and heaped-up above ground level. The insurer stated that it was not responsible for removing the debris from within the foundation walls and that its only responsibility was to pay for removal of debris above ground level and to fill any remaining hole with dirt to level the surface. The company relied upon provision 2.f. under "property not covered": "Covered property does not include...the cost of excavations, grading, backfilling or filling."

The insurer is mistaken in applying the exclusion of coverage for the cost of excavation to the debris removal provision. They are two distinct things. The policy does promise to pay the cost to "remove debris of covered property caused by...a covered cause of loss." The fire was the covered cause of loss, and the resulting debris of the covered property is what must be removed from within the foundation walls. Nothing in the additional coverage limits what debris will be removed.

The cost of excavation exclusion, on the other hand, is found within a list of items that are either uninsurable, such as contraband, or should be insured elsewhere, such as automobiles held for sale. Further, "the cost of excavations" appears within the list of other items commonly associated with new construction, such as grading, backfilling, or filling.

The debris removal additional coverage provision contains only one exclusion: the cost to extract pollutants from land or water or to remove, restore, or replace polluted land or water. Therefore, debris removal from within the foundation walls is covered.

Excavation of Broken Water Pipe Covered?

An insured's building suffered water damage from a broken underground water pipe. The damaged pipe led from the water main in the street to the insured's building. The broken pipe had to be dug up to be repaired in order to avoid continued water damage to the building. The insurance company authorized payment for the water damage to the building but refused to pay the cost of digging up the water pipe to repair it, citing the commercial property provision stating that the cost of excavations, grading, backfilling, or filling is property not covered. Thus, the insurer reasoned that the cost of excavating the pipe to repair it was not covered.

The commercial property policy says that covered property does not include the cost of excavation. The building is covered property, so its insured value does not include the cost of excavation. Excavation is a service that goes into the cost of constructing a building if the building is set in the ground. It is part of the cost of the building, as is the cost of painting it or the cost of cleaning up the construction debris once the building is finished.

The form drafters wanted to cover most costs involved in replacing a building destroyed by a covered cause of loss, but they did not want to cover the portion of the building's cost attributable to excavation. To use policy language to exclude the cost of digging up a broken water pipe is unwarranted. By excavating, the insured is preventing further water damage to his building.

One of the insured's duties in the event of the loss as set out in the commercial property form is to "take all reasonable steps to protect the Covered Property from further damage by a Covered Cause of Loss." The form asks the insured to keep records of expenses incurred in arranging emergency repairs "for consideration in the settlement of the claim." Repairing a broken water pipe that causes water damage to an insured building is the type of emergency repair that the form contemplates.

g.   **Foundations of buildings, structures, machinery, or boilers,** if such foundations are below the lowest basement floor or the surface of the ground, if there is no basement.

> ### Foundations as Property Not Covered
>
> Included under the property not covered section of the commercial property policy are "foundations of buildings, structures, machinery or boilers if their foundations are below: (1) the lowest basement floor; or (2) the surface of the ground, if there is no basement." Some adjusters have said that because of the use of "*their* foundations" instead of "*the* foundations," machinery on a foundation with a top surface below ground level is not covered. If "the" had been used, then coverage would be effective as to machinery but not as to the foundation.
>
> This is incorrect. Only foundations are the subject of the commercial property policy's provision A.2.g regarding foundations as property not covered. The reference goes back to the word *foundation*. Foundations of buildings, structures, machinery, or boilers are not covered property if the foundation is below the lowest basement floor or the surface of the ground, if there is no basement. The use of the word "their" rather than "the" does not affect coverage for the building, structure, machinery, or boiler. Those remain items of covered property and are not included in the scope of property not covered.

h.   **Land, including the land on which the property is located, water, growing crops, or lawns.** Land is generally an uninsurable item. This provision makes clear that the ground upon which the insured property is located is not covered. Water, such as water in a lake on the insured's property, is also not covered. Some losses involving water might involve an on-premises leak in a water pipe that causes a sudden rise in the insured's water bill. While most losses of this type will be of amounts so small that they would never reach litigation, an argument can be made that the excess over the normal water bill is covered. Reading the term in context with the other enumerated items in the list (land, growing crops, lawns) it can be stated that the water referred to would be natural water (such as ponds or lakes).

i.   **Personal property while airborne or waterborne.** There is no coverage for items of the insured while in transit on air or water. Cargo insurance is the appropriate insurance mechanism for this exposure.

j.   **Bulkheads, pilings, piers, wharves, or docks.**

k.   **Property more specifically described in another coverage form.** For example, the building and personal property policy covers equipment and machinery. Boiler equipment would fall under this category. If, however, the insured has a boiler and machinery policy where the boiler machinery is specifically described (listed in the declarations), the item is covered only for any excess amount of loss (whether collectible or not) over the amount of the more specific insurance. Large commercial insureds often have separate policies on boiler machinery, EDP equipment, fine arts, and perhaps others types of property.

l.   **Retaining walls, unless the retaining wall is part of a building.**

m.   **Underground pipes, flues, or drains.**

Outdoor Sprinkler System as Underground Pipes

This policy is written on a special causes of loss basis. The insured has a sprinkler system in the yard, which has pipes underground. The sprinkler heads extend about a quarter of an inch above ground. A windstorm toppled a concrete-footed light pole, which, as it fell, uprooted the sprinkler pipes, damaging the sprinkler system. The insurer denied coverage for damage to the sprinkler system, as underground pipes are specifically property not covered. The insured argued that the loss should be covered as a permanently installed fixture or equipment or as personal property used to maintain the premises.

The commercial property policy will provide only partial coverage for the sprinkler system. There is no coverage for the sprinkler system as permanently installed fixtures or equipment. That coverage is under the building or structure coverage and does not extend to items that are not part of the building or structure. If the underground system extends from the building's plumbing it would ordinarily qualify as "building, including permanently installed fixtures." However, the policy specifies that underground pipes are property not covered.

The insured's argument that the sprinkler system is personal property used to maintain the premises appears to have merit; however, because a fixture to the realty normally cannot be removed without damage to the realty, the sprinkler system would be seen as real, not personal, property. Even if considered personal property, the exclusion of underground pipes prevails. Any damage to the underground pipes is not covered; however, any damage to sprinkler heads or connecting pipes above ground would be covered.

n.   **Electronic data** and

o.   **Cost to Replace or Restore.** Prior to the 04 02 edition of the commercial property policy, the form did not specifically address data itself. Rather, the cost to reproduce the data was addressed. The following is the previous property not covered provision in the CP 00 10 regarding data:

> n.   The cost to research, replace or restore the information on valuable papers and records, including those which exist on electronic or magnetic media, except as provided in the Coverage Extensions;

Previous editions of the CP 00 10 lumped electronic data in with other types of valuable papers and records. With insureds having more and more of their information in electronic format, a better way was needed to cover such data.

The CP 00 10 04 02 deleted the former provision that addressed just the cost of reproduction as property not covered and replaced that provision with the following two provisions under property not covered:

> n.   Electronic data, except as provided under the Additional Coverage—Electronic Data. Electronic data means information, facts or computer programs stored as or on, created or used on, or transmitted to or from computer software (including systems and applications software), on hard or floppy disks, CD-ROMs, tapes, drives, cells, data processing devices or any other repositories of computer software which are used with electronically controlled equipment. The term computer programs, referred to in the foregoing description of electronic data, means a set of related electronic instructions which direct the operations and functions of a computer or device connected to it, which enable the computer or device to receive, process, store, retrieve or send data. This paragraph n., does not apply to your "stock" of prepackaged software;

o.   The cost to replace or restore the information on valuable papers and records, including those which exist as electronic data. Valuable papers and records include but are not limited to proprietary information, books of account, deeds, manuscripts, abstracts, drawings and card index systems. Refer to the Coverage Extension for Valuable Papers And Records (Other Than Electronic Data) for limited coverage for valuable papers and records other than those which exist as electronic data;

These two provisions take the property not covered considerably further than previous editions of the form. Provision n. specifies that the commercial property policy does not cover any types of electronic data, regardless of where it exists. It has expanded the definition to include the data and any systems or applications software. The policy does, however, make an exception for the insured's stock of prepackaged software (necessary for the insured who is a software dealer).

Provision o. then removes coverage for the cost of replacing or restoring data. There is, however, an additional coverage that provides up to $2,500 to restore or replace electronic data, which is addressed in Chapter 3.

Insureds with significant electronic data exposures beyond the reach of the limited coverage of the commercial property form have a need for specific EDP coverage, either by endorsement to the commercial property policy or a separate policy.

p.   **Vehicles or self-propelled machines.** This category removes coverage for vehicles (specifically including aircraft and watercraft) that are licensed for use on public roads or that are operated principally away from the insured premises. However, it makes an exception (thus providing coverage) for the following:

1.   vehicles that the insured manufactures, processes, or warehouses (including autos);

2.   vehicles held for sale (other than autos);

3.   rowboats and canoes out of water at the insured premises; and

4.   trailers, but only to the extent they are covered in the Coverage Extension for Non-owned Detached Trailers.

Exception 4 is a change in the commercial property policy that was first written into the 2000 edition and carried forward. There is a coverage extension for trailers that the insured does not own but uses in his business. Thus, exception 4 applies only to the extent of the coverage extension. For more on this coverage extension, see Chapter 2.

q.   **Property while outside of buildings.** Two types of property are not covered while outside of buildings:

1.   Grain, hay, straw, or other crops, and

2.   Fences, radio or television antennas, including satellite dishes, and their lead-in wiring, masts, towers, trees, shrubs, or plants (other than stock). The commercial property policy picks up limited coverage ($1,000) for such property under the coverage extensions section (see Chapter 2). The high likelihood of loss of or damage to such property makes them either the subject of separately underwritten specialty policies (for example, crop-hail coverage) or uninsurable.

Outdoor signs coverage was revised in the 06 07 edition of the policy. Outdoor signs (other than signs attached to buildings) were previously included in property not covered provision q, except to the extent covered under the outdoor property coverage extension. ISO revised the property not covered and outdoor property coverage extension sections to remove reference to signs. Coverage for detached outdoor signs is subject to the applicable causes of loss form and to a special provision in the limits of insurance condition. The limit of insurance for attached outdoor signs is increased from $1,000 to $2,500 per sign in any one occurrence. The limit of insurance for detached outdoor signs is increased from $1,000 per occurrence (in total) to $2,500 per sign in any one occurrence. Further, coverage for detached outdoor signs is broadened to include all causes of loss otherwise covered under the applicable causes of loss form.

Chapter 2

Additional Coverages, Coverage Extensions, and Optional Coverages

Additional Coverages

Section 4 of the commercial property policy contains additional coverages, providing coverage for consequential or indirect loss not covered by the agreement to cover direct damage (*see* Chapter 1's discussion of direct versus consequential damage). The expenses covered under the additional coverages all result from a direct loss, but are not direct physical damage as required by the insuring agreement. While not directly attributable to the insured peril, they are nevertheless attendant expenses necessary to return the insured to a preloss state and for which insurance coverage has been designed to respond. Examples are that a covered loss leaves debris behind that must be removed, undamaged property must be moved to be protected against further loss, or building codes create increased rebuilding costs. The commercial property policy provides six additional coverages:

- Debris removal

- Preservation of property

- Fire department service charge

- Pollutant clean-up and removal

- Increased cost of construction

- Electronic data

Section 4. Additional Coverages

4.a. Debris Removal

After damage to covered property by an insured peril, often a significant expense to the insured is the expense to remove debris. Since this expense is not a direct result of the peril (consequential, indirect damage), it does not meet the requirement of direct physical damage in the insuring agreement. However, the additional coverage for debris removal provides money for the insured to remove debris.

The CP 00 10 02 00 edition of the commercial property policy introduced a rewritten provision with a much expanded description of how debris removal coverage works and what it pays. It pays the insured's expense to remove debris of covered property that results from a covered peril occurring during the policy period. The expenses must be reported to the insurer within 180 days of the date of loss.

Debris removal coverage, however, specifically does not pay to extract pollutants from land or water. Nor does it cover the expense to remove, restore, or replace polluted land or water.

Debris removal expense is within the limit of liability, except in two situations where the policy may include an additional $10,000 debris removal coverage. In any situation, the most the policy will pay in any loss for both covered loss and debris removal is the policy limit for that type of property (i.e., building or contents), plus $10,000.

The policy caps the amount of debris removal coverage at 25 percent of the total loss (amount of loss payable plus deductible). The policy contains this example to illustrate: assume a limit of insurance of $90,000 with a deductible of $500. Further assume a loss of $50,000, for a loss payable amount of $49,500 (the damage, $50,000, less the deductible of $500). Debris removal expense is $10,000. The total debris removal expense of $10,000 is recoverable because $10,000 is 20 percent of $50,000, which is less than 25 percent of the loss payable ($49,500 plus the $500 deductible). The insured would recover $59,500 ($49,500 for the loss less the deductible plus $10,000 for debris removal expense). In this example, any amount of debris expense over $12,500 would not be covered.

There are cases when the basic debris removal coverage, as described in the previous paragraphs, is not adequate. The sum of the direct damage plus debris removal might be greater than the policy limit, or the amount of debris removal might exceed 25 percent of the total loss. In that case the policy provides an additional flat amount of $10,000 for debris removal. Here is another example under this scenario. Assume everything is the same, except the fire loss is now more serious—$80,000 direct damage, with $30,000 in debris removal expenses. The insurer's payment for the direct damage is $79,500. Even though the initial calculation of debris removal is $20,000 (25 percent of $80,000) the policy will pay only $10,500. That brings the insurer's total payment for direct and indirect damage to the limit of liability, $90,000. Then, the policy pays the additional amount of $10,000 for debris removal. The total debris removal expense payable is $20,500, leaving $9,500 of debris removal expense uncovered. Extra debris removal coverage can be arranged using endorsement CP 04 15.

Debris removal expense is payable if the insured reports the expense in writing to the insurer within 180 days of the physical loss. Former policy editions provided 180 days from the date of the loss or from the end of the policy period, whichever was earlier. The current provision states expense must be reported within 180 days of the date of the loss.

If the insured chooses not to replace the building, the $10,000 flat amount for debris removal is payable. The policy does not require that the building be repaired or replaced before this coverage is available. The policy states that if the sum of the direct physical loss and debris removal expense exceeds the limit of insurance or if the debris removal expense exceeds 25 percent, then an additional $10,000 for each location in one occurrence is available. Neither this additional coverage nor the loss payment conditions require the insured to repair or replace the building. However, if the insured chooses not to replace the building, loss settlement reverts to actual cash value.

Debris Removal Coverage and the Coinsurance Provision

This example illustrates operation of the debris removal provision where the insured does not carry an adequate amount of insurance to meet the coinsurance requirement. A building insured on form CP 00 10 suffered both direct damage and debris removal expense. However the property was underinsured, thus resulting in a coinsurance penalty. The issue is whether the same coinsurance penalty is applied to debris removal payment as to the direct damage payment. The appropriate result is that it is not. An indirect penalty already applies when property is underinsured. The debris removal clause provides up to 25 percent of the amount paid for direct loss, not 25 percent of the amount insured.

With the coinsurance penalty applied to the direct loss settlement the amount payable for debris removal is 25 percent of an already penalized amount.

Debris Removal Coverage—Volunteer Expense

A church insured on form CP 00 10 sustained damage from a fire. The insurance company paid $81,000 for the direct damage. Instead of hiring a contractor to remove the debris, members of the church volunteered their services. The church provided meals to the volunteers while they were taking away the debris. The church submitted the cost of these meals, asking to be reimbursed under the debris removal provision. The insurance company denied payment for the meals, stating that no coverage applied. The argument for covering the meal expense is that the insured kept the overall cost of debris removal down because of free assistance from the members of the congregation. Form CP 00 10 promises to pay the insured's "expense to remove debris of Covered Property caused by or resulting from a Covered Cause of Loss." It does not specify what costs it will pay. The only costs specifically not covered are expenses to remove pollutants from land or water, or the expenses to restore polluted land or water. Additionally, the policy does not specify by whom the work must be done.

4.b. Preservation of Property

Additional coverage b. is preservation of property. If the insured must move property to another location off described premises in order to preserve it from loss or damage the commercial property policy provides protection against direct physical loss during the move and for up to thirty days while it is temporarily stored at another location. The property need not be moved just for protection of property after a covered loss (e.g., after the roof has blown off and contents need to be protected from exposure) but in order to protect the property from damage by a covered loss at all. For example, if fire in a neighboring building causes the insured to move office furniture or equipment to protect it from burning, that property is covered while being moved or stored for up to thirty days. Because the word *any* is used rather than stating that the property is covered for the same perils covered by whichever causes of loss form the insured has, this preservation of property coverage is very broad. For an insured who must move any undamaged property, the policy provides protection for that property against loss or damage from perils such as flood, war, and nuclear hazard, which are normally excluded. In the previous example, assume the insured moves equipment to preserve it from fire in the neighboring building and that the insured's building also burned. The insured moves his property to a warehouse for safekeeping after the fire. Unfortunately the warehouse floods, ruining the property. The commercial property policy will pay for the flood damage—generally excluded—under this additional coverage.

4.c. Fire Department Service Charge

Sometimes an insured must agree upfront in a contract to pay for a fire department's service or a local ordinance may call for such payment. Fire department service charge is an additional coverage that will pay up to $1,000 when the fire department is called to respond to a covered cause of loss and liability for the charges was assumed prior to the loss or is required by local ordinance.

ISO revised the June 2007 edition to provide a mechanism for easily adjusting fire department service charge coverage if the insured needs a larger limit. The provision was changed with the phrase "unless a higher limit is shown in the Declarations," allowing the insured to schedule the necessary amount of economic protection.

This coverage in the commercial property policy differs from similar coverage in the homeowners policy. The homeowners policy does not cover this expense if the covered property is located within the limits of the city, municipality, or protection district that furnishes the protection. The commercial property policy does not restrict where the property may be located. Also, the commercial property policy pays this expense if required by local ordinance. The homeowners policy does not mention this at all.

Fire Department Service Charge Coverage

In rural areas, town fire departments often have contracts with smaller towns, villages, or townships to provide service. The question may arise about the provision in the additional coverage that ties payment for fire department service charges to the insured's liability assumed by contract or agreement. In most cases, the only contract is between the local governments and not between the individual property owner and a government entity. The insured has coverage under such circumstances. No formal contract is required for coverage since an agreement will suffice. According to *Webster's Ninth New Collegiate Dictionary*, an *agreement* is "an arrangement as to a course of action." Simply by being located in the town the insured has made an agreement to abide by local ordinances, regulations, and arrangements for payment of services. The insurance policy does not specify who the parties to the agreement must be. If all property owners of a particular town must pay for services passed down to them for services provided by an out-of-town fire department, coverage applies.

4.d. Pollutant Cleanup and Removal

Pollutant cleanup and removal, the fourth additional coverage, provides an annual aggregate amount of $10,000 for expenses associated with cleanup or removal of pollutants that result from covered losses. The additional coverage covers land and water at the insured location. It responds if a covered peril causes the discharge, dispersal, seepage, migration, release, or escape of pollutants.

The concept of annual aggregate is unusual in property insurance, generally associated with liability insurance. What this means is that the coverage for pollutant cleanup is limited to $10,000 *each year*. For example, an insured gas station suffers vandalism in January, which is the start of the annual policy term. As a result, some petroleum products are spread on the grass around the station. The cost to clean up the ground is $8,000. Note that only cleanup of ground or water is available under this additional coverage—this is not the same as coverage available in the exception to the pollution exclusion, which applies to covered property. If another covered pollutant event occurs before the end of the year, the insured would have $2,000 of coverage remaining for pollutant cleanup. The limit is refreshed to $10,000 at the start of the next annual period.

The policy does not cover the cost of tests to monitor or assess the existence or effects of pollutants. However, it does cover such costs if the testing occurs during the course of the pollutant removal.

4.e. Increased Cost of Construction

Often after a loss an insured must make repairs to damaged buildings or structures to meet current building or zoning laws. An example would be an older warehouse that has knob and tube wiring; local building code now requires the building's owner to rewire with Romex (circuit breakers). The cost for this upgrade was not covered by the commercial property policy unless specifically endorsed until additional coverage e. was introduced in the CP 00 10 10 00. The CP 00 10 10 00 edition added increased cost of construction as the fifth additional coverage. It provides up to $10,000—

above the coverage limit—for increased costs associated with enforcement of building or zoning laws.

In its explanatory comments, ISO stated that the purpose of this coverage is "to respond in some measure to the situation where a building code requires some upgrades but not major construction changes." Of course the insured may still need coverage beyond the $10,000 amount, which can be arranged via endorsement. Note that this coverage applies only to buildings for which the insured has purchased the replacement cost optional coverage.

Increased cost of construction additional coverage responds to expense necessary for compliance with enforcement of an ordinance or law in repairing or rebuilding damaged property. The law must regulate construction or land use at the described premises and must be in force at the time of the loss. If a law required compliance prior to the loss and the insured did not comply, coverage does not apply.

As with debris removal additional coverage, this coverage does not apply to costs for pollutant removal. While it has never covered the costs associated with pollution testing, detoxifying, or cleanup, as of the rollout of CP 00 10 04 02, cost associated with the presence of mold is excluded.

The previous language read as follows:

> Under this Additional Coverage, we will not pay:
>
> > any costs associated with the enforcement of an ordinance or law which requires any insured or others to test for, monitor, clean up, remove, contain, treat, detoxify or neutralize, or in any way respond to, or assess the effects of "pollutants."

An example is a convenience store that sells gasoline. After a fire damages a substantial part of the convenience store, the local ordinance will not permit the owner to rebuild until he certifies that no gasoline is leaking from the tanks. The cost of that certification is not covered by the commercial property policy.

The current version states:

Under this Additional Coverage, we will not pay for:

(a) The enforcement of any ordinance or law which requires demolition, repair, replacement, reconstruction, remodeling or remediation of property due to contamination by "pollutants" or due to the presence, growth, proliferation, spread or any activity of "fungus," wet or dry rot or bacteria; or

(b) Any costs associated with the enforcement of an ordinance or law which requires any insured or others to test for, monitor, clean up, remove, contain, treat, detoxify or neutralize, or in any way respond to, or assess the effects of "pollutants," "fungus," wet or dry rot or bacteria.

The effect is that the policy not only excludes payment for the tank testing, it also excludes payment for any government-ordered mold removal.

The limit for this additional coverage is the lesser of 5 percent of the limit of insurance on the building or $10,000. If the policy provides blanket coverage on several buildings, this coverage is limited to the lesser of $10,000 or 5 percent times the value of the damaged building as of the time of loss times the applicable coinsurance percentage.

The additional coverage for increased cost of construction has its own conditions. It does not pay for the increased cost until the insured actually replaces the damaged property. It also does not pay unless the repairs or replacement are made as soon as reasonably possible, not to exceed two years (this period may be extended with the cooperation of the insurer). The insured may replace at the described premises or any other premises. However, if he chooses to replace at another premises, the policy pays only the amount it would have paid at the old premises for the increased construction costs. If the insured must relocate due to the dictates of a law, the policy pays increased costs at the new location.

By specific term, this additional coverage is not subject to the ordinance or law exclusion to the extent they may conflict.

4.f. Electronic Data

The CP 00 10 04 02 edition introduced the additional coverage for electronic data. This provides an aggregate annual amount of $2,500 for destruction or corruption of electronic data. Electronic data, by specific reference, has the same meaning as in the property not covered section, thereby mirroring the provisions—electronic data is eliminated as covered property under the form and then brought back in as an additional coverage, subject to limits and limitations.

The destruction or corruption must be due to a covered cause of loss. Coverage conditions provisions depend upon which causes of loss form is attached.

Under the special form, the data is covered only against damage from the specified causes of loss as set out and the peril of collapse. If the insured has chosen the broad form perils, electronic data is covered for the broad form perils and for collapse. However, if the insured has purchased extra causes of loss (such as flood or earthquake), those purchased causes do not apply to electronic data.

An important addition under this section is coverage for damage done by a virus to the data. The policy says a *virus* is "designed to damage or destroy any part of the system or disrupt its normal operation." The virus may be introduced by almost anyone from almost anywhere. However, the policy excludes damage manipulation by employees, including leased and temporary employees. It also excludes viruses introduced by or manipulation by anyone the named insured hires to work on the computer system (e.g., a repair technician or IT consultant).

Coverage Extensions

Following the additional coverages is section 5, Coverage Extensions. The coverage extensions operate to allow the insured to extend coverage to certain property or property in certain situations if either of two conditions are met: a coinsurance percentage of 80 percent or a value reporting period symbol is shown on the declarations page. The coverage extensions are as follows:

- Newly acquired or constructed property

- Personal effects and property of others

- Valuable papers and records (other than electronic data)

- Property off-premises

- Outdoor property

- Nonowned detached trailers

Except where specified otherwise coverage extensions apply to property located in or on the described building or in the open or in a vehicle within 100 feet of the described premises. Unlike the additional coverages, the coverage extensions are additional insurance, which represent increased limits of liability.

5.a. Newly Acquired or Constructed Property

The first coverage extension addresses newly constructed or acquired property of the same type already covered. The first part of this coverage extension addresses newly acquired or constructed building property and the second addresses newly acquired business personal property.

If the insured is building a new building on the described premises, this coverage extension covers that building during construction. (Note that the commercial property policy covers additions to existing buildings under building coverage.)

The policy also covers buildings at a different location that the insured acquires. Coverage for these buildings is subject to two conditions:

1. They must be intended for similar use as the described building; or

2. They must be intended for use as a warehouse.

The policy provides up to $250,000 coverage per covered building under the coverage extension. This $250,000 coverage extension amount is available even if the insured carries less insurance on the declared building. For example, the insured's present building is insured for $100,000; however, a new building under construction on the same premises is, or will be, worth $500,000. If this building under construction suffers covered damage, the insured may collect up to $250,000, the limit of this coverage extension, and is not limited to the $100,000 carried on the existing building. This is a per building amount. It applies to a new building under construction on the described premises. It also applies to a building that the insured acquires at another location—as long as he intends to put that building to use in a similar manner as the existing building or intends to use it as a warehouse.

Part 2 part of the newly acquired or constructed property coverage extension was extensively revised in the CP 00 10 10 00 edition; those revisions carry forth into the current edition. If the insured already carries coverage on business personal property, this extension gives the insured up to $100,000 coverage, regardless of the stated policy limit for business personal property at a newly acquired location. This extension does not, however, apply to business personal property at fairs, exhibitions, and trade shows.

While the CP 00 10 06 95 edition of the form promised coverage for business personal property at any location the insured acquires other than fairs or exhibitions, the CP 00 10 10 00 edition added clarifying language. Coverage for newly acquired business personal property is divided into three categories:

1.   Business personal property, including newly acquired business personal property, at any location (with the exception of fairs, exhibitions, and trade shows).

2.   Business personal property in newly constructed or acquired buildings at the described location.

3.   Newly acquired business personal property at the described location.

The extension for newly acquired business personal property does not cover the following:

1.   Business personal property of others upon which the insured is working.

2.   Business personal property of others that the insured has temporarily in his possession while manufacturing or wholesaling.

The coverage extension to newly acquired buildings and business personal property operates for thirty days. The thirty-day period begins when the insured acquires or begins to build new property. It ends after thirty days, at policy expiration, or when the insured reports the values to the insurer, whichever is earliest. The additional premium due for the additional property is calculated from the date the construction begins or the insured acquires the property.

Newly Acquired Location

Property insured under the commercial property policy was damaged by a tornado. In addition to damage at the premises listed on the declarations page, the insured made a claim for property on premises it had rented at a second location. This location, used as a warehouse, had been rented within thirty days prior to the loss. As of the date of loss, the location had not been added to the policy. The question is whether the location qualifies for coverage as a newly acquired location.

One argument is that *acquired* means "to buy" and does not include renting property. The issue is if "to acquire" includes an element of control or must be ownership. Absent a specific policy definition of the word, the insured is entitled to the most favorable common dictionary meaning. "To come into possession of" does not necessarily connote ownership; it is broad enough to encompass other forms of possession, such as renting, leasing, or borrowing. Additionally, the policy uses the word *acquired* rather than *purchased* or some other term meaning "obtaining title." As acquiring is a broader term than purchasing, it is appropriate to include means of obtaining property other than acquiring ownership through purchase.

This additional premises is afforded coverage under the newly acquired property provision to rented locations, provided the insured is legally responsible for damages. Coverage would not extend to the building on the premises absent a legal obligation of the insured.

5.b. Personal Effects and Property of Others

The second coverage extension provides up to $2,500 for damage to property of others. The first part of the extension provides coverage for personal effects belonging to the named insured, and officers, directors, partners, employees, members, or managers of the insured. Recognizing the increased use of the limited liability company formation, members and managers were added to the CP 00 10 10 02 edition. All perils of the policy apply to this personal effects and property of others coverage extension, except theft.

The other part of this extension covers property of others that is in the care, custody, or control of the insured. The $2,500 limit represents goodwill coverage and is insufficient for an insured who regularly takes in property of others for servicing or processing. If the insured has a care, custody, or control exposure, bailees coverage should be arranged. Theft is covered for this second class of others' property.

The first part of this coverage extension provides much narrower coverage than the second. The policy limits coverage for employees, officers, directors, partners, members, or managers to their personal effects. A standard desktop dictionary says that "personal effects" are "privately owned items (as clothing and toilet articles) normally worn or carried on that person."

5.c. Valuable Papers and Records (Other Than Electronic Data)

When a covered peril destroys valuable papers and records at a described location, several separate items must be taken into consideration:

1. The cost of blank paper, film, disks, or other storage media.

2. The cost of actually transcribing or copying such papers and records from available duplicates.

3. The cost of research and other expenses in reconstructing the records if no duplicates exist,.

The third item, the expense of research involved in recompiling data, is the subject of coverage extension 5.c. The insured may apply up to $2,500 for such research costs following destruction of valuable papers and records by an insured peril. Without this extension, the commercial property policy covers only the first two items, new stock and transcription. This extension does not cover the expense associated with data stored electronically. That is addressed by the additional coverage for electronic data.

As well as adding a new additional coverage for electronic data, the CP 00 10 04 02 edition revised the coverage extension for valuable papers and records, other than electronic data. This extension of $2,500 was revised to cover all valuable papers and records other than electronic data. As with the additional coverage for electronic data, an insured with the special causes of loss form is limited to the specified causes of loss for this coverage. Collapse is added for insureds with broad form perils.

The $2,500 limit applies on a per-location basis. Coverage includes cost of blank material on which records are reproduced and labor to do the job. However, those costs are not subject to the $2,500 limit and instead are within the limit applying to business personal property.

5.d. Property Off-premises

The commercial property policy provides $10,000 coverage for property located away from the described premises. The policy lists three places where it covers such property:

1. At a location the insured does not own, lease, or operate.

2. At a leased storage location if the insured entered into the lease after the effective date of the policy.

3. At any fair, trade show, or exhibition.

The coverage provided by number 3 was introduced in the CP 00 10 10 00 edition. Previous editions specifically eliminated property at fairs, trade shows, and exhibitions from this extension. This is not in-transit coverage as property is not covered off-premises while in a vehicle. Further, the extension does not apply to property (samples, usually) in the control of any of the insured's salespersons, unless the salesperson has the property at a fair, trade show, or exhibition. The policy also covers stock off premises under this extension. The policy defines *stock* as "merchandise held in storage or for sale, raw materials, or in-process or finished goods, including supplies used in their packing or shipping."

Meaning of "Locations You Own, Lease, or Operate"

A commercial property insured went to a customer's location to answer a service call. While at the customer's shop, a piece of equipment the insured brought with him fell off a ledge and was damaged to the amount of $2,900. The claim was denied under this provision stating the insured was operating at this location while making the service call. At issue is if coverage extension 5.d. property off-premises applies to the damaged equipment.

The commercial property policy's property off-premises provision allows the extension of coverage (up to $10,000) to apply to covered property that is temporarily at a location that the insured does not own, lease, or operate. Performing a service call at a customer's premises is not equivalent to a location that the insured operates. The phrase "own, lease, or operate" denotes a control feature absent here. Coming onto a customer's premises to perform services does not turn control of that location over to the person coming in. The word *operate* must be viewed in relation to the other words in the provision and interpreted in that context. Therefore, the equipment is covered for up to $10,000 under coverage extension 5.d.

5.e. Outdoor Property

The commercial property policy lists as property not covered a variety of outdoor property that may sometimes be found around a commercial enterprise. This extension restores coverage for direct damage and debris removal for loss to the following types of outdoor property (which are not covered under the basic commercial property policy): outdoor fences, radio and television antennas (including satellite dishes), and trees, shrubs, and plants (other than stock of trees, shrubs, or plants).

Prior to the CP 00 10 06 07 edition, detached signs were eliminated from coverage in the property not covered section and limited coverage was brought back in here. ISO revised the property not covered and outdoor property coverage extension sections to remove reference to detached signs. Coverage for outdoor signs is thereby subject to the applicable causes of loss form and to a special provision in the limits of insurance condition. The limits of insurance condition is revised to increase coverage on outdoor signs from $1,000 per sign to $2,500 per sign in any one occurrence.

This outdoor property extension applies only if loss is caused by fire, lightning, explosion, riot or civil commotion, or aircraft. The total amount available for direct damage and debris removal is $1,000 per occurrence, but only $250 for any one tree, shrub, or plant.

5.f. Nonowned Detached Trailers

The CP 00 10 10 00 edition of the commercial property policy added this sixth coverage extension. ISO explains the addition by stating, "Many insureds have goods delivered by truck and may be held responsible by the trucking company for damage to or theft of detached trailers left on the insured's premises for unloading and retrieval. In addition, insureds who rent detached trailers from others for storage purposes may be held responsible for damage to or theft of the trailers." The current commercial property policy provides no automatic coverage for such trailers. ISO introduced this coverage extension to provide limited coverage on nonowned detached trailers.

The policy provides $5,000 of coverage (with larger amounts available) for nonowned trailers that the insured has on its premises. This additional coverage is excess over any other applicable insurance, whether or not it is collectible.

In order to qualify for this coverage, the nonowned trailer must meet three requirements:

1.　It must be used in the insured's business.

2.　It must be in the insured's care, custody, or control at the described premises.

3.　The insured must have a contractual obligation to pay for damage to the trailer.

Coverage does not apply while the trailer is attached to a motor vehicle or while it is being hitched or unhitched. There is also no coverage if the trailer becomes accidentally unhitched from a motor vehicle.

Optional Coverages

The commercial property policy offers the insured four optional coverages that are so frequently used as to be available in the basic policy: agreed value, inflation guard, replacement cost, and extension of replacement cost to personal property of others. As these are built into the form, no extra endorsements are required. When the insured wants to purchase any of these an indication is made on the policy declarations page.

The optional coverages may be activated on the policy declarations if appropriate or desired. They are contained in section G. of the policy and include the following:

- Agreed value

- Inflation guard

- Replacement cost

- Extension of replacement cost to personal property of others

Section G.1. Agreed Value

When the insured selects agreed value, this coverage provides for a predetermined amount to be paid in the event of a total loss to the described property. If the insured does not desire this option for the entire policy period, he may choose when to make this option effective and when to terminate it. This allows the commercial property policy to be integrated more seamlessly into the insured's business where there may be seasonal differences in inventory or value.

When the insured chooses this option, the coinsurance condition does not apply. However the rules state the insured must carry an amount equal to 80 percent of the building's value or 90 percent for risks written on a blanket basis. Property written on a reporting basis is not eligible for agreed value, nor are builders risk policies. The insured must complete the statement of values endorsement, CP 16 15. Replacement cost values are used if the insured has purchased replacement cost coverage.

If the building is insured on an agreed value basis for $200,000 and it is a total loss, the insurer would simply write the insured a check for $200,000. The insured may also choose to cover some or all contents on this basis.

Section G.2. Inflation Guard

As a protection against the effects of inflation the insured may choose the inflation guard optional coverage to automatically increase limits for designated property, either completed buildings or personal property, by a predetermined annual percentage. Inflation guard may be used on policies written on either a specific or blanket basis. If there is a midterm loss, the limit of liability is increased on a pro rata basis, from either the effective date of the policy or the effective date of the last change in the limit.

The current edition of the commercial property policy contains the following example of how this coverage works:

If : The applicable limit of insurance is $100,000

The annual percentage increase is 8 percent

The number of days since the beginning of the policy year (or last policy change) is 146

The amount of increase is $100,000 x .08 x 146/365, which equals $3,200

Section G.3. Replacement Cost

The insured may purchase replacement cost coverage on various property:

1. Buildings and permanent machinery, fixtures, and equipment that are covered with the building.

2. Business personal property including furniture, fixtures, machinery, and equipment.

3. Merchandise and stock if the including stock option is shown as applicable in the declarations.

4. Tenants improvements and betterments. Specific provision states that for the purposes of replacement cost coverage tenants improvements and betterments are not considered the property of others. Since these items become the property of the landlord, some confusion existed in the past about how to treat them in the event of a loss. This wording makes it clear that a tenant who has purchased this endorsement will receive replacement cost coverage for the improvements he has made to a building.

5. Personal property of others if the extension of replacement cost to personal property of others is shown as applicable in the declarations (discussed later).

The policy specifies the following types of property as not eligible for replacement cost coverage:

1. Personal property of others.

2. Contents of a residence.

3. Works of art, antiques or rare articles, including etchings, pictures, statuary, marbles, bronzes, porcelains, and bric-a-brac.

4. Stock unless the insured includes stock on the declarations.

Replacement cost coverage operates by the insured making a claim for the actual cash value (ACV) of damaged property at the time of loss and requesting replacement cost settlement within 180 days. By first making an ACV claim the insured gets some insurance payment and may engage a contractor to start work. The insured must make repairs or replacement as soon as reasonably possible; the insurer does not make replacement cost settlement until repairs or replacements are completed.

The optional coverage adds two conditions regarding paying replacement cost for tenant improvements and betterments:

1.   If the insured does not replace the improvements or does not replace them as soon as reasonably possible after loss, loss adjustment reverts to the valuation condition (See Chapter 5).

2.   If someone else, such as the landlord, pays to repair or replace the improvements, the policy pays nothing.

The commercial property policy pays the least of the following:

1.   The limit of liability applicable to the damaged property.

2.   The cost to replace the property for the same use, with material of comparable material and quality.

3.   The amount the insured actually spends.

Provision 2 was changed in the CP 00 10 10 00 edition. The wording "on the same premises" was removed because it caused confusion and could be interpreted to mean that the policy required the insured to rebuild on the same location to receive replacement cost, which is not a requirement. The revision added the following wording that clearly allows the insured to rebuild at a new location: "If a building is rebuilt at a new premises, the cost described in e.(2) above is limited to the cost which would have been incurred if the building had been rebuilt at the original premises." For example, if the building cost $300,000 to replace at its current location but the insured chooses to rebuild at a different location where it will cost $350,000, he will receive only $300,000 from the insurer.

Replacement by Substitution — Commercial Property

An insured building was heavily damaged by fire, and the insured found another suitable building, which, after remodeling, would become a replacement for the damaged one. The insurance company agreed to pay the cost of the acquisition but not the cost of improvements. The values of the two sites were generally equivalent, as were the outbuildings. Thus, the transaction represented an even trade from that standpoint. So, in essence, what the insured was requesting of the insurer was to allow him to spend the dollars improving the substitute site that would have been spent in repairing the original. Yet, the insurer balked at the transaction.

When an insured chooses the optional replacement cost coverage, the commercial property policy stipulates three limits. It agrees to pay the least of the following:

(1) The limit of insurance applicable to the lost or damaged property;

(2) The cost to replace the lost or damaged property with other property of comparable material and quality and used for the same purpose; or

(3) The amount the named insured actually spends that is necessary to repair or replace the lost or damaged property.

The third limitation opens the promise to replacement at any site. Consequently, if the third category expenditure is both less than the coverage limit and less or even equal to the price of repairs at the original site, then the conditions of the policy are met and the insured may make the move.

The word *necessary* might seem to be a curious entry in the third limitation. Since it is not defined in the policy, that judgment is left to the insured, which is appropriate. The first limitation protects the insurer. It limits the insurer's payment to no more than the applicable limit stated in the contract. Whether the insured elects to repair the damage to the existing structure or move off site, the insurer's possible maximum loss is not affected.

Replacement Cost—Reconditioned Property

This scenario examines the meaning of comparable material and quality.

A commercial property insured elected the replacement cost option. Lightning destroyed the insured's computerized phone system to the extent it could not be repaired and had to be replaced. The insurer located a used reconditioned phone system of the same make and model as the damaged system and offered to purchase and install it. The insurer believed that this option met the policy obligation since the policy states that the insurer has the option to pay the cost of repairing or replacing the lost or damaged property.

The commercial property policy states that the value of covered property (the phone system) will be determined at replacement cost without deduction for depreciation. A reconditioned phone system is a used phone system and, as such, is depreciated. The policy promises the insured that losses to covered property will be adjusted on a replacement cost basis. so the insured is entitled to a new phone system.

Replacement Cost—New Location

What happens if the replacement cost of a building is less than its actual cash value (ACV), as possible when real estate values decline rapidly?

The insured owned a building that was destroyed. The ACV of the building was $190,000, but the insured had it covered for replacement cost at $300,000. Rather than replacing the building at the same location the insured bought another building at another location. The new building was one-third larger than the destroyed building, yet it cost less. It cost $230,000 and the insured put $20,000 into it to make it usable for a total of $250,000. Since the building is one-third larger than the old building the insurer wanted to pay only 75 percent of the cost of the new building, or $187,500. This figure was less than the ACV on the old building. The insurer claimed that the extra square footage in the new building was a betterment for which the insurer should not pay. Should the insured have been paid full replacement cost, actual cash value, or the value of the new building prorated for the number of square feet in the destroyed building?

This is one of the few examples of a replacement cost settlement on a commercial property loss paying less than an actual cash value settlement. Situations such as this illustrate why the insured is given the chance to choose an actual cash value settlement even though the replacement cost option is in force.

Under paragraph e. of the replacement cost option, the insurer states that it will pay the least of three replacement costs: (1) the limit of the policy; (2) the cost to replace the property with property of comparable material and quality for the same use; or (3) the actual amount spent to replace the property at any location.

In this case, the third option applies and must be used. Since the replacement property was one-third larger than the original property, the cost of actually replacing the destroyed property's square footage is 75 percent of the cost of the new property (That is, 100 sq. ft. x 1.333 = 133 sq. ft.; but 100 sq. ft. = 75 percent of 133 sq. ft., because 133 x .75 = 100). Since the new property cost less per square foot to construct than the old property, the insured receives a lower settlement at replacement cost than if he had chosen the actual cash value valuation.

Section G.4. Extension of Replacement Cost to Personal Property of Others

The option for the insured to extend replacement cost coverage to the property of others was introduced with the CP 00 10 10 00 edition. When the insured chooses this option, it deletes the reference to property of others as not being covered under the replacement cost option.

The insured must be subject to a written contractual obligation governing his liability for the property of others. If such an obligation exists, then the policy covers loss or damage to such property at the amount for which the insured is liable under such contract. The payment is limited to the lesser of the property's replacement cost or the limit of insurance.

Chapter 3

Covered Causes of Loss—Named Perils Forms

Chapters 1 and 2 described and analyzed what is—and is not—covered property for purposes of the commercial property policy. The damage-causing events and incidents that the policy is meant to protect against—the *perils* covered—are determined by the insured's selection of a causes of loss form that enumerates and defines these covered and excluded perils. One of three causes of loss form is attached to the building and personal property coverage form to make a policy, along with endorsements and conditions forms. The options are the *basic form* (named perils), the *broad form* (named perils still, but the number of perils expanded), and the *special form* (any peril not otherwise excluded), also referred to as *open perils* or in older nomenclature, *all risks* (the term "all risks" went out of favor in the 1980s as the term caused policy interpretation problems with judicial decisions vitiating exclusions where the insurer promised "all risks" coverage).

The perils covered by the commercial property policy and several other of the insuring forms comprising the commercial property program depend upon the insured's choice of one of the three causes of loss forms. The basic and broad forms are treated in this chapter; Chapter 4 deals with the special causes of loss form.

The basic form covers eleven basic perils, and the broad form adds three perils and one additional coverage—collapse. Under previous commercial property programs, insureds had to purchase separate coverage for the glass in their buildings using form CP 00 15. That form is no longer in use. ISO simplified the underwriting process and the policy by writing coverage on glass under the commercial property form and subject to the perils applicable to other property.

CP 10 10—Causes of Loss – Basic Form

This form provides named perils coverage and is the most limited of the causes of loss forms. Only those perils specifically included in the form are covered and loss or damage must be directly caused by the peril. The covered perils under the basic form are fire, lightning, explosion, windstorm and hail, smoke, aircraft or vehicles, riot or civil commotion, vandalism, sprinkler leakage, sinkhole collapse, and volcanic action.

Fire. The named peril forms do not limit the peril of fire, however, courts have long held that fire means a *hostile* fire, one that has left its intended confines. Hostile fires are contrasted to the *friendly fire* doctrine. The friendly fire doctrine provides that loss by friendly fires is not insured and that a friendly fire is one that the insured intentionally kindles and that remains in the place it was intended to be. A hostile fire is one that is either not confined to the place intended or one not started intentionally. A minority of courts have expanded the idea of hostile fire to include those that they characterize as excessive, as when a thermostat or other part of a furnace malfunctions and damages either the heating device itself or some other property through extreme heat.

The distinction between friendly and hostile fires applies only to insureds that have purchased named perils coverage. On a special causes of loss form, the doctrine of friendly fire does not apply; coverage is not restricted to named perils but responds to damage unless a specific exclusion applies.

Lightning. As with the peril of fire, the policy does not limit lightning. From the earliest insuring forms lighting has been an accepted corollary of the fire peril.

Explosion. The commercial property policy does not define *explosion*, so it is subject to broad interpretation. The dictionary defines *explosion* as "the act of exploding;" "to burst forth with sudden violence or noise from internal energy" or 'to undergo a rapid reaction with the production of noise, heat and violent expansion," or "to burst violently as a result of pressure from within."

Is a Gunshot an Explosion?

The insured is a gun shop covered on a commercial property policy with the basic causes of loss form, CP 10 10. While the store owner was cleaning a gun it accidentally discharged, causing a large hole in one of the interior walls. Although the agent argued that this constituted an explosion, the insurer denied the claim.

The commercial property policy does not define explosion. In the policy's description of the explosion peril, it does, however, include explosion of gases or fuel in a furnace. It also excludes rupture of pressure relief devices. It does not specifically exclude gunshot from the definition of explosion. A definition of explosion is "a large-scale, rapid, and spectacular expansion, outbreak, or upheaval." That is what happened, and the damage to the shop's wall is covered. The important point is that the form does not say it must be the covered property that explodes; it is damage by explosion that is covered.

Both the basic and broad causes of loss forms exclude two types of explosion peril: operation of pressure relief devices and rupture due to expansion of the contents of any structure caused by water. Steam boiler explosion is also excluded under both forms.

Windstorm or Hail. The commercial policy's coverage for damage by windstorm or hail is limited by three provisions that state coverage does not include the following:

1. Frost or cold weather.

2. Ice (other than hail), snow, or sleet, whether driven by wind or not.

3. Loss or damage to the interior or a building or structure (or the property inside) caused by rain, snow, sand, or dust, whether driven by wind or not. In order for such a loss to be covered the building or structure must first sustain wind or hail damage to the roof or walls through which the rain, snow, sand, or dust enters.

Direct Loss from Windstorm

A subject of coverage argument and litigation has been determining what direct physical loss caused by or resulting from windstorm is. Another topic of significant interest following the hurricane season of 2005, which included hurricanes Katrina, Rita, and Wilma, is the relationship between windstorm coverage and flood insurance and what can be covered as wind damage and what is excluded as flood damage. For more on that topic see Chapter 12.

Forms do not define *windstorm*, so courts are often asked to do so within the circumstances of a particular case. The Arizona Supreme Court said that "a windstorm is a wind of sufficient force to proximately cause damage to the 'ordinary condition of the thing insured.'"

A majority of courts agree that the wind does not need to be the only cause of loss for a loss to be directly related to windstorm. For example, assume damage is not by wind knocking over a covered shed, but from a board picked up by the wind hitting the shed. The rule is that the windstorm must be the proximate cause or the efficient proximate cause of the loss. The minority of courts have followed the rule that any contributing cause to the damage must itself not be excluded by the policy.

Many courts have followed the rule that a direct loss from windstorm occurs when it is shown that the force or strength of the wind caused the damage. Some jurisdictions require that the winds be tumultuous and have the nature of a storm. Courts have also addressed the issue of whether there is direct loss from windstorm when the wind-damaged property was in poor physical condition. Generally, these courts have held that there is covered loss if the windstorm was the proximate cause.

The first part of the exclusionary language reaffirms the policy intent that damage by frost or cold weather is not equivalent to damage by windstorm or hail. However, a windstorm during the winter months that causes damage that is not equivalent to damage by cold weather (e.g., freezing) would be covered.

The policy states that before windstorm or hail damage to the interior of a building is covered, the exterior must suffer damage from wind or hail. Once wind or hail damages the exterior of the building, the policy covers the interior for damage caused by rain, snow, sand, or dust entering the structure. A common type of claim reached by this exclusion is water damage to walls, ceilings, or personal property that occurs during a windstorm but for which there is no apparent source. Sometimes this type of damage results from seepage around window casings or eaves that are of adequate soundness for ordinary weather but not for extraordinary wind events. The argument has been made that absent some kind of damage, temporary though it may be, water would not have seeped through the window or ceiling.

Tarp Blown Off—Damage to Roof?

A business insured under the commercial property policy with the basic causes of loss form contracted to have the roof changed from a flat rolled roof to a metal gable roof. This required the contractor to cut the roof edges to install a new sill plate on the exterior block walls so the new roof trusses could be properly secured. At the end of each day, the contractor covered the edge of the roof with tarps. During construction a windstorm ripped the tarps off the roof and allowed water to enter the building causing damage to contents.

The claim was denied based on the policy language that requires a building to first sustain wind or hail damage to its roof or walls before the policy covers water damage to contents. The insurer's argument is that the tarps used to cover the roof are not part of the roof or walls; because the structure did not sustain damage, there is no coverage for the water damage to the contents.

The basic causes of loss form qualifies the windstorm or hail peril with language that eliminates coverage for loss or damage to the interior of a building or its contents unless the building first sustains damage to its roof or walls through which the rain enters. A standard dictionary defines *roof* as "the cover of a building;" "material used for a roof"; and "something suggesting a roof: as a canopy of leaves and branches." Absent a specific policy definition, the insurance contract is broadly interpreted in favor of coverage. In this case the tarp was acting as a substitute for the actual roof and was, in fact, the roof at the time of the incident.

In *Homestead Fire Ins. Co. v De Witt*, 245 P.2d 92 (Okla. 1952), the court ruled that a canvas covering was a roof, A construction company was building an addition to a school. In order to join the new and old sections an opening was left in the roof of the old building. The construction company covered the opening with canvas to protect the old building. A sudden windstorm arose, ripped off the canvas, and rain damaged the interior.

Even though this case preceded the policies of today, it contained similar language that required roof damage before the insurer would cover water damage to the interior or its contents. The court ruled that because the contractors "evidently considered [as] adequate" the canvas that had been placed on the opening, this "brought it within the provisions of the windstorm clause, since except for the action of the wind, the opening was adequately closed." The canvas was a roof. This case has been cited numerous times over the years and has not been overturned.

However, a California appeals court saw things differently in *Diep v. California Fair Plan Ass'n.*, 15 Cal.App.4th 1205 (1993). The court said: "While 'roof' has many different meanings (e.g., roof of the mouth), dictionary definitions are consistent with respect to that which people usually expect to find on top of a building…a roof is commonly considered to be a permanent part of the structure it covers. Roof is not an ambiguous or vague word…the parties to the insurance contract could not have originally intended the result the plaintiff seeks here."

Windstorm or hail is one of three causes of loss that may be removed from coverage by endorsement (either CP 10 53 or CP 10 54). Insurers doing business in areas such as the South Atlantic or Gulf coast often refuse to write wind coverage or write it subject to high rates and large deductibles. In such areas windstorm coverage is available through a catastrophe pool or similar facility administered by a governmental entity. Endorsement CP 10 53 applies the exclusion only to the coverage parts providing direct physical damage coverage. Endorsement CP 10 54 also applies the exclusion to those coverage parts providing coverage for indirect losses: business income, extra expense, and leasehold interest.

Smoke. The term *smoke*, like *fire*, is undefined in the policy. Many courts have followed a definition similar to this one from *Webster's Tenth New Collegiate Dictionary*: "the gaseous products of burning carbonaceous materials especially of organic origin made visible by the presence of small particles of carbon."

At one time, smoke damage referred only to sudden and accidental smoke from the faulty operation of a heating or cooking unit at the insured premises. Damage resulting from smoke from a fireplace was excluded. The current property forms cover sudden and accidental smoke damage from almost any source, except for agricultural smudging (i.e., the use of smudge pots to produce a smoky fire for protecting certain crops from frost and insects) and industrial operations. The commercial property policy excludes smoke damage from these sources because such operations represent constant or constantly recurring exposures. Damage is certain to occur, so there is no insurable risk; there is a certainty of loss.

Courts usually apply a definition of *smoke* that requires a visible product of combustion. However, in *Henri's Food Products Co. v. Home Ins. Co.,* 474 F. Supp. 889 (E.D. Wis. 1979), the court held that the insured was covered for smoke damage when the outside of bottles of salad dressing stored in a warehouse were contaminated by the vaporization of agricultural chemicals also stored in the warehouse. The court did not discuss its reasoning in any depth, stating simply that it relied on *Words and Phrases* and *Webster's Third New International Dictionary.* Perhaps the court relied on the inclusion of vapor among the dictionary definitions.

A court in another case disagreed with the Wisconsin court's opinion.. In *K & Lee Corp. v. Scottsdale Ins. Co.,* 769 F. Supp. 870 (D.C.Pa.1991), the court held, "An unabridged comprehensive dictionary lists every conceivable usage of words, including those that are arcane, archaic, and obscure. While smoke may result from some chemical reactions, the common usage of the term refers to the products of combustion and, more importantly, to matter that is visible."

The term "industrial operations" raises another interpretation issue. A Georgia appeals court said that the term did not to apply to what the court described as a small neighborhood bakery in *Georgia Farm Bureau Mut. Ins. Co. v. Washington,* 243 S.E.2d 639 (Ga. App. 1978). The insured was a dress shop owner whose merchandise was damaged by smoke that escaped from the faulty exhaust vent of the nearby bakery. The trial court held for the insured, and the court of appeals affirmed with little comment. The trial court held that exclusions and exceptions must be taken more strongly against the insurer and that a layman's reasonable reading of words in an insurance contract—in their plain, ordinary, and popular sense—prevails.

Other than the reference to agricultural smudging or industrial operations, the named perils forms cover smoke damage from any other source as long as the damage is sudden and accidental. There are no other qualifications or limitations with respect to this peril. Thus, even when smoke originates away from the insured premises—at an adjacent building or even at a more distant location—smoke damage is covered.

Aircraft or Vehicles. The aircraft or vehicles cause of loss covers damage done to covered property by physical contact with an aircraft or vehicle. By specific statement this also includes damage done by a spacecraft or a self-propelled missile. It also covers damage from objects that fall from an aircraft or are thrown up by a vehicle although this would not include damage to covered property thrown *from* a vehicle, as by a vandal.

The loss must be caused by an object being thrown up from a vehicle, as by running over the object.

There are many instances in which a vehicle can cause damage without coming into actual contact with the damaged property. From time to time, insureds report losses of the following nature: a truck pulling away from a building to which, unknown to the driver, a chain was attached; a vehicle hitting another object and propelling it into the side of a building; or a vehicle shearing off a water hydrant with resultant severe water damage to property in a nearby building. Due to the peril's requirement of physical contact between the property and the vehicle, these claims are often denied.

However, courts have found coverage under the vehicle peril in situations where, for example, a boom fell off a crane and damaged an insured building. One court stated that "to exclude this loss because contact was only with the boom would be similar to excluding loss caused if a tractor-trailer loaded with piling jackknifed and the projecting piling, but not the trailer, damaged a building. The difference is simply one of degree." The implication is that, in some instances, damage without actual physical contact by the vehicle could be covered even where the policy states that coverage applies only in cases of physical contact.

On the other hand, a court held that no actual physical contact occurred where a truck pulled a cable through a doorway. A boiler on the cable damaged the building. The damage occurred when a barrel that supported a beam or upright to a beam was dislodged, causing the roof to sag eight to ten inches. The insured argued that the term *vehicle* included every accessory piece of equipment attached to the vehicle. The court found the term was not ambiguous and refused to apply the insured's definition to the construction of the policy.

Perhaps the difference in interpretation between this case and the one in the previous paragraph was the nature of the equipment that caused the damage. Whereas a crane cannot be effectively operated without a boom, so that the boom is an integral part of the machine, a cable is more remotely related to the day-to-day operation of a truck. The question of relatedness to the vehicle is one of degree.

The form further states that damage by vehicles owned by the named insured or by vehicles operated in the course of the named insured's business is excluded.

Riot or Civil Commotion. The common definition of *riot,* although it may vary slightly among cases and commentators, can be stated as, "Any tumultuous disturbance of the public peace by three or more persons mutually assisting one another in execution of a common purpose by the unlawful use of force and violence resulting in property damage of any kind." *Black's Law Dictionary* defines *riot* in a much longer passage, but with the same meaning that a riot is a public disturbance of more than one person.

Generally, the courts have not found coverage where the damage was done stealthily or secretly, meaning that a riot must be a public event. An example is *Providence Washington Ins. Co. v. Lynn,* 492 F.2d 979 (1st Cir.1974). In this case three inmates of the maximum security section of the Adult Correctional Institution (ACI), Cranston, Rhode Island, set fire to the facility by pushing a burning mop through a tiled roof. The resulting conflagration caused physical damage to the building exceeding $300,000. They performed the act in secret and intended it to stay that way but were caught. The legal argument by the institution was that a felony like arson is a "tumultuous event offending the peace and dignity of the state" and that the consequences flowing from the arson, rather than the act of setting the fire itself, established a riot.

These consequences included evacuation and transport of displaced prisoners, increased security, excitement and activity occasioned by a major fire, and the presumed fear and confusion caused by a blaze in a prison, particularly among those prisoners who were in lockup when the fire broke out. The court did not agree, stating that a clear doctrine of the common law that a stealthy act of destruction is not transformed into an act of riot because upon later discovery of the damage there is a public disturbance

The meaning of *civil commotion* is more obscure than that of *riot* and has received less attention from the courts. Some authorities doubt that it is possible to conceive of a case in which a loss would be paid as a civil commotion but would not be covered under a policy or endorsement referring only to riot. In *Hartford Fire Ins. Co. v. War Eagle Coal Co.,* 295 F. 663 (4th Cir. 1924), the War Eagle Coal Company was insured on a property form that excluded loss or damage by civil commotion. The United Mine Workers had been organizing in West Virginia, violence had erupted, and the governor declared martial law. The evidence showed conclusively that a conspiracy of five men blew up the mine property as part of union activity. The insured proved that although there had been disturbances in the area, there had been no disorder at the mine or disturbances until the explosion and fire. The explosions and fire were started secretively at one in the morning. The insurer denied coverage, but the trial court held for the insured and the court of appeals affirmed.

The court quoted the following definition of *civil commotion* from the legal commentary in *Corpus Juris*: "An uprising among a mass of people which occasions a serious or prolonged disturbance and an infraction of civil order, not attaining the status of war or an armed insurrection. A civil commotion requires the wild or irregular action of many persons assembled together." The court said that since a serious issue of fact had been raised as to whether the property damage was a consequence of the civil commotion in the general area or was due to the independent initiative of the conspirators it would affirm the lower court's decision.

The policy specifies two events that do constitute a riot or civil commotion: (1) acts of striking employees occupying the described premises, and (2) looting at the time and place of a riot or civil commotion.

Vandalism. *Vandalism* is the willful and malicious damage to or destruction of covered property. In earlier editions of the commercial property policy the peril was phrased as "vandalism and malicious mischief." Malicious mischief is no longer part of the name of this peril although the definition remains the same as that of vandalism or malicious mischief in earlier forms—willful and malicious damage to or destruction of the insured property. Dropping the term "malicious mischief" has no effect on coverage and simplified the contract language.

Remodeling as Vandalism

A building owner discovered that a tenant, who had a lease agreement for two units, renovated the rental space without the landlord's consent as directed by a condition in the lease. The renovations were discovered from a complaint to the building inspector due to discard of debris. The landlord was cited for renovation without proper permits having been secured and directed to fix the problem by tearing it out.

The landlord made a claim under the vandalism and malicious mischief coverage of his building and personal property form, CP 00 10, with a broad causes of loss form, CP 10 20.

The vandalism peril requires a malicious and willful act. While the remodeling was willful, unless there was malicious intent to cause damage, it would not be considered vandalism. The tenant may have violated the terms of the lease, but that is a legal determination that is not addressed by the policy.

The CP 10 10 10 00 edition revised vandalism coverage in the named peril forms in regard to building glass. Previous editions excluded glass breakage caused by vandalism. An insured was required to purchase the broad form perils, which added glass breakage as an additional coverage, or to purchase the glass coverage form, CP 00 15. Now both named peril forms cover glass breakage from any of the named perils, treat glass as part of the building, and include glass coverage within the limit of liability for the building.

Building damage caused by the break-in or exit of burglars is covered, but other loss caused by or resulting from theft is excluded. Burglary, theft, and other crime coverages are addressed by specialized insurance policies.

Under earlier forms of commercial property insurance, vandalism and malicious mischief coverage was optional. Under the current program, the insured may choose to exclude this coverage via endorsement CP 10 55.

Vandalism is one of six causes of loss (sprinkler leakage, glass breakage, water, vandalism, theft, and attempted theft) for which there is no coverage if the building where the loss occurs has been vacant for more than sixty consecutive days.

Sprinkler Leakage. Under earlier commercial property forms, an insured had to purchase this coverage separately, if desired. It is now automatically part of the policy, and the insured may choose to exclude it via endorsement CP 10 56. Coverage is for leakage or discharge from an automatic sprinkler system, including the collapse of the system's tank, if there is one.

Automatic sprinkler system is a defined term within the context of the sprinkler leakage cause of loss. It refers to an automatic fire protective or extinguishing system. The definition includes sprinklers, nozzles, ducts, pipes, valves, fittings, tanks, pumps, and private fire protection mains. It also includes nonautomatic systems, hydrants, standpipes, and outlets supplied from an automatic system.

If the insured's building is covered property, this cause of loss also pays to repair or replace damaged parts of the system. The policy does not specify what must cause the damage to the system. It states only that repair or replacement of damaged parts to the sprinkler system will be made if the damage is a result of sprinkler leakage or is directly caused by freezing. Therefore, damage to the system itself might be from an uncovered cause of loss, but if sprinkler damage results the sprinkler damage is covered and any damaged parts to the system itself will also be replaced or repaired.

The policy also covers the cost of tearing out and replacing part of the structure in order to repair the system if there has been sprinkler damage that necessitates such tearing out or replacement.

Sprinkler leakage is one of six causes of loss (glass breakage, water, vandalism, theft, and attempted theft) for which there is no coverage if the building where the loss occurs has been vacant for more than sixty consecutive days.

Sinkhole Collapse. Coverage for sinkhole collapse was previously available only by endorsement and only in certain regions of the country where sinkholes occur with some frequency. The provision defines *sinkhole* for coverage purposes as "loss or damage caused by the sudden sinking or collapse of land into underground empty spaces created by the action of water on limestone or dolomite." The source of the water that creates the sinkhole is immaterial.

Sinkhole Collapse under the Commercial Property Form

The insured building was covered by the building and personal property form with basic causes of loss. The building had a system of pipes that diverted water runoff from the roof into a retention basin. One of those pipes broke, and the water coming out of it eroded the underlying limestone. A sinkhole was created and part of the building slipped into that sinkhole. The claim was denied, citing the exclusion for collapse into man-made underground cavities.

The commercial property form defines *sinkhole collapse* as the sudden sinking or collapse of land into underground empty spaces. The space is one created by the action of water on limestone or dolomite. The source of the water is not material to the definition. Collapse into underground "man-made cavities" is outside the definition of sinkhole collapse. Thus collapse into a mine shaft or other man-made holes would not be covered.

A standard dictionary defines *man-made* as "manufactured, created, or constructed by man." Those three very active verbs in the definition preclude the notion that a thing can be man-made by accident. An accidental water spill that causes a building to collapse into a sinkhole is covered. Again, the source of the water does not matter.

This peril does not include the cost of filling the sinkhole itself, nor does it include instances where the ground sinks or collapses into man-made cavities in the earth. This exposure is more appropriately the subject of mine subsidence coverage, which is available by endorsement.

Volcanic Action. Volcanic action coverage was also previously available only on an optional basis by endorsement. This peril is now part of the causes of loss forms and covers damage from the above-ground effects of a volcanic eruption—airborne blast and shock waves, ash, dust, particulate matter, and lava flow. It does not include the removal cost of volcanic ash or dust that has not physically damaged insured property. The earth movement exclusion precludes coverage for damage from the seismic effects of a volcanic eruption. This cause of loss considers all volcanic eruptions occurring within a seven day period (168 hours) as a single occurrence.

CP 10 20—Broad Form Causes of Loss

In addition to the eleven named perils of the basic causes of loss form, the broad causes of loss form, CP 10 20, adds coverage for falling objects; weight of snow, ice, or sleet; and water damage. It also provides one additional coverage, collapse.

Falling Objects. Falling objects covers damage by falling objects to buildings or structures and the inside of buildings or property within buildings if the falling object first damages the roof or an outside wall. Damage by a dropped or falling object within a building, such as a chandelier falling on the table below it or a heavy object accidentally dropped on a piece of furniture, does not come within the scope of this peril.

Falling objects coverage also does not apply to personal property in the open. However, as the aircraft/vehicles cause of loss provides coverage for damage by objects falling from aircraft, if an object falling from an airplane damages personal property in the open, that damage is covered.

Weight of Snow, Ice, or Sleet. The weight of snow, ice, or sleet peril applies to all covered property other than personal property outside of buildings or structures. Earlier editions of CP 10 20 did not cover damage to gutters and downspouts. That language has been removed, thus providing coverage for gutters and downspouts from the weight of snow, ice, or sleet.

Reimbursement for Expenses to Prevent Further Loss

A nursing home is insured on a CP 00 10 with CP 10 20 attached. It was hit by a huge snow storm. Due to the weight of ice and snow the roof was sagging, leaking, and causing worry that a collapse was impending. The management of the nursing home had holes cut in the ceilings to allow water and snow to drop in, relieving the pressure. The roof was already damaged and this was done to prevent further damage—or even a major collapse—to the roof.

The nursing home also hired a contractor to clear the ice and snow from the roof, and, based on the policy's requirement that the insured mitigate further loss or damage, submitted a claim for this expense. The insurer refused to reimburse the insured for this action, the adjuster citing the policy language that such expenses should be submitted *for consideration* in the payment of the claim. For the part of the loss that the insurer agreed to pay the figure is considerably less than any estimate the insured has received.

The policy obligates the insured to mitigate further loss and agrees to pay the insured for any expenses incurred in that mitigation. The policy says that the insured should submit receipts for that work for consideration in the payment of the claim. That does not mean the insurer will consider whether or not to pay it. The money spent here is just one more item to be included in overall payment of the claim.

The roof could not be repaired without removal of the snow. Again, that also makes the snow removal payable under the policy. It is analogous to removal of a fallen tree from the roof. The roof cannot be repaired until the tree is removed. Likewise, the insured's roof could not be repaired until the snow was removed.

Suppose there were no damage to the roof prior to the decision to act to relieve the pressure of the weight of ice and snow? Would the policy respond to repair the roof? The policy provides for the payment of expense involved in mitigating against *further* loss to covered property, but without initial damage to the property, this clause in not technically

> invoked. The preservation of property additional coverage pays for dam-
> age to property while being moved or stored temporarily to preserve
> it from covered loss, but that is not the case here either. Contacting
> the insurer's loss protection professionals for guidance in the situation
> would be beneficial.

Water Damage. This provision covers damage done by the accidental discharge or leakage of water or steam when any part of a system or appliance containing water or steam breaks or cracks. The CP 10 20 10 00 edition added an enumeration, carried forward into subsequent editions, of the systems covered: plumbing, heating, air conditioning, or other. Water damage coverage does not encompass leakage or discharge from an automatic sprinkler system, which is the subject of coverage under a separate cause of loss. Nor does it cover discharge from a sump, regardless of what causes the discharge. The form excludes overflow due to sump pump failure or the inability of the sump pump to keep up with the amount of water.

ISO added a provision to the CP 10 20 10 00 edition of the form that also excludes coverage for damage done by water that comes out of roof drains, gutters, downspouts, or similar fixtures or equipment. In its materials ISO says that this change to the policy represents no change in coverage, but it might be argued that it represents a narrowing of coverage. What happens when a roof drain gets clogged and cannot properly remove water from a roof? Under previous forms, the resulting damage would have been covered.

The peril also covers the cost of tearing out and replacing part of the building or structure to repair damage to the system or appliance if the building is covered property. For example, if the accidental discharge was from the sudden rupturing of a pipe in the insured's fire sprinkler system and the system's pipes are within the insured's walls, the cost of tearing out and repairing the walls is covered. The defect that caused the loss or damage is not covered. That would eliminate coverage for the broken pipe itself unless the damage to the pipe was by another covered cause of loss.

The form specifies that it does not cover damage from repeated leakage occurring over a period of at least fourteen days. Added with the CP 10 20 04 02 edition, were mold-inducing hazards as falling under this exception to the water damage cause of loss. Water damage does not include "repeated seepage or leakage of water, or the presence or condensation of humidity, moisture or vapor" that occurs over fourteen days or more.

There is no coverage for plumbing rupture caused by freezing unless the insured maintains heat in the building or structure or has drained the heating equipment and shut off its water supply. Earlier versions of commercial property forms imposed these last conditions on coverage for freezing losses only when the building was vacant or unoccupied. Broad form CP 10 20 makes no such distinction, imposing the conditions with respect to freezing losses regardless of the building's status. Coverage for water damage does not apply after the building has been vacant for sixty days.

Water Damage—Costs to Repair Leak Even if Building Is Undamaged

A pipe burst under the concrete slab of a building insured under the commercial property policy with the broad form causes of loss attached. This break in the pipe caused a loss of water into the ground under the building. The insurer denied the insured's request for coverage for the cost of tearing out and replacing the concrete slab so the broken pipe could be fixed. The denial stated that the policy did not cover this loss because the escaping water ran into the ground and did not damage covered property.

The commercial property policy does, however, cover the costs of tearing out and replacing the slab. The wording of the water damage peril does not require damage to covered property by water before such costs are covered. What it requires is that the damaged system be contained in covered property. In this case, the pipe is part of the system contained within the covered building.

The building coverage insuring agreement also states that the insurer will pay for direct physical damage to covered property caused by or resulting from a covered cause of loss. Destruction of the covered property (the slab) resulted from the covered peril of accidental discharge. Digging up the slab was made necessary by the covered peril. An argument can also be made that the insured was damaged by the increase in his water bill caused by the leaking system.

Exclusions that Apply to Both Named Perils Causes of Loss Forms

Section B of the basic and broad causes of loss forms contains the applicable exclusions. Section B contains three subsections. Subsection one is identical in both forms, with the following exclusions: ordinance or law, earth movement, governmental action, nuclear hazard, utility services, war and military action, and water.

The lead-in language applies concurrent causation language to section B exclusions. Under the efficient proximate cause doctrine, the nonexcluded peril must have been the predominant factor in the loss (e.g., the building was damaged by flood, not the decision of the Army Corps of Engineers to open the dam to stop a build-up of pressure). The concurrent causation doctrine, which arose as a legal concept in the mid-1980s, holds that losses are covered if caused jointly by an excluded peril, such as flooding or earth movement, and some other peril not excluded by the policy, such as negligent construction. As the doctrine developed, coverage began to be adjudicated by courts where the nonexcluded peril played any role in the loss.

Not all states adopted the concurrent causation doctrine, but its development prompted Insurance Services Office (ISO) and insurers filing independent policies to alter property forms in an attempt to avoid recovery in concurrent causation situations.

Another example of concurrent causation is where earth movement causes damage to an insured structure. The commercial property policy specifically excludes earth movement damage, but the insured files a claim stating that the cause of loss was a third party's negligence in preparing the soil under the house for construction, arguably a nonexcluded peril under an policy with a special causes of loss form. Where the concurrent causation doctrine has been accepted coverage would apply. Under the revised concurrent causation lead-in language, the damage would be appropriately excluded as intended.

A provision at the end of the Subsection B.1 exclusions states that the exclusions apply "whether or not the loss event results in wide-spread damage or affects a substantial area." ISO said that it added this language "for the purpose of making this point explicit."

Ordinance or Law. This exclusion eliminates payment for losses arising out of the enforcement of building laws or ordinances, including those that may require the demolition of damaged structures that increase the cost of repairing or rebuilding damaged property. For example, a city's building code may require that any building undergoing substantial renovation or repair after a major loss must be equipped with facilities for handicapped access, or the building code might dictate additional safety features that were not part of the original building. Additionally, the law may require that a building not in conformance with current building codes that is damaged to more than 50 percent of its value may not be repaired but must be demolished and rebuilt. For example, if an insured building were determined to be a 60 percent loss, it could not be rebuilt, and the undamaged portion would have to be demolished. As demolition after loss is not a covered cause of loss, there is no coverage for the cost of demolishing the undamaged portion and removing debris.

The ordinance or law exclusion excludes insurance payment under these forms for the cost of compliance with these requirements. However, the building and personal property coverage form provides a $10,000 of coverage for the increased costs of construction incurred due to the enforcement of a building law (*see* Chapter 2). The insured may also purchase additional coverage via endorsement CP 04 05 (*see* Chapter 8).

Earth Movement. Both named perils causes of loss forms exclude all types of earth movement—such as earthquake, landslide, or mine subsidence—other than sinkhole collapse. The basic and broad causes of loss forms specifically include sinkhole collapse as a specified peril. The policy covers ensuing fire or explosion damage.

Generally, the term *earth movement* applies only to naturally occurring phenomena of a catastrophic nature (e.g., landslide or earthquake). For example, damage to an insured building done by the earth shifting as a result of seismic tremors is readily excluded under the commercial property policy with the basic or broad causes of loss form attached.

Earth Movement Exclusion

The insured's building was situated close to a highway on which the transportation department was doing heavy reconstruction work. Pile driving sent tremors through the earth, cracking walls. The issue is if the earth movement exclusion applies. The earth movement exclusion relates to earth tremors caused by natural forces. Earth movement brought on by an explosion as well as by the action of the pile drivers is of a different nature. The examples of earth movement listed in the exclusion (earthquake, landslide, mine subsidence, or earth sinking, rising, or shifting and volcanic eruption or explosion) provide support that natural causes are the subject of the exclusion. The majority of courts that have considered this issue said the earth movement exclusion relates to earth tremors caused by natural forces.

The earth movement exclusion also eliminates coverage for loss caused by volcanic eruption, explosion, or effusion. However, the policy does cover fire damage occurring as a result of these events. The policy also covers loss attributable to volcanic action—the above-ground effects of volcanic eruption, an insured cause of loss under the basic and broad forms.

Governmental Action. The policy does not cover seizure or destruction of covered property as an act of governmental authority. For example, if the police break down a door or damage walls in executing a search warrant or chasing a fugitive the exclusion is validly applied according to the one court that has decided the issue (*see* "Damage by Police Action"). It does cover the destruction of property when ordered to prevent the more general spread of fire, if the fire itself would be a covered cause of loss (e.g., if fire authorities burn down a building to create a fire break to prevent the spread of a wildfire).

Damage by Police Action

A health clinic covered under the commercial property broad form suffered damage when a man who was trying to evade capture by the police ran into the clinic and took hostages. Eventually he was forced to surrender by the police, who used tear gas and gunfire. In the process of capturing the fugitive damage was done to both the building and personal property of the health clinic.

The insurance company denied coverage under the governmental action exclusion, which eliminates coverage for loss or damage caused directly or indirectly by seizure or destruction of property by order of governmental authority.

Before examining the exclusion, the existence of a covered peril under form CP 10 20 must be addressed. The one that might apply is explosion; exploding tear gas canisters and bullets contributed to the damage. Smoke damage may be another.

Once a named peril that covers the damage is found an analysis of the application of the exclusion for seizure or destruction of property by order of governmental authority is necessary. The aim of the exclusion is to eliminate coverage for the intentional destruction of property by governmental authority because of some hazard that the property presents, such as when the government orders the destruction of vegetables that are infected with the Mediterranean fruit fly or a building burned down to create a firebreak. The type of loss occasioned by this scenario seems to be outside of the scope of the exclusion.

In this case, the destruction done by the police was incidental to the capture of the fugitive. Bullets that damaged equipment were intended to control the fugitive—they were not fired because the equipment posed any danger to people or property. One would not expect the police officer in charge to state that he ordered the destruction of property. For these reasons, the insured might have coverage under the policy. However, a New Jersey court ruled that damage done to an apartment by the police in conducting a duly authorized search was properly excluded under the governmental authority exclusion, so such damage could also be excluded.

Nuclear Hazard. The nuclear hazard exclusion of eliminates coverage of loss by nuclear reaction, radiation, or radioactive contamination, regardless of the cause. The policy does pay for any ensuing fire loss. Radioactive contamination coverage may be purchased with form CP 10 37.

Utility Services. This exclusion was revised in the September 2007 edition of the form. It now applies both to the failure of power or other utility service (e.g., water, communication, or gas) to the insured premises that originates away from those premises and that originates on premises if on-prenises failure involves equipment used to supply the utility services to the described premises from a source away from the premises. For example, a power plant's turbine suffers mechanical breakdown which results in a shutdown of services or a power outage. That power outage results in food spoilage in the refrigerator at an insured's premises. The commercial property policy does not cover the food spoilage. The exclusion operates regardless of the failure's cause—even if the failure is brought about by a covered cause of loss.

The exclusion addresses situations such as a "brown out" or rolling outage, stating "failure of any utility service includes lack of sufficient capacity and reduction in supply." Loss or damage caused by a surge of power is excluded as well if the surge would not have occurred except for the event that caused the power failure, a change added with the September 2007 edition.

If failure or surge of power or other utility service, results in covered cause of loss, that damage is covered. For example, if heat interruption causes pipes to freeze and rupture, and the broad causes of loss form applies, there is coverage.

If, on the other hand, a lightning strike away from the insured premises knocks out the electrical power at the premises consequential property damage on the premises is not covered. Two examples of such losses are spoilage of refrigerated products or of property-in-process depending on continuous heat or cooling. Though lightning is a covered cause of loss, the underlying agreement is to pay for direct physical loss caused by a covered cause of loss. Lightning that strikes off premises and runs in on a line to cause lightning damage directly on premises is covered under these provisions.

The exclusion provides a description of communication services, which include, but are not limited to, Internet-related services and electronic, satellite, and cellular networks.

War and Military Action. This exclusion applies to three related causes of loss: war (including undeclared or civil war); warlike action by any governmental military force; and acts of insurrection, rebellion, revolution, or usurped power. While no court decisions involving the exact language of the war exclusion clause in the current commercial property form have arisen at this time, decisions involving other, past war exclusion clauses that permit reliable conclusions exist. Courts, following British precedent, generally adhere to a strict doctrine of what constitutes war, allowing the exclusion to be applied only in situations involving damage arising from a genuine warlike act between sovereign entities. The two following cases best sum up the idea that for there to be a war, sovereign or quasi-sovereign governments must engage in hostilities.

In *Pan American World Airways, Inc. v. Aetna Casualty & Surety Co.*, 505 F.2d 989 (2nd Cir. 1974), members of a political activist group from Jordan hijacked an aircraft over London and destroyed the aircraft on the ground while in Egypt. The court said the resulting loss to the aircraft was not due to war within the meaning of the term as used in the exclusionary clauses of the all risks policies covering the aircraft. The court reasoned that since the activist group had never claimed to be a state, it could not be acting on behalf of any of the states in which it existed when the plane was hijacked, especially since those states uniformly and publicly opposed hijacking. The hijackers were agents of a radical political group and not a sovereign government. The court concluded that although war can exist between sovereign states, a guerrilla group or radical political group must have at least some incidence of sovereignty before its activities can properly be defined as war.

In a similar case, *Holiday Inns, Inc. v. Aetna Ins. Co.*, 571 F. Supp. 1460 (S.D.N.Y. 1983), a court ruled against the war risks exclusion for a claim brought by an insured hotel in Beirut, Lebanon. The hotel suffered shelling damage during hostilities. The insurer argued that the conflict in Lebanon involved three clearly defined independent entities, each having the attributes of sovereignty or, at the least, quasi-sovereignty, and that the war exclusion could be applied to deny coverage. The court focused on the faction occupying the hotel at the time of the fighting and concluded that it was not a sovereign entity. The court further stated that even if the group possessed the necessary sovereignty, it was not fighting with another sovereign government at the time of the damage, and therefore, the war exclusion clause could not be invoked by the insurer. While there was some discussion of the war exclusion being applied to the September 11, 2001, hijacking and subsequent crashes into the World Trade Center and Pentagon, insurance adjusters and authorities fell back on the traditional interpretations of war acts, deciding that the terrorists were not a sovereign state making an act of aggression against another sovereign state.

Water. The water exclusion clause, which is in all three causes of loss forms, excludes loss caused by flood, surface water, water that backs up from a sewer or drain, and water underground. Though the exclusionary language is quite broad disputes continue to arise when the language is applied to particular situations. Following the 2005 hurricane season which spawned hurricanes Katrina, Rita, and Wilma, disagreement and litigation arose about how the water or flood exclusion applies in the face of windstorm.

Surface water has traditionally been excluded when it occurs naturally. Thus water from a heavy rain that damages a building is not covered. In *Richman v. Home Ins. Co. of New York,* 94 A.2d. 164 (Pa. Super. 1953), the court stated that surface water is commonly understood to mean water on the surface of the ground, usually created by rain or snow that is of a casual or vagrant character. Surface water follows no definite course and has no substantial or permanent existence.

Part three of the exclusion (water that backs up or overflows from a sewer, drain, or sump), became considerably more restrictive with the addition of the words *overflows* and *sump* in the 1995 edition. Previous editions did not address the issue of overflow. And by not specifically excluding water coming from a sump it was left up to interpretation as to whether a sump is a sewer or drain or part of the plumbing system. Not all insurers adopted ISO's wording in this instance and continue to treat water coming from a sump as an overflow of the plumbing system.

Part four of the exclusion eliminates coverage for water that seeps through underground portions of a building (hydrostatic water pressure) and for water that seeps through other openings, such as doors and windows.

If loss from fire, explosion, or sprinkler leakage results, the policy covers that loss, if caused by water, as described previously.

Fungus Wet Rot, Dry Rot, and Bacteria. Mold damage and insurance coverage for mold related expenses became a frequently disputed and litigated issue in the 1990s. Subsequently, insurers attempted to limit exposure to mold-related claims and have clarified the situation by redrafting insurance policies.

To clarify the policy's position on covering mold damage, a fungus, wet rot, dry rot, and bacteria exclusion was added to the commercial property causes of loss forms in the 04 02 editions. In addition, a definition of *fungus* was added to the policy's definitions, in both the causes of loss forms, and the building and personal property coverage form: "Fungus means any type or form of fungus, including mold or mildew, and any mycotoxins, spores, scents or by-products produced or released by fungi."

The fungus exclusion eliminates coverage for mold or fungus losses except in two situations—fire and lightning—or as falls under the additional limited coverage for fungus, wet rot, dry rot, and bacteria.

The exclusion covers the presence, growth, proliferation, spread, or any activity of fungus, wet or dry rot, or bacteria. The exclusion does not apply in the following situations:

- When the fungus results from fire or lightning (this addresses the most common claims-related event—mold growing from water used to put out fire); or

- To the extent coverage is provided under the additional coverage—limited coverage for fungus, wet rot, dry rot, and bacteria.

Subsection B.2. Exclusions

Subsection B.2. of each of the causes of loss forms contains several more exclusions. Unlike the subsection B.1. exclusions, these do not contain the concurrent causation language. The basic form has six exclusions in this part, while the broad form has four because two of the six perils excluded by the basic form are covered perils in the broad form (sprinkler leakage and water damage).

Both forms exclude loss or damage from artificially generated electrical, magnetic, or electromagnetic energy that damages, disturbs, disrupts, or otherwise interferes with electrical or electronic wires, devices, appliances, systems, or networks, or such devices, systems, networks, appliances using satellite or cellular technology. Included in the description of electrical, magnetic, or electromagnetic energy is electric current and arcing, electrical charge produced or conducted by a magnetic field, electromagnetic energy pulse, microwaves, and electromagnetic waves. The list is not an exhaustive one.

ISO changed the language in this exclusion in the 06 07 edition. In its explanatory materials, ISO said, "We are updating this exclusion by explicitly incorporating various terms that reflect current understanding of technology with respect to power sources and associated systems, such as electromagnetic energy (including electromagnetic pulse or waves) and microwaves, and the various risks presented by them." The main objective of the exclusion is to address power surges.

Both cover loss or damage from an ensuing fire. For example, if a power surge causes a piece of office equipment to short, damaging the piece of equipment and causing a fire damaging other property, the fire damage is covered but damage to the piece of equipment caused by the surge is not. Fire damage to the equipment is covered.

Both forms also exclude loss from explosion of steam boilers, steam pipes, steam engines, and steam turbines. If such an explosion causes a fire or combustion explosion, that damage is covered. This exclusion emphasizes the special nature of the exposure presented by boilers, heavy machinery, and equipment of that kind. Equipment breakdown coverage is a specialized coverage necessary for insureds with boiler and machinery exposures.

Both forms also exclude mechanical breakdown but will pay for any loss that results from a covered peril. Again, as in the other exclusions in

B.2., this exclusion is not subject to the concurrent causation language. Therefore if mechanical breakdown leads to otherwise covered damage, there is coverage. For example, an air conditioning unit suffers a mechanical breakdown and causes the unit to catch fire, burning down the building. The loss to the building could not be denied based on the mechanical breakdown exclusion. The only excludable damage would be the damage to the air conditioner directly caused by the mechanical breakdown. All resultant damage would be covered. However, if the air conditioner were consumed in the fire, that would also be covered.

Application of the Mechanical Breakdown Exclusion

A retail business with the basic causes of loss form had a failure in a solenoid switch in the furnace, causing a small fire. The claim was denied citing the exclusion that reads, "We will not pay for loss or damage caused by or resulting from mechanical breakdown" because it was the mechanical breakdown of the solenoid switch that caused the loss.

The mechanical breakdown exclusion's purpose is to prevent the insurer from paying for a maintenance claim. If the insured had found that the solenoid switch was defective, he could not turn to his property insurer and expect payment for a new switch.

The only part of this claim that should be denied is the mechanically unsound solenoid switch itself. The policy does not respond to damage caused by mechanical breakdown. The resultant fire damage is covered. Damage to the solenoid is properly excluded as mechanical breakdown but the fire damage claim that followed is payable because it resulted from a covered cause of loss.

Special Exclusions

The final exclusion section of both forms excludes certain losses where the following coverage forms are made a part of the policy: business income and extra expense, leasehold interest, and legal liability. These exclusions are treated in the chapters in this book dealing with those forms.

Additional Coverages

The basic causes of loss form adds one additional coverage, limited coverage for fungus, wet rot, dry rot and bacteria. The broad form adds two, limited coverage for fungus and collapse.

Collapse

Some time ago, collapse was moved out of the perils section of the policy and set aside as an additional coverage. The broad form covers a building against collapse caused by perils listed.

A shift has occurred in this area of insurance law since the late 1980s. Prior to 1990, only a minority of jurisdictions adopted the view that a collapse occurs when there is a serious impairment to the soundness of a building or a portion of a building. This viewpoint does not limit collapse to a complete falling down or reduction to rubble. This is now apparently the majority viewpoint.

For example, in *Royal Indemnity v. Grunberg*, 553 N.Y.S.2d 527 (1990), the court wrote, "In the view of a numerical majority of American jurisdictions, a substantial impairment of the structural integrity of a building is said to be a collapse." This language has become the test of whether an insurable collapse loss has occurred. The building is not required to fall into rubble to be considered a collapse; instead, if the building is in imminent danger of collapsing, coverage is triggered.

Because of this court decision and others ISO significantly changed the collapse additional coverage. It now includes a definition of what collapse is and is not. Wording is now in place that says collapse is "an abrupt falling down or caving in." This falling down or caving in may be of a building or any part of a building. The result must be that the building cannot be occupied as intended.

The following are not considered *collapse* under the commercial property policy:

1.   A building that is only in danger of falling down.

2.   A part of a building that is still standing, even if it has separated from the rest of the building.

3.   Any building, or part thereof, that is still standing, even if it shows evidence of cracking, bulging, sagging, bending, leaning, settling, shrinkage, or explosion.

In addition to coverage for the perils of the policy, the form lists the following as covered causes of collapse: hidden decay; hidden insect or vermin damage; weight of people or personal property; weight of rain that collects on a roof; and use of defective materials or methods in the construction or remodeling of a building (but the collapse must occur during the construction or remodeling).

Under the hidden decay and insect damage causes, such decay or damage is not a covered cause of collapse if the existence of the decay or damage is known to an insured prior to a collapse. If listed as covered property, the following are covered against collapse of a building insured under the policy: outdoor radio or television antennas (including satellite dishes) and their lead-in wiring, masts or towers; awnings, gutters, and downspouts; yard fixtures; outdoor swimming pools; fences; piers, wharves, and docks; beach or diving platforms or appurtenances; retaining walls; and walks, roadways, and other paved surfaces.

The policy covers personal property if it "abruptly falls down or caves in"—even if it is not the result of a building collapse. However, the collapse of the personal property must be caused by one of the listed causes of collapse, be inside a building, and not be one of the items listed as covered against collapse (e.g., antennas or gutters).

The form states that collapse of personal property does not include settling, cracking, shrinkage, bulging, or expansion. Any payments for collapse are included within the limit of liability for the covered property.

Limited Coverage for Fungus, Wet Rot, Dry Rot, and Bacteria

In addition to revising the exclusionary language related to mold, ISO added an additional coverage to the 2002 causes of loss forms. Under this additional coverage, the commercial property form provides a limited amount of coverage ($15,000) for the cleanup of fungus, wet or dry rot, or bacteria. If the fungus results from fire or lightning, the policy limit applies. If it results from any of the specified causes of loss, the $15,000 applies. The $15,000 is also available for fungus that results from a flood if the policy contains the Flood Coverage endorsement. As a reminder, the policy defines the specified causes of loss as follows:

2. "Specified Causes of Loss" means the following: Fire; lightning; explosion; windstorm or hail; smoke; aircraft or vehicles; riot or civil commotion; vandalism; leakage from fire extinguishing equipment; sinkhole collapse; volcanic action; falling objects; weight of snow, ice or sleet; water damage.

a.   Sinkhole collapse means the sudden sinking or collapse of land into underground empty spaces created by the action of water on limestone or dolomite. This cause of loss does not include:

    (1)   The cost of filling sinkholes; or

    (2)   Sinking or collapse of land into manmade underground cavities.

b.   Falling objects does not include loss or damage to:

    (1)   Personal property in the open; or

    (2)   The interior of a building or structure, or property inside a building or structure, unless the roof or an outside wall of the building or structure is first damaged by a falling object.

c.   Water damage means accidental discharge or leakage of water or steam as the direct result of the breaking apart or cracking of a plumbing, heating, air conditioning or other system or appliance (other than a sump system including its related equipment and parts), that is located on the described premises and contains water or steam.

Additional coverage E provides coverage for three things:

1.   Direct damage done by fungus to the covered property;

2.   The cost to tear out and replace any part of the covered property in order to get at the fungus; and

3.   Testing after either of the first two are complete, if there is "reason to believe" that fungus is still present.

The policy provides $15,000 (within the limit of liability for the covered property) for this additional coverage.

Chapter 4

Special Causes of Loss Form (CP 10 30)

The special causes of loss form (CP 10 30) provides insurance protection for "risks of direct physical loss, unless the loss is excluded in the exclusions section," which means the insured does not have to make a claim stating a specific cause of loss, but rather, all losses are covered unless a policy exclusion applies. This is referred to as open perils coverage. This form offers the insured the broadest possible protection.

At one time the special form was referred to as the all risks form. However, a line of court cases held that a policy touting all risks coverage should provide just that—coverage against all risks of loss, regardless of any exclusions or limitations; that it is reasonable for the insured to expect coverage against any and all exposures, based on the policy language pledging to cover all risks. To counter this expectation, ISO adopted phrasing that eliminated the all risks phrasing. These revised policies have been called open perils forms to distinguish them from named perils forms. In the commercial property program, open perils coverage is designated as the Special Causes of Loss form, CP 10 30. The last version of the CP 10 30 to use the word *all* in the perils section was the 01 83 edition when ISO was still using nonsimplified versions of commercial property forms. In October of 1983 (still in the nonsimplified versions), the word was dropped. That form insured against "risk of physical loss," instead of "all risks of physical loss." The current wording was adopted in the first readable version (November 1985), which insured against "risks of physical loss unless the loss is excluded...or limited."

The special causes of loss form's insuring agreement is not defined by a listing of named or specified causes of loss insured by the policy. Instead, the form states that when "special" is shown in the declarations, the covered causes of loss are "Risks of Direct Physical Loss, unless the loss is excluded in the Exclusions section or limited in the Limitations section." Therefore the scope of covered perils is not defined by what is listed as a covered peril but by what is excluded under the otherwise broad coverage of the policy.

A maxim of insurance policy interpretation is that coverage grants are interpreted as broadly as reasonably possible in favor of the insured and that exclusions are read as narrowly as reasonably possible in favor of the insured. This adage provides an advantage to the insured in proof-of-loss situations. While it is the insured's obligation to prove a loss falls under the coverage of a named peril, it is the insurer's obligation to prove the applicability of exclusions. Open perils coverage generally creates a situation where a loss may be assumed to be covered unless the insurer can show the applicability of a policy exclusion.

Similarities to Named Perils Forms

The first set of exclusions in the special causes of loss form (clauses B.1.a. to B.1.h.) is identical to those found in the basic and broad named perils forms: ordinance or law, earth movement, governmental action, nuclear hazard, utility services, war, and water. See Chapter 3 for a discussion of these exclusions pertinent to all causes of loss forms. The lead-in language applies concurrent causation language developed to avoid covering losses where a nonexcluded peril operates in conjunction with an excluded peril to cause damage. The concurrent causation theory is first described in Chapter 3 and later again in this chapter.

Like the other two forms, the special form gives back coverage for losses from fire, glass breakage, and volcanic action caused by a volcanic eruption. Coverage for volcanic action is provided in the basic and broad forms as a named peril; in the special form it is an exception to the earth movement exclusion.

Heavy Construction and the Earth Movement Exclusion

A building located near a highway under construction was covered by a special causes of loss form. The reconstruction of the highway required pile driving. The tremors from the pile driving damaged the building. The claim was denied under the earth movement exclusion.

> While the earth movement exclusion might seem to apply to exclude coverage, generally the exclusion is found to apply only to earth tremors caused by natural forces. Most courts agree with the opinion expressed in *Rightley v. Lebanon Mutual Ins. Co.*, 1992 WL 562578 (Pa. Co. Pl. 1992), wherein the court said that "the earth movement exclusion applies only to spontaneous, natural, catastrophic earth movement and not movement brought about by other causes." Earth movement that might be brought on by an explosion or the action of a pile driver is another matter. The examples of earth movement listed in the exclusion (earthquake; landslide; mine subsidence; earth sinking, rising, or shifting; and volcanic eruption or explosion) provide support for the notion that natural causes are the subject of the exclusion. The *ejusdem generis rule* (that items in a list must be viewed in context with each other) would apply.

Like the named perils form, the open perils form adds a provision that the described exclusions apply regardless of how widespread a loss is.

Open Perils Exclusions—Section B.2.

Exclusion provisions B.2.a. through B.2.m, the second set of exclusions, has traditionally been called the all risks or open perils exclusions. Some eliminate coverage for events that are historically uninsurable, such as wear and tear or mechanical breakdown—occurrences that happen over time with some certainty, contrasted to sudden and accidental occurrences. Others exclude loss more appropriately handled by specialized coverage such as the boiler explosion or employee dishonesty exclusions (which can be covered by equipment breakdown and fidelity coverage). Still others exclude exposures that, as a matter of underwriting policy either due to the enormous potential economic consequences of the event or because of the morale hazard, the drafters of the commercial property policy decided against covering. Examples of such exposures include the release of pollutants or the voluntary entrustment of property (again, specialized coverage forms have been developed to handle some of these exposures).

Artificially Generated Electrical, Magnetic, or Electromagnetic Energy. As in the named perils forms, the special form also excludes damage to electrical devices, appliances, systems, networks—including those that use cellular or satellite technology—or wires caused by artificially generated electrical, magnetic, or electromagnetic energy. This exclusion applies to any manmade electrical current, so a lightning strike on a building that damages electrical devices would not be subject to this exclusion.

Any ensuing fire damage resulting from artificially generated electrical, magnetic, or electromagnetic energy is covered.

Delay; Loss of Use; Loss of Market. This exclusion emphasizes the commercial property policy's intent to cover direct and not consequential loss. Delay and loss of use or market are indirect losses that are the result of a covered loss, such as a restaurant losing customers with the attendant loss of revenue while rebuilding after a fire, or retail customers finding other places to shop while repairs are performed and not returning. The insured may purchase business income and extra expense insurance to cover some of this exposure.

Smoke, Vapor, or Gas from Agricultural Smudging or Industrial Operations. This is the same exclusion that appears in the named perils forms under the peril of smoke. The commercial property policy does not pay for this type of damage because such operations represent constant or constantly recurring exposures. Damage is certain to occur, so there is no risk but a certainty of loss given time.

Section 2.d.(1) to (7) Exclusions

Several exclusions of a similar nature are grouped together in section 2.d. of the special causes of loss form, listed as 2.d. (1) through 2.d. (7). These are causes of loss that are generally uninsurable, in that, given time, the event will occur. A component will wear out or an inherent defect will eventually reveal itself as damage.

In this regard, the special form excludes loss or damage caused by the following:

1. wear and tear;

2. rust, or other corrosion, decay, deterioration, or a hidden or latent defect. In short any quality in property that causes it to damage or destroy;

3. smog;

4. settling, cracking, shrinking, or expansion;

5. nesting or infestation, or discharge or release of waste products or secretions of birds, insects, rodents, or other animals;

6.   mechanical breakdown, though resulting elevator collision is covered;

7.   with respect to personal property, marring or scratching, dampness or dryness of atmosphere, and changes in or extremes of temperature.

If any of these excluded events causes resulting damage from building glass breakage or from one of the specified causes of loss listed in definitions section F of the form (Specified Causes of Loss, reproduced in the next paragraph), that resulting loss is covered. For example, if mechanical breakdown in a piece of machinery causes a fire that destroys the machinery and damages the building, the resulting fire damage to both the machinery and building is covered, excluding any damage to the machinery that was directly caused by the mechanical breakdown.

The following are the *specified causes of loss*: fire; lightning; explosion; windstorm or hail; smoke; aircraft or vehicles; riot or civil commotion; vandalism; leakage from fire extinguishing equipment; sinkhole collapse; volcanic action; falling objects; weight of snow, ice, or sleet; or water damage.

The form defines the specified causes of loss for the following perils:

1.   *Sinkhole collapse* means the sudden sinking or collapse of land into underground empty spaces created by the action of water on limestone or dolomite. This cause of loss does not include the cost of filling sinkholes or sinking or collapse of land into mine shafts or other manmade underground cavities.

2.   *Falling objects* does not include loss or damage to personal property in the open or to the interior of a building or structure, or property inside a building or structure, unless the roof or an outside wall of the building or structure is first damaged by a falling object.

3.   *Water damage* means accidental discharge or leakage of water or steam as the direct result of the breaking or cracking of any part of a system or appliance containing water or steam.

Wear and Tear, Cracking and Shrinking, and Mechanical Breakdown

Some of the excluded items in the list found in B.2.d.—the so-called "wear and tear" exclusions—deserve further analysis.

Applying the wear and tear exclusion can be confusing. For example, a rusted-out pipe inside a wall bursts and causes water to leak into an office. The initial reaction might be to deny the claim based on the wear and tear exclusion, as the loss was caused by the wear and tear on the pipe. However, the only property that is not covered is the pipe itself; the damage done by the water as well as the cost to repair the damage to the wall necessary to remove and replace the leaking pipe is covered.

The purpose of the wear and tear exclusion (sometimes referred to as the maintenance exclusion) is to avoid payment for things that the insured should maintain as a matter of course. In the previous example, if the insured had discovered the rusted pipe before it actually burst he could not look to his insurance policy to replace the pipe. The wear and tear exclusion precludes insurance recovery for normal maintenance. However, once wear and tear causes a covered loss, that loss is covered.

Wear and Tear Exclusion—Damage to Shower Stall

The insured is an apartment complex insured on a commercial property policy with special causes of loss. One of the tenants was a very large individual. This tenant stepped into the shower enclosure and, due to his excessive weight, cracked the floor area of the shower. There was immediate and direct damage to the apartment below. The crack required replacement of the shower/tub unit, as well as cleanup of the damage.

The insured entered a claim for replacement of the shower unit and repair of the ceiling in the apartment below. The carrier extended coverage for the ceiling damage but denied coverage of the shower enclosure due to the wear and tear exclusion, although the shower unit was relatively new.

The damage to the ceiling and shower unit are covered. The wear and tear exclusion does not apply. The wear and tear exclusion is one of a number of exclusions in the commercial property's special causes of loss form that eliminate coverage for what are essentially nonfortuitous losses— losses that are certain to happen and as such are not appropriate subjects for insurance coverage. If something is used long enough it will wear out. This is not an insurable event. However, a sudden and accidental breaking of a new shower unit by a very large individual is not wear and tear, but is direct damage.

The exclusion of settling, cracking, shrinking, or expansion has engendered litigation by raising the issues of, specifically, what is the difference among settling, cracking, shrinking, or expansion and collapse?

A Florida appeals court found that collapse must be defined independently of the language of the settling exclusion in *Auto Owners Insurance Co. v. Allen*, 362 So.2d 176 (Fla. App. 1978). The court held that restrictions on coverage contained in the exclusion do not limit the definition of collapse. The court stated, "The provision at issue here is clear in only one regard as to the meaning of collapse. Coverage is not provided for loss from 'settling, cracking, shrinkage, bulging or expansion' which is occasioned by other than a direct result of collapse of the building."

In one instance, a motel was in imminent danger of falling down when the claim was brought. While a trench was being dug next to the back wall of the motel in order to lay sewer pipe, sandy soil fell away from the footings supporting the wall. Rejecting the argument that the exclusion was specifically designed to avoid ambiguity by limiting the insurer's liability to cases where the building fell down, the court said, "We cannot accept this construction. If [the insurer] had intended to limit its liability as it argues, it would have been a simple matter to include in the policy a restriction of coverage to a flattened form or rubble. Other than the exclusion for [settling, etc.] there is no attempt to define what a collapse is or is not."

However, the Kansas Supreme Court came to a different conclusion. In *Krug v. Miller's Mut. Ins. Assn. of Illinois*, 495 P.2d 949 (Kan. 1972), the court determined that the term collapse was not ambiguous when qualified by the exclusion pertaining to settling and cracking. Where collapse coverage is so qualified, the court determined that collapse does not take place unless more than settling or cracking has occurred.

Like the other causes of loss forms, the special form also has a mechanical breakdown exclusion. However, the CP 10 30 has a clarifying provision that the exclusion does not apply to any resulting loss or damage caused by elevator collision.

Mechanical breakdown is another area that has caused confusion. When a piece of machinery breaks down, ensuing loss from a covered peril is covered. However, claims have been denied for such loss citing the mechanical breakdown exclusion. The purpose of this exclusion is the same as that for the wear and tear exclusionary provision. If a piece of machinery just stops working the insured may not look to his insurer to repair it. However if that machine breaks down and causes a covered loss, that loss should be paid.

Mechanical Breakdown Exclusion and Concurrent Causation

Air conditioning units on a church insured under a commercial property coverage form with the special causes of loss form were damaged by freezing. The insurer-engaged engineer reported that there were two causes of loss: (1) failure of the pump-down solenoid, which allowed the compressors to run during freezing conditions, eventually resulting in the freezing of the circulating chilled water system and destruction of the system; and (2) a control rod did not close on the louver vent economizer system, which allowed the very cold outside air into the church. The engineer concluded that the failure of the system was due to the mechanical failure of these devices. The insurer denied the loss, stating that the concurrent causation language in the policy removed coverage for any damage resulting from mechanical breakdown.

Analysis discloses the loss is not appropriately denied in its entirety for several reasons. First, the concurrent causation language of the CP 10 30 does not apply to the mechanical breakdown exclusion. The lead-in language to section B. Exclusions, clause 2.—where the mechanical breakdown exclusion is located—reads, "We will not pay for loss or damage caused by or resulting from any of the following." This is not concurrent causation language; in fact, this was the original lead-in to both B. sections 1 and 2, which was changed because of the development of the concurrent causation doctrine.

Because the concurrent causation language does not apply to this set of exclusions, if mechanical breakdown causes damage not otherwise excluded to something other than the item that actually broke down, any subsequent damage is covered. In this case, the loss to the air conditioning system was not caused by mechanical breakdown but was due to freezing resulting from the mechanical breakdown. The failure of the solenoid may have set the stage, but it did not cause the loss. Freezing did.

By way of example of how the mechanical breakdown exclusion works, apply these facts to a peril other than freezing. Suppose that the breakdown of the solenoid caused heat to build up and the entire building burned down rather than damaging just the components of the air conditioning system. The loss would not be denied for the fire damage due to the mechanical breakdown of the solenoid.

Other Exclusions

Explosion of Steam Boilers, Steam Pipes, Steam Engines or Steam Turbines. This exclusion applies to steam equipment that the insured owns, leases, or operates. Ensuing loss from fire or combustion explosion is covered. Again, as in the basic and broad causes of loss forms, this exclusion reiterates the fact that boiler equipment and industrial type machinery is beyond the scope of the commercial property policy and is more appropriately covered by an equipment breakdown policy.

Continuous or Repeated Seepage or Leakage of Water. An exclusion of damage from continuous or repeated seepage or leakage of water over a period of fourteen days or more modifies coverage for plumbing discharge under special form coverage, just as it does the named cause of loss of water damage in broad form CP 10 20. Some have argued that the fourteen-day period should begin when the insured first discovers the leakage, but it is damage caused by the undiscovered leak that the policy specifically excludes. The fourteen-day period begins with the onset of the leakage and not when the insured discovers the leak or damage. Also excluded is damage from the presence or condensation of humidity, moisture, or vapor.

Repeated Seepage or Leakage

The floors in an insured building were becoming soft. Investigation in the crawl space under the floor disclosed a leak in a hot water pipe, which caused moisture damage to the floor above. The damage was calculated at $123,000. The claim was denied due to the special causes of loss form's exclusion of repeated seepage or leakage over a period of more than fourteen days. The insured could not hear or see the water leak and had no way of knowing what was going on under the floor. The insured disputed application of the exclusion, stating that the fourteen-day period should begin at the discovery of the leak or damage and not from the date of the beginning of the occurrence.

The exclusion is appropriately applied. This type of loss is the type meant to be excluded by the commercial property policy's repeated seepage or leakage exclusion. The fact that the insured could not easily make himself aware of the impending damage does not make it any the less a nonfortuitous loss or bring it outside of the clear language of the exclusion.

Water, Other Liquids, Powder, or Molten Material. The policy does not cover damage by water, other liquids, powder, or molten material if, due to freezing, they leak or flow from plumbing, heating, air conditioning, or other equipment, except fire protective systems. The exclusion applies unless the insured does his best to maintain heat in the building or structure or drains the equipment and shuts off the supply if the heat is not maintained. If the insured meets these conditions, the exclusion does not apply. The form does not exclude all damage by water, other liquids, powder, or molten material. It excludes only damage by these items if caused by freezing, and only then if the insured has not maintained heat or drained and shut off the system. This reinforces the necessary maintenance concept.

Dishonest or Criminal Acts. This exclusion eliminates coverage for dishonest or criminal acts committed by the named insured, partners, employees, directors, trustees, or authorized representatives of the named insured, or anyone to whom the named insured entrusts covered property. The CP 10 30 10 00 edition added members, officers, and managers in order to recognize the limited liability company form of organization. This exclusion applies whether the person commits the act alone or in collusion with others and regardless of whether the act occurs during working hours.

While it obviously excludes employee theft—a subject for fidelity coverage—it specifically does not exclude loss from acts of destruction committed by such individuals. Therefore, while the form does not cover an employee stealing office equipment, if an employee damages or destroys a photocopying machine as an act of revenge the policy will respond.

A court applied the exclusion to arson committed by a shareholder and corporate officer in *Minnesota Bond Ltd. v. St. Paul Mercury Ins. Co.*, 706 P.2d 942 (Or. 1985). A partner with a 50 percent interest set the building on fire, hoping to collect the insurance so she could pay a debt. The trial court originally refused to apply the exclusion to this case and held that the "context of a 'willful or dishonest act' is described by the remainder of the language in the exclusion, which speaks to unexplained or mysterious disappearance of property or the voluntary parting with titled possession of property as a result of a fraudulent scheme. This Court concludes that this exclusion is inapplicable to the factual situation."

The Supreme Court of Oregon overturned that decision without any discussion of the coinsured's position. In its reversal, the court said, "Although it may have been unwise for this insured to purchase a policy with such a far-reaching exclusion as contained in exclusion No. 4, nevertheless that decision was made by the plaintiff corporation when it chose to insure its property under this policy. The exclusion is clear and unambiguous and fully applicable to this loss. There is no coverage for this loss under the policy."

This case involved individuals who have such control over the corporation that their acts essentially constitute the acts of the corporation; where a regular employee (not an officer, director, or partner) commits an act of arson, the policy would respond.

Voluntary Parting with Property (Trick or Device). This provision eliminates coverage where the insured has been tricked out of property; for example, voluntarily turning over a car for a test drive, and the prospective customer absconds with it. This exclusion applies if the insured or anyone to whom the property has been entrusted has been induced to part voluntarily with the property by fraudulent scheme, trick, device, or false pretense. This exclusion reiterates the intent of the commercial property policy to provide coverage for direct loss to property and not fidelity or theft coverage (which is available under the crime insurance program).

In the typical trick or device loss, the insured is defrauded. An example of such a scheme would be where a customer pays for an item with a bad check or stolen credit card and obtains possession of the property. The insured cannot look to the commercial property policy for coverage in such situations.

Rain, Snow, Ice, or Sleet Damage to Personal Property in the Open. The commercial property policy covers personal property in the described building or structure or in the open within 100 feet of the described premises. The policy also covers personal property temporarily off premises at certain locations (*see* Chapter 2). The exclusion modifies this coverage and is another example of a nonfortuitous loss. Personal property left out in the open in rain, snow, ice, or sleet will be damaged. Risk management techniques other than insurance are more appropriate to this exposure (for example, bringing it inside).

Collapse. The grant of collapse coverage (limited by its terms) coexists with a broad exclusion of collapse. That is, collapse is excluded, except to the extent that coverage is provided under the terms of the additional coverage. Under the additional coverage, coverage is provided for an abrupt falling down or caving in, subject to the terms of that additional coverage. ISO most recently revised the exclusion in the CP 10 30 06 07 to describe various conditions affecting property, to reinforce the relationship between the exclusion (broad) and the coverage grant (which builds back limited coverage). ISO also revised the exclusion to specify that it does not apply to "specified causes of loss" (defined in the form as various named perils), building glass breakage, weight of rain that collects on a roof, and weight of people or personal property. Previously, this exception was conveyed under the additional coverage for collapse by way of stating that the criteria defining a covered collapse do not limit coverage otherwise provided for the aforementioned perils. In other words, there is coverage for loss or damage by the aforementioned perils, whether the loss or damage involves collapse, subject to any other applicable policy provisions.

Discharge, Dispersal, Seepage, Migration, Release, or Escape of Pollutants. The pollution exclusion originally read "release, discharge, or dispersal of pollutants or contaminants." This phrasing was replaced by an exclusion that removed coverage for loss or damage caused by or resulting from the release, discharge, or dispersal of pollutants unless the release, discharge, or dispersal is itself caused by any of the specified causes of loss. Resulting loss or damage by the specified causes of loss was covered.

The policy was revised again in 1990 with a modification by adding the words *seepage*, *migration*, and *escape* of pollutants as well, thus giving stronger emphasis to the exclusion of nonsudden pollution losses. This change was in accord with changes made in the Building and Personal Property Coverage form (CP 00 10 10 90). This phrasing has been carried forward. The effect of the exclusion is to limit pollutant cleanup and removal coverage in the commercial property program to those sudden and accidental occurrences brought on by the specified causes of loss—the broad form perils.

CP 10 30 10 00 added an exception. The exclusion does not apply to damage to glass done by chemicals that are applied to the glass. This is part of the simplification of glass coverage. Damage done by chemicals was covered by the old glass form. Since that form has been removed, the policy now provides the coverage by means of this exception to the exclusion.

Neglect. The CP 10 30 10 00 edition added the exclusion for neglect By eliminating coverage for damage caused by the insured's neglect to protect property post-loss against further damage, it emphasizes the insured's responsibility to protect his property from further loss at the time of the initial loss.

Concurrent Causation Exclusions

The special form contains a third set of exclusions (designated 3.a., b., and c.) that preclude coverage under the doctrine of concurrent causation. Concurrent causation is a legal doctrine developed in case law to find coverage despite common property policy exclusions, such as earth movement or flooding. For example, a third-party contractor is negligent in the preparation of the soil prior to the construction of an office building. After the building is completed and occupied, it suffers earth movement damage. While earth movement is excluded, using the doctrine of concurrent causation the building owner could claim that the loss was caused by the negligence of the contractor that prepared the soil. Without these exclusions, the claim would be payable under the special causes of loss form because third-party negligence is not an excluded peril.

To avoid otherwise unintended insurance recovery in concurrent causation situations, ISO included concurrent causation lead-in language ("such loss is excluded regardless of any other cause or event") to a number of exclusions and added this concurrent causation exclusion with three subparts. These include loss or damage caused by weather conditions; acts or decisions (or failure to act) of individuals and groups; and faulty, inadequate, or defective planning, design, defective materials, or maintenance.

They do not defeat coverage for a covered cause of loss that happens to involve damage by the excluded cause of loss. For example, a building suffers flood damage because of negligent maintenance of a dam. The flood damage is excluded under the surface water exclusion, and the concurrent causation exclusion operates to defeat coverage for a claim of negligent maintenance. If the building also suffers vandalism as a result of the flood, that vandalism is covered because the policy does not exclude vandalism.

There is no coverage for ensuing losses caused by one of the three special exclusions if the ensuing losses fall under one of the excluded risks. Thus, there would be no coverage if faulty construction (one of the special exclusions) caused natural subsurface water damage to the foundation.

Weather Conditions Exclusion

The weather conditions exclusion applies only if weather conditions contribute in any way with a cause or event excluded in exclusion section 1 (ordinance or law, earth movement, nuclear hazard, utility services, war and military action, and water). Assume heavy rain causes a landslide, which in turn damages an insured structure. The policy excludes earth movement, and the claim should be denied. However, at court the insured argues that it was not earth movement that caused the damage to the house, but instead, the cause of damage was the rainfall (a weather condition). Prior to the adoption of the concurrent causation exclusions this argument sometimes prevailed. ISO adopted the concurrent causation exclusions to retain the original intent to not cover damage by earth movement or the other excluded causes of loss, regardless of what caused the earth to move, subject to the caveat regarding natural versus manmade earth movement, discussed prior.

Acts or Decisions and Faulty Planning Exclusions

The second of the concurrent causation exclusions eliminates as a cause of loss the acts or decisions, including the failure to act or decide, by persons, groups, or governmental bodies. For example, governmental officials fail to act in a crisis and allow a dam to overflow and damage insured property. Under a seminal concurrent causation case, the court allowed the nonexcluded peril of negligent decision-making to override the policy's flood exclusion and found coverage under these same facts. The current version of the commercial property policy eliminates this possibility.

Part c. of these exclusions eliminates coverage where the cause of loss is inadequate, faulty, or defective planning, zoning, development, surveying, siting, design, specifications, workmanship, repair, construction, renovation, remodeling, grading, compaction, maintenance or materials used in repair, construction, renovation, or remodeling.

All three parts of the exclusion are subject to the provision that if loss or damage by a covered cause of loss results from one of these excluded perils, coverage applies to the resulting loss or damage. For example, if faulty workmanship in the electrical system of a building results in fire, the resulting fire loss is covered. Or, if earth movement causes a fire, the fire damage is covered. Or, if the failure of the fire officials to act in creating firebreaks causes a building to burn, the fire damage is covered.

ISO introduced a clarifying new exclusion in the special causes of loss form with the 06 07 edition related to production errors. Some examples of errors in production are introduction of foreign matter, addition of a wrong ingredient or element, or wrong measure of a particular element. An error in the production process is a business risk; it is not a peril intended to be insured under fire/allied lines property insurance. In certain circumstances, some claims may involve errors in production and allege that the need to destroy a now useless product constitutes physical loss or damage to that product, thereby asserting a broad and nontraditional interpretation of the concept of physical damage under an insurance contract.

To avoid this result, ISO inserted new Additional Exclusion 5, which applies only to the specified property and is entitled Loss or Damage to Products:

> We will not pay for loss or damage to any merchandise, goods or other product caused by or resulting from error or omission by any person or entity (including those having possession under an arrangement where work or a portion of the work is outsourced) in any stage of the development, production or use of the product, including planning, testing, processing, packaging, installation, maintenance or repair. This exclusion applies to any effect that compromises the form, substance or quality of the product. But if such error or omission results in a Covered Cause of Loss, we will pay for the loss or damage caused by that Covered Cause of Loss.

Special Exclusions

The final exclusion section of the commercial property policy excludes various losses on business income and extra expense, leasehold interest, and legal liability coverage forms. These exclusions are treated in the chapters in this book dealing with those forms.

Limitations

Under this section (C), the form (1) clarifies that it does not cover loss or damage to certain types of property; (2) places dollar limits on certain types of property; and (3) limits coverage on other types to the specified causes of loss.

Steam Boilers, Steam Pipes, Steam Engines, or Steam Turbines. The policy does not cover these items for damage that results from a condition or event inside the equipment. As mentioned earlier, ensuing loss from fire or combustion explosion is covered.

Steam Boilers—Condition or Event Inside

Property covered under a special causes of loss form suffered the following loss: water was seen coming out an unoccupied building, and the fire department was notified. They turned off the water and asked the power company to turn off the power. The management company was notified a few days later, and on inspection, found the boilers had frozen and were damaged.

Loss did not result from any condition or event inside the equipment, as contractually required. The event that caused the damage was the power company turning off the power, something outside the equipment and not reached by the exclusion. The limitation in the policy concerns loss caused by a condition or event inside the equipment.

The limitations in Part C must be read in context. The limitations apply to items that should be separately insured and to losses that are foreseeable and therefore uninsurable. For example, if the boilers were damaged due to lime buildup, the loss could have been prevented through proper maintenance and is therefore not covered. The freezing loss was outside the insured's control and is covered.

Hot Water Boilers or Other Water Heating Equipment. As with the steam equipment previously discussed, the special form does not cover these items for damage caused by or resulting from any condition or event inside the equipment other than an explosion. Therefore, explosion damage, regardless of whether the explosion is caused by an internal condition or event, is covered.

Building Interiors and Personal Property in a Building. The special form does not cover these items for damage caused by rain, snow, sleet, ice, sand, or dust unless the building first sustains damage by an insured peril to its roof or walls through which the rain, snow, sleet, ice, sand, or dust enters. The form also covers such damage caused by the thawing of snow, ice, or sleet on the building.

Water Damage and Boarded-Up Windows

A building covered by a special causes of loss form suffered rain damage to an unoccupied second floor. The second story windows were boarded up with plywood to prevent water from entering through any broken panes. Extremely heavy storms accompanied by heavy winds and wind-driven rain knocked the plywood boarding loose, resulting in water penetrating the window openings and damaging the insured's business personal property stored on the second floor.

The loss was denied coverage under the limitation on water damage that requires the building must first suffer damage to its roof or walls by a covered cause of loss through which the rain enters. In supporting the denial, the adjuster compared the boarding being blown in to that of a windowpane being blown open. The adjuster stated that coverage would not apply in this similar situation unless the windowpane would be blown out or damaged.

According to *Merriam-Webster's Dictionary*, a window is the opening in a wall, covered by a material, typically glass (the glass is called a windowpane). The windows, including the boarding, are part of the wall, and the material covering the openings does not have to be glass. Wind is a covered cause of loss, and it damaged the wall by blowing out the window covering, triggering coverage for the damage to the insured's interior business personal property. The loss is covered.

Building Materials. The policy does not cover building materials for theft unless they are held for sale by the insured. The inventory at a lumber yard or hardware store, for example, is not covered. This limitation also does not apply to business income or extra expense coverage.

Missing Property. The policy does not pay for missing property if the loss can be documented only because of an inventory shortage, or there is no physical evidence to show what happened to the property.

Missing Property—No Physical Evidence

A hospital insured under the special causes of loss form submitted a claim for a scientific video monitor used in the intensive care unit. Hospital officials claimed that the monitor was stolen. The claim was denied based on the following exclusion: "We will not pay for loss or damage to...property that is missing, but there is no physical evidence to show what happened to it, such as a shortage disclosed on taking inventory."

Limitation of coverage 1.e. does not require visible signs of forcible entry, which is a requirement for coverage under the peril of burglary in the crime policy. This limitation refers instead to the loss of property that could not be recognized except by reference to written records. For example, if the hospital had a storage room filled with hundreds of monitors and one were stolen, that theft probably could not be recognized by physical evidence alone. The physical absence of one monitor out of hundreds could not be seen without counting the monitors and comparing the total to a known number.

In this case, the absence of the monitor could be immediately noticed by anyone familiar with the room. It is physically missing and the hospital does not have to rely on an inventory to know that it is gone. The purpose of the limitation of the coverage in question is to prevent claiming theft when the loss might, in fact, be due to poor record keeping. The limitation is not intended to exclude theft, which might be thought of as the disappearance of property from a specific place during a specific time period.

Transferred Property. There is no coverage for property transferred to an off-premises person or place on the basis of unauthorized instructions. This is similar to the trick or device exclusion and eliminates what is more appropriately covered under crime or fidelity policies.

Property Limited to Specified Causes of Loss

The following types of property are covered only for loss or damage due to the specified causes of loss: animals, fragile articles, and owned builders equipment or tools.

Animals. The policy covers animals only if they are killed or if they must be destroyed.

Fragile Articles. Earlier editions stated that the limitation on fragile articles did not apply to glass that is part of a building. However, with the revised treatment of building glass in the CP 00 10 10 00 edition, that exception to the limitation is no longer necessary and has been removed. The current form also removes the exception for photographic or scientific instrument lenses, thus making them subject to the fragile articles limitation. Now the only exceptions to the fragile articles limitation are glass and containers of property held for sale.

Builders' Machinery, Tools, and Equipment. The limitation on owned tools does not apply to property located on or within 100 feet of the described premises unless the premises is insured under the builders risk form; nor does it apply to business income or extra expense coverage.

Marble Slab as Fragile Article

An insured covered by a a special causes of loss form had a marble slab resting on a platform. The platform collapsed and the marble slab broke into pieces. The insurer denied the claim due to limitation C.2.c., which eliminates coverage for breakage of fragile articles such as glassware, statuary, marbles, chinaware, and porcelains unless damage is caused by one of the defined specified causes of loss. The issue is whether the limitation's specific reference to marbles places the marble slab in the fragile articles category and precludes coverage for this loss.

The loss to the unrefined marble slab does not fall under the scope of the fragile articles limitation. The operative word in the provision is *fragile*, and the items listed in the exclusion are examples, not definitions. Although a delicate piece of marble artwork is a fragile article, a large block of marble is outside the limitation. Many things (such as concrete blocks or bricks) may be breakable given sufficient force. However, they would hardly be considered fragile articles.

Special Theft Limits

Special Theft Limits. The following items are subject to a special limit for any one occurrence of theft. The special limit shown for each category is the total limit for loss or damage to all property in that category, no matter the number of items involved.

a. $2,500 for furs, fur garments, and garments trimmed with fur.

b. $2,500 for jewelry, watches, watch movements, jewels, pearls, precious and semiprecious stones, bullion, gold, silver, platinum, and other precious alloys or metals. This limit does not apply to jewelry and watches worth $100 or less per item.

c. $2,500 for patterns, dies, molds, and forms.

d. $250 for stamps, tickets, including lottery tickets held for sale, and letters of credit.

The final policy limitation precludes coverage for the cost to repair any system from which any liquid or molten material escapes. Fire extinguishing equipment is covered for discharges or for loss caused by freezing.

Additional Coverages and Limitation

As does the broad causes of loss form, the special causes of loss form provides two additional coverages: collapse and limited coverage for fungus, wet rot, dry rot, and bacteria.

These additional coverages are exactly the same in both forms. For a complete discussion, see Chapter 3.

Additional Coverage Extensions

Form CP 10 30 provides three additional coverage extensions: property in transit; water damage, other liquids, powder, or molten material damage; and glass.

The form allows the insured to extend coverage on business personal property in transit more than 100 feet from the described premises. The extension does not apply to property in the care of the insured's salespersons. The property must be located in or on a vehicle that the named insured owns, leases, or operates within the coverage territory.

The policy covers property in transit for the following perils: fire; lightning; explosion; windstorm or hail; riot or civil commotion; vandalism; vehicle collision, upset, or overturn (but not contact with the roadbed); and theft of an entire bale, case, or package. Theft is covered only in the case of forced entry into a securely locked body or compartment of the vehicle. The insured must show visible marks of the forced entry.

The limit of liability for this additional coverage extension is $5,000. This amount is in addition to the limit of liability.

Property in Transit

An insured plumber's tools were stolen from his van while parked on his home driveway. The tools were valued at more than $2,000. A claim was made for $1,000 under the property in transit additional coverage extension. The claim was denied.

Property in transit coverage is not designed for the insured's tools and business property; this coverage is intended for the insured's goods while being shipped or delivered to another location. The coverage applies to personal property of the insured in transit more than 100 feet from described premises, while in or on a motor vehicle. Damage must be by one of the described perils. Loss caused by theft is covered only where theft is of an entire bale, case, or package. The vehicle or compartment must be locked and there must be visible marks of forced entry.

Therefore, tools left loose in the vehicle do not qualify. If all the tools were contained in a case, and that case was stolen by someone leaving visible marks of forced entry, coverage would apply. If the tools were not packaged or in a case, there would be no coverage.

The second additional coverage extension applies in case of a covered loss due to water, other liquids, powder, or molten material. The insurer agrees to pay the cost to tear out and replace any part of the building in order to repair the appliance or system from which the material escaped.

Added with the 2000 edition was additional coverage extension 3, glass. When the insured suffers a loss to building glass, this coverage pays for temporary plates or other coverings if the repair is delayed. The limit of insurance provided by this extension is included in the limit of liability.

Chapter 5

Conditions

Commercial Property General Conditions

Common Policy Conditions form, IL 00 17, of the ISO commercial property program contains six conditions that must be incorporated into any policy written and that apply to all the policy's coverages. Most of these common policy conditions are restatements of provisions, modified in varying degree, that have been standard features of property provisions since the advent of the standard fire policy. The common policy conditions form has not been revised nearly as often as the building and personal property coverage form and the causes of loss forms. The two editions that have been released are the IL 00 17 11 85 and IL 00 17 11 98.

Cancellation

The cancellation provision gives the named insured the ability to cancel the policy at any time by notifying the insurer. The notification may be that the insured's copy of the policy is returned or a lost policy release is signed. Because the insured requests the cancellation, the return premium is calculated at rates less than pro rata.

The insurer may also cancel the policy at any time with appropriate written notice mailed to the insured. Cancellation for nonpayment requires a ten day notice; for any other reason, thirty days must be provided. When the insurer cancels, the return premium is figured on a pro-rata basis. Jurisdictions may have different statutory requirements regarding form and timing for insurance policy cancellations. These requirements are tracked in *FC&S Cancellation and Nonrenewal*, an annual compendium published by The National Underwriter Company.

The policy calls for cancellation notices to be to or from the *first named insured* (the person or entity whose name appears first on the policy).

Changes

This condition stipulates that any changes in the terms of the policy can be made only by endorsement issued by the insurer. Any change requests by the insured must be by the first named insured.

Examination of Your Books and Records

This condition gives the insurer the right to audit books and records of the insured relating to the policy. The examination or audit may be made during the policy period or any time within three years after the policy period ends. The condition does not allow the insurer to go randomly through the insured's records. Rather, the insurer may examine only the records that relate to the policy. Such related records may involve finances, safety, inventory, and so on.

Inspection and Surveys

The first part of this condition (D.1.a through c) gives the insurer the right to conduct inspections, surveys, and reports, and to make recommendations. These may be part of the underwriting process or may involve the insurance company's loss control or safety programs. They might relate to risk management, insurability, or conditions on the premises.

The second part of the condition (D.2.) makes clear that the insurer is not accepting liability related to these inspections, surveys, and reports. This acts as a disclaimer of liability so that liability for conditions existing in the insured's operations that may or may not be discovered or disclosed in an insurer's inspection cannot be passed on to the insurance company. Inspections, surveys, or reports the insurer performs do not act as a guarantee.

The forms states:

> We are not obligated to make any inspections, surveys, reports or recommendations and any such actions we do undertake relate only to insurability and the premiums to be charged. We do not make safety inspections. We do not undertake to perform the duty of any person or organization to provide for the health or safety of workers or the public. And we do not warrant that conditions:

a. Are safe or healthful; or

b. Comply with laws, regulations, codes or standards

This condition makes the point that an insurance inspection for underwriting or other purposes is not meant as a warranty from the insurer that the insured's operations are safe or healthful. Nor does it warrant that the insured is in compliance with legal requirements that may pertain to those operations.

Another part of the condition brings any rating, advisory, or similar organization—such as Insurance Services Office (ISO) or American Association of Insurance Services (AAIS)—who may make inspections or reports under the liability disclaimer.

The inspection and surveys condition was called into play in the 1977 litigation involving a fire at the Beverly Hills Supper Club in Kentucky that killed 165 people. The property insurer had recently inspected the building. Based on this inspection, some plaintiffs' attorneys attempted to hold the insurer and ISO liable for the deaths and injuries sustained in the fire. The courts, however, did not allow the suit to go forward. (The cause of the fire was eventually determined to be due to faulty aluminum wiring.)

Premiums

This condition specifies that the first named insured is responsible for paying the policy premium. It also calls for any return premiums to be sent to the first named insured.

Transfer of Rights and Duties under This Policy

The final common policy condition requires the insurer's written consent in order to transfer the insured's rights and duties under the policy to another person. The only time the written consent of the insurer is not needed is upon the death of a named insured. When a named insured dies his rights and duties are transferred to the named insured's legal representative. In such cases, the legal representative exercises the deceased insured's rights and duties while acting as legal representative. Until a legal representative is appointed, rights and duties of the deceased insured with respect to the deceased insured's property pass to anyone having proper temporary custody of that property. Such individuals might include a spouse, a partner, or a corporate officer.

Commercial Property Policy Conditions

In addition to the common policy conditions, the Commercial Property Policy Conditions form is attached to form a commercial property policy. The current edition of this form is the CP 00 90 07 88, meaning that these conditions have had no revisions since July 1988. The following conditions comprise this form:

1. Concealment, Misrepresentation, or Fraud

2. Control of Property

3. Insurance under Two or More Coverages

4. Legal Action Against Us (the insurer)

5. Liberalization

6. No Benefit to Bailee

7. Other Insurance

8. Policy Period, Coverage Territory

9. Transfer of Rights of Recovery Against Others to Us

Concealment, Misrepresentation, or Fraud

This condition voids coverage if, at any time pre- or post-loss, the named insured commits a fraudulent act relating to the policy. Misrepresenting the use or occupancy of the building—representing the property as a pharmacy when in reality it is an illegal methamphetamine lab, for example—or misrepresenting the value of destroyed equipment to boost insurance recovery is fraud. Such an act before or after loss voids coverage. *Void* does not mean that the policy is canceled or suspended, but that a contract between the insurer and insured never existed. In other words, a bargain was never struck due to the misrepresentation or fraud of the party.

The policy is also void if the named insured or any other insured intentionally conceals or misrepresents a material fact about the coverage, the covered property, a claim under the policy, or the named insured's interest in the property.

Fraud of *any* type by the named insured related to the policy voids coverage. Concealing or misrepresenting *material facts* by the named insured or any other insured also voids coverage.

The phrase *any other insured* does not void the policy only for the person committing the misrepresentation or concealment. It is possible that the act of any insured could void the policy as to all other insureds, including the named insured. A number of courts have interpreted the language *the insured* under the concealment, fraud, or neglect provisions of the standard fire policy as applying only to the individual insured guilty of the fraud, giving coverage to other innocent insureds. However other court decisions have interpreted language similar to the ISO *any other insured* phrase in certain fire policies as unambiguously precluding coverage to innocent, as well as guilty, insureds. In *Employers Mutual Casualty Company v. Tavernaro,* 4 F. Supp.2d 868 (E.D. Mo.1998), the Tavernaros owned a business covered on a businessowners policy (with the same wording as the commercial property policy). Mr. Tavernaro set the building on fire and Mrs. Tavernaro attempted to collect the insurance proceeds as an *innocent coinsured.* The court concluded that "the language clearly precludes recovery by either party in this case."

Control of Property

This condition protects the insured from the acts of others. It provides that acts or neglect by any person that are not under the direction or control of the named insured will not affect coverage. For example, if an employee of the named insured causes intentional damage the damage will be covered, despite the intentional acts exclusion (i.e., the intentional act is not imputed to the insured).

The language of the second part of the control of property condition states that a breach of any condition at one or more locations does not affect coverage at any location where the breach does not exist at the time of loss. For example, a breach of the vacancy condition at one insured location will not spill over to affect coverage at a second insured location.

Additionally, as there is no specific exemption regarding the fraud, misrepresentation, or concealment condition, it is reasonable to assume that the second part of the control of property condition applies equally to the fraud provision. If an employee of the insured commits fraud in connection with a claim, that will not bar the insured from recovering under the policy.

Insurance under Two or More Coverages

In the event that more than one of the commercial property policy's coverages applies to a loss, this condition prevents double payment. It limits the amount of payment to the actual amount of loss or damage. For example, a piece of business equipment might be covered under both the building and contents section of the commercial property policy. The insured cannot recover under both. However, if the amount of coverage left under one section is insufficient to pay the entire loss, it could be paid under either or both sections, up to the actual amount of loss or damage.

Legal Action against Us

If the insured wishes to bring suit against the insurer, she must first fully comply with all the policy terms. The insured must bring the suit within two years following the loss or damage (not two years after a formal denial of the claim). Earlier policies that incorporated the standard fire policy language gave the insured one year in which to bring suit.

Liberalization

The commercial property policy states that if the insurer liberalizes the policy (i.e., broadens or adds coverage) without any corresponding premium increase, the revisions automatically apply to the insured's unrevised policy. This provision applies to any liberalizations adopted by the insurer during the policy term or forty-five days prior to the inception date. For example, the current version of the commercial property policy provides $250,000 for a newly acquired or constructed building. If an insurer changes its policy to provide $300,000, without increasing the premium, all existing policyholders receive the $300,000 coverage.

No Benefit to Bailee

The commercial property policy is intended to protect the insured's property; there is no insurance under the policy for the benefit of others to whom insured property may be entrusted. If the insured owns a clothing store and sends some of the clothing out to be dry cleaned, the dry cleaner is responsible for the clothing while it is in his care. If the clothing is damaged while at the dry cleaner, the dry cleaner cannot look to the clothing owner's commercial property policy for coverage. While the commercial property policy insurer may eventually settle with its own insured, it would still retain the right to enter into subrogation proceedings against the dry cleaner to recover the insurer's payment and would make no payment to the insured or the bailee for the benefit of the bailee.

Other Insurance

While this condition does not prohibit an insured from carrying more than one property policy—and, in fact, states that the insured may have other insurance subject to the same plan, terms, conditions, and provisions—it spells out how a loss is handled in such a situation.

If the insured has more than one policy that covers the same plan, terms, conditions, and provisions, then any loss will be split pro rata by limits. For example, the XYZ Company headquarters is insured for $1 million with two policies covering the same plan, terms, conditions, and provisions. ABC Insurance has a policy for $750,000; DEF Indemnity has a policy for $250,000. If the XYZ building suffers a $400,000 fire loss, the payments would be split as follows: ABC—$300,000; DEF—$100,000. The insured would be responsible for two deductibles under this scenario.

The second part of this condition makes the commercial property policy excess over any other policy that does not cover the same plan, terms, conditions, and provisions. The commercial property policy is excess even if the insured cannot collect from the other insurer.

Policy Period, Coverage Territory

The commercial property policy covers losses that commence during the policy period, which is shown on the declarations page of the policy. The loss must also commence within the coverage territory—the United States (including territories and possessions), Puerto Rico, or Canada.

Transfer of Rights of Recovery against Others to Us

This condition defines the insurer's subrogation rights when it makes a payment under the policy. To expedite the claim process, many times an insurer will, pay its insured for property that was damaged by someone else. This condition allows the insurer to pursue the responsible party to recover the amount it paid to the insured.

The subrogation condition also preserves the rights of the insurer when it comes to third parties such as a bailor or mortgagee. The insurer is first in line to get money back from the responsible party (at least for the amount it paid).

At any time *prior to a loss* an insured may waive, in writing, possible recovery rights against anyone. However, once a loss has occurred the insured may waive those rights against only another insured, a business that the insured owns or controls (or owns or controls the insured), or a tenant of the insured.

Other Relevant Provisions of the Commercial Property Policy

While not designated as conditions, there are several provisions in the Building and Personal Property Coverage form that operate as conditions.

Limits of Insurance

The policy states that the most it will pay for loss or damage in any one occurrence is the limit of liability shown on the declarations page. Unlike commercial general liability policies, the commercial property policy is not subject to annual aggregate limits (meaning that once the limit is exhausted during the policy period, it is gone); instead, the commercial property policy's limits are per occurrence. For example, if the insured's building is insured for $100,000 and suffers fire damage in the first month of the policy period of $75,000, full policy limits of $100,000 are available for windstorm that may occur in the eleventh month.

The limits section goes on to indicate that the amounts of insurance applicable to Fire Department Service Charge, Pollutant Clean-up And Removal, Increased Cost Of Construction, and Electronic Data are in addition to the declared policy limits.

The section also provides $2,500 coverage for outdoor signs attached to buildings.

The limits section concludes by putting the additional coverage of Preservation of Property within the policy limits. Debris Removal was included here, as well in previous editions, but the Debris Removal additional coverage now describes the maximum payable under that coverage (see Chapter 2).

Deductible

One deductible applies per loss occurrence, i.e., not per insured peril or each item of building or personal property damaged. A loss may involve both fire and windstorm damage—only one deductible applies; or, the loss may involve damage to (1) the insured's building; (2) a structure on the premises; and (3) items of personal property—again, one deductible applies.

By policy provision, the amount of loss is first reduced (if required) by the coinsurance condition or the agreed value option coverage. If this adjusted amount of loss is less than the deductible, the insurer pays nothing on the claim. If the adjusted amount of loss exceeds the deductible, the deductible is subtracted from the adjusted amount of loss and that is the amount the insured recovers, subject to the applicable policy limits.

The deductible condition explains the application of the deductible when the occurrence involves loss to more than one item of covered property and separate limits apply to those items. For example, a building on the property has a $60,000 limit and another has a value of $80,000. Both are damaged in the same occurrence, building #1 with damage totaling $60,110, and loss to building #2 is $90,000. The losses to each building are not combined in determining the application of the deductible, but the deductible is applied only once per occurrence (see the following example from the policy).

Deductible	$250
Limit of insurance—building #1	$60,000
Limit of insurance—building #2	$80,000
Loss to building #1	$60,100
Loss to building #2	$90,000

The amount of loss to building #1 ($60,100) is less than the sum of the limit of insurance applicable to building #1, plus the deductible ($60,250). The deductible is subtracted from the amount of loss in calculating the loss payable for building #1 ($60,100 - $250) for a loss payable on building #1 of $59,850.

Because the deductible applies only once per occurrence, it is not subtracted in determining the loss payable for building #2. The loss payable for building #2 is its limit of insurance ($80,000). The insured still has an uninsured loss in the amount of $10,000 (because the loss was $90,000 and the limits are $80,000) and a deductible is not applied to building #2.

In policy example no. 2, the deductible and limits are the same as in example no. 1. In this example,

Loss to building #1	$70,000 (which exceeds the limit and deductible)
Loss to building #2	$90,000 (which exceeds the limit and deductible)
Loss payable on building #1	$60,000 (limit of insurance)
Loss payable on building #2	$80,000 (limit of insurance)
Total amount of loss payable	$140,000

Deductible—How to Apply

The insured property is a hotel located on the coast of North Carolina. The hotel is insured on a commercial property form CP 00 10 with Special Causes of Loss form, CP 10 30. The amount of building coverage is $6,905,000 with a deductible of $353,193. In order to get the insurance the hotel owners had to agree to a manuscripted change in the form. It excludes hail damage to some types of outdoor property, such as exterior paint, landscaping, and parking lots.

When Hurricane Floyd hit the Carolinas, this hotel suffered severe damage. The amount of the loss is $5 million; out of that $5 million, $1.3 million is uncovered damage to exterior property. Of the remaining $3.7 million only about $800,000 is damage to covered property.

The difficulty is the application of the deductible. The adjuster says that it applies to the amount of the covered loss. Thus, the deductible of $353,193 applies to the $800,000 that is payable, leaving an amount payable of $446,807.

The policy says the deductible applies "in any one occurrence of loss or damage (herein referred to as loss)." This is not otherwise qualified by "covered loss" or "the amount of loss covered by this policy." The deductible in a commercial property policy applies to the total amount of the loss as respects the insured —not to the limit of liability or special sublimits of liability.

The deductible is applied to the total amount of the loss, $5 million, leaving $4,646,807 as the amount of loss. However, that amount is further limited by the exclusion of damage to certain types of exterior property. Thus, the $1.3 million in uncovered hail damage is taken from that, leaving a final amount of $3,346,807.

Even if the insurer prevails at appraisal and is correct that only $800,000 is payable under the policy, the deductible still applies to the amount of the loss—$5 million. If the insurer prevails in appraisal and the amount payable is reduced to $800,000, the insurer will still owe the full $800,000: amount of loss ($5 million); less the deductible ($353,193) for an initial amount payable of $4,646,807; less the $1.3 million in uncovered hail damage (leaving $3,346,807); less $2,546,807 that the insurer claims is not covered (leaving a total amount payable of $800,000). No further deductions would be taken.

For example, a standard limitation in the CP 10 30 is $2,500 for the theft of patterns, dies, molds, and forms. A thief breaks into a machine shop covered by a CP 00 10 and CP 10 30. The deductible is $1,000.

The thief takes $4,000 worth of patterns, dies, molds and forms. The $1,000 deductible first applies to the loss, leaving $3,000 payable. However, that amount is further limited to $2,500 by the above provision. This insured is owed $2,500 by his insurer. If the deductible of $1,000 were applied to the sublimit of $2,500, the insured could collect only $1,500. If this were the case, the policy would never pay its full limits.

Loss Conditions

In addition to the common policy conditions and the commercial property conditions, the commercial property policy contains a set of loss conditions that operate in case of a loss.

Abandonment and Appraisal

Abandonment. The first loss condition is abandonment. The insured may not simply abandon damaged property to the insurance company. The insurer has the right to the salvage value of property for which it makes total payment but cannot be compelled to take damaged or destroyed property.

Appraisal. The second loss condition, appraisal, provides a method to settle differences between insured and insurer regarding the valuation of damaged property or the amount of the loss. In this event each party selects its own appraiser. Then the two appraisers select an umpire. If the appraisers cannot agree on an umpire they may request that the umpire be chosen by a judge of a court having jurisdiction. The appraisers then separately value the property and set the value of the loss. If the appraisers are unable to agree the matter goes to the umpire. A decision to which any two agree (either both appraisers or an appraiser and the umpire) is binding on both parties. The condition states that each party must pay its own appraiser. The costs of the umpire and of the appraisal process are shared equally.

The condition ends with these words: "If there is an appraisal, we will still retain our right to deny the claim." The inclusion of this statement helps the insurer avoid the implication that by participating in the appraisal process there is an implied agreement to pay the claim. It also prevents the insured from claiming that entering the appraisal process keeps the insurer from denying the claim further on down the road. Appraisal applies to the value of property, not whether the loss is covered.

Appraisal of a Loss

A commercial property insured suffered a major fire loss. The insured first hired a public adjuster, submitted a proof of loss, and awaited the insurer's decision. When the insured and the insurer could not agree on the amount of the loss, the dispute was submitted to appraisal.

The appraisers reached a decision favorable to the insured. At that point the insurer decided that it wanted to readjust the claim, but that is contractually impermissible. Once a claim goes through the appraisal process and an amount is set, the insurer no longer has the options it had. The language clearly says that the decision of any two of the three (appraisers and umpire) is binding on all parties.

An insured must submit a proof of loss so that the insurer may investigate the claim. That was already done in this case. The policy says that the insurer will pay a loss within thirty days after receiving the proof of loss and an appraisal award has been made. In this case, the appraisal award was made. The insurer cannot now decide to settle the claim in a different manner.

Appraisal Clause and Disinterested Appraisers

The insurer and insured disputed resolution of a fire loss claim. There is no dispute as to the cause of the fire loss and the insured prepared a building estimate. The dispute was over the extent and valuation of the loss.

The insured instituted the appraisal process under the policy and submitted the name of a disinterested builder and asked the insurer to do likewise. The insurer selected the original builder with whom the insured could not agree about the amount of damages.

The appraisal clause states that "each party will choose a competent appraiser." If these two cannot reach an agreement, they select an umpire. Having one of the original parties to the dispute chosen as an appraiser seems to build a barrier in the appraisal process, but the policy requires only that the appraiser must be competent; it does not require that each party select a disinterested appraiser.

The hope is that because the appraisers are competent professionals who are one step removed from the dispute, they will reach an agreement despite a certain natural bias in favor of their employer. If they cannot, the policy offers a mechanism for them to choose an umpire who decides which of the appraisers is right. If they cannot agree on an umpire, the policy provides for a court to select the umpire. These contingencies for involving an umpire are based in part on the recognition that the appraisers chosen by the parties might not be completely unbiased.

The Insured's Duties in the Event of Loss

The policy lists eight things an insured must do in the event of loss or damage under the policy. It also specifies the right of the insurer to examine the insured under oath without any other insured being present. The policy specifies that the insured must:

1. Notify the police if a law was broken.

2. Send the insurance company a notice of loss that includes a description of the property. The provision does not specify that the description must be in writing but it must be given promptly. The condition begins with the word *give* not *send*, so presumably notice to the insured's agent of loss by telephone is sufficient to fulfill this condition.

3. Provide a description of how, when, and where the loss or damage took place. This must be done as soon as possible.

4. Protect the covered property from any further damage and keep track of costs for emergency and temporary repairs to do so. This includes separating damaged from undamaged property if feasible. The insured must document expenses incurred in preserving the property from further loss. Such documentation is necessary for consideration in the settlement of the claim. These expenses are subject to the limit of insurance. "For consideration in the settlement of a claim" does not mean that the insurance company can consider whether to reimburse the insured for expense to protect covered property from further damage; consideration here can be taken in the contract context of *consideration*, meaning "due consideration" in a pecuniary sense.

    The insured must protect the covered property from any further damage, not just damage from a covered peril. However, the insurer is not liable for subsequent loss or damage resulting from any uncovered cause of loss.

5. Compile an inventory of damaged and undamaged property if the insurer so requests.

6. Allow the insurer to inspect the property, including the insured's books and records. The insurer may also take samples of damaged and undamaged property. Comparing these types of property helps in the investigation of a loss.

7. Submit a signed, sworn proof of loss, if requested.

8. Generally cooperate with the insurance company. Cooperation includes submitting to questions under oath. It also includes allowing the insurer to examine the insured's books and records. Any insured answering such questions in writing must sign his answers.

The form states that the insurer may examine the insured under oath (a term that courts have held encompasses both oral and written examination). The insurer may examine insureds separately and out of the presence of other insureds. In *USF&G v. Hill,* 722 S.W.2d 609 (Mo. App. 1986), the court found the insurer's right to examine insureds separately had to be made explicit in the policy or the insurer had no such right this language was added to the form.

Loss Payment

After a covered loss, the insurer has four settlement options; the policy specifically gives the insurer the selection of which option to employ. Settlement will be effected using one of these options:

1. **Pay the value of the property**. Prior editions of the commercial property policy did not define the word *value*, but the CP 00 10 10 00 edition added a paragraph in the provision stating that the insurer will determine the value of the damaged property or the cost to repair or replace in accordance with the valuation condition.

2. **The cost to repair or replace the damaged property.** The policy reiterates the ordinance or law exclusion by specifically eliminating insurance recovery for any extra costs due to the operation of building or zoning laws.

3. **The insurer may take the property at an agreed or an appraised value.**

4. **The insurer may actually repair, rebuild, or replace the property with that of "like kind and quality."** This option also excludes any extra costs due to the operation of building laws.

Within thirty days of receipt of the sworn proof of loss, the insurer must advise the insured which option it chooses. Whichever option is chosen, the insurer will not pay the insured more than the insured's financial interest in the property.

Property of others is also subject to the same four options. The insurer deals directly with the owner of the property in the insured's stead. Again, the insurer owes the owner of the property no more than his financial interest in it.

Sometimes the owners of damaged property may bring suit against the insured. The insurer promises to defend such suits at its own expense.

Once the insurer receives the signed, sworn proof of loss and reaches an agreement with the insured regarding the value of the property, the loss will be paid within thirty days. Reaching an agreement on the value includes the award of an appraisal.

ISO added a loss payment condition to address exposures related to party walls in the CP 00 10 06 07 edition. A party wall is generally defined as a wall that divides two adjoining properties and in which each of the owners shares the rights. Ownership of a party wall may or may not be shared; there are numerous legal variations including tenancy in common and unilateral ownership with easement rights. A coverage issue may arise when one owner of a party wall refuses or is unable to repair his side of a party wall following loss or damage.

The policy was revised to identify the exposure and convey loss adjusting procedures for it. In this provision, loss payment relating to a party wall reflects the insured's partial interest in that wall. However, if the owner of the adjoining building elects not to repair or replace that building (and the building insured under this insurance is being repaired or replaced), this insurance will pay the full value of the party wall, subject to all other policy provisions.

Actual Cash Value Defined

Actual cash value (ACV) has three meanings in actual usage:

1. **Fair market value,** which is usually described as the price a willing buyer would pay to buy property from a willing seller in a free market.

2. **Replacement cost less depreciation**, which is generally accepted to mean the cost to replace property at the time of the loss minus its physical depreciation.

3. **The broad evidence rule,** which involves a judicious application of either one or two to the unique circumstance of the claim, whichever is more favorable to the insured.

State laws vary considerably on the definition. In California, an appeals court decided that ACV means fair market value in *Cheeks v. California Fair Plan,* 61 Cal. App. 4th 423 (1998). The court admonished insurers: "If it [the insurer] wants to determine actual cash value on the basis of replacement cost less depreciation, all it has to do is say so in the policy." Courts in Pennsylvania have taken the opposite view that ACV means replacement cost, such as in *Judge v. Celina Mut. Ins. Co.* 449 A.2d 658 (Pa. Super. 1982).

Fair market value, *replacement cost*, and *depreciation* are all fairly common and have commonly accepted meanings. They have been used over and over in establishing the value of damaged property.

The broad evidence rule, on the other hand, tries to bring other factors into consideration. *McAnarney v. Newark Fire Ins. Co.,* 247 N.Y. 176 (1928) is a leading case on this question. The case involved the fire destruction of an old brewery that could not be used because of the National Prohibition Act. The building apparently had no other economic use, and the owner advertised it for sale, unsuccessfully, for a fraction of the amount of insurance carried. In striking a compromise between the insured and the insurer, the court said: "Where insured buildings have been destroyed, the trier of fact may, and should, call to its aid in order to effectuate complete indemnity, every fact and circumstance which would logically tend to the formation of a correct estimate of the loss. It may consider original cost and cost of reproduction; the opinions upon value given by qualified witnesses; declarations against interest which may have been made by the insured; the gainful uses to which the buildings may have been put; as well as any other reasonable factor tending to throw light on the subject." In so reasoning, the court decided on a value between replacement cost less depreciation and the market value of the building.

The most important point regarding the broad evidence rule was quoted in *McAnarney*. The court said that "every fact and circumstance which would logically tend to the formation of a correct estimate of the loss," including the economic value of the property, should be considered in determining the actual cash value.

Valuing Business Personal Property

Valuing business personal property may be less difficult because the value of the contents is not tied to the value of the land as with a building. The problem with using replacement cost less depreciation is that business personal property is often diverse, is acquired over a period of time, and depreciates at various rates. Often receipts are unavailable. Market value is also not a reliable guide. Few businesses would want their fairly new office furniture replaced with similar furniture that had been rented to others.

Another problem for businesses is the value of stocks of merchandise and raw materials. These items usually do not suffer depreciation. In such a case the proper measure of recovery is the cost of replacing them at the current market value, less any salvage value. Merchandise that has become shopworn and has deteriorated in value should be subject to depreciation. The measure of recovery might be more or less than the original cost; however, the standard of recovery is the cost to the insured not the price at which it is expected to sell. Rules in most states permit use of a market value or selling price clause that converts, for some insureds such as manufacturers and retailers, finished stock from actual cash value to selling price less discounts and unincurred expenses. Form CP 99 30 provides for valuation based on selling price, less any applicable discounts and expenses, for all completed stock (not just finished stock that is sold but not delivered, as in the building and personal property coverage form).

Recovered Property

This condition provides a method for loss readjustment in case stolen property is recovered. If either party recovers any property after loss settlement prompt notice must be given to the other party. The insured has the option to return the amount of claim payment in return for the original item. The insurer cannot require the insured to return payment and take back recovered property. Recovery expenses and necessary repairs to the property are borne by the insurance company up to the applicable limit.

Vacancy

The vacancy provision contains two parts. The first defines *building* for both an owner-occupant and a tenant as meant in the vacancy provision. The second describes the manner in which losses to vacant buildings are handled.

The form defines *building* for a tenant as that portion rented or leased to the insured. The tenant's portion is vacant when it does not contain enough business personal property to conduct customary operations, which would mean its normal business.

When the policy is issued to the owner or general lessee rather than a tenant, the policy says that a building is vacant if the insured does not rent at least 31 percent of the floor space to others or if the insured does not use at least 31 percent of the floor space for his own operations.

Under prior editions a building with the furniture and fixtures of a business—but from which the stock had been removed—would be considered vacant since customary operations are not possible without stock. In post-2000 editions, a building containing fixtures, fittings, and business personal property would still be considered vacant if it were being under-utilized. The vacancy provision could be an issue for insureds where a storefront operation is the only going concern in a multiple story building. Despite the going concern on the first floor, if less than 31 percent of the building is unrented or not used for customary operations, the building is considered vacant and the provisions related to vacant property are applicable.

Prior to 1995, only buildings under construction were exempt from the vacancy provision. The 1995 version added buildings under renovation. The times when the building and personal property coverage form applies—by coverage extension—to a building under construction are rare and are limited by the provisions of the form (thirty days). An existing structure, on the other hand, can be subject to renovation at any time with no requirement of notice to the insurance company since it will not be considered vacant. However, the insured must be careful of a coinsurance problem if much value is added prior to notifying the insurer.

The second part of the vacancy condition describes how losses are handled when the building has been vacant for more than sixty consecutive days, or longer, if so endorsed. There is no coverage for damage from vandalism, building glass breakage, water damage, theft or attempted theft, or sprinkler leakage, unless steps have been taken to protect the system against freezing. The policy covers loss from a covered peril in a vacant building at a reduction of 15 percent in what it otherwise would pay.

Valuation

The commercial property policy covers loss to covered property at actual cash value unless some other valuation method (such as replacement cost) has been arranged. The policy does, however, provide four exceptions. Valuable papers and records were at one time a fifth exception, but the CP 00 10 04 02 edition's treatment of electronic data and valuable papers and records necessitated its removal from this section. The exceptions are as follows:

1. If the insured meets the coinsurance requirement, the policy covers any loss under $2,500 at replacement cost. However, the following building items are still subject to ACV adjustment: awnings, floor coverings, appliances, outdoor equipment, and furniture. Replacement cost does not include any extra cost due to the operation of building laws.

2. Stock sold but not delivered is valued at selling price less any applicable discounts and normally incurred expenses. For example, if the insured sells widgets at $100 each and offers a discount of 2 percent if paid within ten days, entire amount due within thirty days, with $10 in shipping expense, the recovery on the $100 item might be $88 ($100 selling price less 2 percent discount minus shipping fee of $10). Trade and business practice, along with examination of books and records, determines actual valuation.

3. The policy provides for replacement of damaged glass with safety glass if required by law.

4. Tenants improvements and betterments are adjusted at ACV if repairs are made promptly. If the insured does not make repairs promptly to improvements and betterments the insurer offers a proportional settlement via the following formula. The original cost of the improvement times the number of days from the loss to the lease's expiration or the expiration of the renewal option period, if applicable. The amount computed is then divided by the number of days from the installation of the improvement to the expiration of the lease or the expiration of the renewal option period. The inclusion of renewal option periods addresses the long standing question of whether such periods should be considered during loss settlement calculations to provide a better restitution for an insured's use interest in a damaged improvement.

    Assume a tenant holds a one-year lease for a commercial building that expires on July 31. The lease contains a one-year renewal option. On March 3, the tenant installs paneling costing $1,500. A fire occurs on June 2 that causes damage so extensive that the insured closes the business permanently. Had no loss occurred, the tenant would have stayed in business and exercised the renewal option.

    Without taking the renewal option period into consideration, the insured stands to receive a $600 payment for the improvement ($1,500 x 60/150 = $600; where 60 equals the days from loss to lease expiration and 150 equals the days from improvement installation to lease expiration). When the renewal option period (365 days) is included in the calculation, the result of the proportional loss settlement is $1,238—[$1,500 x (60 + 365/150 + 365)] = $1,238—a significant difference.

These formulas come into play only if the insured does not make the repairs promptly, thus disqualifying him from actual cash value recovery. The insured receives nothing from the insurer if someone other than the tenant (the landlord, for instance) repairs damaged improvements.

Valuation and Selling Price

A load of nonalcoholic beer was damaged when the load shifted during transit. The insured's customer made a claim against the insured for replacement of the shipment and a dispute over the value of the beer ensued.

Even though the buyer of the beer was to pay $4,300 for it replacement cost for the damaged goods to the insured was $10,260. It is standard practice in that industry to reduce the price on one product and increase prices on other products in order to maintain (or increase) profit margins.

The insurer took the position that it would pay the smaller of the replacement cost or actual cash value at the time of the loss. At the time of the loss, the value was the selling price, $4,300.

However, because the insured sold the beer for less than it cost does not reduce the value to that amount. What needs to be established is the ACV of the beer. The insured needs to demonstrate that this practice of selling certain items for less than their cost is a standard business practice in this industry.

Additional Conditions

The commercial property policy contains two additional conditions: coinsurance and mortgageholders.

Coinsurance

The principle of coinsurance says that in exchange for a reduced rate the insured must agree to maintain a specified relationship between property values and amount of insurance (e.g., 80 percent). For example, a building with a value of $1,000,000 must be insured for at least $800,000. If the insured agrees to carry this amount of coverage, the rate charged may be fifty cents per thousand dollars of coverage; however, if the insured chooses to carry only $500,000, that rate might increase to seventy-five cents or a dollar.

The form explains the mechanics of coinsurance with a step-by-step description. It also examines the ramifications of a coinsurance penalty. Examples show the effects of coinsurance computations in three different situations: where limits are inadequate, where limits are adequate, and where a blanket limit exists.

Since 1986, every version of the coinsurance provision found in the CP 00 10 applies the deductible after the calculation of the coinsurance penalty. The wording in the 2000 policy was rearranged to emphasize this point. Prior to 1986, the forms applied the deductible prior to the calculation of the coinsurance penalty, a manner more advantageous to the insured.

The following is an example of the interaction between the deductible and the coinsurance clause: Two insureds each have a $50,000 loss under policies with a $250 deductible. Insured A is in compliance with the coinsurance requirement and recovers $49,750 ($50,000 minus $250). Insured B is underinsured and must accept 25 percent of the loss as a coinsurer. Insured B will collect $37,500 (75 percent of $50,000) less the $250 deductible for a net recovery of $37,250. Had insured B been covered under a pre-1986 commercial property form, he would have collected $37,316 (75 percent of $49,750). Subtracting the deductible before calculating the coinsurance penalty makes a difference of $66 for the insured.

Mortgageholders

This condition spells out the rights and duties of any mortgagees or trustees (here referred to as mortgageholders) that are named on the declarations. In the event of a claim, any listed mortgageholder receives payment for losses as interests may appear. However, the insured must be in compliance with all coverage terms. Even if foreclosure proceedings or similar actions have begun on a building that suffers a loss, a mortgageholder may collect a loss payment.

Further, even if the insurer denies a claim to the insured due to the insured's actions or lack of compliance with the terms for coverage, the mortgageholder may still collect. The mortgageholder must pay any premium due and submit the appropriate proof of loss. Additionally, a mortgageholder must notify the insurance company of any known change in ownership, occupancy, or increase of hazard. When these conditions are satisfied, all terms of the building and personal property coverage form become applicable to the mortgageholder.

If partial claim payment is made to a mortgageholder and not to an insured, the insurance company inherits a proportion of the mortgageholder's rights under the mortgage based on the extent of claim payment, and the mortgageholder retains subrogation rights and may attempt to recover the full amount of the claim.

The insurance company may, at its option, pay the mortgageholder the full amount of the principal and interest on the mortgage in exchange for transfer of the mortgage to the insurance company. In this case, the insured continues mortgage payments, but to the insurance company instead of the original mortgageholder.

If the insurer cancels the policy, it must send written notice to the mortgageholder thirty days before the effective date of cancellation. If the cancellation is due to nonpayment of premium by the insured, then notice to the mortgageholder is only ten days. In the event of nonrenewal, the insurer must also send a ten-day notice to the mortgageholder.

Loss during Foreclosure

A large warehouse was insured for over $1 million. The mortgageholder foreclosed on the property. Shortly after the foreclosure a fire caused nearly $700,000 in damage to the warehouse. The agent wondered about the insurer's obligation to the mortgageholder.

The amount of the loss does not determine the insurer's obligation to the mortgageholder; the amount of debt still owed on the property does. That amount is the mortgageholder's insurable interest.

The insurer's obligation to the named insured owner is the value of the loss limited to the former owner's insurable interest. If the owner of the building has complied with all the policy conditions, the insurer owes the loss to the named insured and the mortgageholder as their interests may appear. The amount of each of their interests is a legal.

Chapter 6

Builders Risk

Buildings under construction are not eligible for coverage under the building and personal property coverage form, which forms the basis for a commercial property policy. Due to the different exposures faced by a building under construction, such as an increased risk of theft and vandalism, different rates and forms must be used. The Builders Risk Coverage Form, CP 00 20, is combined with one of the causes of loss forms to cover buildings under construction. It can also be used to cover additions and alterations, foundations, temporary structures, materials and supplies owned by the insured, and on a limited basis, building materials and supplies of others.

As with the building and personal property coverage and causes of loss forms, the builders risk policy has been revised by Insurance Services Office (ISO) from time to time. The builders risk editions are as follows (the date is the last four digits of the form number):

- CP 00 20 07 88

- CP 00 20 10 90

- CP 00 20 10 91

- CP 00 20 06 95

- CP 00 20 02 00

- CP 00 20 10 00

- CP 00 20 04 02

- CP 00 20 06 07

ISO Eligibility and Rules

Buildings in the course of construction are eligible for the builders risk coverage form. The rules recognize that even some buildings that, once occupied, are not eligible for the commercial property policy because use occupancy may still be covered on the CP 00 20 while under construction. ISO includes three examples in the rules of such exposures—boarding or rooming houses of one to four units, farm properties, and dwellings. The rules state that "the following are some examples of risks which are eligible during the course of construction but which may not be eligible when occupied," so the list is noncomprehensive.

Builders risk coverage is written for a minimum one-year term to cover a new building or structure under construction or an existing structure undergoing additions, alterations, or repairs. The rules state that policy inception should begin no later than the date that construction starts above the level of the lowest basement floor, or, if there is no basement, the date construction begins. The rules permit pro-rata cancellation when construction is completed whether insurance on the completed structure is rewritten with the same company or companies. If the policy is cancelled before the structure is completed, the general cancellation provisions found in the common policy conditions apply.

Blanket insurance covering more than one building or structure is subject to the rating rules for such coverage. Blanket coverage is useful for housing projects and other large risks with several units being erected at the same time.

A builders risk policy is written for the completed value of the insured building. This amount should include the value of all permanent fixtures and decorations that will become part of the building. The rules include the following warnings: "Contract price does not necessarily equal the full value at completion" and, "Failure to maintain the proper limit of insurance may cause the insured to share proportionately in a loss." The rates contemplate the fact that the insurer does not face the total amount of exposure for the entire policy term.

While not described as a coinsurance penalty, the builders risk form does penalize the insured in the event of a loss when the limit of liability is inadequate. The need for adequate insurance provision calls for a reduction in loss payment by the percentage the customer is underinsured. If the building has a completed value of $200,000 but is only insured for

$100,000, any loss payment will be reduced by 50 percent. The provision says, "We will not pay a greater share of any loss than the proportion that the Limit of Insurance bears to the value on the date of completion."

The builders risk insured with more than one location may choose to cover all locations on a blanket basis. The countrywide rules contain a formula for calculating the blanket average rate.

Value of the Building on the Completion Date

The Builders Risk Coverage form, CP 00 20, contains what amounts to a 100 percent coinsurance clause based on the value of the building on its completion date but it is not always clear what comprises the completed building's value. More specifically, assume construction of a building that has a great deal of asphalt blacktop and a sizable volume of poured concrete in the footings and base slabs. The insured might not feel that these items should be included in the amount of insurance, although they are included in the contract price of the building.

The following is an example of why these items need to be insured. Keep in mind that these items will be excluded upon completion.

The builders risk coverage form applies to the building described in the policy declarations while in the course of construction. It does not contain the exclusion of foundations below the lowest basement (or, lacking a basement below the surface of the ground) found in the building and personal property coverage form. In fact, the builders risk form explicitly states that it covers foundations: "(1) Covered Property...Building Under Construction, meaning the building or structure described in the declarations while in the course of construction, including: (a) Foundations; (b) The following property...(3) Your building materials and supplies used for construction; provided such property is intended to be permanently located in or on the building... or within 100 feet of its premises."

Unlike with a completed structure, there is a time during the course of construction when the footings and slabs the insured would like to exclude are exposed to loss. Fire or wind could destroy the forms before the concrete is poured and cause a legitimate builders risk loss. If construction has not yet begun—and insurance should be in place before construction begins—the insured and the underwriter might agree to write an endorsement eliminating coverage for foundations, materials, and supplies connected with them in exchange for an appropriate reduction in the amount of insurance. If construction is beyond the foundation stage, the insured has had the protection of the insurance while it was needed and there would be no justification for eliminating foundation values from the completed building value.

The same can be said for the asphalt blacktop. The builders risk form affords coverage for building materials and supplies used in construction, provided the materials are to remain permanently in or on the building or structure described in the declarations or within 100 feet of its premises. Perhaps the reason insureds generally decline this type of coverage is that the risk of damage or loss to the materials seems low. Instead, insureds often prefer to carry the risk themselves. Again, if the underwriter agrees, the value of the blacktopping might be removed from the completed value of the building in a preconstruction agreement if the insured is willing to accept an endorsement excluding coverage of materials and supplies used in that operation.

Covered Property

The builders risk form covers direct loss or damage to covered property. The list of covered property is short compared to the list of covered property in the building and personal property coverage form because the property covered by the commercial property policy is being put to its intended use while a builders risk policy covers property under construction.

The builders risk form covers the building under construction as described in the declarations and its foundation. It also covers fixtures and machinery and equipment used to service the building and the insured's building materials and supplies used for construction. The insured must intend that these items be permanently located in or on the building or within 100 feet of the premises.

The form does not define the phrase *in the course of construction*; therefore common usage applies. According to *Webster's New International Dictionary*, *construction* is "the act of putting together to form a complete integrated object: fabrication."

However, in *Patton v. Aetna Insurance Co.,* 595 F. Supp. 533 (D.C. Miss. 1984), the court expanded the meaning. The court ruled that the term includes activities related to, but prior to commencement of construction. The case concerned a builders risk policy issued to cover a building scheduled for renovation. A fire destroyed a large portion of the building. At the time of the fire only preparatory work towards the renovation had been done. This included removing the furnace and lattice work, unhooking the gas and plumbing lines, and engaging in discussions with contractors regarding the lowering of the building. The court determined that since the insured and the insuring company understood that renovation of the house was intended, it was reasonable to interpret construction to mean alterations of any type, whether additions or removals. As a result, the activities of the insured were considered construction and covered under the provisions of the builders risk policy.

There is no coverage for business personal property. Nor is there any coverage for the property of others. The builders risk form does, however, provide an additional coverage in the amount of $5,000 for material and supplies owned by others.

Temporary structures built on the premises are covered property if there is no other insurance on them. Such structures include cribbing, scaffolding, and construction forms.

Property Not Covered

As with the property covered section, the property not covered section is also rather short as compared to the commercial property policy. Again, much of the property indicated as not covered under the commercial property policy is property that would be present only at a business already in operation. The form specifically excludes land and water. It also excludes lawns, trees, shrubs, plants; radio or television antennas, including lead-in wiring, masts or towers; and detached signs. Coverage may be bought back via endorsement.

Although the builders risk form excludes land and water, it provides the same additional coverage for pollutant cleanup as does the commercial property policy (*see* Chapter 2). The form provides $10,000 of annual coverage for the cost to extract pollutants from land or water at the described premises. *Pollutants* is defined as in the commercial property policy as, "any solid, liquid, gaseous or thermal irritant or contaminant, including smoke, vapor, soot, fumes, acids, alkalis, chemicals and waste. Waste includes materials to be recycled, reconditioned or reclaimed."

Covered Causes of Loss

The builders risk form is combined with one of the causes of loss forms: CP 10 10, CP 10 20, or CP 10 30. For a discussion of these forms, see Chapters 3 and 4.

Additional Coverages

The builders risk form provides four additional coverages: debris removal, preservation of property, fire department service charge, and pollutant cleanup and removal. These coverages are identical to those contained in the commercial property policy. (See Chapter 2.)

Coverage Extensions

The builders risk form provides two coverage extensions: building supplies and materials of others and sod, trees, shrubs, and plants.

The first extension pays up to $5,000 per location for material and supplies owned by others. The insured may purchase a higher amount by making an entry on the policy declarations. This is an additional amount of insurance and applies at each described premises. These losses are settled for the account of the property owner. This coverage extension applies when the property of others is in the insured's care, custody, or control and is located in or on the described building or within 100 feet of the premises.

In order for this extension to apply, the insured must intend to make the property a permanent part of the building (e.g., air conditioning or heating equipment), thus precluding coverage for the builder's machinery and equipment used in the construction. The builders risk coverage form was released in 1986 with no separate item of coverage for builders machinery, tools, and equipment as found in previous versions. According to explanatory information from ISO, the provision was deleted because broader coverage is available to builders and contractors through inland marine policies.

However, the current edition provides limited coverage for builders machinery, tools, and equipment when Special Causes of Loss form, CP 10 30, is attached to the builders risk coverage form. The property must be owned by or entrusted to the insured. Found in the limitations section of the CP 10 30, it provides coverage against the specified causes of loss to builders' machinery, tools, and equipment.

Trees, Shrubs, and Plants

Sod, trees, shrubs, and plants are not covered under the builders risk policy. However, coverage extension b provides limited coverage for these items. It covers trees, shrubs, and plants for the perils of fire, lightning, explosion, riot or civil commotion, and aircraft. Coverage is limited to $1,000 per occurrence, regardless of the type or number of items lost, with a limit of $250 for any one tree, shrub, or plant.

Limits of Insurance

The limits of insurance as shown on the declarations page apply to covered property on a per occurrence basis. A sublimit of $2,500 applies per outdoor sign per occurrence.

The amounts payable under the coverage extensions—building supplies and materials of others and sod, trees, shrubs, and plants—apply in addition to the limit of liability. Likewise, two additional coverages are outside the limit of liability: fire department service charge and pollutant cleanup and removal (see Chapter 2).

The amounts payable under the other two additional coverages, debris removal and preservation of property, are included in the limit of liability. The debris removal provision contains the same $10,000 extra amount payable under certain conditions as in the commercial property policy (see Chapter 2).

Deductible

The deductible applies after any deduction required by the additional condition—need for adequate insurance (discussed later in this chapter).

Loss Conditions

The following builders risk loss conditions are exactly the same as those found in the commercial property policy: abandonment, appraisal, duties in the event of loss or damage, and recovered property.

The 2000 edition added wording to the loss payment condition. It specifies that the insurer determines the value of covered property in accordance with the applicable terms of the valuation condition. The only valuation method used is actual cash value (ACV). Remember that the policy does not define ACV.

The builders risk form was revised in the 06 07 edition identically to the building and personal property coverage form as regards party walls. A party wall is generally defined as a wall that divides two adjoining properties and in which each of the owners shares the rights. Ownership of a party wall may or may not be shared; there are numerous legal variations including tenancy in common and unilateral ownership with easement rights. A coverage issue may arise when one owner of a party wall refuses or is unable to repair his side of a party wall following loss or damage. The 06 07 edition revised the builders risk form to identify the exposure and convey loss adjusting procedures for it. Provisions were added under loss payment relating to a party wall reflecting the insured's partial interest in that wall. However, if the owner of the adjoining building elects not to repair or replace that building (and the building insured under this insurance is being repaired or replaced), this insurance will pay the full value of the party wall, subject to all other policy provisions.

The vacancy loss condition, found in the commercial property policy, is not present in the builders risk form because any building under construction is usually vacant. The rates for builders risk contemplate this increase in exposure.

Additional Conditions

The builders risk form contains four additional conditions: mortgage-holders, need for adequate insurance, restriction of additional coverage—collapse, and when coverage ceases.

Mortgageholders. This condition is the same as that found in the commercial property policy.

Need for adequate insurance. This additional condition resembles the coinsurance condition of the commercial property policy and operates in the same fashion. It serves to penalize the insured in the event of a loss if he does not insure the building to 100 percent of its completed value. The policy calls for a reduction in loss payment by the percentage the customer is underinsured. If the building has a completed value of $200,000, but is insured only for $100,000, any loss payment will be reduced by 50 percent.

Restriction of collapse coverage. The broad and special causes of loss forms include collapse as an additional coverage. One of the covered causes of collapse is use of defective material or methods in construction, remodeling, or renovation if the collapse occurs during the course of the construction, remodeling or renovation. The builders risk form eliminates this covered cause of collapse. Thus, the builders risk policy provides no coverage for collapse caused by the use of defective material or methods.

When coverage ceases. The builders risk coverage form says that coverage ceases when one of the following first occurs:

a.   the policy expires or is cancelled;

b.   the property is accepted by the purchaser;

c.   the named insured's interest in the property ceases;

d.   the named insured abandons the construction with no intention to complete it;

e.   unless the insurer specifies otherwise in writing:

    (1)   ninety days after construction is complete; or

    (2)   sixty days after any building described in the declarations is:

        (a)   Occupied in whole or in part; or

        (b)   Put to its intended use.

Builders risk rates do not contemplate the increased exposures of occupied premises. However, the policy does not define *occupied*. Courts have often held that a building is not considered occupied until it is put to the practical and substantial use for which it was designed. This definition of *occupied*, then, becomes synonymous with a building being put to its intended use. The builders risk policy has employed the current policy language since 1985.

Previous editions of the builders risk form covered property in transit for $5,000 if subject to the Special Causes of Loss form, CP 10 30. The previous edition of form CP 10 30 covered only this property for $1,000. This additional coverage has been removed from the builders risk form because the CP 10 30 now provides this coverage in the amount of $5,000.

Builders Risk Coverage Options

The builders risk form provides six optional endorsements to modify the basic form. They include building renovations, builders' risk reporting form, separate or subcontractor's interests, collapse during construction, theft of building materials, fixtures, machinery, equipment; and building materials and supplies of others.

Building Renovations

When renovations are made to existing buildings, builders risk coverage can be amended to exclude the value of existing realty. This endorsement, Builders Risk Renovations, CP 11 13, changes the definition of *covered property*. Instead of insuring the building under construction, this endorsement covers renovations under construction. It provides coverage only for the value of building improvements, alterations, or repairs under construction. Unlike the CP 00 20, the CP 11 13 does not cover foundations. It does cover fixtures, equipment used to service the building, and building materials. These items must be intended for use in the building or within 100 feet of the premises. This endorsement adds the value of buildings or structures existing prior to construction of the improvements, alterations, or repairs to property not covered.

This endorsement also modifies the need for adequate insurance condition. This condition acts like a 100 percent coinsurance clause in that it requires insurance in the full amount of the completed value of the structure. Since a completed structure already exists, that condition becomes impractical. Instead, form CP 11 13 requires the insured to carry 100 percent of the value of the improvements, alterations, or repairs at the described premises. When using this endorsement, the when coverage ceases condition does not apply.

Builders Risk Reporting Form

The insured may choose to report monthly values of the building under construction using endorsement CP 11 05. The form requires the insured to choose a date when values will be reported each month. This choice must be made within thirty days of coverage inception.

If the insured does not make the required reports on form CP 11 06, the policy lists two different penalties. Being late with a report relegates loss adjustment to the last reported value. If the insured does not file any reports, the building is valued at ACV as of the inception date.

Endorsement CP 11 05 removes the need for adequate insurance condition. However, losses will still be adjusted by the proportion of values last reported to the ACV of the property at the time of loss. Total loss payment is limited to the limit of liability—even if the reported values exceed that amount.

Because the values at risk change, the premium changes as well. The initial premium is based on the ACV of the property at policy inception. Subsequently the insurer makes adjustments based on the reported values.

Separate or Subcontractors Interest

The insured may choose to exclude the interests of other contractors or subcontractors by endorsement CP 11 14. This endorsement adds the value of the installation that the contractor makes at the described location to the definition of property not covered. Such value includes labor, materials, and supplies. The endorsement also removes such an installation from the requirements under the need for adequate insurance condition.

Endorsement CP 11 15 covers the interests of other contractors or subcontractors. It does the opposite of CP 11 14. It adds labor, materials, and supplies to the definition of *covered property* and specifies that the installation described is the only item to which the need for adequate insurance condition applies.

Collapse during Construction

If the insured chooses broad or special causes of loss, the builders risk form removes coverage for collapse during construction. Endorsement CP 11 20 restores this coverage for an additional premium. The rates for this coverage are published in the multistate pages of the Commercial Lines Manual. However, if the policy covers an architect, engineer, or building trade contractor as an insured or additional insured, the rate is increased five times.

Theft of Building Materials, Fixtures, Machinery, Equipment

Endorsement CP 11 21 provides theft and attempted theft coverage for building materials, fixtures, machinery, and equipment that are intended to become a permanent part of the building if they are located within 100 feet of the building. The amount of insurance shown on this endorsement is separate from the amount of coverage shown on the declarations as applicable to the building. The minimum deductible for this form is $1,000 and applies separately from the deductible under the builders risk policy. In order for coverage to apply, a watchman must be on duty during the hours when no construction is being conducted. If no watchman is on duty, there is no coverage.

The endorsement describes what does not constitute theft or attempted theft:

1. dishonest or criminal acts by the named insured; any of the named insured's partners, employees, directors, trustees, or authorized representatives; any contractors or subcontractors or their respective employees; or anyone to whom the property is entrusted.

2. voluntary parting with any property by the named insured or anyone else to whom the property is entrusted, if induced to do so by any fraudulent scheme, trick, device, or false pretense.

3. property that is missing, where the only evidence of loss or damage is a shortage disclosed on taking inventory, or other instances where there is no physical evidence to indicate what happened to the property.

Building Materials and Supplies of Others

For an additional premium, the insured may choose to increase the coverage provided for these items. The basic amount is $5,000. The increase is indicated on the declarations page.

> ### Need for Builders Risk on Renovations to Existing Building
>
> The question arises of when, if at any time, would a builders risk policy need to be written in conjunction with a commercial property form on an existing building undergoing remodeling or renovation?
>
> For a building owner, there is no reason to have separate builders risk coverage applying in conjunction with a standard commercial property policy on renovations to an existing covered building. The standard commercial property form covers additions under construction, alterations, and repairs to the building or structure. It further covers materials, equipment, supplies, and temporary structures on or within 100 feet of the described premises, used for making additions, alterations, or repairs

to the building. However, coverage for these items applies only if not covered by other insurance. Therefore, if the owner bought separate builders risk coverage on such a project, there would be no coverage under the commercial property form.

The policy, however, covers only property owned by the insured. There would be no coverage, for example, for a contractor's equipment or tools unless the tools could be said to be in the care, custody, or control of the insured, which is not generally the case, and therefore covered as personal property of others.

Chapter 7

Business Income Coverage Forms

Business income insurance, also referred to as business interruption or time element, and in older nomenclature use and occupancy coverage, protects the business income of the insured, the money that would be earned absent the (covered) event. The purpose is to replace what the business would have financially received had no loss occurred during the period of business interruption. Loss of net income, the prime source of money for continuing operating expenses, as well as profit, if any, is the subject of coverage. Business income forms cover the net income plus continuing normal operating expenses that businesses would have earned had no direct property damage loss occurred.

The purpose of this chapter is to discuss coverage under the Insurance Services Office (ISO) business income forms, as they form part of the commercial property protection program. Aspects of business income coverage are complex A much more comprehensive treatment of the subject can be found in *The Business Interruption Book,* also published by the National Underwriter Company.

There are three ISO forms available to cover an insured's business income and extra expense exposures. The edition date is current with the commercial building and personal property coverage form—06 07.

- Business Income (And Extra Expense) Coverage Form, CP 00 30

- Business Income (Without Extra Expense) Coverage Form, CP 00 32

- Extra Expense Coverage Form, CP 00 50

Like other forms in the commercial property program, there have been various edition dates for the ISO business income forms. In large, the various edition dates are the same as the edition dates for revisions in the building and personal property coverage form and the causes of loss forms.

Coverage for Business Income

Visualizing a profit and loss statement is helpful in understanding business income insurance. In a mercantile operation, for example, the retailer's operating expenses and profit are derived from resale at a markup of goods purchased. The merchant buys goods from a manufacturer or wholesaler for sale to the consumer. The dollar difference between sales income and cost of goods purchased provides funds for operating expenses and profit—the basis of insurable interest under business income coverage. Similarly, a manufacturing operation derives its income from the increase in value of materials that it converts into its product.

ISO rules for business income coverage define a *mercantile or non-manufacturing risk* as "one in which the business consists principally of the sale or storage of merchandise, or the furnishing or rendering of a service." Some businesses provide services with little or no sale of merchandise. Examples include banks, bowling alleys, laundries, and legal or accounting firms. In these businesses, cost of goods or raw materials purchased is minimal, consisting mainly of consumable supplies, so nearly all of the income from the sale of the services is used to pay expenses and provide a profit.

According to ISO rules, a manufacturing risk is "one in which the operation consists principally of changing raw stock into finished stock by aging, assembling, converting or seasoning through the use of hand or machinery processes or the application of mechanical, electrical, thermal or chemical energy. Property including grain elevators, grain storage buildings, grain tanks and/or equipment for drying grain is a manufacturing risk." By specific rule provision, "building service machinery or the use of machinery for packing and shipping, or minor repairing or altering incidental to a predominantly mercantile or non-manufacturing risk does not require the occupancy to be classified as a manufacturing risk."

Since the subject for business income insurance is the income of the business, it is fundamental to this type of insurance that there be earnings and that earnings continue to be possible. If a business is idle and likely to remain that way for a long time, there are neither present nor prospective earnings and no need for business income coverage. But the mere fact that a business is not operating does not necessarily eliminate the need for this coverage. If a business is definitely scheduled to resume operations but the property is damaged or destroyed by an insured peril, there will be a loss of income and, hence, a business income exposure. The exposure commences on the date operations were scheduled to resume. A seasonal business, such as an ice cream shop in a vacation area, is one example of this situation.

Similarly, insurance can be written for a business operator whose premises are under construction. Loss to an uncompleted building postpones the date of occupancy and any loss of earnings from the date business operations should have begun can be insured.

Coverage can properly be written for businesses whose earnings are sufficient to meet all or part of the operating expenses but not sufficient to show a profit. Some businesses, although currently unable to produce a profit, still have a substantial exposure in the form of continuing expenses if a suspension of business occurs. Coverage is in order to the extent that those expenses were being earned prior to loss. But, for businesses not operating at a profit, close underwriting scrutiny is necessary. In addition, the amount collectible will be reduced by the normal net loss.

When Coverage Applies

Another consideration of business income insurance is that recovery applies only for the time required to repair or replace damaged property with the exercise of due diligence and dispatch, or as required in the business income coverage form, "with reasonable speed" so that normal operations can be resumed. This criterion is the yardstick that measures the amount of loss to be paid. The restoration period applies for the time required to rebuild or repair the buildings and equipment, replace the merchandise or raw materials, and, for a manufacturing establishment, bring unfinished products to the same point of manufacture that had been reached at the time of the covered loss or triggering event.

Within this standard of reasonable speed, the actual time required to rebuild or replace can vary considerably, depending upon conditions at the time of loss. For example, weather, availability of materials, labor, and transportation can and often do affect the time needed to restore the property. Considering all the variables involved, chances are that even the most reasonable and well intentioned estimators will not be in exact agreement as to the day or perhaps even to the week when the business could be resumed.

The thrust of the provision is two-pronged. It puts the insured on notice that any unreasonable delay in construction will affect the amount of insurance recovery, thereby eliciting the insured's cooperation and giving the insurance company an avenue to escape the consequences of unreasonable delays in the restoration. But, the insurer also has an incentive to adjust the property and business income claims promptly, enabling the insured to proceed with restoration, as delay in claim settlement extends the time given the insured to restore operations and increases the amount of the loss.

Extra Expense

Some businesses must make every effort to continue operating no matter how serious the damage and regardless of the cost. A prime example is the *New Orleans Times-Picayune* and its efforts to resume publishing immediately in the days after Hurricane Katrina in 2005. Other examples are dairies, insurance agencies, and banks. For such risks, the principal need is extra expense insurance.

These types of businesses also may not be able to avoid a temporary suspension following severe damage. To avoid long-term loss of customers they will spend substantial amounts of money to get back into operation. Other businesses have some operations that must go on and others that could be suspended. One example is a newspaper and printing firm in which the newspaper publication must continue but job printing can be interrupted. For such an operation, a combination of business income and extra expense insurance is needed.

Extended Loss after Operations Resume

A common complaint about recovery under older forms of business income coverage was that the full loss to the business was limited to the time required to restore the property. For example, a popular restaurant in a remote location, if damaged and forced to close, would need regular business income insurance to cover the loss during reconstruction, but it would undoubtedly suffer an additional loss beyond that time until its clientele was fully reestablished. Losses occurring during the lag between physical reopening and the time when business was operating at the level it was before the loss occurred were not covered under the standard business interruption forms. To insure such losses under business income policies, an optional endorsement was used, extending the period of indemnity to include this lag. Under the current ISO business income coverage, this feature is built into the form with a thirty-day limit and the option to increase the number of days of coverage as needed.

Blanket Coverage

When an insured has interdependent operations in two or more separately rated buildings or at more than one location and a loss at one location will curtail business at other locations, blanket business income insurance is ordinarily recommended.

Blanket coverage may also be arranged when the separate locations are independent of one another, but the principal advantage here, if any, is cost. If the average rate results in lower overall costs than would be the case with each location covered separately, then blanketing might be advised. Otherwise, the necessity of adjusting any loss on the basis of the business being done at all covered locations (for coinsurance purposes) may offset any blanketing advantage.

Incidentally, blanket business income insurance should not be confused with business income from dependent properties coverage. Blanket insurance covers two or more separately rated units of the insured's own operations. Income from dependent property insurance covers the loss that the insured will suffer if the operation of a key supplier, customer, or leader property on which the insured's operations are dependent is shut down by an insured peril.

ISO Simplified Business Income Program

As previously noted, there are three basic ISO forms available for use in covering an insured's business income and extra expense exposures: Business Income (And Extra Expense) Coverage Form, CP 00 30; Business Income (Without Extra Expense) Coverage Form CP 00 32; and Extra Expense Coverage Form CP 00 50.

The definition of *business income* under the forms is (a) the net income (net profit or loss before income taxes) that would have been earned or incurred, and (b) continuing normal operating expenses incurred, including payroll. For manufacturing risks, net income includes the net sales value of production.

The use of a two-item definition of business income has created a problem of interpretation in cases where a business operates at a loss. A court ruled that the two items—net income and continuing normal operating expenses—are separate, unrelated items of covered business income and that a negative net income should not be used to offset continuing expenses. For instance, in *Continental Ins. Co. v. DNE Corp.*, 834 S.W.2d

930 (Tenn. 1992), the court found that adding DNE's net income to its continuing expenses yielded a negative number so there was no business income recovery.

Three elements included in the Section A coverage provision are required for coverage to apply: (1) a necessary suspension of business operations during the period of restoration; (2) a direct physical loss of or damage to property at the described premises caused by or resulting from a covered cause of loss; and (3) an actual loss of business income.

Pre-2000 forms did not define *necessary suspension*. As some insurers' policies still use previous editions or independently filed forms containing variations, a look at litigation surrounding this definition is helpful. Courts have divided on the meaning. For instance, in *American States Ins. Co. v. Creative Walking, Inc.*, 16 F. Supp.2d 1062 (E.D. Mo. 1998), the court found that necessary suspension meant a complete cessation of business operations. Creative Walking suffered direct physical damage due to a water main break, leaving its premises untenantable. It moved to a temporary facility a few weeks later and made the temporary facility its new headquarters. Creative Walking submitted a business income and extra expense claim to the insurer stating that it suffered a business slowdown for about eighteen weeks following the loss. The court said, "If the insured is able to continue its business operations at a temporary facility, it has not suffered 'necessary suspension' of its operations." Therefore, Creative Walking was entitled only to compensation for the two-week period before moving to the new location and the expenses incurred in relocating.

Similar rulings were made in these cases: *Keetch v. Mutual of Enumclaw Ins. Co.*, 831 P.2d 784 (Wash. Ct. App. 1992) (motel experienced only a partial interruption of business, not enough to trigger coverage, due to eruption of Mt. St. Helens burying it in six inches of volcanic ash); *Quality Oilfield Products, Inc. v. Michigan Mutual Ins. Co.*, 971 S.W.2d 635 (Tex. App. 1998) (slowdown of business following burglary of design information, computer disks, process orders, and other key operational materials did not constitute the necessary interruption of business required for coverage to apply); and, *The Home Indemnity Co. v. Hyplains Beef*, 893 F. Supp. 987 (D. Kan. 1995) (failure of computer system resulting in less efficiency and a slowdown in operations at a cattle slaughter and processing company did not qualify as a necessary suspension of operations).

However, a court has found that companies can recover expenses for mitigating damages. In *American Medical Imaging Corp. v. St. Paul Fire and Marine Ins. Co.*, 949 F.2d 690 (3d Cir. 1991), the court ruled that a business that set up temporary offices with a reduced phone capacity suffered a necessary or potential suspension of operations. Following a fire that caused smoke and water damage, American Medical Imaging relocated to an alternate site for six weeks while its facilities were unusable. The company relied on fewer telephone lines at the temporary location and claimed that it lost nearly $1 million and incurred extra expenses. The court said that American Medical was entitled to coverage because it acted promptly to mitigate the damages and that its operations had been suspended.

To clarify the issue the 2000 business income/extra expense form added a definition of *suspension*:

a. The slowdown or cessation of your business activities; or

b. That a part or all of the described premises is rendered untenantable, if coverage for Business Income including "Rental Value" or "Rental Value" apples.

This resolved the contract interpretation argument over whether a slowdown of business activities is sufficient to trigger coverage, and not complete cessation.

The first required element for coverage also specifies that the suspension of business operations occur during the period of restoration. *Period of restoration* is a defined policy term. The period includes a time deductible, with coverage beginning seventy-two hours after the time of direct physical loss for business income insurance. The time deductible does not apply to extra expense coverage and that recovery is available immediately after the time of direct loss. The period ends on the date when the property at the described premises should be rebuilt, replaced, or repaired with similar quality and reasonable speed or when the business resumes at a new permanent location, whichever is earlier. The period is not terminated by the policy expiration date, meaning that business income coverage may extend past the policy term.

The second element required for coverage is that the loss must result from direct physical damage to or loss of property at premises described in the declarations resulting from a covered cause of loss. Causes of loss will vary depending upon which of the three commercial property causes of loss forms is selected by the insured. As in the building and personal property coverage form direct physical damage and loss is not defined.

Courts have upheld that physical damage is necessary for business income coverage to apply. For example, a North Carolina appeals court held that inability to access a business did not trigger business income coverage when no physical damage occurred in *Harry's Cadillac-Pontiac-GMC Truck Co. v. Motors Ins. Corp.*, 486 S.E.2d 249 (N.C. Ct. App. 1997). When a snowstorm struck, Harry's car dealership could not be reached for a week. The court said that business income insurance "does not cover all business interruption losses, but only those losses requiring repair, rebuilding, or replacement."

Likewise, the court in *St. Paul Mercury Ins. Co. v. Magnolia Lady, Inc.*, No. 2:97CV-153-B-B, 1999 U.S. Dist. LEXIS 17895 (N.D. Miss. Nov. 4, 1999) decided that loss of earnings could not be reimbursed if the insured location suffered no direct physical loss or damage. A barge collided with a bridge near a casino-hotel owned by Magnolia Lady. State authorities closed the bridge for three weeks following the collision, which Magnolia Lady argued caused a dramatic decrease in business. Because the casino-hotel remained accessible and suffered no damage, the court said no coverage was available.

Actual loss of business income is the third requirement for a business income loss. If there is no loss of business income coverage is not triggered. The Tennessee Supreme Court affirmed this element in *Continental Ins. Co. v. DNE Corp.*, 834 S.W.2d 930 (Tenn. 1992). DNE owned a plant that had been operating at a loss when it was damaged by a tornado. During the period of restoration, DNE paid continuing operating expenses as defined by its business income coverage. The insurance promised recovery only if a loss of actual business income was sustained, which is the net income that would have been earned had business not been interrupted plus continuing operating expenses. The addition of DNE's net income and continuing expenses yielded a negative number, and the court found that there was no coverage.

Business Income—Bomb Threat?

A bomb threat necessitated the evacuation of insured premises, effectively shutting down operations. The insured questioned whether the shut down was covered under its business income policy.

Business income coverage under the standard business income coverage form is triggered by a suspension of operations "caused by direct physical loss" of or damage to property at the premises described in the declarations. Absent physical damage there is no coverage for suspension of operations caused by threats. A bomb threat does not trigger business income coverage.

Extra Expense

Extra expense is not a defined term in the policy definitions section, but the term is given a specific policy meaning for coverage purposes in section A: "necessary expenses you [the insured] incur during the period of restoration that you would not have incurred if there had been no direct physical loss or damage to property caused by or resulting from a covered cause of loss." Most frequently the kinds of expenses for which coverage is afforded are rental of a temporary office or store, computer or communications rental equipment, and items of that kind.

The policy provides coverage for two categories of extra expenses:

1. Extra expense to avoid or minimize the suspension of business and to continue operations at the insured premises or at replacement premises or temporary locations. Included are relocation expenses and costs to equip and operate a replacement or temporary location. The costs to rent, move, and set up a temporary facility or obtain temporary or replacement equipment would be paid by this portion of the policy.

2. Extra expense incurred to minimize suspension of business if operations cannot be continued. The hiring of additional workers or paying existing employees overtime in order to reopen the business would be covered here.

The form also provides coverage for extra expenses necessary to repair or replace property but only to the extent the amount of loss otherwise payable is reduced.

Covered Causes of Loss

As with the building and personal property coverage form, insurance protection can be arranged on three levels: basic, broad, and special. The forms used are the same used with the building and personal property coverage form. These causes of loss forms are the topics of Chapters 3 and 4.

Exclusions and Limitations

Each of the covered causes of loss forms also contains a section of special exclusions applicable to the business income coverage and extra expense coverage forms only.

Excluded are business income and extra expense losses caused directly or indirectly by power or other utility service failure that do not result in a covered cause of loss. For example, a storm causes a power outage to an insured premises, and the lights and cash register will not operate. Business income coverage is not triggered because there is no physical damage to the property.

The utility service exclusion was substantially revised in the 06 07 editions of the business income forms. The existing utility services exclusion for time element applies to the failure of power or other utility service supplied to the described premises if the failure occurs outside of a covered building. In the 06 07 edition reference to power and other utilities is expanded to make explicit mention of water and communication services, which are common services and currently addressed in optional coverage endorsements.

The pre-06 07 exclusion precluded coverage in the case of failure that occurs away from the described premises, whereas the revised exclusion focuses on events that involve an off-premises supplier and embraces certain events originating on-premises as well. Often, occurrences of utility service failure involve equipment failure. Equipment used or supplied by an off-premises utility service provider may be located at the site of the utility company's facility (away from the insured premises) and (in the case of such things as transmission lines and cables) at various sites in the area being supplied, including the insured premises. ISO revised the exclusion to address utility failure that originates at the described premises when such failure involves equipment used to provide utility service supplied by an off-premises provider. This revision is consistent with the focus of the exclusion previously described with respect to precluding coverage for utility failure related to an off-premises provider. The revised exclusion applies to all coverage forms and eliminates the distinction between the property damage and time element versions of the exclusion. The exclusion newly applies to utility failure that originates at the described premises when such failure involves equipment used to provide utility service supplied by an off-premises provider. The aforementioned statement is relevant to the covered building since the current time element exclusion already includes failure originating on the described premises outside a covered building.

There is also a broadening of coverage, in that on-premises failure is limited to situations where the failure involves equipment used to supply utility service from an off-premises source.

A provision was added in the 06 07 edition to make it explicit that the exclusion encompasses power surge related to the power failure event and that communication services include electronic network access and internet service.

Losses that arise from direct physical loss or damage to radio or television antennas and their lead-in wiring, masts, or towers are also not covered. However, this exclusion may be eliminated with the purchase of endorsement CP 15 50.

Another exclusion prohibits business income coverage for any loss caused or resulting from damage or destruction of finished stock or the time required to reproduce such stock. *Finished stock* is defined as "stock you have manufactured," including whiskey and alcoholic beverages being aged, but not manufactured stock held for sale at any retail outlet insured on the form. This exclusion does not apply to extra expense coverage.

Interference at the insured premises by strikers or others with rebuilding or replacing the property or with the resumption or continuance of business is specifically excluded as well. Because the reference is to delay by interference at the premises, an increase of loss caused by a strike elsewhere—such as one affecting material suppliers, transportation lines, or the availability of workers to do the restoration—is covered.

Suspension, lapse, or cancellation of any license, lease, or contract not directly caused by the suspension of operations is also excluded. Extra expenses incurred beyond the period of restoration due to suspension, lapse, or cancellation of any license, lease, or contract are not covered, either. Any other consequential losses are also excluded (see the discussion in Chapter 1 for the distinction between direct and consequential losses).

Accounting Documentation—Who Pays?

Loss adjustment may involve an insurance company request that the insured provide accounting documentation to support the claim. To comply with the request the insured might incur professional services costs from an accountant to accumulate the data and provide the report to the company.

There is nothing in the wording of the business income portion of the policy that obligates the insurance company to pay the insured's accounting cost to determine the extent of the business income loss. The policy promises to pay for "the actual loss of Business Income you sustain due to the necessary suspension of your 'operations' during the 'period of restoration.'" *Business income* is defined in the policy to mean "a.Net Income (Net Profit or Loss before income taxes) that would have been earned or incurred; and b. Continuing normal operating expenses incurred, including payroll." The accountant's fee is neither net income nor continuing normal operating expenses.

However, the form also provides extra expense coverage. *Extra expense* is defined as "necessary expenses you incur during the 'period of restoration' that you would not have incurred if there had been no direct physical loss." The accounting fees in question would not have been incurred had there been no loss. The policy also requires that the extra expense be incurred to "avoid or minimize the suspension of business and to continue 'operations.'" It is fair to assume that the insurance company would not have paid the business income loss if the insured had not submitted the requested accounting information. The insured's business also would have continued to be suspended or operated at reduced income if the insured had not been paid for the business income loss.

Therefore, it seems reasonable to conclude that accounting fees incurred at the request of the insurance company are an insured extra expense as intended under the policy.

Additional Limitation

Forms CP 00 30 and CP 00 32 contain an additional limitation for interruption of computer operations. This limitation points out the specialized exposures computer operations and data present. Specific computer and electronic data coverage has evolved to protect against the economic effects of these types of loss.

If a suspension of operations is caused by destruction or corruption of electronic data or any loss or damage to electronic data, coverage for business income does not apply. If action is taken to avoid or minimize a suspension of operations caused by the destruction or corruption of electronic data or any loss or damage to electronic data, coverage for extra expense does not apply.

Electronic data is "information, facts or computer programs stored as or on, created or used on, or transmitted to or from computer software (including systems and applications software), on hard or floppy disks, CD-ROMS, tapes, drives, cells, data processing devices or any other repositories of computer software which are used with electronically controlled equipment."

There is an exception to this limitation, a modest give-back of coverage. The interruption of computer operations limitation does not apply to losses covered under the interruption of computer operations additional coverage, which is discussed subsequently in this chapter.

Additional Coverages

There are four additional coverages on form CP 00 30: civil authority, alterations and new buildings, extended business income, and interruption of computer operations. Form CP 00 32 contains additional coverage for expenses to reduce loss, civil authority, and alterations and new buildings. These additional coverages extend the basic business income coverage without increase in the limit of insurance unless noted otherwise.

Civil Authority

Additional coverage for civil authority extends the business income and extra expense coverage to include loss caused by action of civil authority that prohibits access to the described premises "due to direct physical loss of or damage to property, other than at the described premises, caused by or resulting from any covered cause of loss." If, for instance, a fire at a building down the block from the insured location causes the police to close the street for a week for inspections and debris removal, coverage will apply. Coverage for business income begins seventy-two hours after action by civil authorities, immediately after civil action for extra expense. The coverage applies for up to three consecutive weeks from the date of the action, and, for extra expense, when business income coverage ends.

The pre-2000 ISO business income and independently filed policies have slightly different civil authority additional coverage language, requiring damage to adjacent property, rather than the "damage to property, other than at described premises" phrasing later adopted in the CP 00 30 04 02 and CP 00 32 04 02. Under the "adjacent property" wording, courts have held that damage to adjacent property must occur to trigger business income coverage.

In *Syufy Enterprises v. The Home Ins. Co.*, No. 94-0756 FMS, 1995 U.S. Dist. LEXIS 3771 (N.D. Cal. March 21, 1995), the court said that a company that closed during an officially imposed curfew period did not experience a business income loss. Syufy Enterprises owned and operated several theaters in Los Angeles, San Francisco, and Las Vegas. Civil authorities in those cities imposed dusk-to-dawn curfews following rioting and looting. Access was not denied to the theaters by authorities, no property next door to or across the street from the theaters was damaged, and no property located within two blocks of the theaters was damaged as a direct result of the riots. Syufy contended that any property damage within the curfew zones should have been sufficient to elicit business income coverage. The court, though, maintained that "Syufy opted to close its theaters as a direct result of the city-wide curfews, not as a result of adjacent property damage." Because there was no riot-induced damage within close proximity to Syufy's theaters and because the theaters were voluntarily closed, there was no coverage.

Language in the current edition, though, is broader than the more specific language requiring a covered loss involving property adjacent to the insured premises, as upheld in the *Syufy* opinion. With the current form, the property damage producing the action of civil authority need not be in the insured's immediate vicinity. For example, loss from a fire or explosion in a chemical plant located several miles from the insured's premises that forces evacuation of a large area around the plant would be covered by the current form, but not by the policy language in *Syufy*.

This issue was revisited again with the 06 07 editions, clarifying coverage issues that arose after the September 11, 2001, terrorist attacks on the World Trade Center and the Pentagon. In its explanation of changes ISO stated, "Historically, this Additional Coverage, in general, provided coverage in cases where there was a prohibitive action of civil authority due to damage by a covered peril in close proximity to the insured premises. However, in more recent times, situations have arisen where civil authority actions are taken in response to an event taking place far from the insured premises."

ISO revised the civil authority additional coverage on its time element coverage forms so that it applies if the insured premises are not more than one mile from the damaged property and the action of civil authority is taken in response to dangerous physical conditions resulting from the damage or continuation of the covered cause of loss that caused the damage, or the action is taken to enable a civil authority to have unimpeded access to the damaged property. This settles the issue for the type of business income losses that occurred on 9-11.

The use of a radius of one mile to circumscribe civil authority coverage is from a technical (though not historical) perspective, a reduction in coverage—that is, a narrowing of the circumstances under which this coverage may be triggered. A companion rule filing addresses use of optional endorsement CP 15 32 to modify the radius. Civil Authority coverage is broadened, in that the basic coverage period is increased from three weeks to four weeks. The current option to further increase the coverage period (under endorsement CP 15 32) will remain in effect

Additionally, the civil authority coverage period is extended in these coverage forms from three weeks to four.

Airports Closed by Order of Civil Authority

The terrorist attacks on September 11, 2001, created some business income loss scenarios that had not been addressed before. In the wake of the attacks, and for the first time in the nation's history, the federal government shut down all airports in the country. Even as the airports reopened, many people were fearful of flying and stayed away from airports and the businesses located in them. Were these businesses eligible for business income coverage?

ISO's policy has a time deductible of seventy-two hours. If the airports reopened by September 14, that deductible would not have been met to allow coverage to take effect. However, Reagan National Airport remained closed longer than other airports, so businesses located there may have been eligible for coverage.

The closures met the policy's requirements of direct physical loss or damage to property other than at the described premises—the World Trade Center towers and the Pentagon—and that access was prohibited by civil authority. The reduced traffic after the airports reopened, though, would not meet the criterion that access was denied by civil authority. Courts have held that complete cessation of business is necessary for the civil authority additional coverage to kick in. A mere fall off of business is not sufficient to trigger this coverage.

Businesses dependent on airlines for deliveries or other aspects of their operations would also find no coverage in a standard business income policy. Likewise, businesses, such as hotels and travel agencies, that saw a drastic drop in clients and profits after the attacks would find it difficult to recover their losses under standard business income policies. Without direct physical loss or damage to their premises or nearby property, and if an order of civil authority did not specifically deny access to their premises, they do not meet the requirements for business income coverage to apply.

Alterations and New Buildings

Additional coverage for alterations and new buildings extends the business income coverage to cover loss of business income sustained due to direct physical loss or damage at the described premises by any covered cause of loss to:

1. new buildings or structures, whether complete or under construction;

2. alterations or additions to existing buildings or structures; and

3. machinery, equipment, supplies, or building materials located on or within 100 feet of the described premises and used in the construction, alterations, or additions, or incidental to the occupancy of the new buildings.

If the covered damage delays the start of operations, the period of restoration for which loss is payable begins on the date that operations would have begun except for occurrence of the loss.

To illustrate, suppose that an insured is expanding its suite of offices in order to house two additional practitioners and that the new offices are scheduled to be operational on January 1. On December 15, there is a small fire and the offices cannot be occupied until February 1. Any extra expense the insured undertakes to speed up the repairs is covered under the basic insuring agreement. The expenses associated with the additional coverage start on January 1, the date when the offices would have been available and applies to expenses such as the cost of acquiring temporary office space for the two new persons during the delay.

Extended Business Income

This coverage pays for additional loss of business income that exists after damaged property, other than finished stock, is actually repaired and operations are resumed. It provides business income recovery until the business can be restored, with reasonable speed, to the condition that existed before the loss occurred. Loss caused by unfavorable business conditions is not covered.

Extended business income is designed to enable the insured to recapture market position following completion of repairs and resumption of operations. For example, a retailer that endured a long closure for repairs may not see its customers return right away. It may need to entice customers back from other stores or wait for new customers to be found. The loss of income during this period is covered by extended business income.

The basic coverage applies for up to thirty consecutive days after resumption of operations. In form CP 00 30, though, another provision states that a longer extended period of indemnity can be provided by inserting a higher number in the space provided on the declarations. That number of days then replaces the customary thirty-day extension.

Interruption of Computer Operations

While the forms contain a limitation for interruption of computer operations, this additional coverage gives back a small amount of business income coverage for losses arising from certain types of computer interruptions. Coverage is extended, subject to the provisions of the additional coverage, when the suspension of operations caused by an interruption in computer operations results from a covered cause of loss.

For instance, up to $2,500 of business income coverage may be available if a hacker tampers with a company's network and causes it to crash, temporarily interrupting business operations.

Depending on which form is used, the covered causes of loss are subject to the following:

- For the special form, the additional coverage is limited to the specified causes of loss as defined and collapse.

- In the broad form, the additional coverage applies to collapse.

- If an endorsement adds a covered cause of loss, the additional covered cause of loss does not apply to the coverage provided under this additional coverage.

- This additional coverage applies if the covered causes of loss include a virus, harmful code, or similar instruction introduced into or enacted on a computer system, electronic data, or a network to which it is connected, designed to damage, destroy, or disrupt any part of the system or its operation. No coverage is extended, though, if an employee, including a temporary or leased employee, manipulates the insured's computer system or electronic data. Coverage also does not apply to manipulation of computer systems or electronic data by another entity that inspects, designs, installs, maintains, repairs, or replaces the system and is retained by the insured.

The amount of additional coverage is limited to $2,500 for all loss sustained and expense incurred during any one policy year. The limit applies no matter how many interruptions occur or the number of insured premises or computer systems involved. The additional coverage does not extend beyond the period of restoration. The limit for this additional coverage is separate from the policy limit.

Expense to Reduce Loss

Unlike the full extra expense coverage of form CP 00 30, coverage under this item of form CP 00 32 is limited to payment of expenses incurred to reduce the business income loss that would otherwise be payable under the coverage. Recovery is restricted to no more than the amount by which the business income loss is reduced by incurring the added expenses.

Restaurant Closed Due to Robbery

A small restaurant was robbed at 9:30 PM on a Saturday night. Everyone was locked in a cooler by the robbers while they emptied the cash drawer and smashed the computer that operates the cash register and customer order system. Because the computer was down, the restaurant remained closed Saturday night and did not open again until its normal opening time of 11:00 AM Monday morning. The computer had been fixed by this time. The insured carried a Business Income Coverage form (Without Extra Expense) with the extended business income option and a Special Causes of Loss form. The insurance company paid the business income loss for the balance of Saturday night and Sunday but denied the extended business income option for the decrease in business the insured suffered during the week following the robbery. Business was down by one-third that week.

In the insurance company's adjustment, the decrease in business during the week following the robbery was due to patrons' fear of bodily injury and was not caused by the time required to repair the physical damage to the computer. The insurer maintained that the short-term closing was not long enough to cause the loss of customer base intended to be covered by the extended business income option.

In this scenario, all of the elements required for a covered extended business income loss are present. Business was suspended because of direct physical loss or damage to the computer ordering system. The loss was caused by a covered cause of loss. The insurance company adjustment supports this by paying the business income loss suffered from Saturday night until Monday morning. An additional loss of business income began on the date the property was repaired and operations were resumed and ended at the end of the week when the insured's operations were restored to the condition that would have existed if no direct physical loss or damage occurred.

The motives of the customers who stayed away from the restaurant are not relevant. All that is required is a covered loss and a decrease in business during the time period allowed by the policy.

Coverage Extension

Both forms provide a coverage extension to newly acquired locations (except fairs or exhibitions) if 50 percent or higher coinsurance is shown in the declarations for the business income coverage. The extension's limit is separate from the policy's limit. It is not subject to the coinsurance clause.

The limit paid under the extension for both business income and extra expense is $100,000 per location. The coverage begins when a new location is acquired or construction is begun and ends when the first of the following occurs: (a) the policy expires; (b) thirty days elapse after date of acquisition or start of construction; or (c) values for the location are reported to the insurer. Additional premium is charged for the new location from the date of acquisition.

This coverage parallels coverage provided for buildings and personal property and is useful as a temporary form of automatic coverage for newly acquired or constructed locations until permanent coverage can be arranged. But for locations acquired just before policy expiration, perhaps after renewal coverage has been ordered without knowledge of the new location, the coverage will expire with the policy. There is no provision for carrying the coverage over to the new policy for the remainder of the thirty days or until the location is recognized and values reported.

Application of Negligent Work Exclusion

A motel's power lines were cut by a sewer subcontractor while doing work on the premises. The insurer denied an ensuing business income loss claim stating that the damage was caused by negligent work of the sewer contractor and the policy does not provide coverage for this loss.

However, business income coverage is triggered by suspension of the insured's operations caused by "direct physical loss of or damage to property at the premises described in the declarations." The direct loss or damage to property on the insured's premises is the damage to the power lines. Therefore, absent a validly applied exclusion, this loss is covered. Damage to property on the insured's premises caused a suspension of operations.

Limits of Insurance

The limits of insurance section provides that payment of loss in any one occurrence is limited to the applicable limit of insurance shown in the declarations, except that the limit applicable to the interruption of computer operations and the coverage extension for newly acquired locations are separate from the limit of insurance.

The clause also provides that payments under certain additional coverages do not increase the applicable limit of insurance. The limit is not increased by payments under additional coverages for alterations and new buildings, civil authority, extra expense, and extended business income for business income coverage; nor for payment under alterations and new buildings and civil authority for extra expense coverage.

Loss Conditions

The loss conditions section of forms CP 00 30 and CP 00 32 are similar to those of the building and personal property coverage form.

The section on appraisal stipulates that either party may make a written demand for appraisal if they disagree on the amount of the loss or net income and operating expenses. Each party selects an appraiser, who in turn selects an umpire. Each appraiser states the amount of the loss or net income and operating expenses. If the appraisers do not agree on the amount, they submit the differences to the umpire. A decision agreed by any two will be binding. Each party pays for its appraiser and split the cost of the appraisal and the umpire. Submitting to an appraisal does not negate the insurer's right to deny the claim.

The section on duties in the event of loss of business income lists the following requirements of the insured:

1. Notify the police if a law may have been broken.

2. Give the insurer prompt notice of the loss or damage, including a description of the property.

3. Give a description of how, when, and where the damage or loss occurred.

4. Keep a record of expenses and take all reasonable steps to protect the property from further damage. Also, the damaged property should be set aside if possible.

5. Permit the insurer to inspect the property; examine and make copies of books and records; and take samples of damaged and undamaged property for testing, inspection, and analysis.

6. Send a signed, sworn proof of loss within sixty days of the insurer's request.

7. Cooperate with the insurer in the investigation and settlement of the claim.

8. Resume operations as quickly as possible if the business is to continue.

The policy further states that the insurer may examine any insured under oath, while not in the presence of other insureds, and that the answers must be signed.

Loss Determination

The condition for loss determination explains how business income loss and extra expense payments are determined. This section reads as follows:

a. The amount of business income loss will be determined based on:

(1) The net income of the business before the direct physical loss or damage occurred;

(2) The likely net income of the business if no physical loss or damage had occurred, but not including any Net Income of the business that would likely have been earned as a result of an increase in the volume of business due to favorable conditions caused by the impact of the Covered Cause of Loss on customers or other businesses;

Therefore, for example, if a lumber yard was put into a cessation-of-business condition in a hurricane-wrecked area and, but for the damage to the business, would have been able to serve the rebuilding needs of the entire area, that presumed increase in net income would not be a factor in adjusting the business income loss of the lumber yard.

(3) The operating expenses, including payroll expenses, necessary to resume "operations" with the same quality of service that existed just before the direct physical loss or damage; and

(4) Other relevant sources of information, including:

(a) Your financial records and accounting procedures;

(b) Bills, invoices, and other vouchers; and

(c) Deeds, liens, or contracts.

b. The amount of extra expense will be determined based on:

(1) All expenses that exceed the normal operating expenses that would have been incurred by "operations" during the "period of restoration" if no direct physical loss or damage

had occurred. We will deduct from the total of such expenses:

(a) The salvage value that remains of any property bought for temporary use during the "period of restoration," once "operations" are resumed; and

(b) Any extra expense that is paid for by other insurance, except for insurance that is written subject to the same plan, terms, conditions, and provisions as this insurance; and

(2) Necessary expenses that reduce the business income loss that otherwise would have been incurred.

Part b. is on form CP 00 30 only.

Resuming operations in whole or in part by using damaged or undamaged property at the described premises or elsewhere reduces the business income amount of loss determined in this section. Damaged or undamaged property includes stock and merchandise. For extra expense losses, the amount is reduced to the extent operations return to normal, thus discontinuing the need to incur extra expense. If operations are not resumed as quickly as possible, recovery will be based on the amount of time necessary to restore operations as quickly as possible.

Other Loss Conditions

Other loss conditions include resumption of operations and loss payment. The loss payment provision states that loss will be paid within thirty days after the insurer receives the sworn proof of loss, provided the insured has complied with all terms of the coverage and agreement has been reached on the amount of the loss or an appraisal award has been made.

The resumption of operations clause provides that the insurer will reduce the amount of business income loss, other than extra expense, to the extent the insured can resume operations in whole or part by using damaged or undamaged property including merchandise or stock at the insured premises or elsewhere, and extra expense loss to the extent the insured can return operations to normal and discontinue such extra expense. If the insured does not resume operations or does not resume operations as quickly as possible, CP 00 30 will pay based on the length of time it would have taken to resume operations as quickly as possible.

The resumption of operations clause on CP 00 32, Business Income Coverage form (Without Extra Expense), reads the same as that on CP 00 30, except that reference to extra expense is deleted.

Coinsurance

The coinsurance additional condition applies if a coinsurance percentage is inserted on the declarations page. The application of the coinsurance clause in forms CP 00 30 and CP 00 32 bases the coinsurance measurement on the twelve months following inception or last previous anniversary of the policy, whichever is later. This is advantageous to insureds as they are required to anticipate values only for the current policy year and insure accordingly.

Business growth during the policy year, not anticipated when the initial insurable values were estimated, can cause underinsurance if the amount of insurance is not increased appropriately after the accelerated growth has become apparent.

The coinsurance clause is based on the sum of net income (net profit or loss before income taxes) and all operating expenses, including payroll expenses, that would have been earned by the operations at the insured premises for the twelve months of the current policy term had no loss occurred.

The clause includes a list of expenses that are deducted from the total of all operating expenses, including prepaid freight; returns and allowances; discounts; bad debts; collection expenses; cost of raw stock and factory supplies consumed, including transportation charges; cost of merchandise sold, including transportation charges; cost of other supplies consumed, including transportation charges; cost of services purchased from outsiders, not employees, to resell that do not continue under contract; power, heat, and refrigeration expenses that do not continue under contract, all ordinary payroll expenses or the amount of payroll expenses excluded; and special deductions for mining properties.

Included in the coinsurance section are examples of how it operates, both when enough insurance is carried and when there is a deficiency (see the business income form included in the back of the book for these examples).

Optional Coverages

Forms CP 00 30 and CP 00 32 include four optional coverages activated by appropriate entries on the commercial property declarations page. Their use is an alternative to coinsurance.

The first three options, maximum period of indemnity, monthly limit of indemnity, and agreed value, are mutually exclusive—any one of them, but only one, may be applied to any one item of business income coverage. The fourth option, extended period of indemnity, may be used alone or with options two or three but not with option one.

Maximum Period of Indemnity

The first optional coverage is called maximum period of indemnity. This option is most advantageous to businesses that are not likely to suffer an interruption longer than four months. When this option is selected the coinsurance provision is deleted and a provision substituted stating that the most the insurer will pay for loss of business income is the smaller of the amount of loss sustained during the 120 days immediately following the direct physical loss or damage, or the limit of insurance shown in the declarations.

Monthly Limit of Indemnity

The second optional coverage is monthly limit of indemnity. This option deletes the coinsurance provision and substitutes a monthly limit of insurance, which can be either one-third, one-fourth, or one-sixth of the total limit of insurance shown in the declarations. To activate this option, the appropriate fraction is entered in the space provided on the declarations page.

Included in optional coverage two is an example on the form itself of how the fractional limit for each thirty days of loss applies to an actual situation. In the example, the limit of insurance is $120,000 and the monthly limit is one-fourth; the most the insurer will pay for loss in each period of thirty consecutive days is $30,000. If the actual loss for the first thirty days is $40,000, the second thirty days is $20,000, and the third thirty-day period is $30,000, then the insurer will pay $30,000 for the first period, $20,000 for the second period, and $30,000 for the last period.

Unlike the maximum period of indemnity option, which applies to the first 120 days immediately following the loss, coverage with the monthly limit of indemnity option applies for the entire period that it takes to resume operations (and, under the extended business income additional coverage of the basic form, thirty days beyond). The only limitations are the actual stated limit of insurance and that the coverage for loss of business income shall not exceed the indicated fraction of the total limit for each thirty consecutive days after the beginning date of the loss. So, with a one-fourth monthly limit, if the actual loss in any of the thirty-day periods is less than one-fourth of the limit of insurance, loss extending beyond the 120 days could be covered (again subject to the one-fourth monthly limit) until the limit of insurance is exhausted.

The example cited applies only to loss of business income and does not illustrate the way the insurance applies to extra expense, which is not subject to the fractional monthly limit. With a loss involving only extra expense, the entire coverage limit can be applied to extra expenses incurred to maintain or quickly restore production, regardless of when they are incurred.

This option is best suited for small businesses that can easily predict what net profits and continuing expenses will be. For instance, a seasonal business like a family-run miniature golf course may operate from April to September, with July being its best month. If net profits and continuing expenses for July are expected to be $10,000, then that amount is set as the monthly limit. The insured would estimate the duration of a shutdown and choose the one-third, one-fourth, or one-sixth monthly limit. If this business chose one-sixth, then the amount of insurance purchased would be $60,000, or six times the monthly limit of $10,000.

Agreed Value

The third optional coverage, agreed value, provides the means for suspending the coinsurance provision on a year-to-year basis. Businesses that are in a growth mode or anticipate growth or increased sales would benefit from this option.

This optional provision is activated by entering the amount of the agreed value in the appropriate space on the declarations page and by attaching a completed Business Income Report/Worksheet form, CP 15 15, showing actual business income values for a twelve-month period already completed and estimated values for the twelve months after inception of the agreed value provision. The agreed value must equal or be more than the appropriate coinsurance percentage times the coming year's estimated values. As long as at least this amount of insurance is carried, the application of the coinsurance provision is suspended for the twelve months covered by the report, unless the policy expires before the end of that time.

If less insurance is carried than the agreed value, the insured's recovery of loss is reduced in proportion to the deficiency, regardless of whether or not the amount of insurance carried is adequate to satisfy the coinsurance provision. Thus, in a time of declining business in which the initial current policy year estimate proves to be too high, the insured may wish to reduce the amount of insurance to reflect the reduced business. Under the agreed value option the insured must complete a new worksheet with the revised estimate and change the agreed value amount shown in the policy before reducing the amount of insurance. Otherwise, the reduced amount of insurance will be insufficient to provide for complete recovery of loss.

When the business income coverage is divided among two or more policies, the total amount of the agreed value is shown in the space for agreed value on the declarations, rather than each insurer's individual portion of the total. The sum of the limits of insurance for all of the individual policies of the insured (or business income coverage parts) sharing the coverage should equal the agreed value.

Form CP 15 15 carries a statement certifying that the report is a true and correct report of values as required under the policy for the periods indicated and that the agreed value for the period of coverage is the stated dollar amount based on the stated coinsurance percentage. The statement must be signed by a company official. The business income report/work sheet becomes a part of the policy provisions, so an understatement of values, when there is evidence of deliberate intent, could be viewed as material misrepresentation. The insurance would be entirely voided rather than the amount of recovery being reduced. In the absence of such evidence, though, there is no penalty for understating values.

The agreed value optional coverage is not to be used with policies having the following forms attached: Business Income from Dependent Properties—Broad Form, CP 15 08; Business Income from Dependent Properties—Limited Form, CP 15 09; and Business Income Premium Adjustment endorsement, CP 15 20.

Extended Period of Indemnity

The fourth optional coverage, extended period of indemnity, is used to extend the period of coverage under the extended business income additional coverage from the thirty days provided in the basic form to any of seven longer options up to 360 days. Businesses such as hotels or restaurants in competitive locations that require a longer period of time to recapture customers following a shutdown may choose to extend the period of indemnity using this option. Thirty-day increments are available up to 180 days, then ninety-day increments up to 360 days.

This extension option is activated by inserting the appropriate number of days in the space provided on the declarations page. A separate endorsement is not necessary.

Extra Expense Insurance

Contrasted with Business Income Coverage

What will be the insured's most pressing need if a fire or other disaster interrupts normal business operations? If normal relations with customers are interrupted for a time, what will be the effect on the insured's operations over the long term? Does the insured deal in services of a type that can be readily transferred to a new location so that the prospect of an interruption of significant duration need not even be contemplated? The answers to these issues provide the strongest guide in determining whether business income coverage or extra expense insurance is the primary need.

Most insureds that anticipate a temporary suspension of operations will also anticipate only a temporary suspension of the flow of customers. It is even possible that, in the case of retailers, the interest generated by fire sales and by a gala reopening of remodeled premises can have a beneficial effect on the business. Firms that are able to anticipate that the customer flow will resume in step with the resumption of operations are those that, in general, market their goods or services broadly to a wide and general market. Such firms are most in need of funds to replace the income that the business would have generated and that it will need to meet the unavoidable financial obligations that continue during a business shutdown. They need business income coverage.

Other firms, especially those dealing in services, may face a permanent loss of customers if the service is interrupted for any significant length of time. Banks and newspapers are frequently cited as examples of businesses that cannot tell their customers to go elsewhere for a month or two and expect them to return. Far more numerous are firms that expect brief interruptions because their operations are readily transportable to a temporary location. For example, firms that offer professional services and depend more on persons than on facilities can more easily operate from temporary locations. Firms in this category primarily need extra expense insurance. As long as they have a source of funds to support the extraordinary expenses of staying in business, they should not experience a drop in income from the business.

Insured May Need Both

Having determined that the primary need is for either business income coverage or extra expense insurance, the insured that chooses the latter should also give careful consideration to the extent of the business income exposure and perhaps arrange some coverage for that exposure also. The same process is not required of the insured that purchases business income coverage with extra expense because that form automatically provides extra expense insurance. Since the loss of income from interruption of operations is not covered by the extra expense insurance, the insured may want to purchase business income coverage to apply to those operations.

Because some business income forms have extra expense insurance built in, consideration might be given to using those forms in lieu of the extra expense form. In most cases, however, the insured who has a need only for extra expense insurance will find it both more economical and more convenient to choose the extra expense form. For example, an enterprise might have an exposure of $200,000 per month in terms of business income coverage, but $50,000 per month in terms of extra expense. If by an emergency expenditure of $50,000 the insured can avoid the $200,000 loss of business income, then the purchase of extra expense insurance (instead of business income coverage) is clearly the proper choice. Such a decision requires adoption of a recovery plan that provides a blueprint for an immediate resumption of operations.

Extra Expense Coverage Form, CP 00 50

The current edition of the extra expense coverage form is CP 00 50 06 07, corresponding to the other form editions in the ISO commercial property program. The coverage agreement of the extra expense form is to pay to the insured "the actual and necessary extra expense you sustain due to direct physical loss of or damage to property at premises described in the declarations." Described premises include the area within 100 feet of the site at which described premises are located. The loss or damage must be caused by or result from any covered cause of loss, which will depend upon the causes of loss form selected by the insured.

Extra expense is defined as "necessary expenses you incur during the period of restoration that you would not have incurred if there had been no direct physical loss or damage to property." This is a broad definition allowing the insured flexibility in getting the business back into operation, subject only to the requirement that the extra expense be necessary. Renting equivalent office space to restore operations would qualify; renting larger office space with plans to expand business would not.

The period of restoration begins with the date of covered direct physical loss or damage and ends when the property should be repaired if reasonable speed is applied to getting the property back to its preloss condition or when business is resumed at a new permanent location.

The term limit of the policy has no bearing on this period of time; that is, the expiration of the policy will not end the time for restoration of the property. On the other hand, the operation of any building or zoning law or ordinance that interferes with repairs or reconstruction will not extend the time when extra expense coverage is payable. Likewise, any environmental protection ordinance that regulates the prevention or cleanup of pollution damage does not increase the period of restoration. The period of restoration remains based on that period of time during which repairs should be accomplished.

Insureds who have a building ordinances exposure are able to obtain an increased period of restoration via endorsement CP 15 31. The endorsement allows for the operation of laws affecting construction, repairs, or demolition as legitimate factors in the computation of restoration time. This endorsement does not extend the period of restoration as regards the operation of environmental protection laws, though.

Interference by strikers or others at the site of repairs or reconstruction that causes a delay in the resumption of operations is excluded from consideration in the period of restoration as well. This is stipulated in the causes of loss forms and is one of several special exclusions that are applicable to extra expense insurance. See the causes of loss section later in this analysis.

The coverage agreement also applies to money spent to minimize the suspension if it cannot be avoided and to facilitate the repair or restoration of property to the extent that the latter reduces the amount that would otherwise have been necessary to spend. For example, the cost of air shipment of a vital part is covered as a legitimate extra expense if air shipment will reduce the period of restoration and save payment of other expenses that would otherwise be at least equal to the cost of air shipment.

However, restoring the damaged property is secondary to the central concern of the coverage. The major extra expenses that the policy insures are those having to do with keeping the insured enterprise in operation at the described premises or getting it moved and operating at a new location.

Causes of Loss

Whether property damage at the insured premises triggers extra expense coverage depends upon whether the triggering peril is covered. This is determined by the causes of loss form that is a necessary part of the policy.

In addition to setting up the perils and the applicable exclusions, the causes of loss forms all contain one set of exclusions that specifically apply to extra expense insurance. The exclusions are essentially the same as those for business income discussed earlier, with a few exceptions. For example, the exclusion for finished stock does not apply to extra expense coverage.

There is also no coverage for extra expense associated with the termination of any license, lease, or contract beyond the period of restoration. Just as there is no coverage for any other consequential loss with the business income coverage, the same is true for extra expense coverage. If, for example, an advertising agency insured is prevented from soliciting a new account because a fire destroys the layout on the day before a scheduled presentation, the consequential loss exclusion rules out coverage under the extra expense form.

Additional Limitation—
Interruption of Computer Operations

The extra expense coverage form contains an additional limitation for interruption of computer operations that is similar to that discussed in the business income section, without reference to limitation for business income coverage, of course.

Coverage Extension and Additions

If the insured acquires a new location during the term of the policy, the extra expense form automatically provides limited coverage at the new location. The added coverage is in addition to the coverage at the locations described in the declarations. This automatic insurance expires thirty days from the date of acquisition of the property or on the date the acquisition is reported to the insurance company, whichever occurs first. Expiration of the policy terminates the coverage as well.

The form addresses four other areas of exposure under the additional coverages section.

Alterations and new buildings. One of the additional coverages relates to alterations and new buildings on the described premises. Coverage for these eventualities might be inferred from the basic insuring agreement, which covers extra expense losses caused by physical damage to insured property at described locations (including personal property in the open or in vehicles within 100 feet of the described locations). Additions and new construction are distinguished in terms of additional coverage because the time frame for the extra expense loss is different. If an already existing structure is damaged, extra expense insurance runs from the date of damage through the time the damage should be repaired. If a new structure or an alteration is damaged, extra expense insurance begins to run on the date that the new property would have been operational if no loss had occurred.

Civil authority. Additional coverage also applies when damage by an insured peril occurs away from the insured's premises and civil authorities seal off the area or otherwise prohibit the insured's access to the described premises. Firefighters cordoning off a city block during and after a fire on neighboring property is an example of an interruption by civil authority during which extra expense insurance applies. There is coverage for up to three weeks of such blocked access.

This additional coverage responds only to blockades imposed by civil authority. Extra expense insurance does not provide for coverage if access to the insured's premises is reduced or cut off by some other means—as when weather conditions or heavy construction activity near the insured's premises discourages customers or clients. Likewise, blockage by civil authorities in the face of an uninsured cause of loss, such as flood, does not activate this additional coverage. The changes to this form track the civil authority clause of the business income form, discussed in this chapter.

While the form contains a limitation for the interruption of computer operations, it also includes an additional coverage for interruption of computer operations. Again, it is similar to the provision found on the business income forms, with variations depending on the causes of loss form chosen, as previously indicated. The coverage applies to the destruction or corruption of electronic data due to a covered cause of loss. For example, a customer may send an email with an attachment containing a virus. If the attachment is opened and infects essential operating files, which then causes a suspension of business activities, the extra expense incurred to clean up the network and return to normal operations will be covered. If, however, an employee or contractor working for the company hacks into the system and manipulates electronic data, no coverage for extra expense is available.

Limits

The system of recovery under extra expense insurance requires careful attention. There is a limit set out in the declarations that specifies the most that the insurance company will pay on an extra expense loss. However, the declarations also specify percentages of the policy limit that are recoverable in thirty day intervals. A 40-80-100 arrangement is the most common. With this, the insured may not recover more than 40 percent of the policy limit when the recovery period is thirty days or less; 80 percent when the recovery period is over thirty but less than sixty days; and 100 percent of the limit only when the recovery period exceeds sixty days.

As an example, the extra expense form itself contains a limit on loss payment provision that shows what happens when proven expenses do not line up favorably with the selected limits. The insured in the form's example recovers only $80,000 on a $90,000 loss even thought the policy limit is $100,000. The insured cannot recover $10,000 of proven expenses. The time for recovery—the period of restoration—is forty-five days, and the insured had a 40-80-100 arrangement. Thus, the most the insured could recover for a restoration period of sixty days or less was 80 percent of the $100,000 limit, even though extra expenses had amounted to $90,000.

The insured has the option—and the challenge—of selecting the number of thirty day intervals and the percentages of the overall limit that will become available at each limit. Endorsement CP 15 07 is used when four or more recovery intervals are contemplated. The 40-80-100 arrangement commonly shown on the declarations page can often be altered on the page itself.

The most foolproof arrangement is to have 100 percent of the coverage available during the first thirty days. The time of recovery could extend beyond thirty days, in which case the full amount of the policy is still available. Even a one-day period of restoration is sufficient to bring the total policy limit into play. However, this arrangement is also significantly more expensive. The cost of the coverage decreases as the limit is spread through longer intervals into the policy term. An insured who could realistically expect a very slow recovery and a gradual payout of extra expenses might choose a 300-day recovery with 10 percent of the policy limit becoming available every thirty days. The premium would be relatively inexpensive, but few insureds are in a position to take advantage of that extended arrangement. Only a careful examination of maximum expenses during the first thirty-day interval, maximum expenses during the second thirty-day interval, and maximum time of restoration can guide the insured in determining the firm's individual and special requirements.

Other Insurance

In the Commercial Property Conditions form, CP 00 90, extra expense insurance holds itself as excess to recovery of the same expenses that the insured receives from another source unless the other source "is written subject to the same plan, terms, conditions and provisions as this insurance." As mentioned earlier, many insureds may need both business income coverage and extra expense insurance although business income coverage has some extra expense insurance built in.

An examination of the business income forms reveals close parallels between the coverage of those forms and the plan, terms, conditions, and provisions of the extra expense form. The parallels are sufficient to call into question the interoperation of the two forms. In that context, it is important to know that the drafters of the extra expense insurance form express the opinion (according to ISO explanatory material) that the coverage of the extra expense form is excess to the extra expense recovery of the business income coverage form.

Other Exposures

Although the following exposures are not addressed in ISO's program, they may be contained in independently filed or manuscripted policies and should be considered when embarking on the management of business income and extra expense exposures.

Ingress and Egress

Ingress refers to access or entrance to one's premises. In turn, egress means the freedom to exit or leave those premises. Some situations may prevent businessowners, customers, or both from coming or going. A tornado, for instance, may make roads to a business impassable because of fallen trees, thus blocking access to the business. The case previously discussed where heavy snow blocked access to an auto dealership, and the court held there was no physical damage and thus no trigger for business income coverage, is a example of an ingress and egress exposure. Because no direct physical damage or loss to property occurs, ISO business income and extra expense coverages will not address these losses.

Manuscript and company-specific policies may add an ingress/egress clause to provide coverage. The court found coverage under such a provision in *Fountain Powerboat Industries v. Reliance Ins. Co.*, 119 F. Supp.2d 552 (E.D. N.C. 2000). Fountain Powerboat could not reach its manufacturing facility and headquarters because the sole road approaching them was inaccessible after Hurricane Floyd dumped heavy rainfall in the area. Reliance paid claims for physical damage to the premises but denied business income coverage, arguing that the physical losses to the insured property were not the cause of the business income losses. The court, though, stated that the clause clearly provided coverage even though no direct physical damage or loss had occurred.

Flood

Commercial property policies generally exclude the peril of flood. National Flood Insurance Plan (NFIP) forms do not include provisions for business income or extra expense, so a gap could exist even if direct flood damage to a property is covered by an NFIP-based policy. The greatest losses to businesses as a result of flood are not usually property damage but lost income because the premises is shut down for flood cleanup and extra expenses incurred from operating at a temporary site.

Absence of Profits

Calculating a business income loss for a company that is operating at a net loss is particularly important for certain types of companies. Start-up companies, which may not have established a predictable earnings flow, and high-tech companies, which may be relying on grant money and stockholders equity during their developmental stages, are two examples of companies that may be operating at planned net losses at the time of a covered loss.

Consider a high-tech company that raised operational money through a public offering. This company's business plan includes operating in the red for five years. It will take the company that much time to develop a product from research it has licensed, work out the bugs, take the product to market, and begin to earn income from it. During this time, the money raised through the public offering is funding operations. If business is suspended by a loss for six months in the middle of the five-year plan, it continues to draw on stockholders equity in order to stay alive. But it will not make any progress in its business plan during the interruption, causing it to fall short of plan and, possibly, fail.

In addition, a high-tech company may be especially exposed to a high level of continuing expenses because it needs to keep its technical employees on the payroll during the down time. The standard business income coverage form would not adequately cover these continuing expenses because the loss calculation combines the net profit or loss with the continuing expenses. If the net loss is $200,000 a month and continuing expenses are $250,000 a month, the insured would be able to collect only $50,000 a month, well short of the $250,000 necessary to cover continuing expenses. In severe cases, no business income recovery would be possible.

A method to handle this situation is with a valued business income coverage form.

This form is appropriate in the situation described because it pays a set amount for each period of business suspension as specified in the policy declarations. The time period could be twenty-four hours, one week, or one month.

Because the limit is established prior to the loss, there is no need to perform a lengthy calculation to establish the amount of loss after it occurs. This means that the issue of a net loss or net profit is addressed prior to the insurance being purchased. There also is no coinsurance clause.

Professionals are cautious of using the valued form of coverage for several reasons, including:

1. fear that the form promotes a moral hazard;

2. the possibility of miscalculating the limit and not purchasing sufficient coverage; and

3. possible settlement problems if only a partial interruption triggers the coverage.

Careful underwriting of a company's business plan is necessary to counter the possibility of promoting a moral hazard. The form should be used as a tool to craft coverage that is suited to companies in their developmental stages, and careful review of the company's business plan is necessary. It should not be used just because a company is operating at a net loss.

Insureds assume the burden of setting the limit of coverage. Even though this method does not rely on the insured's internal financial data when adjusting the loss, it does require careful preparation of a business income worksheet by the insured when the coverage is underwritten. Special attention must be given to the amount of anticipated continuing expenses, as well as any extra expense that might be incurred. The insured must realize that the limit established for each unit of recovery (day, week, or month) is the maximum amount recoverable during each recovery unit.

In addition to the per unit limit, the form also lists a maximum amount recoverable. As an example, a form may provide for a loss payment of up to $5,000 per day with a maximum payable of $900,000. This means that the insured could recover up to $5,000 per day for a total of 180 days. However, if less than $5,000 a day is paid during a partial suspension, the $900,000 cap still applies.

Companies with seasonal swings, or companies that are directly affected by outside economic factors, also need to take special care in developing the limit of insurance. Since there are maximum limits payable per unit and per loss, it is important that the limit accurately reflect seasonal and economic upswings.

In the event of a partial suspension of business, the form pays a percentage of the per unit limit. It is important for companies to understand that the amount paid each day will be decreased proportionately when a partial shutdown occurs. This percentage is equal to the value of lost production or income divided by its normal value prior to the loss. The formula for a partial suspension is as follows:

Lost Production x Working Day Limit = Partial Loss Payment

The partial loss formula would be triggered when only a portion of the business is suspended because of a loss. It also comes into play as a company begins to resume operations after a total suspension.

The premium charged for a valued form could be higher than for a standard business income form. However, in certain situations the benefit would greatly outweigh the possibly higher premium. It is a useful tool in designing coverage that is suited to a particular type of insured.

Chapter 8

Other Coverage Forms

In addition to the coverage forms already discussed, the commercial property program offers other coverage forms modified to meet the particular needs of the business type being covered: Leasehold Interest, CP 00 60; Mortgageholders E&O, CP 00 70; Tobacco in Sales Warehouses, CP 00 80; Condominium Associations, CP 00 17; Condominium Commercial Unit-Owners, CP 00 18; and Legal Liability, CP 00 40.

Leasehold Interest Coverage Form, CP 00 60

A building tenant may have a favorable lease; however if property at the location suffers damage, the tenant may lose the advantage of that favorable lease (the leasehold interest). This coverage form refers to *property* and not to *covered property*. Thus, the damage leading to insurance recovery may be to the building owned by someone else or to the insured's property located in the rented location. Leasehold interest insurance protects the tenant from this possibility. A building owner, on the other hand, would look to his business income coverage to pay his rental income in case of covered loss to the property.

The leasehold interest coverage form has not been revised as often as other forms in the ISO commercial property program. The current edition of the leasehold interest coverage form is CP 00 60 06 95. It also exists as the CP 00 60 07 88 and CP 00 60 10 91.

What Is Insured—Types of Leasehold Interest

The form defines four types of leasehold interest—tenants lease interest, bonus payments, improvements and betterments, and prepaid rent.

Tenants lease interest may take one of two forms:

1. The tenant occupies the premises under a favorable lease. This means that the insured holds a lease on premises that is under the market price of comparable premises. For example, the premises may be rent-controlled or, because of the terms of a long-term lease entered into years previously, comparable premises rent in the current market for substantially more. The leasehold interest is the difference between the actual rental value of the premises and the rent payable for the unexpired term of the lease. To illustrate, the insured has a lease with three years remaining at $250 per month. The current market price of comparable premises is $400 per month. A complete fire loss to the building causes the lease to be terminated. The insured would collect $5,400 ($400 actual rental value minus favorable lease amount, $250, equaling $150 x 36 months of the unexpired term of the lease).

2. The tenant has a valuable lease and sublets the premises at a higher rental. The leasehold interest is the profit the tenant-insured receives through subleasing for the unexpired term of the sublease.

Bonus payments. For the second type of leasehold interest, an insured may pay an upfront bonus to obtain a favorable lease. If the bonus is nonrefundable, the monthly leasehold interest on such cash bonus is the original cost of the bonus divided by the number of months remaining in the lease at the time the bonus was paid. For example, if the bonus paid at the inception of the lease is $5,000 and the lease is for three years, the monthly leasehold interest is $138.89 ($5,000 divided by 36). A bonus does not include rent, whether or not prepaid, or security.

Improvements and betterments. If a tenant makes improvements to the premises, the unamortized portion of payments for those improvements represents a leasehold interest. The monthly leasehold interest in the improvements and betterments is the original cost of the improvements and betterments divided by the number of months remaining in the lease at the time of installation. If the installation of the improvements and betterments increases the rental value of the premises, the monthly leasehold interest is the increase in rental value divided by the number of months remaining in the lease at the time of installation.

For example, an insured currently leases his retail outlet for $1,000 per month. In the third month of the lease, he adds improvements and betterments to the store that result in an increase in the rental value of $6,000 per year. This insured's increase in monthly leasehold interest would be calculated by dividing $6,000 by 9 months, or $666.

Prepaid rent. The fourth and final type of leasehold interest is prepaid rent. If the insured has prepaid rent and it is not refundable, the unamortized portion is insured. However, this does not include the customary rent due at any rental period (monthly or otherwise).

Causes of Loss, Exclusions, and Limitations

For these items, the leasehold interest form refers to the appropriate causes of loss form. In order for leasehold interest to be payable, property at the insured premises must suffer direct damage by a covered cause of loss.

Each of the basic, broad, and special causes of loss forms contains an identical special exclusions section regarding the leasehold interest coverage form with two provisions:

1. The building ordinance or law exclusion does not apply to claims for leasehold interest. Therefore, if zoning prohibits rebuilding, the leasehold interest loss is covered.

2. There is no coverage if the insured cancels the lease; if there is a suspension, lapse, or cancellation of any license that causes the cancellation of the lease (liquor sales licenses, for example); or from any other consequential loss.

Thus leasehold interest applies if a lease is canceled due to the operation of building laws, as long as a covered cause of loss causes the physical damage to the building. However, other consequential loss is not covered.

Leasehold Interest—Terms in a Lease

Terms in a lease can have an appreciable effect on insurance and warrant close attention when advising an insured on proper coverage. Any questions should be addressed with a leasing professional. For example, an insured with a lease that is totally silent on both continuing rents and cancellation of the lease may have a problem. If damage to property at the described premises from a covered cause of loss leads the insured to cancel his lease, there is no coverage. A special exclusion in the causes of loss form is used with the leasehold interest coverage form to prevent coverage where the insured cancels the lease ("we will not pay for any loss caused by: (a) your canceling the lease.").

Therefore, the insured cannot cancel the lease and turn to the policy for recovery. A lease that is silent on the matter of cancellation can prove troublesome to the tenant for many reasons, particularly where the tenant has a lease on untenable premises with no contractual provision to protect him. Again, the advice of a leasing professional should be sought.

In short, the leasehold interest coverage form will not respond where the insured cancels the lease. Where the lease is favorable, the insured will not want it canceled, and should be further protected with business income and expense coverages to maintain business income in the event the leased premises are unusable for some period.

Limits of Insurance

In two clauses, the policy describes separate limits of insurance for tenants lease interest and for bonus payments, improvements and betterments, and prepaid rent.

Tenants lease interest. The most the insurer will pay because of the cancellation of a lease is the net leasehold interest. The ISO rules state this amount as the present value of the gross leasehold interest (difference between monthly rental value and actual rent payable for the unexpired term of the lease of the insured's premises) as of the policy inception date. This amount decreases automatically each month. The amount of net leasehold interest at any time is the gross leasehold interest multiplied by the leasehold interest factor for the remaining months of the lease. For any period of less than a month a proportionate factor is used. The leasehold interest coverage policy always contains a table of leasehold interest factors.

Alternately, the net leasehold interest is the amount that placed elsewhere at the assumed rate of interest would be equivalent to the insured's receiving the gross leasehold interest for each month of the unexpired term of the lease.

Bonus payments, improvements and betterments, and prepaid rent. The most the insurer will pay because of the cancellation of a lease is the net leasehold interest. A proportionate share of the monthly leasehold interest applies to periods of less than a month. After cancellation, if the landlord allows the tenant to stay under a new lease or other arrangement, the insurance covers the difference in rent between the canceled lease and the rent under the new arrangement.

Loss Conditions

The loss conditions of the leasehold interest form are similar to those in the commercial property policy. However, because the leasehold interest form does not cover tangible property, the provisions are modified to eliminate property abandonment, the inventory requirement, recovered property, and valuation.

Loss payment. Covered loss is paid within thirty days after receipt of the sworn proof of loss if the insured has complied with the terms of the leasehold interest coverage part and an agreement has been reached on the amount of loss or an appraisal award made.

Vacancy. The first portion of the vacancy clause specifies that it applies only to the area actually leased to the insured. The insured's suite or unit is vacant "when it does not contain enough business personal property to conduct customary operations." A building under construction is not considered vacant. Vacancy and customary operations are discussed in Chapter 5.

If the insured subleases the premises to someone else, the vacancy clause applies somewhat differently. If the sublet building has been vacant for more than sixty consecutive days before the loss, there is no coverage for leasehold interest loss caused by vandalism, sprinkler leakage (by freeze rupture in spite of the insured having protected the system against freezing), building glass breakage, water damage, theft, or attempted theft. Any other covered loss is paid with a reduction of 15 percent. If there is no sublease agreement at the time of loss, the policy will not pay any leasehold interest loss.

Cancellation

The leasehold interest form contains an additional condition relating to cancellation. This cancellation provision supersedes the cancellation clause of the common policy conditions form.

The difference between the two cancellation provisions is in the method provided for computing return premium. Because the amount of leasehold interest decreases steadily from inception to expiration, the daily earned premium is greatest early in the policy term. Cancellation must be computed based on the higher average net leasehold interest between inception and the date of cancellation, rather than the lower average leasehold interest for the full original term of the policy, the basis of the original premium. Only the difference between original premium and the earned premium for this higher average amount of insurance is returnable. As in the common policy conditions, the refund may be more favorable if the insurer, rather than the insured, cancels.

The ISO Commercial Lines Manual sets out the steps for premium determination and computation of earned premium at cancellation.

Schedule Form CP 19 60

Along with leasehold interest form CP 00 60, a Leasehold Interest Schedule, CP 19 60, applies. This form shows the necessary information about the lease and the way the amount of leasehold interest insurance is developed. The schedule includes spaces to enter the inception and expiration dates of the lease, the number of months remaining at inception of the policy, and the percentage of interest that applies.

The schedule also shows the amount of gross leasehold interest, monthly leasehold interest, net leasehold interest at policy inception, and premium.

Leasehold Interest Factors

A table of leasehold interest factors used in determining the tenant's net leasehold interest is attached to each leasehold interest policy. Form CP 00 60 states that the tenant's net leasehold interest is the amount that, placed at the applicable interest rate, would provide the insured with the equivalent of the gross leasehold interest for each month of the unexpired lease term. ISO provides a series of endorsements (CP 60 05 through CP 60 15) for interest rates ranging from 5 to 15 percent.

The appropriate form, reflecting the current level of interest rates, is selected. The interest rate should be selected carefully in consultation between agent and insured. If interest rates change dramatically during the course of the policy, a rewrite should be considered. If for example, form CP 60 10, showing a 10 percent interest rate is selected, 10 percent is also entered in the interest space on form CP 19 60. The table shows interest factors for months numbered from 1 to 400. These factors are used to compute the amount of net leasehold interest coverage for tenant's lease interest at inception, throughout the policy term, for cancellation, or to determine the amount of loss payable under the policy if the lease is cancelled due to a covered cause of loss.

Mortgageholders Errors and Omissions Coverage Form, CP 00 70

Mortgageholders (banks, mortgage companies, credit unions, and other mortgage lenders) have insurance in place on property under mortgage to them in the event of loss or damage, generally in the event the borrower has not complied with mortgage terms to keep appropriate insurance coverage on the property.

Mortgageholders Errors and Omissions, CP 00 70, covers a lending institution or other mortgage servicing agency against losses arising out of the failure to have proper insurance in force to protect the mortgaged property as a result of error or accidental omission. Such a lack of insurance is usually the result of a mistake in the mortgagee's office procedure. A policy might be entered incorrectly into the mortgagee's data systems or misfiled, for example, and subsequently expire without being renewed. If a fire destroys the property and the mortgagor is unable to continue payments, the institution holding the mortgage would have nothing but ruins upon which to foreclose.

Mortgageholders errors and omissions insurance covers lenders against both direct damage and legal liability losses that may arise out of error or accidental omission in its customary mortgage-handling procedures. It offers four coverage agreements: A and B deal with property coverage, while C and D describe liability coverage. The form itself lists the applicable causes of loss under the provisions for each individual coverage so that no separate causes of loss form needs to be attached.

The CLM specifies that the Commercial Property Conditions form, CP 00 90, is not to be used with form CP 00 70. Instead, the form itself includes a modified version of those commercial property conditions that apply in addition to the common policy conditions of form IL 00 17. The rules specify that no causes of loss form is attached; rather, each coverage agreement is subject to a different set of perils.

The declarations page indicates the estimated number of mortgages that the insured will own or service during the policy period. The policy is to cover one named insured only and may not be endorsed to the names of servicing agents or other interests.

The Four Coverage Agreements

The four coverages in this form are as follows:

1. Coverage A—Mortgageholder's Interest

2. Coverage B—Property Owned or Held in Trust

3. Coverage C—Mortgageholder's Liability

4. Coverage D—Real Estate Tax Liability

Coverage A—Mortgageholder's Interest

Coverage A promises to pay for loss of the insured's mortgageholders interest. The form defines this interest as the insured's "interest, as mortgageholder, in real or personal property, including your interest in any legal fiduciary capacity." It protects the insured against loss arising from errors and accidental omissions by the insured or a representative in requiring, procuring, or maintaining valid insurance to protect its interest.

Covered property for coverage A may be real property (such as a building where business is conducted), or personal property secured in connection with that real property. Such personal property might include the contents of a business purchased as a going concern; for example, an existing dry cleaner with all the attendant machinery. Coverage A applies during and after the named insured's foreclosure. It also applies to property sold under an agreement whereby the named insured retains title (such as a conditional sales agreement).

Coverage A lists property not covered as accounts, bills, currency, deeds, evidences of debt, money, notes, or securities. The form specifies that food stamps are evidences of debt (and excluded) and that lottery tickets held for sale are not securities (and not excluded). The form also states that land (including the land where the property is located), water, growing crops, or lawns are not covered property.

Covered causes of loss under coverage A are those that the named insured customarily requires mortgagors to insure. This may range from named perils to unspecified risk of physical loss (special form or open perils). What is customarily required by the mortgageholder is the rule of thumb. In the event of a dispute over what the named insured customarily requires its customers to insure, the Common Policy Conditions, IL 00 17, contains the examination of your books and records provision. By allowing the insurer to examine the mortgageholder's records, what it customarily requires can be readily ascertained.

The form specifies that the causes of loss do not include losses insured under mortgage loan guarantee insurance—insurance that protects the mortgageholder in the event that the mortgagor defaults (often called private mortgage insurance or PMI)—or under title, life, health, or accident insurance policies.

Coverage A extends to losses arising from mortgages owned by others and serviced by the named insured, as if the named insured owned the mortgageholder's interest. This servicing by the named insured must be done through a written contract. Losses are payable jointly to the named insured and the mortgageholder.

Coverage B—Property Owned or Held in Trust

While coverage A protects the insured against loss to property on which it has loaned money, coverage B protects the insured against loss to property it actually owns or in which it has a fiduciary interest.

Coverage B pays for loss to covered property if the loss is not otherwise insured. The absence of insurance must be due to error or accidental omission in the named insured's customary procedure in procuring valid insurance payable to the named insured as owner or trustee. If an insured buys both coverage A and coverage B, recovery under both coverages may be possible. For example, coverage A includes real property "during and after your foreclosure." Since coverage B covers property owned by the insured, a property that has been foreclosed on would fall under both coverages, allowing the insured to collect any remaining balance under B if the limits under A prove inadequate. However, the limits of coverage A and B cannot be combined to collect an amount greater than the insured's loss.

The list of property not covered is identical to that under Coverage A.

While the covered causes of loss under Coverage A are quite broad (whatever the named insured normally requires its customers to purchase), the perils under Coverage B are limited to fire, lightning, explosion, windstorm or hail, smoke, aircraft or vehicles, riot or civil commotion, sinkhole collapse, and volcanic action. For a further discussion of these perils see Chapter 3.

Vandalism and sprinkler leakage are not covered under Coverage B, presumably because the insured lender actually owns often vacant property, and these perils become much more of a risk to the insurer.

The additional conditions in form CP 00 70 state that Coverage B protection ends on the earlier of (1) ninety days after the date that the insured acquires the property or the insured's fiduciary interest begins, or (2) the day that other insurance is obtained.

Coverage C—Mortgageholder's Liability

In some cases, a mortgageholder may decide to purchase insurance on a mortgaged property instead of having the customer purchase it. For those instances, the insured lending institution needs Coverage C.

Like the previous coverages, this protects the lender from damages due to errors or omissions in obtaining insurance. However, this time the insurance is purchased for the benefit of the mortgagor. Coverage C is similar to Coverage A in that the perils covered are those that the lender normally requires its customers to purchase. There are exclusions, including losses insured under mortgage guarantee insurance policies or programs or title, life, health or accident insurance policies. Collapse coverage is limited.

If the insured, in its capacity as a mortgageholder, mortgage fiduciary, or mortgage servicing agency, has agreed with the mortgagor to procure and maintain insurance against loss, thereby relieving the mortgagor of those responsibilities, and then fails to obtain such insurance, Coverage C will pay the legal obligations that subsequently may befall. The duty to defend is also included under Coverage C, although this duty ends when the Coverage C limit is used up in settlements or judgments.

In addition to the limits of liability shown, Coverage C provides supplemental payments for the following:

1. All expenses of the insurer.

2. Cost of bonds.

3. Expenses incurred by the insured at the request of the insurer, including loss of earnings of up to $100 per day.

4. Costs taxed against the insured in the suit.

5. Pre- and post-judgment interest.

Coverage C extends to additional insureds, such as the named insured's partners, executive officers, trustees, directors, managers, and stockholders. They are covered only in their capacity as such. Newly acquired organizations (other than partnerships, joint ventures, or limited liability companies) are automatically insured. Coverage for newly acquired organizations is limited to ninety days from the date of acquisition. The policy specifies that it does not apply to errors and omissions that occurred before the insured acquired the organization.

Coverage D—Real Estate Tax Liability

Some mortgages are set up so that the lending institution pays the real estate taxes on the property. This arrangement may be for the convenience of the borrower, who then makes monthly payments toward the tax, rather than two large payments per year. Or, it may be that the lender has some concerns about payment of the taxes and it may take the responsibility itself. With the proliferation of home mortgages now available with little money as a down payment, lenders routinely require that they collect and pay the real estate taxes via an escrow account until the owner's equity in the home reaches 20 percent.

Problems can arise in such an arrangement if the lender does not pay the taxes. In such a case, the property owner may suffer damages. These damages are insured by Coverage D. The policy limits the amount payable to not more than 15 percent of the limit of insurance for damages in connection with any single mortgage. Explanatory information from ISO states that this limit is expressed as a percentage rather than a dollar amount in order to reflect that property values, upon which real estate taxes are based, usually affect the amount of insurance selected by the mortgagee and thus the revised computation will be more accurately tied to the mortgagee's insurance needs. The 15 percent limit also corresponds to the requirements for real estate tax errors and omissions liability coverage of the Federal National Mortgage Association (Fannie Mae).

Exclusions

The following exclusions apply to all coverages under form CP 00 70: ordinance or law; earth movement; governmental action; nuclear hazard; utility services; war; water damage; fungus, wet or dry rot, and bacteria.

These exclusions apply "regardless of any other cause or event that contributes concurrently or in any sequence to the loss" (the concurrent causation wording).

The policy excludes damage from the "discharge, dispersal, seepage, migration, release or escape of 'pollutants,'" without the concurrent causation wording. However, if the lender customarily requires its customers to insure the property under the Special Causes of Loss form, CP 10 30, pollution losses caused by one of the specified causes of loss defined in the policy are covered. Following the language that has been added to other forms in the commercial property program, *pollutants* are defined as "any solid, liquid, gaseous or thermal irritant or contaminant, including smoke, vapor, soot, fumes, acids, alkalis, chemicals and waste." Waste includes materials to be recycled, reconditioned, or reclaimed.

Losses caused by artificially generated electrical, magnetic, or electromagnetic energy are excluded but resulting fire loss is covered. Also excluded is any event that occurs thirty or more days after a lender knows that an error or omission may have occurred.

The policy excludes loss or damage caused by or resulting from the insured's failure to obtain, maintain, or process title insurance, mortgage guarantee, life, or health or accident insurance.

The neglect exclusion removes coverage if the insured does not use reasonable means to protect property from further loss.

A set of exclusions that was introduced to avoid coverage under the concurrent causation doctrine corresponds to exclusions already found in the CP 10 30. Excluded as part of this group are loss or damage caused by or resulting from collapse (except as modified by the additional coverage for collapse); weather conditions; acts or decisions (and the failure to act or decide) of individuals or groups; and faulty, inadequate, or defective (1) planning, zoning, development, surveying, siting; (2) design, specifications, workmanship, repair, construction, renovation, remodeling, grading, compaction; (3) materials used in repair, construction, renovation, or remodeling; or (4) maintenance—in regard to any property, whether on or off the described premises. However, if loss or damage by a covered cause of loss results from one these excluded events, coverage applies to the resulting loss or damage. This same exclusion is treated in more detail in Chapter 4.

The 06 07 edition introduced a production errors exclusion. Some examples of errors in production are introduction of foreign matter, addition of a wrong ingredient or element, and wrong measure of a particular element. An error in the production process is a business risk; it is not a peril intended to be insured under fire/allied lines property insurance. In certain circumstances, some claims may involve errors in production and allege that the need to destroy a now-useless product constitutes physical loss or damage to that product, thereby asserting a broad and nontraditional interpretation of the concept of physical damage under an insurance contract.

ISO added the following provision to address errors in production, shown in the context of CP 10 30, the Causes of Loss - Special Form:

B. Exclusions

    5.   Additional Exclusion

The following provisions apply only to the specified property.

    Loss Or Damage To Products

      We will not pay for loss or damage to any merchandise, goods or other product caused by or resulting from error or omission by any person or entity (including those having possession under an arrangement where work or a portion of the work is outsourced) in any stage of the development, production or use of the product, including planning, testing, processing, packaging, installation, maintenance or repair. This exclusion applies to any effect that compromises the form, substance or quality of the product. But if such error or omission results in a Covered Cause of Loss, we will pay for the loss or damage caused by that Covered Cause of Loss.

The impact is that coverage intent is reinforced, with an explicit provision, in light of sporadic claims being asserted in contradiction of intent. With respect to individual insurers, impact may vary based on past claims and loss settlement history.

Limits of Insurance

In the event of a covered loss, the most the insurer will pay is the amount shown on the policy declarations, subject to certain limitations.

Under Coverage A—Mortgageholder's Interest, or Coverage B—Property Owned or Held in Trust, limit of insurance is the least of the following:

1. The amount that would have been payable by the borrower's property insurance if no error or accidental omission in its procurement or maintenance by the lender had occurred. The mortgageholders E&O policy reduces this payment by the amount of any other insurance payable to the lender.

2. The amount that would have been payable under policies that the lender should have obtained but failed to do so.

3. The amount of the lender's mortgageholder's interest.

For Coverage C—Mortgageholder's Liability, the insurer's limit of liability is shown on the declarations page. For Coverage D (Real Estate Tax Liability), the insurer's limit of liability is 15 percent of the amount of insurance as shown on the declarations page. This limit applies on a per mortgage basis.

Additional Coverage—Collapse

Collapse coverage applies under CP 00 70 for covered property. The coverage is for an *abrupt* collapse, which the form describes as "an abrupt falling down or caving in of a building or any part of a building with the result that the building or part of the building cannot be occupied for its intended purpose."

Collapse is covered if due to hidden decay; hidden insect or vermin damage; use of defective materials or methods in construction, remodeling, or renovation if the collapse occurs during construction, remodeling, or renovation; use of defective materials or methods in construction, remodeling, or renovation if the collapse occurs after the construction, remodeling, or renovation, but only if caused by hidden decay or hidden insect or vermin damage, a specified cause of loss, breakage of building glass, weight of people or personal property, or weight of rain that collects on a roof.

As in the building and personal property coverage form, the 2000 edition added a caveat to the hidden decay and insect damage causes. Such decay or damage is not a covered cause of collapse if the existence of the decay or damage is known to an insured prior to a collapse. Under previous wording, an insured may have known about the damage, but if it was hidden the commercial property policy would cover resulting collapse.

The coverage does not apply to buildings or parts of buildings that are in danger of falling down; a part of a building that is standing; or a building that is standing or any part of a building that is standing even if it shows evidence of sagging, bending, cracking, bulging, leaning, expansion, shrinkage, or settling.

As with other causes of loss forms, personal property must be located inside a building to be covered for collapse. The collapse must be due to one of the covered causes of collapse.

Additional Coverage—Limited Coverage for Fungus, Wet Rot, Dry Rot, and Bacteria

This additional coverage was introduced in the CP 00 70 04 02, at the same time mold and fungus treatment was revised in other parts of the commercial property program.

This coverage applies when fungus (a defined term) or rot or bacteria is the result of a specified cause of loss other than fire or lightning or is caused by flood, provided the flood coverage endorsement applies.

The coverage applies to the following:

- Direct physical loss or damage caused by fungus, wet or dry rot, or bacteria, including the cost of removal;

- The cost to tear out and replace any part of the building or other property as needed to gain access to the damaged area;

- The cost of testing performed after removal, repair, replacement, or restoration, provided there is a reason to believe that fungus, wet or dry rot, or bacteria is present.

This coverage is limited to $15,000 in an annual period for all loss or occurrences. With respect to particular occurrences that result in fungus, wet or dry rot, or bacteria, the insurer will not pay more than $15,000 even if the fungus continues to be present or recurs in a later policy period.

Another clause makes clear that this is an additional coverage but does not increase the overall limit of insurance. For example, if fungus and other covered damage exceed the limit, no more than the limits will be paid (not the limit plus $15,000).

Additional Conditions

Form CP 00 70 contains one additional condition that applies only to coverage A, four additional conditions that apply to coverage B, and two additional conditions that apply to coverages C and D.

The insurer may, in concert with other insurers on the risk, pay the lender the full outstanding amount of any mortgage, even if that amount is greater than the amount of the loss. Then, the insured lender must assign the mortgage and all other securities pertaining to it to the insurance company.

In the event of loss or damage under coverage B, the insurer reserves the choice of four options:

1. Pay the value of lost or damaged property;

2. Pay the cost of repairing or replacing the lost or damaged property;

3. Take all or any part of the property at an agreed or appraised value; or

4. Repair, rebuild, or replace the property with other property of like kind and quality.

In any case, the policy restricts the insured's recovery to its financial interest in the covered property. Furthermore, the value of lost or damaged property is determined at actual cash value as of the time of loss or damage.

If either the insured or insurer recovers lost property, it must notify the other party. The option of whether the insured takes back the property remains with the insured. If the insured chooses to take the property back, the amount of the claim must be repaid to the insurer. The insurer, on the other hand, agrees to pay recovery expenses and to pay for repairs to the property (up to the limit of liability).

As mentioned under the discussion of coverage B, the protection ends on the earlier of (1) ninety days after the date the insured acquires the property or the insured's fiduciary interest begins, or (2) the day that other insurance is obtained.

Coverages C and D (mortgage holders liability and real estate tax liability) contain two additional conditions: bankruptcy and separation of insureds. Even if the insured declares bankruptcy, the insurer is still obligated under Coverages C and D. The separation condition clarifies that the policy applies separately to each insured except for the limits of liability.

Conditions Applicable to All Coverages

The following conditions apply to the entire policy, though some apply differently to different portions:

1. **Abandonment**. As with other property policies, no property may be abandoned to the insurer.

2. **Appraisal (Coverages A and B Only).** As with other property policies, the mortgageholders E&O form sets up a procedure for settling differences regarding the value of a loss. If the parties cannot agree, each hires its own appraiser and the two appraisers then hire an umpire. After reviewing the facts, the decision of any two of the three is binding on all parties.

3. **Duties in the Event of Loss**. Because this form covers both property and liability, different conditions exist for the different coverages. In the event of a loss under the property coverages (A and B), the insured must do the following:

   a.   Notify the police in the event of a crime;

   b.   Give prompt notice to the insurer;

   c.   Protect the property from further damage and keep a record of expenses in connection with this activity (Although anything spent by the insured in this regard does not increase the limit of liability, the insurer will not pay for subsequent losses from perils not covered. The insured must also separate the damaged and undamaged property for inspection by the insurer.);

   d.   Provide the insurer with inventories of both the damaged and undamaged property;

e.   Allow the insurer to examine his/her books and records; and permit the insurer to take samples of damaged and undamaged property for testing and analysis;

f.   Submit a signed, sworn proof of loss within sixty days of request by the insurer ;

g.   Cooperate with the insurer.

The policy gives the insurer the right to examine any insured under oath about the claim "while not in the presence of any other insured." Courts have held that the term *examine* encompasses both oral and written questioning, and the right to isolate the insured from others was made explicit after a Missouri court ruled that the insurer had no such right without an explicit provision.

In the event of a claim under coverages C or D, the insured must do the following:

a.   Give the insurer prompt notice of the claim or suit;

b.   Send the insurer copies of all correspondence and other papers in connection with the claim;

c.   Authorize the insurer to obtain any necessary information;

d.   Cooperate with the insurer;

e.   Assist the insurer in enforcing its right of subrogation; and

f.   Give a signed statement of facts regarding the claim.

The insured may not make any payment or assume any obligation without the consent of the insurer.

4.   **Insurance under Two or More Coverages.** It is possible that more than one of the form's coverages may apply. In this case, the insurer still pays no more than the actual amount of the loss.

5.   **Legal Action against Us.** Under coverages A and B, no one may bring a suit against the insurer unless all terms of the policy have

been met. No suit may be brought later than two years after the insured discovers the error or omission.

As with Coverages A and B, under Coverages C and D no one may bring a suit against the insurer unless all terms of the policy have been met. Also, the policy prohibits anyone from joining the insurer in a suit against the insured.

After an agreed settlement or actual trial resulting in a judgment against the insured, suit may be brought to recover the amount due. The form defines an *agreed settlement* as a settlement and release of liability signed by all parties.

6. **Liberalization.** If within the forty-five days prior to the policy's inception the insurer adopts a policy provision that broadens coverage without an additional premium that provision automatically applies.

7. **Loss Payment.** Once the insured submits a proof of loss and the parties reach an agreement or an award is made in arbitration as to the amount of the loss, the insurer will pay the loss within thirty days.

8. **Other Insurance.** The policy shares pro rata with other insurance containing the same plan, terms, conditions and provisions. However, it is excess over any other type of insurance—*whether or not* the insured can collect on the other policy.

9. **Policy Period, Coverage Territory.** Coverage under the mortgageholders coverage form is occurrence-based. Coverage applies to loss or damage, claims or suits (including arbitration proceedings) arising from an event that "occurs during the policy period shown in the Declarations." Therefore, even if an error or accidental omission happens outside the policy period, this coverage applies as long as the loss or damage occurs within the policy period.

    This form specifies the territory by limiting the location of the mortgaged property to the United States, its territories and possessions, and Puerto Rico.

10. **Transfer of Rights of Recovery against Others to Us.** The insured transfers any rights to recover from another under all

coverages to the insurer, to the extent of the insurer's payment. In addition, the insured must do nothing to impair the insurer's rights.

Under coverages A and B, the insured may—prior to any loss— waive his rights against another party if the waiver is in writing. The insured may make a post-loss waiver against any of the following:

a.   Someone else covered by the policy;

b.   A firm that owns or controls the insured;

c.   A firm that the insured owns or controls;

d.   The insured's tenant.

11. **Vacancy.** The insurance does not cover damage to buildings that have been vacant for more than sixty days prior to the loss. It also does not cover suits arising out of such buildings. Under the policy, a vacant building as one where at least 31 percent of its square footage is not rented and used by the tenant to conduct normal operations or where at least 31 percent of the square footage is not used by the building owner.

12. **Your Duties.** In addition to the specific duties after a loss, the insured has other, ongoing duties. This condition requires the insured to make every reasonable effort to procure and maintain valid insurance (either a valid policy or other evidence of insurance) on the mortgaged property. In the case of Coverage D, the insured must make prompt payment of real estate taxes on behalf of the mortgagor.

Definitions

The policy concludes with the definitions of six terms. *Fungus, pollutants, specified causes of loss,* and *suit* are defined the same as in the commercial property policy.

Mortgageholder's interest is what the policy protects—the lienholder's (named insured) interest in mortgaged property. *Valid insurance* refers to what must be missing in order for the mortgageholders E&O policy to be activated.

Tobacco Sales Warehouses Coverage Form, CP 00 80

The Tobacco Sales Warehouses Coverage form, CP 00 80, is an annual reporting form that covers direct physical loss of or damage to tobacco in sales warehouses. The tobacco warehouse and any other business personal property must still be covered on the commercial property policy CP 00 10. The form is revised occasionally as are other forms in the commercial property program. The edition history includes the following:

- CP 00 80 07 88

- CP 00 80 10 90

- CP 00 80 10 91

- CP 00 80 06 95

- CP 00 80 02 00

- CP 00 80 10 00

- CP 00 80 06 07

Because tobacco is stored in a warehouse only long enough to be sold at auction and shipped, the policy term is different from other property policies. The coverage applies only at the described premises and begins at 12:01 A.M. of the fifteenth day before the opening of the regular auction season. It ends at 12:01 A.M. of the fifteenth day following the official closing date of the regular auction season. The length of the auction season varies according to local custom.

The tobacco sales warehouses form requires the insured to report tobacco sales at each location and to pay premium on the amount of sales reported. These reports must be filed within thirty days of the close of the auction season. Reports may be in any format provided they are in writing.

Covered Property

Tobacco in the described warehouse is the only type of property covered by this form. The tobacco may be "leaf, loose, scrap and stem." It may either be the tobacco of others of which the insured has care, custody, or control (a bailment situation) or it may be tobacco that the insured has purchased and is holding for resale. The tobacco is covered for whatever causes of loss the insured chooses (basic, broad, or special).

The form specifies the following types of property as not covered:

a. Growing crops or water.

b. Tobacco insured elsewhere that is more specifically described.

c. Tobacco outside buildings or structures.

d. Tobacco while waterborne.

e. Contraband or property in the course of illegal transportation or trade.

Additional Coverages

The tobacco in sales warehouses form provides additional coverages for debris removal, preservation of property, fire department service charge, and pollutant clean up and removal. These are the same as the additional coverages in the commercial property policy.

A rare conflict could theoretically arise under the additional coverage of preservation of property. For example, a fire occurs at a tobacco warehouse located next to a river. The insured must move the undamaged tobacco away in order to protect it. If the insured moves the tobacco onto a boat and it becomes damaged while on the boat, a possible conflict exists because the definition of covered property excludes tobacco that is waterborne. The additional coverage of preservation of property provides thirty-day coverage for any direct physical loss or damage to the tobacco while it is being moved or stored at another location. Whether this would include the tobacco being temporarily stored on the boat might give rise to a coverage dispute.

A more plausible scenario might be that the no-coverage status for tobacco outside of buildings and structures might give rise to a conflict with the preservation of property additional coverage. Say, for example, the insured removes tobacco from a burning warehouse and temporarily stores it under tarps. Rain subsequently damages the tobacco before it can be moved inside. Close cooperation with the insurer's loss teams in such a case would be desirable.

Coverage Extension

As in the commercial property policy, the tobacco in sales warehouses form provides $10,000 coverage for property off premises.

Exclusions and Limitations

These are described on the appropriate causes of loss form.

Additional Conditions

Although this section is near the end of the form, some of the previous provisions make reference to its terms, hence its discussion here.

Reports of Value: The tobacco in sales warehouses form is a reporting form. The policy requires a report within thirty days of the close of the auction season that contains the total weight in pounds of the tobacco that the insured sold or resold during the season and the total price per pound.

Premium Adjustment: The insurer then bases the final premium for the policy on the information contained in these reports and charges additional premium or makes a refund.

Need for Full Reports: While not labeled a coinsurance penalty, the policy operates to penalize the insured in the event the report does not equal 100 percent of the values at risk. In this case, the reported value is divided by the actual value at risk. That figure is then multiplied by the amount of the loss to arrive at a final payment.

For newly acquired locations (those acquired after the last report of values), the values at all locations are divided by the values at risk at all locations (including the new locations) and then multiplied by the amount of the loss to arrive at a final payment.

Deductible

The deductible condition is the same as that in the commercial property policy with one exception. The policy applies the deductible after any deduction calculated under the "need for full reports."

Loss Conditions

The loss conditions of form CP 00 80 are the same as in the commercial property policy, except for the valuation clause. Damaged tobacco is valued at the average price for similar grades and types. The average is based on the sale price on the day of the loss, two days prior to the loss, and two days following the loss.

The prices are those at the warehouse nearest to where the loss occurs. Total sales are divided by total number of pounds sold to arrive at an average price. The final price is determined by subtracting any unearned warehouse charges, unearned auction fees, and unpaid government taxes from the coverage price.

Definitions

The only word defined is *pollutants*. It is the same definition as in the commercial property coverage form: "any solid, liquid, gaseous or thermal irritant or contaminant, including smoke, vapor, soot, fumes, acids, alkalis, chemicals and waste. Waste includes materials to be recycled, reconditioned or reclaimed."

Condominium Associations Coverage Form, CP 00 17

Even though condominiums are typically occupied by their owners as a residence, the building (being owned in common by all unit-owners) must be insured on a master policy. For property owned by condominium associations (such as buildings, clubhouses, and pools), ISO has form CP 00 17. The condominium associations policy editions history is as follows:

- CP 00 17 07 88

- CP 00 17 10 90

- CP 00 17 10 91

- CP 00 17 06 95

- CP 00 17 02 00

- CP 00 17 10 00

- CP 00 17 04 02

- CP 00 17 06 07

Form CP 00 17 is similar to CP 00 10 in most respects. It has been modified to better fit the needs of the condominium association. This discussion centers on those differences.

Covered Property

Like the commercial property policy, the condominium association form covers items such as the building, completed additions, and permanently installed equipment. The commercial property policy covers appliances used for refrigerating, ventilating, cooking, dishwashing, or laundering. The condominium association form limits coverage to those items not contained within individual units. This places the responsibility for insuring such items on the unit-owner—the person who actually owns the equipment but would provide coverage for association-provided facilities.

Form CP 00 17 adds a sixth class of covered property, consisting of certain items within individual units if the condominium association agreement or bylaws requires the association to insure such property. This property consists of the following:

1. Fixtures, improvements and alterations that are a part of the building or structure; and

2. Appliances, such as those used for refrigerating, ventilating, cooking, dishwashing, laundering, security, or housekeeping.

The important wording here is "if the condominium association agreement or bylaws requires." When writing coverage for a condominium association, it is always important to review the association agreement and the bylaws to be certain about whose responsibility it is to insure various items.

Carpeting in Condominiums

Inexperienced adjusters may have problems adjusting losses to carpeting, wallpaper, and paint inside a condominium unit under form CP 00 17. Conventional wisdom is that if the condo master deed and bylaws require the association to insure, for example, all units, common elements, and limited common elements, the CP 00 17 would pick up coverage for carpet, wallpaper, and paint. Although association agreements vary, typically limited common elements are outside of the building but serve only one unit. These include porches, sidewalks leading to the door, and areas between privacy fences.

In many losses, the damage is confined to a single unit and it is necessary to replace vinyl or carpet and padding because of the buckling of the sub flooring. Confusion occurs in trying to determine which policy covers the damage.

The HO-6 (condominium unit-owners) policy contains a statement making it excess over any recoverable insurance held by the association. The CP 00 17 is specific that it is primary and not contributing. There is some question regarding the interaction with the HO-6 in the case of a large deductible on the CP 00 17. Specifically, if the damage is under the amount of the deductible on the CP 00 17, would the HO-6 become primary?

At one time condo unit-owners were considered to have purchased air space and everything from bare walls out was considered the owner's responsibility to insure. Now the condo association master policy may cover individual unit owners' fixtures, improvements, and alterations that are part of the building structure as long as the association agreement requires it. Improvements and alterations that are part of the building include, but are not limited to, paint, wallpaper, lighting fixtures, and counters. Appliances, such as dishwashers, are also covered.

Coverage for carpeting follows the same logic. If wall-to-wall carpeting is included in the mortgage, it is part of the realty and thus falls under the improvements and alterations that are part of the building structure. If not so designated, then generally where carpet is laid over an unfinished floor it is considered part of the building and would be covered as such. If the carpet is laid over a finished floor, and its removal would not materially damage the floor, courts have generally considered it contents. Coverage would therefore be found under the HO-6.

If the unit-owner receives no payment from the association policy because the loss is under the deductible, then the unit owner's coverage becomes primary. The purpose is to prevent double payment for a loss, not to prevent payment for a claim.

The coverage for business personal property is more limited on the condo association form than on the commercial property policy. Like the CP 00 10, the CP 00 17 covers the following:

1. The insured's interest in the labor, materials, or services that the condo association furnishes or arranges on personal property of others.

2.   Leased personal property that, via contract, is the insured association's responsibility to insure.

3.   Personal property of others in the condo association's care, custody, or control. Such property must be located in or on the building described in the declarations or in the open (or in a vehicle) within 100 feet of the described premises.

The unique provision of the CP 00 17 is that, in addition to covering the personal property owned by the association, it also covers personal property owned indivisibly by all unit-owners (such as pool furniture). The form specifies that property belonging to a unit-owner is not covered.

The property not covered section is the same as in form CP 00 10.

Other Provisions

As with the CP 00 10, the CP 00 17 covers the property for whatever causes of loss form is attached. The condominium association form provides the same additional coverages: debris removal, preservation of property, fire department service charge, pollutant cleanup and removal, increased cost of construction, and electronic data (see Chapter 2). CP 00 17 also provides the same extensions of coverage as the CP 00 10: newly acquired or constructed property, personal effects and property of others, valuable papers and records (other than electronic data), property off-premises, outdoor property, and nonowned detached trailers (see Chapter 2). The limits of insurance provision also reads the same in both forms (see Chapter 6).

The loss conditions are the same in both forms with three exceptions. Often, a condominium association appoints an insurance trustee to handle claims with its insurer. If that is the case, then the insurer agrees to pay the trustee.

The second difference addresses the issue of a unit-owner's insurance. If a unit-owner has insurance on property that is also covered by the association policy, the association policy is primary and does not contribute with the unit-owner's policy. The unit-owner's policy then becomes excess coverage.

The final difference is that the insurer agrees up-front to waive any subrogation rights against any unit-owner. In other commercial property forms, it is a simple matter for a building owner to waive subrogation rights against a tenant after a loss. The condo association form requires such a waiver.

The condominium association form has the same two additional conditions as does the commercial property policy: coinsurance and mortgage-holders.

The final two sections contain identical optional coverages: agreed value, inflation guard, replacement cost, and replacement cost for personal property of others (see Chapter 2.); and a definition of *pollutants*: "any solid, liquid, gaseous or thermal irritant or contaminant, including smoke, vapor, soot, fumes, acids, alkalis, chemicals and waste. Waste includes materials to be recycled, reconditioned or reclaimed."

Commercial Condominium Unit-Owners Coverage Form, CP 00 18

ISO provides for the needs of the commercial condominium unit-owner under a separate coverage form, CP 00 18. The current edition is CP 00 18 06 07, and the edition history is the same as the condominium association form outlined in the previous section. The form is available for business or professional firms that own commercial condominium units. The form closely follows building and personal property coverage form CP 00 10 but is modified to fit the needs of commercial condominium unit owners. In addition, ISO has provided an optional endorsement, form CP 04 18, offering loss assessment coverage and miscellaneous real property coverage.

The following is a discussion of the current form, with differences from the previous form and the CP 00 10 noted.

Property

The first difference between the CP 00 10 and the CP 00 18 is that the condominium unit-owners form has no provision to cover any building property other than coverage on building fixtures, improvements, and alterations owned by the unit owner. It begins with "your business personal property."

Property not covered includes fixtures, improvements, and alterations that are a part of the building, and appliances "such as those used for refrigerating, ventilating, cooking, dishwashing, laundering, security, or housekeeping," when the condominium association agreement requires that such property be insured by the association. Note that this provision is an absolute exclusion—unlike the provision of form HO 00 06 (covering owner occupied condos used as a residence) where the unit-owners coverage is excess over the association coverage in the same situation—and it applies even when the association insurance is not properly written and does not, in fact, provide the coverage required by the agreement.

Additional Coverages and Coverage Extensions

The unit-owners form offers these additional coverages, just as does the commercial property policy: debris removal, preservation of property, fire department service charge, pollutant cleanup and removal and electronic data. The similar coverage extensions are newly acquired property, personal effects and property of others, valuable papers and records (other than electronic data), property off-premises, outdoor property, and non-owned detached trailers.

Limits and Deductible

The limits of insurance and deductible provisions of the CP 00 18 are the same as in the building and personal property policy.

Loss Conditions

The loss conditions of form CP 00 18 duplicate those in the building and personal property policy with one addition, condominium association insurance. The unit-owner's policy is excess of such other insurance. It is not intended to contribute with the other policy.

Other Provisions

Finally, these provisions of the CP 00 18 are identical to those in the building and personal property policy: additional condition - coinsurance, and the optional coverages of agreed value, inflation guard, replacement cost, and replacement cost for the property of others.

The terms *pollutants* and *stock* are defined terms in the unit-owners policy as they are in the building and personal property policy.

Legal Liability Coverage Form, CP 00 40

There are situations where something different than direct property damage coverage is called for. Businesses may have leased machinery and equipment that the lease calls on the business to insure or perhaps leases real property for all or part of its operations. Although the legal liability coverage form CP 00 40 is part of the ISO commercial property program, it is actually a liability coverage and closer in format to the commercial general liability policy.

The legal liability coverage form edition history includes the following:

- CP 00 40 07 88

- CP 00 40 10 90

- CP 00 40 06 95

- CP 00 40 10 00

- CP 00 40 04 02

- CP 00 40 06 07

The legal liability coverage form covers the insured's legal liability for loss or damage to real and personal property of others. The property must be in the insured's care, custody, or control, and the damage must be caused by an insured peril. It also covers loss of use of the property and provides defense coverage. The loss to covered property must be caused by accident, thus eliminating coverage for intentional damage brought about by the insured. The loss must be caused by an insured peril, as indicated on the appropriate causes of loss form.

Coverage can be applied to commercial property—mercantile or manufacturing, building or contents—in the care, custody, or control of the insured. However, ISO rules say that form CP 00 40 cannot be used for a contractor while working on a building. A contractor needs a commercial general liability (CGL) policy. However, such a policy still excludes damage to work performed. The CGL covers the contractor for damage done to a part of the building not directly being worked on.

Manual rules state that the policy declarations (which is designated Legal Liability Coverage Schedule form, CP DS 05) must include a precise description of the insured's business operations, location, and the property of others for which the insured may be legally liable. In actual practice, it is most often written for the tenant of a commercial building, where the tenant is—by lease terms—responsible for damage to the building.

Legal liability coverage may be written under a separate policy or included as a separate item in the same policy with property coverages.

The declarations page must indicate a definite description of the insured's business operation and location, a description of the property of others for which the insured may be legally liable, and separate limits of liability that apply for this coverage on or in each building.

The amount of insurance is usually based on replacement cost of the property, though consideration should also be given to the fact that coverage contemplates protection for the insured's liability as respects loss of use as well as damage or destruction of the property itself. Thus, the lessee of a building that has a replacement cost of $100,000 and earns $2,000 per month in rental fees might purchase fire legal liability insurance with a limit of $112,000—replacement cost plus rent for a maximum of six months of reconstruction. Obviously, a good deal of speculation and investigation is involved in the final selection of the amount of coverage. What are the chances of the building being totally destroyed, what are the prospects for speedy reconstruction, what does the lease have to say about continuation of rent payments while the building is shut down, and so on?

Tenants of multi-occupant buildings purchase fire legal liability coverage (in the CGL policy) on *that part of the building* in their care, custody or control. Coverage for their liability as respects the remainder of the building is properly the subject of general liability insurance—with attention to the matter of adequate property damage limits.

Many times the named insured under the form may be required to add different entities as additional insureds under the policy. Such entities may include someone buying the building under a land contract; co-owners of the premises, with respect to their liability as such; and mortgagees, assignees, or receivers. The ISO rules state that most may be added without an extra premium charge. However, adding the following additional insureds requires a surcharge of 25 percent: (1) general lessees, managers, or operators of premises in policies covering tenants or lessees of such premises; and (2) employees other than executive officers or partners in policies covering their employers. A general lessee of a multi-tenant building cannot purchase a policy and include the interests of each of the tenants as additional insureds. However, each of the tenants can purchase a policy in which the interest of the general lessee is covered as an additional insured.

The following may not be added as additional insureds at any time: (1) contractors or subcontractors in policies covering tenants or lessees of premises and (2) tenants, lessees, concessionaires, or exhibitors, in policies covering general lessees, managers, or operators of premises.

Coverage

The insuring agreement of form CP 00 40 requires the insurer to "pay those sums that the insured becomes legally obligated to pay as damages because of direct physical loss or damage, including loss of use, to covered property caused by accident and arising out of any covered cause of loss."

The form describes covered property as "tangible property of others in your care, custody or control and described in the declarations." There is no coverage for electronic data under the legal liability coverage form. The form's definitions of *electronic data* and *computer programs* are the same as in the building and commercial property coverage form.

The phrase *legally obligated* is used in the insuring agreement to emphasize that the insurance is in no way direct coverage. The policy does not cover damage to the property; it covers the insured's responsibility following damage as imposed by law. Naturally, the insurer will use whatever legal defenses are available to the insured in resisting the assessment of responsibility. The policy reserves the insurer's right to investigate and settle any claim or suit.

The second aspect of fire legal liability coverage is that the insurer has the right and duty to defend any suit seeking damages and will bear the cost of defending a suit against the insured. A suit includes an arbitration proceeding. Payment of legal expenses is in addition to the limit set forth in the policy.

The insurer agrees to pay the cost of defense attorneys and court costs. The amount payable for these expenses is limited only by the provision that the insurer's obligation to defend ends when the insurer has paid the limit in payment of judgments or settlements. In other words, the insurer must pay whatever the insured's legal expenses are (even if they exceed the policy limit) until a judgment or settlement is reached and the amount of the limit has been paid out in the judgment or settlement.

The form also agrees to make the following supplemental payments in addition to the limit of liability:

1.   All expenses that the insurer incurs;

2.   The cost of bonds to release attachments;

3.   All reasonable expenses incurred by the insured at the insurer's request. This includes actual loss of earnings up to $250 a day because of time off work;

4.   All costs taxed against the insured in the suit;

5.   Prejudgment interest awarded against the insured;

6.   All interest on the full amount of any judgment that accrues after entry of the judgment.

Coverage Extensions—Additional Insureds and Newly Acquired Organizations

If the named insured is a partnership or corporation, partners, executive officers, trustees, directors, and stockholders are additional insureds while acting within the scope of their duties, as are the managers of a limited liability company. Other employees may be named as additional insureds by endorsement, subject to an additional premium charge equal to 25 percent of the policy premium. Coverage under this extension does not increase the limit of insurance.

If the policy is appropriately endorsed, it is permissible (with two exceptions) to include others as insureds. The exceptions are a policy issued to a tenant or lessee may not also cover the insurable interest of a contractor or subcontractor, and a policy issued to a general lessee (one who leases an entire premises and sublets to others) or manager may not include the interest of a tenant, concessionaire or exhibitor.

The legal liability form covers newly acquired organizations within the applicable limit of insurance for legal liability arising out of direct physical loss that occurs after the insured acquires or forms the organization. An insured includes any organization (other than a partnership, joint venture, or limited liability company) that the insured newly acquires or forms and over which the insured maintains ownership or majority interest, provided there is no other insurance available to that organization. This extension of coverage runs for ninety days after the acquisition or formation of the organization, unless the policy expires first.

Newly Acquired Property

Form CP 00 40 allows for limited automatic coverage for property (building and personal) that comes under the insured's care, custody, or control during the policy period. In order for a building to be covered by this provision, it must be intended for similar use to the one described in the declarations or for warehouse use. Coverage under the extension ends at the earliest of policy expiration; thirty days after the insured acquires care, custody, or control; or the insured reports values to the insurer. Additional premium is charged and payments under the newly acquired property extension are in addition to the limits of insurance.

Coverage for a total loss of all newly acquired covered buildings arising out of one accident is limited to $250,000 at each building. The building limit can be increased by adding endorsement CP 04 25.

Newly acquired personal property must be either at a location owned by or in the care, custody, or control of the insured at the time of loss. There is no provision for adding newly acquired property that is in the insured's care, custody, or control at fairs or exhibitions. Total coverage for loss to this personal property resulting from one accident is $100,000 at each building. Endorsement CP 04 25 cannot be used to increase this limit.

Perils and Exclusions

Under the legal liability form any of the three causes of loss forms used with the commercial property program may be employed (basic, broad, or special). However, the Special Causes of Loss form, CP 10 30, may not be attached when coverage is written for personal property of others in the insured's care, custody, or control, or warehouse risks involving personal property. Presumably these ineligible risks involve *business personal property* of others. However, the rules do not specify that limitation.

Since most if not all of the perils covered (extended coverage, vandalism and malicious mischief, or the open perils of form CP 10 30) typically involve either fortuitous events or acts of others, insureds sometimes question the logic of including these perils in their legal liability protection. Some would argue that the likelihood of their becoming legally involved seems remote. Nevertheless, the chance is there and it is just as expensive to defend a groundless suit as any other kind. The cost of defense and coverage, contrasted with the normally very slight expense of adding these perils, is usually enough to balance the decision. And the extended coverage perils of smoke, vehicle damage, and explosion are clearly valid items for inclusion in the legal liability contract.

Both the basic and broad causes of loss forms exclude damage from a vehicle owned or operated by the named insured in the course of business. Employees are outside the scope of the exclusion except with respect to vehicles owned by the insured.

In relation to legal liability coverage, all three causes of loss forms contain a contractual liability exclusion. This exclusion provides that the insurer will not "defend any claim or 'suit', or pay damages that [the insured is] legally liable to pay, solely by reason of [the insured's] assumption of liability in a contract or agreement."

Certain exclusions in each of the causes of loss forms do not apply to the legal liability coverage form: ordinance or law, governmental action, nuclear hazard, utility services, and war and military action. The nuclear hazard exclusion of the applicable causes of loss form is replaced by one that pertains only to the legal liability coverage form. Unlike the generally applicable nuclear exclusion, the exclusion used with the legal liability form does not provide coverage for resulting loss or damage by fire.

The reason for specifically stating that some of the other exclusions do not apply is less clear. For example, just as damage by war is beyond the insured's control, so are many causes of earth movement; yet the earth movement exclusion is left fully intact. However, the elimination of the ordinance or law exclusion and governmental action exclusions is more significant. If the insured negligently damages a building to such a degree that a building ordinance requires its complete demolition, the total liability would not be covered without the elimination of the ordinance or law exclusion. Similarly, if the insured accidentally causes an unsafe condition on the premises that results in seizure and destruction of the property by local authorities, the insured would not receive full liability coverage without the elimination of the governmental action exclusion. For example, the insured negligently rents his building to someone operating a drug lab. If it is destroyed by the police in a raid, the insured would receive no coverage without the elimination of this exclusion.

Loss Conditions

Since the CP 00 40 covers liability, the loss conditions read more like those of the CGL than those of the commercial property policy. The form imposes the following conditions on the insured in the event of a loss:

1. Duties

    a. Notify the insurer of how and when the accident occurred and the names of any possible witnesses;

    b. Provide the insurer with prompt notice of any claim or suit;

    c. Send copies of any demands, summons, or other legal papers to the insurer;

    d. Authorize the insurer to obtain any necessary information;

    e. Cooperate with the insurer;

    f. Assist the insurer in the enforcement of its subrogation rights; and

    g. The insured may not, except at its own expense, make any settlement or offer any payment.

2. Legal Action Against the Insurer—no one may join the insurer in a suit against the insured and no one may sue the insurer under this form until all terms have been met.

3. Other Insurance—this policy responds pro rata with other like insurance.

4. Subrogation—the insured must do nothing to impair the insurer's subrogation rights. If the insurer requests, the insured must bring suit to help enforce those rights.

Additional Conditions

The following four conditions apply in addition to the commercial property conditions:

1. Amendment of commercial property conditions: the only commercial property conditions that apply to the legal liability form are:

    a. Condition A., Concealment, Misrepresentation or Fraud;

    b. Condition C., Insurance Under Two or More Coverages; and

    c. Condition E., Liberalization.

2. Bankruptcy of the insured does not relieve the insurer of its obligations.

3. Policy period, coverage territory: the policy period is shown on the Declarations page and the territory is the United States, Canada, and Puerto Rico.

4. Separation of insureds: the insurance applies separately to all insureds, except for the limits of liability.

Chapter 9

Commercial Property Endorsements

ISO offers many endorsements to tailor the commercial property coverage form to the needs of the insured. This chapter alphabetically lists and explains many of the endorsements that are available to add, delete, or modify coverage under the commercial property business and personal property coverage form.

Additional Building Property, CP 14 15

Business personal property items that are owned but not permanently installed may be designated as building items on this endorsement. See Chapter 1 for a discussion of issues related to business personal property coverage under the building section of the form.

Additional Covered Property, CP 14 10

The insured may purchase coverage for certain excluded items of both building and personal property on this endorsement. Coverage applies only to those items scheduled and only at the premises designated. This endorsement adds coverage for certain building items, generally at the building rate (unless special class rates apply). The following may be added to building coverage: cost of excavations, grading, backfilling, or filling; certain foundations; underground pipes, flues, or drains; bulkheads, pilings, piers, wharves, or docks; fences; freestanding retaining walls; bridges, roadways, walks, patios, or other paved surfaces.

ISO Commercial Lines Manual (CLM) rule 30 allows for vehicles or self-propelled machines (including aircraft and watercraft) and animals to be covered (and that the commercial property policy otherwise excludes).

For vehicles to be covered, they must be licensed for road use and operated principally away from the described premises. The insured may not manufacture, process, warehouse, or hold any of these vehicles for sale. The endorsement also adds coverage for animals.

The endorsement adds only these items as covered property under the CP 00 10. That form limits personal property coverage to that property on or within 100 feet of the described premises. The coverage is for physical damage only and is not as broad as coverage under the comprehensive coverage of a commercial auto policy or an open perils inland marine policy.

Additional Exclusions, CP 10 50

This endorsement can be used with any of the causes of loss forms (basic, broad, or special) and contains a schedule of premises and buildings where a windstorm or hail, vandalism, or sprinkler leakage exclusion is added. If loss or damage for another covered cause of loss results, that loss is covered.

Additional Insured and Loss Payee (Building Owner), CP 12 18 and CP 12 19

In 2007 ISO introduced two mutually exclusive options for recognizing the interest of a building owner under a tenant's property damage insurance: new endorsement CP 12 19, enables adding the building owner as an additional named insured under a tenant's building coverage. Endorsement CP 12 was revised to add an option, building owner loss payable, to identify the building owner and recognize that entity as a loss payee. Each of these new options broadens coverage under a policy to which the option applies.

Additional Locations Special Coinsurance Provisions, CP 13 20

Some insureds may want to make use of multiple location average rating, but their personal property values at each location do not fluctuate enough to warrant use of value reporting form CP 13 10. Endorsement CP 13 20 extends business personal property coverage to include personal property at all reported, acquired, and incidental locations. It does not cover property at fairs or exhibitions.

CLM rule 35 says that the following types of property are eligible for this endorsement:

1. Merchandise and stock (raw, in process, or finished) that the insured owns;

2. All business personal property that the insured owns;

3. Personal property owned by others in the care, custody, or control of the insured.

The CLM also specifies that property subject to the following rating schedules is ineligible for this endorsement:

1. Petroleum Properties Schedule;

2. Petrochemical Plants Schedule;

3. Public Utility Electric Generating Stations Schedule;

4. Public Utility Natural Gas Pumping Stations Schedule; and

5. Rating Plan for Highly Protected or Superior Risks.

The endorsement applies a coinsurance percentage (at least 90 percent is required) to an overall limit of insurance. The overall limit is the sum of the total values from each individual location, including any reported, acquired, and incidental locations. It is shown in the Declarations or on the Reported—Acquired—Incidental Locations Schedule, CP DS 04. The average rate and premium are derived from the overall limit. It is not a blanket limit; however, each location possesses its own individual limit. A sample loss settlement is included on the endorsement to clarify the use of the overall limit.

Additional Property Not Covered, CP 14 20

The insured may choose to exclude items of building or business personal property by scheduling them on this endorsement. The underwriter may not write the risk without excluding certain items of property or that the insured is willing to exclude certain items to get a lower insurance cost. CLM rules 30 and 31 describe the types of property that may be excluded:

Building items that may be excluded include the following:

a. Awnings or canopies of fabric or slat construction, including their supports;

b. Brick, metal, stone, or concrete chimneys or stacks that are not part of a building; or metal smokestacks;

c. Crop silos;

d. Swimming pools, diving towers, or platforms;

e. Waterwheels, windmills, wind pumps, or their towers;

f. The value of improvements, alterations or repairs (including labor, materials, and supplies) being performed by a named individual or organization; (This includes existing real property that will be demolished or permanently removed in the course of making the improvements, alterations, or repairs) and

g. Any other type of property for which more specific property damage coverage is available.

Business personal property items that may be excluded include the following:

a. Personal Property contained in safes or vaults;

b. Contents of crop silos;

c. Glass that is not part of a building or structure;

d. Metals in ingots, pigs, billets, or scraps;

e. Ores, gravels, clay, or sand;

f. Property of others;

g. Property stored in open yards;

h. Signs inside the premises;

i. Vending machines or their contents;

j.   Any other type of property for which more specific property damage coverage is available;

k.   The following types of property contained within a condominium unit and covered under CP 00 18 whether owned by the Condominium Association or by the unit-owner, unless the Condominium Association Agreement requires the Condominium Association to insure this property:

(1) Fixtures, improvements, and alterations that are part of the building and

(2) Appliances.

Agricultural Products Storage, CP 13 30

Insureds who store grain (such as grain elevator operators) may cover it with endorsement CP 13 30. This endorsement covers grain or grain products on the premises and part of stock at a manufacturing, warehousing, processing, or finishing plant. Rice, flaxseed, beans, soybeans, seeds, or seed grain are also eligible.

This endorsement amends the property not covered provision of the property coverage forms pertaining to grain, hay, straw, or other crops outside of buildings. If such property is harvested and not in storage, it is covered under CP 13 30.

This form does not cover agricultural products stored at fairs or exhibitions or in transit; nor does it cover storage or elevator charges or unpaid customs duties on agricultural products.

In case of loss to covered property in terminal grain elevator plants, payment is made jointly to the named insured and anyone else with an established interest in the property. Such interest may be established by ownership, having a pledge for property, or holding or having a pledge for warehouse receipts. For losses to property stored at other locations, all liens, storage tickets, and warehouse receipts must be satisfied and released before payment occurs.

The endorsement values damaged or destroyed agricultural products at the market value of the covered property less any unincurred expenses such as commissions, loading and unloading charges, and freight. Loss to other commodities (those commodities for which market value is inappropriate) is figured at actual cash value of the property as of the time and place of the loss.

Alcoholic Beverage Tax Exclusion, CP 99 10

This endorsement has two purposes:

1.   It excludes the value of taxes and custom duties paid on alcoholic beverages if the beverages suffer damage from a cause of loss other than theft. These taxes and custom duties are refundable under law when the beverages are damaged by a cause of loss other than theft.

2.   When theft is a covered peril (as it is only under the Special Causes of Loss form, CP 10 30), endorsement CP 99 10 includes the value of taxes and custom duties in the loss valuation. The insured cannot receive government reimbursement for such costs in the case of theft and therefore needs insurance protection.

A special theft limit may be scheduled at each covered location under business personal property, stock only, or personal property of others.

The distilled spirits and wines market value endorsement, CP 99 05, also excludes the value of taxes and duties, so endorsement CP 99 10 does not need to be added for that purpose when endorsement CP 99 05 applies. However, if the insured has theft coverage under the special causes of loss form, endorsement CP 99 10 may be used in conjunction with CP 99 05. The addition of both endorsements allows for valuation at market value with different limits for theft versus causes of loss other than theft.

Blanket Insurance – Margin Clause Option, CP 12 32

One advantage of blanket insurance is that the insured can be fully covered at individual locations without insuring 100 percent of the total value of all locations. However, blanket coverage typically requires insurance to value of 90 percent for blanket coverage, which is often not met and results in the potential for payment of a disproportionate part of the blanket limit the insured suffers a partial loss. Total blanket value is also often difficult to determine at the time of loss, which impedes application of the policy's coinsurance requirement.

To address such issues, ISO introduced a margin clause in 2007 in an optional endorsement for use on blanket policies. Under the endorsement, loss payment on an individual property under the blanket coverage is limited to its stated value plus a percentage of that value. The insured still has the advantages of blanket coverage, but the most that is payable on individual properties is limited. The margin may vary by location and type of property but does not increase the blanket limit of insurance. If there is a partial loss, this endorsement may reduce the amount of loss payment in comparison to a blanket policy without a margin clause.

Brands and Labels, CP 04 01

When an insurer takes the salvage of damaged property, an attempt to sell the salvaged property is made in order to recoup some of its payment. Such a situation, however, might place the insurer in direct competition with its customer, since the customer is still trying to sell new, undamaged merchandise of the same kind.

The brands and labels endorsement provides the original manufacturer with two options in this situation:

1.   He may stamp such merchandise as salvage material.

2.   The insured may remove the brands or labels if doing so does not damage the merchandise.

The endorsement provides that the insurer will cover such expenses within the limit of liability that applies to the covered property.

Broken or Cracked Glass Exclusion Form, CP 10 52

The broken or cracked glass exclusion endorsement identifies, at policy inception, any broken or cracked glass on the insured premises. It clarifies that no coverage applies for damage caused by or resulting from the existing cracks. It also eliminates coverage for damage done by the extension of these cracks. The insured may identify the existing damage either via a diagram of the glass or by a written description of the damage

Building Glass Under Tenant's Policy, CP 14 70

The glass coverage form, CP 00 15, was withdrawn in 2000 when that edition of the commercial property form was updated to include building glass. Prior to its withdrawal, the form was sometimes used when a tenant was contractually required to provide coverage for glass that is part of the building, but the tenant's policy did not insure the building itself. An entry on the declarations could limit building coverage to building glass. With the 2007 edition, ISO introduced endorsement CP 14 70, Building Glass - Tenant's Policy, to enable coverage of building glass under a tenant's policy that does not otherwise cover the building.

Business Income Changes – Beginning of the Period of Restoration, CP 15 56

Chapter 7 addresses changes made in the 06 07 policy edition to civil authority coverage in the underlying business income policy. The changes include use of a one-mile radius as one of the qualifications to trigger civil authority coverage and a basic coverage period of four weeks. ISO revised endorsement CP 15 56, Business Income Changes - Beginning of the Period of Restoration because it referred to a three week coverage period for civil authority coverage. The endorsement amends the definition of *period of restoration* to eliminate the 72-hour time deductible. An option for a 24-hour time deductible was also added. That option was previously contained in endorsement CP 15 55, Business Income Changes - Time Period, which has been withdrawn.

Business Income – Discretionary Payroll Expense, CP 15 04

In the 2007 revision of the Commercial Property program, ISO introduced a new endorsement, CP 15 04, Discretionary Payroll Expense. The business income forms state that the amount of loss is partly based on "the operating expenses, including payroll expenses, necessary to resume 'operations' with the same quality of service that existed just before the direct physical loss or damage." Payroll expense for only certain job classifications or employees is covered as business income loss. However, insureds may want to keep other employees in other job classifications on the payroll. This endorsement was introduced to address such situations.

Under this endorsement, discretionary payroll may be specified in terms of job classification or individual employees. Payroll coverage may be available for the entire period of restoration or limited to a specified maximum number of days; the days do not need to be consecutive. If not identified in the schedule, other job classifications and employees not affected by the terms of this endorsement.

Business Income – Landlord as Additional Insured (Rental Value), CP 15 03

If a rental or lease agreement requires the tenant to carry insurance for loss of rental income for the benefit of the landlord in situations where the premises cannot be used for business purposes because of a covered loss, the 2007 commercial property program revision introduced a new optional endorsement that provides coverage for loss of rental income for a landlord under a tenant's policy. This option broadens coverage.

Business Income — Ordinary Payroll Limitation or Exclusion, CP 15 10

Endorsement CP 15 10 excludes or limits ordinary payroll expense, which is defined as "payroll expenses for all your employees except: 1. Officers; 2. Executives; 3. Department managers; 4. Employees under contract; and 5. Additional Exemptions, shown in the Schedule as: a. Job Classifications; or b. Employees. 'Ordinary payroll expenses' include: (1) Payroll; (2) Employee benefits, if directly related to payroll; (3) FICA payments you pay; (4) Union dues you pay; and (5) Workers' compensation premiums."

Coverage begins following the date of direct physical loss or damage. The number of days do not need to be consecutive but must occur during the period of restoration. The schedule must indicate a number of days or there is no coverage.

Burglary and Robbery Protective Safeguards, CP 12 11

The Burglary and Robbery Protective Safeguards endorsement identifies safeguards that protect the insured's property from burglary and robbery. According to rating procedures in the CLM, such devices warrant rate credits.

The endorsement refers to only four different types of systems:

1. BR-1: [for 'burglary and robbery'] Automatic Burglary Alarm, protecting the entire building, that signals to:

    (a) An outside central station or

    (b) A police station.

2.   BR-2: Automatic Burglary Alarm, protecting the entire building, that has a loud sounding gong or siren on the outside of the building.

3.   BR-3: Security Service, with a recording system or watch clock, making hourly rounds covering the entire building, when the premises are not in actual operation.

4.   BR-4: The protective safeguard described in the Schedule.

Previous versions of the endorsement required the insured to notify the insurer immediately in the event of any malfunction of the protective systems (burglar alarms, gongs, security services) at the premises. That requirement no longer appears. Rather, the requirement is that the insured must maintain the protective devices and/or services listed in the Schedule.

The insured must also give notice of any failure to maintain such systems. If the insured does not make the notification or does not maintain the systems in working order, the theft coverage is suspended.

Cap on Losses from Certified Acts of Terrorism, IL 09 52

This endorsement is one of the terrorism provisions created for the commercial property program following the terrorist acts of September 11, 2001.

The endorsement includes the following provision:

A.   Cap On Certified Terrorism Losses

"Certified act of terrorism" means an act that is certified by the Secretary of the Treasury, in concurrence with the Secretary of State and the Attorney General of the United States, to be an act of terrorism pursuant to the federal Terrorism Risk Insurance Act. The criteria contained in the Terrorism Risk Insurance Act for a certified act of terrorism" include the following:

1.   The act resulted in insured losses in excess of $5 million in the aggregate, attributable to all types of insurance subject to the Terrorism Risk Insurance Act; and

2.   The act is a violent act or an act that is dangerous to human life, property or infrastructure and is committed by an indi-

vidual or individuals as part of an effort to coerce the civilian population of the United States or to influence the policy or affect the conduct of the United States Government by coercion.

If aggregate insured losses attributable to terrorist acts certified under the Terrorism Risk Insurance Act exceed $100 billion in a Program Year (January1 through December 31) and we have met our insurer deductible under the Terrorism Risk Insurance Act, we shall not be liable for the payment of any portion of the amount of such losses that exceeds $100 billion, and in such case insured losses up to that amount are subject to pro rata allocation in accordance with procedures established by the Secretary of the Treasury.

Changes – Electronic Data, CP 01 70

This endorsement reflects the change in treatment of electronic data coverage made in the CP 00 10 04 02 edition. This endorsement is attached to previous editions to reflect the changes.

Via this endorsement, covered property does not include electronic data, except as provided under Limited Coverage – Electronic Data.

The cost to replace or restore the information on valuable papers and records, including those that exist as electronic data, is not covered property. Proprietary information, books of account, deeds, manuscripts, abstracts, drawings, and card index systems are considered valuable papers and records, but this is not an exhaustive list.

The endorsement does provide limited coverage for valuable papers and records, other than those that exist as electronic data, under the Limited Coverage – Valuable Papers and Records (Other Than Electronic Data).

Additionally, the endorsement contains the provisions for the limited coverage for electronic data, valuable papers and records (other than electronic data), and the limited coverage for interruption of computer operations. These policy provisions are discussed in Chapter 2.

Changes – Fungus, Wet Rot, Dry Rot and Bacteria, CP 01 71

This endorsement reflects the change in treatment of mold-related damage coverage made in the CP 00 10 04 02 edition. This endorsement is attached to previous editions to reflect the changes. The fungus, wet rot, dry rot, and bacteria exclusion is added and the limited coverage for fungus, wet rot, dry rot, and bacteria is added back by way of additional coverage. See Chapter 2.

Civil Authority Change(s), CP 15 32

Chapter 7 addresses changes made in the 06 07 policy edition to civil authority coverage in the underlying business income policy. The changes include use of a one-mile radius as one of the qualifications to trigger civil authority coverage and a basic coverage period of four weeks. At the same time ISO revised CP 15 32, Civil Authority Change(s), so that the one-mile radius or the four-week coverage period of civil authority coverage can be changed. The endorsement previously addressed only the coverage period.

Condominium Commercial Unit Owners Optional Coverages, CP 04 18

The owner of a commercial condominium unit may purchase either of the additional coverages, loss assessment or miscellaneous real property, on this endorsement. In the event of loss to property that all unit-owners hold in common, the association may assess each owner a share of the loss. Such an assessment may include a portion of the master insurance policy's deductible. The association may also assess a portion of the loss itself if there is either no insurance or inadequate insurance. The endorsement covers all assessments, up to the limit of liability. However, it limits payment for the insured's share of any deductible to $1,000.

Depending on the terms of the association agreement, bylaws, and condominium declaration, the unit-owner may also need to insure some or all of the real property in the condominium. Endorsement CP 04 18 offers miscellaneous real property coverage for such property in the insured's unit only. This coverage is excess over the association coverage on the property, whether the insurance is collectible or not.

The endorsement's schedule was updated in the 2007 revision so that each unit for which coverage applies can be indicated.

Contributing Insurance, CP 99 20

If the insured has coverage with more than one company, the contributing insurance endorsement clarifies the amount for which the insurer is liable.

The endorsement indicates the company's percentage of the total of all contributing insurance. The endorsement also shows the property and coverages to which it applies and the total limits for all contributing insurance.

Debris Removal Additional Insurance, CP 04 15

Debris removal additional insurance provides an additional amount of insurance for debris removal expenses incurred due to loss or damage to covered property from a covered cause of loss. The endorsement increases the $10,000 limit that the policy currently provides to the amount shown on the endorsement.

Deductible Limitation, CP 03 10

The deductible limitation endorsement allows the insured to select an annual accumulation amount for the deductible. The insurer agrees not to subtract any more than this amount for all losses the insured has in any one policy year. Losses that are less than 10 percent of the deductible do not count towards this annual figure. After the annual accumulation amount is reached, the insured must notify the insurer of any loss of more than $250. The insurer deducts $250 for such losses. Form CP 03 10 does not apply to any earthquake deductible.

Dependent Properties, CP 15 08

Dependent properties must be identified in the schedule are divided into the following categories: contributing locations, recipient locations, manufacturing locations, and leader locations. An unscheduled dependent location deductible may also be applied to a small portion of the limit. These unscheduled or miscellaneous locations encompass business entities or organizations that become, contributing, recipient, leader, or manufacturing locations in mid-policy term with respect to the insured's operations. Miscellaneous locations coverage recognizes other situations as well, such as where certain entities or organizations do not represent a significant dependency or are temporary. In the 2007 revision, ISO added language to the description of miscellaneous locations to make it clear that highways

and other transportation conduits are not considered miscellaneous locations. ISO also added references to the business income's policy limit in
the 2007 revision.

Disclosure Pursuant to Terrorism Risk Insurance Act, IL 09 85

Under provisions of the federal Terrorism Risk Insurance Act (TRIA),
insurers are required to provide insureds with a notice disclosing the portion
of the premium, if any, attributable to coverage for terrorist acts certified
under that Act. The portion of the premium attributable to such coverage is
shown in the schedule of this endorsement or in the policy declarations.

B.   Disclosure Of Federal Participation In Payment Of Terrorism
     Losses

     The United States Government, Department of the Treasury,
     will pay a share of terrorism losses insured under the federal
     program. The federal share equals 85% of that portion of the
     amount of such insured losses that exceeds the applicable
     insurer retention. However, if aggregate insured losses attribut-
     able to terrorist acts certified under the Terrorism Risk Insurance
     Act exceed $100 billion in a Program Year (January 1 through
     December 31), the Treasury shall not make any payment for any
     portion of the amount of such losses that exceeds $100 billion.

Distilled Spirits and Wines Market Value, CP 99 05

This endorsement changes the valuation of distilled spirits and wines
from actual cash value to market value. Such items may be either the
insured's stock or the property of others in the insured's care. The insured
schedules on the endorsement the locations to which the endorsement
applies.

The endorsement lists five categories of distilled spirits:

1.   Bottled winery products—wine that is either in a bottle or unbot-
     tled. If not bottled, it must be irreplaceable and it must be of the
     kind that the insured would normally bottle or have in his posses-
     sion.

2.   Bulk wine—anything other than bottled wine.

3. Irreplaceable bulk distilled spirits—distilled spirits aged in wood, not replaceable, and held by the insured for sale to others.

4. Older bulk distilled spirits—irreplaceable bulk spirits that have reached a certain age.

5. Younger bulk distilled spirits—irreplaceable bulk other than older bulk spirits.

Valuation for distilled spirits is essentially market price at the time and place of loss less any discounts and expenses the insured otherwise would have had.

The form divides wines into two categories:

1. Bottled winery products—valued at the price they would have been sold as case goods; and

2. Bulk wine—valued at the lesser of:

   a. the price it could have been sold for; or

   b. the market price of replaceable bulk wine of like kind and quality.

Values exclude federal taxes, discounts, and expenses the insured otherwise would have had, but include state, county, and local taxes.

Certain insureds covered by the Special Causes of Loss form, CP 10 30, may want to add endorsement CP 99 10 when this endorsement is used. For insureds with other types of stock subject to market value, another endorsement, CP 99 31, is available.

Earthquake and Volcanic Eruption Endorsement Form, CP 10 40

Until 1999, this endorsement was known as causes of loss-earthquake form. The insured may purchase earthquake and volcanic eruption coverage—otherwise specifically excluded—via this endorsement. It covers as one occurrence all shocks or eruption that occur within a 168-hour time period.

The insured may choose specific or blanket earthquake coverage. When choosing specific coverage, the declarations page must indicate the property to which the earthquake coverage applies. Even if the insured chooses blanket earthquake coverage, there may be some buildings it does not wish to cover. In that case, the declarations should, again, reflect the property to which the coverage applies.

Typically, the deductible for earthquake coverage is a percentage of the limit of liability applicable to the covered property. The deductible is calculated separately for and applies separately to the following:

1. Each building, if two or more buildings sustain loss or damage;

2. The building and to personal property in that building, if both sustain loss or damage;

3. Personal property at each building, if personal property at two or more buildings sustains loss or damage;

4. Personal property in the open.

Because a building made of masonry veneer is more likely to sustain heavy damage in an earthquake, the endorsement does not include the value of the veneer when calculating the deductible or applying the coinsurance condition. This limitation does not apply if the building's exterior is less than 10 percent masonry veneer or if the description of the premises specifically includes masonry veneer. The limitation does not apply to stucco.

Earthquake Inception Extension, CP 10 41

Use of this endorsement avoids a coverage gap when an expiring policy and new policy both include earthquake coverage. The endorsement specifically covers damage that occurs on or after the inception of the new coverage if the damage is caused by earthquake shocks or volcanic eruptions that began within seventy two hours before the new policy takes effect.

Electrical Apparatus, CP 04 10

This endorsement modifies the electrical apparatus exclusion in the basic, broad and special causes of loss forms. Those forms exclude damage caused by artificially generated electrical currents. However, an exception allows coverage for any resulting fire damage.

Endorsement CP 04 10 extends this exception to include coverage for damage to electrical equipment or devices from resulting explosions. It also covers damage by electricity after the fire or explosion. In order for such coverage to apply, the fire must continue even after the electrical current is turned off. Unless a higher amount is shown on the declarations, coverage under this endorsement is subject to a $1,000 deductible.

In 2007 ISO updated the artificially generated electrical current exclusion in the causes of loss forms to incorporate various terms reflecting current technology with regard to power sources and associated systems. This endorsement was revised to reflect the changes in the causes of loss forms.

Electronic Commerce (E-Commerce), CP 04 30

This endorsement covers various e-commerce exposures of the insured against data corruption and other electronic exposures. The ISO rules state that electronic commerce, for purposes of this endorsement, is "commerce conducted via the Internet or other computer-based interactive communications network. This includes business-to-business commerce conducted in that manner."

Section 1 of the endorsement covers electronic data that is owned, licensed, or leased by the insured; originates and resides in computers located in the coverage territory; and is used in the e-commerce activity of the insured's business described in the schedule.

The form covers the cost to replace or restore electronic data that has suffered loss or damage by a covered cause of loss. The endorsement states that loss or damage to electronic data means destruction or corruption of electronic data.

Section II provides electronic commerce time element coverage. Coverage is for the actual loss of business income sustained and extra expense incurred due to the necessary suspension (slowdown or cessation) of the e-commerce activity of the business described for the applicable period of time specified. Loss must be caused by a covered loss under section 1 or interruption in normal computer network service or function caused by a covered cause of loss.

If the suspension of e-commerce activity is caused by a loss covered under Section I, the period of coverage begins twenty-four hours after the time of such loss and ends on the earliest of the time when ecommerce activity is resumed, the time when the electronic data is restored, or ninety days after the date of loss.

If the suspension is caused by interruption in normal computer network service or function caused by a covered cause of loss, the period of coverage begins twenty-four hours after the time of the interruption, which is when service to the insured's Web site is disrupted. The period ends at the earliest of when e-commerce is resumed, service is restored, or two weeks after the interruption began.

The special causes of loss form, modified by provisions of the e-commerce endorsement, provides the covered causes of loss. The utility services exclusion does not apply with respect to power or communications supply services, provided that there is an interruption in utility service caused by a specified cause of loss; the exclusion of artificially generated electrical, magnetic, or electromagnetic energy, does not apply; and the exclusion of mechanical breakdown does not apply with respect to the breakdown of the insured's computers and their related equipment, but this exception is limited to the effect of such mechanical breakdown on electronic data.

The e-commerce endorsement adds eight exclusions:

(1) A virus, malicious code or similar instruction introduced into or enacted on a computer system (including electronic data) or a network to which it is connected, designed to damage or destroy any part of the system or disrupt its normal operation. But this exclusion does not apply if the insured's e-commerce activity is conducted via a computer system that is equipped with virus-scanning or anti-virus software, or if the Anti-Virus Waiver is indicated as applicable in the Schedule. When this exclusion does not apply, then coverage also extends to shut-down of the computer system if the shut-down is undertaken in response to the detection of a virus or other incident by virus-scanning software, to mitigate or avoid attack, infiltration or infection of the system;

(2) Unauthorized viewing, copying or use of electronic data (or any proprietary or confidential information or intellectual property in any form) by any person, even if such activity is characterized as theft;

(3) Errors or omissions in programming or processing electronic data;

(4)   Errors or deficiency in design, installation, maintenance, repair or modification of your computer system or any computer system or network to which the insured system is connected or on which the insured system depends (including electronic data);

(5)   Manipulation of the insured computer system, including electronic data, by an employee, volunteer worker or contractor, for the purpose of diverting electronic data or causing fraudulent or illegal transfer of any property;

(6)   Interruption in normal computer function or network service or function due to insufficient capacity to process transactions or to an overload of activity on the system or network. But this exclusion does not apply if such incident is caused by a virus, malicious code or similar instruction introduced into or enacted on a computer system or network;

(7)   Unexplained or indeterminable failure, malfunction or slowdown of a computer system, including electronic data and the inability to access or properly manipulate the electronic data;

(8)   Complete or substantial failure, disablement or shut-down of the entire Internet, regardless of the cause.

In 2007 ISO updated the artificially generated electrical current exclusion in the causes of loss forms to incorporate various terms reflecting current technology with regard to power sources and associated systems. This endorsement was revised to reflect the changes in the causes of loss forms.

Flood Coverage Endorsement, CP 10 65

The property program allows flood coverage to be endorsed to a policy. In order to provide flood coverage in excess of that on a National Flood Insurance Program (NFIP) policy, this endorsement and the flood coverage schedule, CP DS 65, are added. The CP DS 65 allows for specific or blanket limits. It also shows the limits and deductibles applying at each location. The insured may choose to blanket several items of covered property, several different coverages (such as property and time element), or several different premises.

The rules state that the following are ineligible for this coverage:

1.   Property subject to the builders risk form;

2.   Certain property as defined in the following Federal Statutes:

   a.   The Coastal Barrier Resources Act and

   b.   The Coastal Barrier Improvement Act.

The endorsement itself defines those properties in number two, as property not covered.

The endorsement defines *flood* as follows:

1.   The overflow of inland or tidal waters;

2.   The unusual or rapid accumulation or runoff of surface waters from any source; or

3.   Mudslides or mudflows which are caused by flooding as defined in C.2. above. For the purpose of this covered cause of loss, a mudslide or mudflow involves a river of liquid and flowing mud on the surface of normally dry land areas as when earth is carried by a current of water and deposited along the path of the current

Many times another peril, such as fire, accompanies a flood. The limits of insurance section specifies that the limit shown on the DS 65 is the most the endorsement will pay and that the limits cannot be stacked.

The endorsement applies as excess over any NFIP coverage. It also is excess of any NFIP coverage that should be in place. If the insured is eligible for NFIP coverage but does not purchase or maintain it, the ISO endorsement pays only in excess of the maximum amount available under the NFIP. For an additional premium, the insured may purchase a waiver of this requirement.

Functional Building Valuation, CP 04 38

Insureds may add this endorsement to the commercial property or the condominium association coverage form to provide an alternate method of valuation for building property. It provides for the replacement of a scheduled building with similar property that performs the same function but is less costly. The endorsement also provides building ordinance coverage at no charge.

The coinsurance condition does not apply. However, the rate for this coverage is 30 percent above the rate charged for buildings subject to the 80 percent coinsurance rule.

If the insured chooses to repair or replace the building, the insurer pays the least of four different amounts. The first choice is the limit of liability. If the building suffers a total loss, the insurer pays the cost to replace the building on the same site with one that is functionally equivalent. If the insured must rebuild on a different site, the endorsement pays to build on that different site.

In the event of a partial loss, payment by the insurer has two components:

a. the cost to repair or replace the damaged portion in the same architectural style with less costly material (if available); and

b. the amount the insured spends to demolish the undamaged portion of the building and to clear the site.

The insurer's fourth option is to pay the amount that the insured actually spends to repair or replace the building with less costly material (if available). The insured must contract for the repairs within 180 days of the loss unless the insured and insurer agree otherwise.

If the insured does not select repair or replacement (or does not do so within the 180 day time period), the endorsement pays the smallest of the following:

a. The limit of liability;

b. The market value (not including the value of the land) at the time of loss. The endorsement defines *market value* as "the price which the property might be expected to realize if offered for sale in a fair market";

c. A modified form of actual cash value (the amount to repair or replace on the same site with less costly material and in the same architectural style, less depreciation).

Unlike former endorsement CP 04 35, this endorsement and the manual rules do not specifically exclude functional replacement cost coverage for certain fixtures and personal property used to service the premises. The previous form and rules excluded these items because they are subject to rapid depreciation. The current endorsement does not exclude this property. Therefore, items such as awnings or floor coverings; appliances for refrigerating, ventilating, cooking, dishwashing, or laundering; or outdoor equipment or furniture (treated as building property under the property coverage form) can be valued at functional replacement cost. Functional replacement cost coverage may be more favorable for such items than actual cash value.

In the event of other insurance using the same type of valuation, form CP 04 38 responds on a pro-rata basis. Coverage is excess when other insurance covering the loss is not subject to the same plan, terms, conditions (such as valuation), and provisions.

Functional Personal Property Valuation Other Than Stock, CP 04 39

Similar to endorsement CP 04 38, CP 04 39 provides an alternate method of valuation for business personal property. It is used when an item of personal property cannot be replaced with the same type of property (as when the damaged property is technologically obsolete), or when actual cash value would be inappropriate because the item depreciates quickly in value.

Coinsurance does not apply to this endorsement and blanket insurance is not allowed. The rate is 25 percent above that for personal property written with 80 percent coinsurance. Any items scheduled on this endorsement should be excluded from coverage under the building and personal property coverage form.

The insured may cover the property for more or less than its actual cash value. For example, a metal stamping plant uses an older piece of machinery with an actual cash value of $50,000. The closest thing available today is one that costs $100,000. Using endorsement CP 04 39, the insured could choose a limit of $100,000 to cover the cost of the new machinery.

The situation is the same when the values are reversed. An insured suffers a fire loss to the central computer. That computer (purchased two years ago) has an actual cash value of $50,000. However, due to advances in technology, the same computer may now be purchased for $30,000.

Using endorsement CP 04 39, the insured may cover this computer for $30,000.

The insured must contract for repair or replacement within 180 days of the loss (a time period that may be altered by consent of the insurer and the insured). If the insured does so, the insurer pays the least of the following amounts under functional replacement cost:

1. The endorsed limit;

2. The cost to replace, on the same site, with the most equivalent property available; or

3. The amount the insured spends to repair or replace the property.

If the insured chooses not to repair or replace (or does not do so within the 180 day time period), the insurer pays the smallest of the following:

1. The limit of liability;

2. The market value at the time of loss; or

3. The amount to repair or replace with material of like kind and quality, minus an allowance for physical deterioration and depreciation.

The endorsement defines *market value* as "the price which the property might be expected to realize if offered for sale in a fair market."

Grain Properties—Explosion Limitation, CP 10 51

This endorsement restricts the peril of explosion found in the basic and broad causes of loss forms, CP 10 10 and CP 10 20. It specifies that if a grain elevator or processing plant building or structure ruptures or bursts as a result of a change in temperature, the resulting damage is not covered as part of the explosion peril.

Household Personal Property Coverage, CP 99 92

This endorsement extends the definition of *covered property* to include household personal property that belongs

• to the insured,

- to a member of the insured's family, or

- to a domestic employee of the insured.

It also covers household personal property for which the insured is legally liable. This includes property purchased through installment plans.

The insured may extend up to 10 percent of the applicable limit to such property away from the premises. According to explanatory information from ISO, this endorsement applies only to owner-occupants of three and four family dwellings.

Leased Property, CP 14 60

The insured may need to insure personal property that he leases. If he chooses not to include such property under the commercial property policy, this endorsement covers it. The leased property must be specifically described on the schedule. Any property covered by this endorsement should not be included when calculating a value for the insured's personal property or the property of others.

The insured may cover losses under this endorsement for an agreed value. However, unlike the optional agreed value coverage available in the property forms, coinsurance provisions still apply. This endorsement allows the insured to select a valuation other than actual cash value (such as replacement cost) on an item-by-item basis for leased property.

Legal Liability Coverage Schedule, CP DS 05

The legal liability coverage schedule is used in conjunction with form CP 00 40, legal liability coverage form (see Chapter 7). The form describes the insured's location and occupancy, the property to which coverage applies, and the limits of insurance.

Loss Payable Provisions, CP 12 18

When someone other than the named insured has an insurable interest in the covered property, form CP 12 18 protects that interest in one or more of the following ways:

1. Loss payable—this is very similar to loss payable provisions in other policies. Under this provision, any losses payable are payable to the insured and a named loss payee as their interests may

appear. Under this provision, the loss payee has no further rights than does the insured.

2. Lender's loss payable—like a mortgage clause, this provision establishes separate rights of the loss payee and insured. Even if the insured breaches any policy condition, the loss payee will still collect on a covered claim. This provision is used when a mortgage holders clause is not applicable. The insured and loss payee may document the loss payee's interest in the property by written instruments such as warehouse receipts; a contract for deed; bills of lading; financing statements; or mortgages, deeds of trust, or security agreements.

3. Contract of sale—this clause protects the duplicate interests of the insured and another party with whom the insured has entered into a contract for the sale of covered property. The endorsement amends the definition of the word *you* to include the loss payee.

4. Building owner—names the building owner as a loss payee and recognizes the owner's interest under a tenant's property damage coverage. Losses for tenants' improvements and betterments will be adjusted with the tenant. The 2007 revision added this clause.

There is no additional premium charge for use of endorsement CP 12 18.

Manufacturers Consequential Loss Assumption, CP 99 02

As with other consequential loss endorsements, this one covers indirect damage. It covers the reduction in value of physically undamaged stock in the process of being manufactured. Such a reduction in value must result from a covered direct loss to other unfinished stock. The rate for this coverage is 25 percent above that for business personal property. When the policy does not break out stock from other personal property, the increase factor is 15 percent.

For coinsurance purposes, the value of stock in process at the insured location includes the additional value that it represents in stock at other locations. The minimum coinsurance amount is 80 percent.

Manufacturer's Selling Price (Finished Stock Only), CP 99 30

This endorsement amends the method at which loss to stock is adjusted. It provides for valuation based on selling price less any applicable discounts and expenses for all completed stock. Unlike the commercial property policy, such adjustment is not limited to finished stock that is sold but not delivered.

Market Value Stock, CP 99 31

This endorsement amends the method by which loss to certain types of stock is adjusted. It covers stock subject to market value. Such stock is defined as the "kind that is bought and sold at an established market exchange where the market prices are posted and quoted." Stocks of wines and distilled spirits are not eligible for this endorsement (see CP 99 05 earlier in this chapter).

The endorsement agrees to set the value of such stock at the market price less any applicable discounts and expenses.

Molten Material, CP 10 60

The molten material endorsement adds the accidental discharge of molten material from equipment as a covered peril. It also covers damage done by the heat released from the discharged molten material. It applies only to the basic, CP 10 10, or broad, CP 10 20, causes of loss forms, because the special form, CP 10 30, contains no exclusion for this cause of loss.

The endorsement excludes the following:

1. Loss of or damage to the discharged material;

2. The cost to repair any defect that caused the discharge; or

3. The cost to remove or recover the discharged material.

Multiple Deductible, CP 03 20

The multiple deductible endorsement allows the insured to schedule different deductible amounts at different locations. It also allows the choice of different deductibles for the perils of wind or hail and theft.

Multiple Location/Premium and Dispersion Credit Application, CP 13 70

Insureds use this endorsement for calculating a provisional premium for use with a reporting form or for determining a multiple location average rate.

Newly Acquired/Constructed Property-Increased Limit, CP 04 25

The policy automatically provides an extension in the amount of $250,000 for newly acquired/constructed property. This endorsement increases that limit. It must be written for the same causes of loss as the underlying policy and it must apply to all policies providing coverage on the same building property.

Off-Premises Services-Direct Damage, CP 04 17 1091

This endorsement provides coverage for damage to covered property caused by an interruption of utility service. The utility interruption must be caused by a covered peril to any of the following (when so indicated on the endorsement):

1. Water supply services—damage to pumping stations or water mains.

2. Communication supply services—damage to property that provides these services, including telephone, radio, microwave or television services. Examples of covered property include communication transmission lines, including fiber optic transmission lines; Coaxial cables; and microwave radio relays, except satellites.

3. Power supply services—damage to property that supply electricity, steam, or gas to the described premises:

    a. Utility generating plants;

    b. Switching stations;

    c. Substations;

    d. Transformers; and

    e. Transmission lines.

Coverage for damage to overhead transmission lines is available under numbers 2 and 3 by indicating in the appropriate box on the endorsement.

Ordinance or Law Coverage, CP 04 05

The ordinance or law coverage endorsement responds if the enforcement of any building, zoning, or land use law results in added costs that are not covered as direct loss. The insured indicates on the declarations which of three distinct coverages is desired:

1. Coverage A, Loss to the Undamaged Portion of the Building—covers the loss of value to the undamaged portion of the building caused by the enforcement of certain ordinances or laws. Such laws require demolition of a building after it suffers a certain percentage of direct damage. They also regulate construction, repair, zoning, or land use (such as laws that do not allow the same type of land use upon rebuilding as the insured had before the loss). For coverage to apply, the ordinance or law must be in force at the time of loss (a requirement that does not apply to Coverages B and C). However, there is no coverage if the insured was required to comply with an ordinance and failed to do so. Coverage A is not an additional amount of insurance but merely an extension of the existing policy limit. Thus, recovery is limited to the lesser of actual cash value or the building coverage limit if replacement cost coverage does not apply. Replacement cost will not apply if an insured chooses not to repair or replace, or if the insured did not buy the coverage.

    The insured must purchase coverage for at least 80 percent of the property's replacement cost value if the insured has added Coverage C (see below), or 80 percent of actual cash value if Coverage C is not included. Since coverage C requires that the underlying policy include the replacement cost option, the rules effectively require insurance equal to 80 percent of the property's replacement cost when Coverage C is selected.

2. Coverage B, Demolition Cost Coverage—if the insured must demolish the undamaged portion of the building, this coverage pays the cost of that demolition. It also pays to clear the site of undamaged parts of the property. The CP 04 05 limits the amount of debris removal coverage to the lesser of the amount actually

spent to demolish and clear the site or the coverage B limit. Coinsurance does not apply to Coverage B.

3. Coverage C, Increased Cost of Construction—if the insured actually repairs or replaces the building (either at the same or another location), Coverage C pays the increased cost of construction at the same premises or the coverage C limit (whichever is less). The coverage does not require replacement at the same location. It only limits payment to the cost to replace *at that location*. If the insured chooses to rebuild elsewhere, the loss payment is figured on the cost to rebuild at the original location.

    However, if the ordinance or law requires relocation to another location, coverage C pays the lesser of the increased cost of construction at the new premises or the applicable limit. The form limits the time to rebuild to two years. However, that limit may be extended by another two years.

    The endorsement provides an extensive description of "proportionate loss payment." Many losses involve damage from both covered and uncovered perils. When a building suffers damage from both a flood and a fire, the CP policy covers only the fire damage. The wording on the CP 04 05 emphasizes that any increased costs due to the operation of building laws will be covered on a proportionate basis for damage from the covered perils only.

    A statement clarifies that the endorsement responds only to the minimum requirements of that law. It specifically excludes costs of "recommend actions" in excess of what the law actually requires.

Outdoor Trees, Shrubs and Plants, CP 14 30

The building and personal property form provides up to $1,000 coverage, subject to a limit of $250, per item for outdoor trees, shrubs, and plants. It covers these items only for the perils of fire, lightning, explosion, riot or civil commotion, or aircraft.

This endorsement increases the coverage on these items and expands it to make them subject to the perils of the policy. The insured may choose to exclude loss caused by vehicles.

Even with open perils coverage, this endorsement still does not cover damage to trees, shrubs, and plants from ice and snow, insects, or animals. The CP 14 30 does not cover outdoor trees, shrubs, and plants for loss from the following:

1.   Dampness or dryness of atmosphere;

2.   Changes in or extremes of temperature; or

3.   Rain, snow, ice, or sleet.

Trees, shrubs, and plants that the insured grows for commercial purposes are not eligible for this coverage, nor is standing timber.

Outdoor Signs, CP 14 40

In the 2007 edition of the commercial property forms, ISO increased the limit of insurance for outdoor signs from $1,000 to $2,500, thus increasing coverage. Coverage was also broadened to include all causes of loss otherwise covered under the applicable causes of loss form.

The Outdoor Signs endorsement, CP 14 40, was revised in accordance with the broadening of coverage on the underlying policies. The endorsement can be used to and to increase the dollar limit.

The schedule contains information about the covered signs' location, materials from which they are constructed, individual limits, coinsurance percentage, applicable causes of loss form, and additional premium.

The endorsement clarifies that the limit in the basic policy no longer applies. Any unscheduled signs, however, remain subject to the limit of liability and the limited causes of loss in the coverage extension.

Peak Season Limit of Insurance, CP 12 30

Some businesses experience seasonal fluctuations in the value of business personal property. This endorsement addresses that issue by providing increased coverage during designated periods of time.

The insured chooses the property that increases in value, the amount of the increase, and the applicable time period.

Reporting form policies are not eligible for this endorsement. Also, the time periods indicated must not extend beyond the expiration date of the policy (the anniversary date if payable in annual installments).

Pier and Wharf Additional Covered Causes of Loss, CP 10 70

Piers and wharves are specifically eliminated as covered property in the property not covered section of the building and personal property form. Such items are covered only if added to the policy via endorsement CP 14 10. They face unusual exposure to certain causes of loss not covered by the basic or broad causes of loss forms. This endorsement extends those causes of loss forms to cover loss caused by floating ice or collision of any vessel or floating object.

All pier and wharf structures are eligible for this endorsement except floating structures or equipment not incidental to a fixed pier or wharf. This endorsement is not used with the special causes of loss form CP 10 30.

Pollutant Cleanup & Removal Additional Aggregate Limit of Insurance, CP 04 07

CP 04 07 provides an additional annual aggregate limit of insurance applicable exclusively to the costs to remove pollutants from land or water at the insured's premises in excess of the $10,000 additional coverage annual aggregate in the property damage forms.

The unendorsed policy provides an aggregate amount of $10,000 to cover the costs of pollutant cleanup and removal. The commercial property policy provides coverage if a covered cause of loss causes the discharge, dispersal, seepage, migration, release, or escape of pollutants. This endorsement increases that annual aggregate amount.

The minimum deductible for this endorsement is $1,000, but it should not be less than the largest direct damage deductible for any of the locations shown on the endorsement. This deductible is independent from the direct damage deductible.

Endorsement CP 04 07 does not come into play until both the underlying amount of $10,000 and the scheduled deductible are exceeded. For example, an insured fuel oil distributor suffers an oil spill. This insured purchased CP 04 07 in the amount of $35,000 with a $5,000 deductible.

Earlier in the year, he used $7,000 of the policy's coverage to pay for another oil spill.

If the current spill involves cleanup charges of $40,000, payment by the insurer is calculated as follows:

$40,000   Cleanup charges

- 3,000 Amount of coverage remaining under CP policy

_- 5,000_ Deductible on endorsement CP 04 07

$32,000 Payment by insurer under the CP 04 07

Protective Safeguards, IL 04 15

As a condition of writing a risk, an insurer may require the installation of protective safeguards or the use of some other type of security device. This endorsement identifies the fire protection safeguards that exist on the insured's property. Such devices fall into one of the following five categories, as enumerated on the endorsement:

P-1 Automatic Sprinkler System, including related supervisory services, meaning:

    (1)   Any automatic fire protective or extinguishing system, including connected:

        (a) Sprinklers and discharge nozzles;

        (b) Ducts, pipes, valves and fittings;

        (c) Tanks, their component parts and supports; and

        (d) Pumps and private fire protection mains.

    (2)   When supplied from an automatic fire protective system:

        (a) Non-automatic fire protective systems; and

        (b) Hydrants, standpipes and outlets.

P-2 Automatic Fire Alarm, protecting the entire building, that is:

> (1)   Connected to a central station; or
>
> (2)   Reporting to a public or private fire alarm station.

P-3 Security Service, with a recording system or watch clock, making hourly rounds covering the entire building, when the premises are not in actual operation.

P-4 Service Contract with a privately owned fire department providing fire protection service to the described premises.

P-9   The protective system described in the Schedule.

The endorsement also clarifies the insured's duties with respect to the maintenance of such systems. The insured must keep the systems in operation and notify the insurance company if they are not working properly.

If the insured does not notify the insurer, coverage is suspended. If an automatic sprinkler must be shut down due to breakage, leakage, freezing conditions, or the opening of sprinkler heads, the insured has forty-eight hours to restore the systems before they must notify the insurer.

Radio or Television Antennas, CP 14 50

The CP policy provides $1,000 coverage for these items but only for limited causes of loss. This endorsement provides an additional amount of coverage, as well as expanding coverage to the perils of the policy. Use of this endorsement removes antennas from the outdoor property coverage extension and adds them as covered property.

This endorsement subjects antennas to the three additional exclusions of dampness or dryness of atmosphere; changes in or extremes of temperature; or rain, snow, ice, or sleet.

Radioactive Contamination, CP 10 37

This endorsement extends coverage for loss caused by sudden and accidental radioactive contamination or resultant radiation damage to the described property. Such damage must arise from material used or stored on the described premises.

The endorsement provides two types of radioactive coverage:

1. Limited—the radioactive contamination must be caused by a covered cause of loss.

2. Broad—does not require that the radioactive contamination be caused by a covered cause of loss.

The location and type of property must be scheduled on the endorsement and the type of coverage desired. However, only broad form coverage may be elected if the insured has the Special Causes of Loss form, CP 10 30.

The endorsement describes three instances where the coverage does not apply:

1. If the described premises contains a functioning nuclear reactor.

2. If the described premises contains any new or used nuclear fuel intended for or used in such a nuclear reactor.

3. If the radioactive material causing the contamination is not located at the described premises.

Report of Values, CP 13 60, and Supplemental Report of Values, CP 13 61

These endorsements are used for submitting reports of property values according to the provisions of the Value Reporting form, CP 13 10. The CP 13 60 no longer refers to itself as an endorsement. ISO says that the word *endorsement* implies a change to the policy and the CP 13 60 makes no changes. Thus, they call it a report.

Spoilage Coverage, CP 04 40

The insured may choose to extend direct coverage for spoilage of perishable stock via this endorsement. ISO lists types of property or occupancy for spoilage coverage, identifying them by class 1, 2, and 3.

Class 1 includes bakery goods, cheese shops, delicatessens, fruits and vegetables, and restaurants. Class 2 includes dairy products (excluding ice cream), grocery stores, meat and poultry markets, pharmaceuticals—non-manufacturing, and supermarkets. Class 3 includes dairy products (including ice cream), florists, greenhouses, and seafood. For other types of property or occupancies not included in any of the three classes, ISO rules say to refer to specific company manuals.

The endorsement offers coverage for loss or damage caused by the following:

    a.   Breakdown or Contamination:

        1.   Change in temperature or humidity resulting from mechanical breakdown or mechanical failure of refrigerating, cooling or humidity control apparatus or equipment, but only while such equipment or apparatus is at the described premises; and

        2.   Contamination by the refrigerant.

    b.   Power outage, meaning change in temperature or humidity resulting from complete or partial interruption of electrical power, either on or off the described premises, due to conditions beyond the insured's control.

If the insured chooses breakdown or contamination coverage, he must keep a refrigeration maintenance agreement in force. If the insured voluntarily terminates the agreement, the coverage is suspended at that location.

This endorsement has a deductible separate from the rest of the policy. The insured may select to value the property at selling price. In that case the insurer determines the value of the property at selling price less any discounts and expenses.

Sprinkler Leakage Exclusion, CP 10 56

An insurer or an insured may wish to exclude sprinkler leakage coverage from some items of property. The declarations indicate such property. If a covered cause of loss results, that damage is covered.

This endorsement may be used with any of the causes of loss forms. On the basic and broad forms, sprinkler leakage is excluded unless caused by a covered cause of loss. Also under the broad form, this endorsement deletes sprinkler leakage as a covered cause of collapse.

The endorsement also makes the following changes to the CP 10 30:

1.   It eliminates coverage for damage done by liquids, powder, and other listed causes that leak or flow from plumbing, heating, air conditioning equipment, and other listed equipment, unless the insured does his best to maintain heat in the structure or drains the system and shuts off the supply if the heat is not maintained.

2.   It agrees to pay for damage to fire extinguishing equipment, if the damage was caused by freezing and the insured:

     a.   does his/her best to maintain heat in the structure; or

     b.   drains the system and shuts off the supply, if the heat is not maintained.

3.   It removes leakage from fire extinguishing equipment from the definition of specified causes of loss.

The 2007 revision added a schedule to this endorsement.

Sprinkler Leakage-Earthquake Extension, CP 10 39

This endorsement adds sprinkler leakage loss or damage caused by earthquake or volcanic eruption as a covered causes of loss. It is not necessary to use the endorsement with causes of loss-earthquake form, CP 10 40, since that form already includes sprinkler leakage coverage.

Storage or Repairs Limited Liability, CP 99 42

This endorsement modifies the term *actual cash value* as it relates to personal property of others in the valuation condition. In the event of a covered loss to such property, the insurer pays the lesser of the property's actual cash value or the value shown on the receipt the insured issued to the owner before the loss.

Tentative Rates, CP 99 93

Used only on specifically rated property, this endorsement states that the premium rates for the commercial property coverage part are tentative and that the insurer will adjust the premium once the rates are determined. If the policy is a renewal, the previous specific rate may need to be changed due to materially changed conditions. The endorsement provides that premium adjustment is effective from the renewal date once the rates are promulgated.

Terrorism Endorsements

Following the September 11, 2001, terrorist attacks and subsequent federal Terrorism Risk Insurance Act (TRIA) ISO developed a series of endorsements to the commercial property program forms related to terrorist acts. A discussion of these endorsements constitute part of Chapter 12.

Theft Exclusion, CP 10 33

If an insurer or insured wishes to exclude theft from a policy subject to the Special Causes of Loss form, CP 10 30, this endorsement is attached. With this endorsement attached, there is no coverage for theft. However, to the following are covered:

1. Loss or damage due to looting at the time and place of a riot or civil commotion;

2. Building damage caused by the breaking in or exiting of burglars; or

3. Any damage caused by a resulting covered cause of loss.

Utility Services - Direct Damage, CP 04 17

This endorsement provides coverage for loss or damage to covered property that results from interruption of water, communication, or power supply services if a covered cause of loss damages any of the properties furnishing these services. The insured may elect to cover one or all of the three exposures.

The form allows the insured to extend coverage for losses resulting from damaged transmission lines listed under both communication and power supply services to lines that are overhead. This coverage is subject to the limit of liability for the covered property.

Vacancy Changes, CP 04 60

The policy says that a building is vacant when at least 31 percent of its square footage is not rented or being used. This endorsement allows that percentage to be reduced to as low as 10 percent. In its explanatory material ISO says this endorsement provides a tool to recognize risks where a lower level of occupancy is sufficient in averting the hazards associated with vacancy.

Endorsements CP 04 50 and CP 04 60 may not be written on the same risk.

Vacancy Permit, CP 04 50

The commercial property policy covers a vacant building for sixty days. After sixty days of vacancy, there is no coverage for loss from vandalism, sprinkler leakage, building glass breakage, water damage, and theft or attempted theft. Also, after sixty days of vacancy, the policy reduces payment for any other covered claim by 15 percent. If the insured desires coverage for a longer period, this endorsement must be attached.

Coverage for direct physical loss or damage applies only to the locations and for the permit periods scheduled on the form or on the declarations. The insured may also exclude vandalism or sprinkler leakage as covered causes of loss during the vacancy for a reduction in premium.

Endorsements CP 04 50 and CP 04 60 may not be written on the same risk.

Value Reporting Form, CP 13 10

The purpose of the value reporting form is to allow an insured who has property that fluctuates in value to be fully protected at all times and to pay a premium based on the values actually at risk—provided the insured reports values correctly and promptly and maintains a sufficient limit of insurance to cover the highest value at any one time. In other words, if the insured follows the policy requirements, the endorsement provides complete and automatic coverage, avoidance of the dangers of both underinsurance and overinsurance on the property, and no necessity of increasing and decreasing amounts of insurance as values move up and down.

The policy indicates how often reports of value must be made to the insurer: daily, weekly, monthly, quarterly, or by policy year. For daily, weekly, monthly, or quarterly reporting, the first report must be made within sixty days of the end of the first reporting period. Subsequent reports must be made within thirty days of the end of each reporting period. A policy with an annual reporting period requires the report to be made within thirty days of the end of the period. At policy expiration, the insurer charges either an additional premium or tenders a refund, based on the average of the insured's reports of value.

The value reporting form contains a 100 percent coinsurance requirement. The insured must report specific insurance on any items. The insurer then subtracts the specific insurance from the values reported when computing the final premium.

If the insured does not submit the necessary reports, the policy calls for two types of penalty. The first is if the insured does not submit an initial report. In that case, any loss payable is reduced by 25 percent. If the insured fails to submit subsequent reports, any loss is adjusted based on the value last reported.

Vandalism Exclusion, CP 10 55

For a reduction in premium, the insured may choose to exclude vandalism. Also, adding this endorsement may transform an otherwise unacceptable underwriting risk into an acceptable one.

Although the endorsement excludes vandalism, it does cover any resulting loss that is not excluded. The endorsement also deletes vandalism from the list of specified causes of loss.

The 2007 revision added a schedule to this endorsement.

Water Exclusion, CP 10 32

Following litigation surrounding the aftermath of 2005's Hurricane Katrina, ISO introduced this 2008 endorsement to replace the water exclusion on the commercial property coverage part or the standard property policy. The purpose of the endorsement is to reinforce the scope of the water exclusion. Also, tsunami and storm surge were added to the list of excluded water. "Otherwise discharged" was added to backup and overflow of sewer, drain, or sump as being excluded. Sump pump and related equipment are new additions, as well.

Watercraft Exclusion, CP 10 35

This endorsement excludes damage by watercraft to the following types of property:

1.   Retaining walls that are not part of a building;

2.   Bulkheads; or

3.   Pilings, piers, wharves, or docks.

This endorsement may be used only with the Special Causes of Loss form, CP 10 30.

Windstorm or Hail Percentage Deductible, CP 03 21

This endorsement allows the insured to choose a deductible for the perils of windstorm or hail, apart from the deductible that applies to all other perils. The available deductibles are 1 percent, 2 percent, or 5 percent of covered property. This deductible is calculated as follows:

A.   Calculation Of The Deductible – All Policies

    1.   A Deductible is calculated separately for, and applies separately to:

        a.   Each building that sustains loss or damage;

        b.   The personal property at each building at which there is loss or damage to personal property;

        c.   Personal property in the open.

        If there is damage to both a building and personal property in that building, separate deductibles apply to the building and to the personal property.

Windstorm or Hail Exclusion - Direct Damage, CP 10 53

An insurance company or an insured may desire to exclude certain property, identified in the declarations from coverage for these perils.

This endorsement modifies the causes of loss forms to eliminate payment for loss caused directly or indirectly by windstorm or hail, regardless of any other cause or event that contributes concurrently or in any sequence to the loss or damage.

It also excludes damage done by rain, snow, or dust resulting from a windstorm. However, any resulting loss that is not excluded is covered.

The endorsement also excludes windstorm or hail damage as a covered cause of collapse and as a specified cause of loss. It also removes windstorm and hail as a covered cause of loss for property in transit.

Windstorm or Hail Exclusion, CP 10 54

The windstorm or hail exclusion extends the windstorm or hail exclusion to also apply to indirect losses covered under: business income coverage forms, extra expense coverage forms, and leasehold interest form.

The 2007 revision added a schedule to this endorsement.

Your Business Personal Property Separation of Coverage, CP 19 10

The various categories of business personal property (stock, contents except stock, machinery and equipment, furniture, fixtures, tenant's improvements and betterments) may be assigned individual limits of insurance by using this endorsement. It also functions as a way to exclude certain types of personal property since any categories not listed with an individual limit of insurance are not covered at the specified locations. Care must be taken in specifying a limit on one class of property at a scheduled location (e.g., stock), so that coverage is not inadvertently voided at that location on another category (e.g., all business personal property except stock).

Chapter 10

The Commercial Properties Program of American Association of Insurance Services (AAIS)

Another major insurance services association that provides loss cost services and policy form development is the American Association of Insurance Services (AAIS). AAIS is a national insurance advisory organization that develops policy forms and rating information used by more than 600 property/casualty insurers throughout the United States. Many insurers that do not subscribe to Insurance Services Offices (ISO) services use the resources of AAIS.

The AAIS program for commercial property exposures is similar to that of ISO, although there are some differences. This chapter highlights those differences.

ISO does not specify what risks are eligible or ineligible for their commercial property program. The AAIS rules manual does contain such a listing. AAIS includes these as eligible risks: habitational, mercantile, nonmanufacturing, and warehousing properties; not eligible for the AAIS commercial properties program are manufacturers and processors, farm operations, and dwellings. AAIS offers other programs for such risks, such as the commercial output program, farm properties program, and dwelling properties program.

In addition to the Building and Personal Property Coverage Part, CP-12, AAIS offers: Builders Risk, CP-14 or CP-15; Condominium Buildings, CP-19; Condominium Unit Coverage, CP-21; Personal Property Coverage Part -Reporting form, CP-25; Earnings Coverage, CP-60; Extra Expense Coverage, CP-69; and Income Coverage, CP-70. This chapter examines the differences between AAIS and ISO in the primary form, the building and personal property coverage part, and in the most often employed causes of loss form, the special perils form, equivalent to ISO's CP 10 30. Having not been revised since its introduction—other than by the development of additional endorsements—the current edition is designated CP-12 Ed. 1.0.

Building and Personal Property Coverage Part

Covered Property

The AAIS form covers essentially the same building property as the ISO form. In addition to the described building, the CP-12 covers the following:

1. Completed additions;

2. Fixtures, machinery, and equipment that are a permanent part of the building;

3. Outdoor fixtures. ISO separates fixtures from machinery and equipment and does not require that fixtures be permanent. However, use of the word *permanent* may be redundant, as the definition of fixture implies permanence;

4. Personal property that the insured owns and uses to maintain or service the building. In addition to fire extinguishing apparatus, floor coverings, and various appliances, AAIS adds air conditioning equipment to the list of examples. Window-unit air conditioners are specifically covered as part of the building;

5. Additions, alterations, and repairs to the building. Also covered are the materials and supplies used to make the alterations. The policy covers these items only if not covered elsewhere.

AAIS provides simplified coverage for business personal property. Instead of a list of the types of personal property covered, the AAIS policy says that it covers the named insured's business personal property in the buildings and structures described. Like ISO, the AAIS form also covers the following:

1. The insured's interest (labor, material, and services) in the property of others;

2. The insured's use interest in improvements and betterments that he makes to a rented building; and

3. Leased personal property for which the insured is obligated to provide insurance.

The final category of covered property is property belonging to others in the insured's care, custody, or control. As with ISO, the AAIS policy provides $2,500 coverage for property of others as a supplemental coverage when the business personal property supplemental coverage is indicated on the declarations page.

Property Excluded and Limitations

The section is similar to the ISO property not covered section, containing many of the same items. This section of the AAIS form also refers to the section of supplemental coverages where property for items otherwise limited or excluded is found.

The AAIS policy lists the following types of property as either excluded or limited in some fashion:

1. **Animals**—like the ISO form, the policy does not cover animals, unless owned by others that the insured boards or animals belonging to the insured that he holds for sale. Unlike ISO, the AAIS policy does not require animals held for sale to be located in buildings.

2. **Antennas, Awnings, Canopies, Fences, and Signs**—AAIS covers these items under supplemental coverages. This portion is more restrictive than ISO because ISO places no limit on awnings or canopies.

3. **Contraband**.

4. **Foundations, Retaining Walls, Pilings, Piers, Wharves, or Docks**—unlike ISO, AAIS does not include bulkheads as property not covered. Also, AAIS does not further define *foundations* as those of buildings, structures, machinery, or boilers.

5. **Land; Water; Growing Crops or Lawns; Cost of Excavation, Grading, of Filling; Paved Surfaces; or Underground Pipes, Flues, or Drains**—although the meaning of *paved* is fairly clear, ISO shows the following as examples: bridges, roadways, walks, patios. AAIS adds driveways and parking lots, but does not specify patios.

6. **Money and Securities**—ISO also excludes deeds, while AAIS does not mention that item.

7. **Property More Specifically Insured**.

8. **Trees, Shrubs, and Plants**—AAIS covers these items under supplemental coverages.

9. **Valuable Papers and Records—Research Cost**—AAIS covers these items under supplemental coverages.

10. **Vehicles, Aircraft, and Watercraft**. The AAIS policy makes an exception for the following (thus providing coverage):

    a. vehicles the insured manufactures, processes, warehouses, or holds for sale (other than autos held for sale) and

    b. rowboats or canoes that are at the described premises and not in the water.

The ISO policy excludes personal property while airborne or waterborne. AAIS has no such exclusion.

Additional Coverages

The AAIS building and personal property coverage part contains the following additional coverages:

1. **Debris Removal**—the policy covers debris removal for up to 25 percent of the amount spent for the direct damage. This amount is included in the limit of liability. Unlike ISO, AAIS makes no mention of the deductible, thus limiting the insured's cover-

age for debris removal to 25 percent of the paid loss. The AAIS policy provides an additional $5,000 of debris removal when the total loss exceeds the limit of liability or when the 25 percent is not adequate.

2. **Emergency Removal**—this is like ISO's preservation of property provision, but AAIS covers the moved personal property for ten days (ISO's policy covers for thirty days).

3. **Fire Department Service Charges**—$1,000..

4. **Pollutant Clean Up and Removal**—$10,000

Supplemental Coverages

AAIS offers several supplemental coverages that are comparable to ISO's coverage extensions. These coverages are available only if a coinsurance percentage of 80 percent or more is shown on the declarations. Unless otherwise indicated, all of these supplemental coverages represent additional amounts of insurance.

These coverages are available only when a limit is shown for either building or business personal property:

a. **Antennas, Awnings, Canopies, Fences, and Signs**—$1,000 coverage for loss caused by fire, lightning, aircraft, riot or civil commotion, or explosion. AAIS specifically includes antenna masts, towers, and lead-in wiring. The $1,000 includes direct damage and debris removal.

b. **Property Off-Premises**—$5,000 for property temporarily off-premises, including stock (merchandise held for sale). ISO provides $10,000. This supplemental coverage does not apply to property in a vehicle, in the care of the insured's salespersons, or at a fair or exhibition.

The following coverages are available only when a limit is shown for building property:

a. **Increased Costs - Ordinance or Law**—up to $5,000 for each described premises to cover such costs. ISO's policy contains $10,000 coverage in the basic policy.

b. **Newly Acquired Buildings**—this coverage applies to buildings that are either built or acquired during the policy period. It is broader than ISO's similar provision. Unlike the ISO policy, AAIS does not restrict coverage for buildings being constructed "on the described premises." The limit available under AAIS is an amount equal to 25 percent of the current building limit, with a maximum of $250,000.

c. **Trees, Shrubs, and Plants.** The AAIS policy covers these for $1,000, subject to a maximum of $250 for any one tree, shrub, or plant. It provides coverage for these items for the perils of aircraft, civil commotion, explosion, fire, lightning, or riot.

The following coverages are available only when a limit is shown for business personal property:

a. **Condominium Units**—if the described premises is a condo, AAIS provides up to 10 percent of the limit (maximum of $20,000) for fixtures, improvements, and alterations. This amount is included in the limit of liability. ISO has no similar coverage.

b. **Extra Expenses**—$1,000 to cover extra expense incurred in order to continue business after a covered loss. ISO offers this coverage only as part of the business income and extra expense form.

c. **Personal Effects**—$500 for personal effects owned by the named insured or his officers, partners, or employees. The per person limit is $100. ISO offers up to $2,500 per described premises with no per person maximum.

d. **Personal Property - Acquired Locations**—thirty-day coverage for personal property at acquired locations. AAIS provides this coverage in the amount of 10 percent of the business personal property limit, with a maximum of $100,000. This coverage does not apply to property at fairs or exhibitions.

e. **Personal Property of Others**—$2,500 coverage. Unlike ISO, the AAIS policy also covers this property for the peril of theft.

f. **Property in Transit**—$1,000 coverage for property in vehicles that the insured owns, leases, or operates. This coverage is available only with the special causes of loss form under the ISO program. The AAIS policy requires visible marks of forced entry.

g. **Valuable Papers and Records-Research Cost**—$1,000 coverage, compared to ISO's $2,500.

What Must Be Done in Case of Loss

The AAIS policy lists the following loss conditions:

a. **Notice**—prompt notice must be given to the insurer or the agent. ISO makes no mention of agent, although in general practice it is notice to the agent or broker that triggers notice to the insurer.

b. **Protect Property**.

c. **Proof of Loss**—while ISO merely says that the proof of loss must contain the information that the insurer requests, AAIS spells out what must be included in the proof:

 1. Time, place, and circumstance of loss;

 2. Other policies that might cover the loss;

 3. The insured's interest in the damaged property as well as the interests of any others;

 4. Changes in the title or occupancy;

 5. Detailed estimates for repair or replacement of the covered property;

 6. Plans and specifications of buildings or structures;

 7. Detailed estimates of income loss and expenses; and

 8. Inventory of damaged and undamaged property. AAIS does not require an inventory of the undamaged property if the loss is less than $10,000 or less than 5 percent of the total limit.

d. **Examination under Oath.**

e.   **Records**—these must be produced if the insurer requests.

f.   **Damaged Property**—must be available for inspection.

g.   **Volunteer Payments**—the insured must not make any voluntary payments, except at his own expense. This provision does not appear in ISO's policy.

h.   **Abandonment.**

i.   **Cooperation.**

Valuation

The AAIS form specifies that if replacement cost is not shown on the declarations page, all losses are adjusted at actual cash value (ACV). This provision describes seven other valuations:

1.   **Limited Replacement Cost**—as with ISO, if the building meets the coinsurance requirement and the loss is less than $2,500, replacement cost applies.

2.   **Glass**—safety glass is used when required by law.

3.   **Merchandise Sold**—at selling price less all discounts and unincurred expenses. ISO refers to this as stock sold but not delivered.

4.   **Valuable Papers and Records**—the cost of blank materials and the labor to transcribe the records.

5.   **Tenant's Improvements**—at ACV if repaired within a reasonable time. If not repaired, the value is based on a portion of the original cost new. This provision is the same as ISO.

6.   **Pair or Set/Loss to Parts**—neither of these clauses appears in ISO's policy.

7.   **Replacement Cost**—this is an option, as with ISO. AAIS specifies that replacement cost does not apply to objects of art, rarity, or antiquity, or to property of others. It also does not apply to paragraphs two through six.

How Much We Pay

This section details six things that determine the amount of loss payable.

1. **Insurable Interest**—AAIS' "insurable interest" is the same as the ISO policy concept of "financial interest."

2. **Deductible**—Unlike ISO, the AAIS form applies the deductible before application of the coinsurance penalty. This formula results in a more favorable result for the insured.

3. **Loss Settlement Terms**—the AAIS policy agrees to pay the lesser of the following:

    a. the value of the property, as described in the valuation provision;

    b. the cost to repair, replace, or rebuild with materials of like kind and quality; or

    c. the limit applicable.

4. **Coinsurance**—the principle is the same as in ISO. To figure a loss divide amount of insurance carried by amount required and multiply by the amount of the loss. The difference from ISO is how the deductible is applied. ISO applies it after application of the coinsurance penalty; AAIS applies it before the coinsurance penalty. AAIS's method is more favorable to the insured, as shown in the following example:

    Value of the property: $2,000,000

    Coinsurance percentage: 80%

    Amount of Insurance Carried: $1,000,000

    Deductible: $10,000

    Amount of loss: $ 400,000

ISO Method:

Step 1: $2,000,000 times 80% = $1,600,000 (amount required)

Step 2: $1,000,000 divided by $1,600,000 = .625

Step 3: $ 400,000 x .625 = $250,000

Step 4: $ 250,000 - $10,000 = $240,000 (payment by the insurer)

AAIS Method:

Step (1): $2,000,000 x 80% = $1,600,000 (amount required)

Step (2): $1,000,000 divided by $1,600,000 = .625

Step (3): $ 400,000 - $10,000 = $390,000

Step (4): $ 390,000 x .625 = $243,750 (payment by the insurer)

5. **Insurance Under More Than One Coverage**—same as ISO.

6. **Insurance Under More Than One Policy**—same as ISO.

Loss Payment

The AAIS policy provides the insurer with the same four options that ISO provides:

1. Pay the value of loss;

2. Pay the cost of repairing or replacing the loss;

3. Rebuild, repair, or replace with property of equivalent kind and quality, to the extent practicable; or

4. Take all or any part of the damaged property at an agreed or appraised value.

The insurer must advise the insured of its intentions within thirty days of receipt of the proof of loss.

Payment for the insured's losses are adjusted with the insured unless another loss payee is named in the policy. A covered loss is payable thirty days after the following:

1. The insurer receives a satisfactory proof of loss;

2. The amount of loss has been agreed to in writing; an appraisal award has been filed with the insurer; or

3. A final judgment has been entered.

Payment for loss to property of others may be adjusted with the insured on behalf of the owner or directly with the owner.

Other Conditions

The AAIS policy is subject to four additional conditions:

1. **Appraisal**—similar to ISO's condition, but the AAIS policy imposes certain time limits. After the demand for the appraisal each party has twenty days to give the name of its appraiser to the other. The appraisers then have fifteen days to select an umpire, or either party may then submit the umpire choice to a court.

2. **Mortgage Provisions**—identical to ISO, which calls its provision "Mortgageholders."

3. **Recoveries**—this is called "Recovered Property" in ISO. This condition is similar to ISO's, with one exception. If the insurer's payment for the original loss is less than the agreed loss due to a deductible or other limiting term in the policy the AAIS policy calls for any recovery to be prorated between the insurer and the insured.

4. **Vacancy-Unoccupancy**—the AAIS policy imposes one of two penalties on the insured if a building is vacant for more than sixty consecutive days. It also imposes a penalty if the building is unoccupied for the longer of sixty consecutive days or the usual

or incidental unoccupancy period for the described premises. The penalties are as follows:

a.   No payment at all for loss from theft, attempted theft, glass breakage, sprinkler leakage, vandalism, or water damage; and

b.   Any other loss payable is reduced by 15 percent.

Special Causes of Loss Form

The AAIS Special Perils Part, CP-85, is similar to ISO's Special Causes of Loss form, CP 10 30.

The AAIS form provides three additional definitions: *sinkhole collapse*; *specified perils*; and *volcanic action*. The definitions of *sinkhole collapse* and *specified perils* are the same as in ISO, but ISO includes *sinkhole collapse* within the definition of specified perils. *Volcanic action* is the same as in ISO, but ISO includes it within the earth movement exclusion, the effect being the same.

The AAIS form covers risks of direct physical loss subject to the following exclusions:

1.   **Ordinance or Law**.

2.   **Earth Movement or Volcanic Eruption**.

3.   **Civil Authority**—this is called "Governmental Action" in ISO.

4.   **Nuclear Hazard**.

5.   **Utility Failure**—called "Utility Services" in ISO. AAIS also excludes "reduced or increased voltage, low or high pressure, or other interruptions of normal services."

6.   **War**—like ISO, but AAIS adds that the discharge of a nuclear weapon, even if accidental, is an act of war.

7.   **Water**—AAIS's form contains two differences from ISO. It does not include mudslide or mudflow as types of water damage and AAIS does not exclude water that backs up or overflows from a sump. This second difference is a significant benefit to the policyholder, who under an ISO form does not even have

the opportunity to buy-back coverage for sump-pump overflow. (That option is available in the ISO homeowners program.)

These seven items are excluded regardless of other causes or events that contribute to or aggravate the loss (concurrent causation language).

The following exclusions also apply, but any subsequent loss is covered if not excluded elsewhere:

1. **Animals**—the only subsequent losses that are covered must be caused by a specified peril or glass breakage.

2. **Collapse**—except as provided in the additional coverage.

3. **Contamination or Deterioration**—this includes "corrosion, decay, fungus, mildew, mold, rot, rust, or any quality, faulty, or weakness in property that causes it to damage or destroy itself." As with ISO, subsequent losses caused by a specified peril or glass breakage are covered.

4. **Criminal, Fraudulent, or Dishonest Acts**—as with ISO, losses caused by such acts of the insured, partners, and directors are not covered. AAIS adds the category of "others who have an interest in the property." For instance, such acts committed by the mortgagee might not be covered.

5. **Defects, Errors, and Omissions**—in things such as land use, design, construction, and workmanship. Any ensuing loss not excluded is covered.

6. **Electrical Currents**. ISO calls this exclusion "Electrical, Magnetic, or Electromagnetic Energy."

7. **Explosion**—of steam boilers, steam pipes, steam turbines, or steam engines owned or operated by the insured.

8. **Freezing**—of water, other liquids, powder, or molten material.

9. **Increased Hazard**—not contained in ISO.

10. **Loss of Use**—includes loss of market.

11. **Mechanical Breakdown.**

12. **Neglect**—to save covered property at the time of a loss or when covered property is endangered by a covered peril.

13. **Pollutants.**

14. **Seepage** of steam.

15. **Settling, Cracking, Shrinking, Bulging, or Expanding**—AAIS adds bulging to this list.

16. **Smog, Smoke, Vapor, or Gas.**

17. **Temperature/Humidity.**

18. **Voluntary Parting.**

19. **Wear and Tear.**

20. **Weather.**

Additional Property Excluded and Limitations

1. **Animals**—are covered only if their death or destruction is caused by a specified peril or glass breakage. ISO covers animals if they are killed or their destruction is made necessary.

2. **Boilers.**

3. **Building Materials**—are covered only if held for sale by the insured.

4. **Furs**—covered for $2,500 per occurrence of theft.

5. **Glass Breakage**—$100 per pane, $500 per occurrence. For loss by the specified perils, the policy provides unlimited glass coverage (other than for loss by vandalism).

6. **Glassware/Fragile Articles**—breakage is covered only if caused by one of the specified perils.

7. **Gutters and Downspouts**—not covered for loss due to weight of ice, sleet, or snow.

8. **Interior of Buildings**—not covered for damage from rain, snow, sleet, ice, or dust unless the exterior first suffers damage from a specified peril or the loss is caused by thawing.

9. **Sub-Limits on Certain Types of Property**—theft of jewelry, watches, jewels, pearls, precious stones, and metals is limited to $2,500 per occurrence; theft of patterns, dies, molds, models, and forms is also limited to $2,500 per occurrence; theft of tickets, stamps, or letters of credit is limited to $250 per occurrence. ISO also limits theft of furs to $2,500 per occurrence, but AAIS's policy does not contain such a limitation.

10. **Builders Machinery, Tools, and Equipment**—same as ISO.

11. **Missing Property**—same as ISO.

12. **Personal Property in the Open**—same as ISO.

13. **Transferred Property**—same as ISO.

14. **Valuable Papers and Records**—same as ISO.

Additional Coverages

The AAIS policy contains two additional coverages:

1. **Collapse**—same as ISO for the causes of collapse. However, the AAIS form does not define collapse nor does it limit collapse by defining what is not collapse.

2. **Tearing Out and Replacing**—same as ISO.

Other Coverage Parts

In addition to the building and personal property coverage part, AAIS offers the following:

1. Builders Risk - Completed Value

2. Builders Risk - Reporting Form

3. Condominium Building Coverage Part

4. Condominium Unit Coverage Part

5. Personal Property Coverage Part - Reporting Form

6. Earnings Coverage Part

7. Extra Expense Coverage Part

8. Income Coverage Part

9. Basic and Broad Form Perils

10. Earthquake Perils

Endorsements

The following endorsements are available under the AAIS commercial property program:

1. Alcoholic Beverages Manufacturers - Finished Stock, CP-611

2. Alcoholic Beverages Valuation, CP-110

3. Antenna Coverage, CP-606

4. Automatic Increase, CP-111

5. Biological and Chemical Non-certified Act of Terrorism Exclusion, CL-0550

6. Brand or Label Permit, CP-112

7. Certified Terrorism Losses, CL-0500

8. Certified Act of Terrorism Exclusion, CL-0610

9. Conditional Terrorism Exclusion, CL-1630

10. Condominium Buildings Exclusion - Entire Units, CP-119

11. Condominium Buildings Exclusion – Improvements, CP-120

12. Condominium Loss Assessment Coverage, CP-121

13. Condominium Units Exclusion, CP-122

14. Contributing Insurance, CP-124

15. Debris Removal Coverage, CP-125

16. Deductible Schedule, CP-127

17. Electric Utility Coverage - $1,000 Deductible, CP-129

18. Electronic Information, CP-147

19. Equipment Breakdown Coverage, CP-0629

20. Expanded Restoration Period - Extra Expense, CP-77

21. Explosion Limitation for Grain Risks, CP-612

22. Explosion Limitation for Public Utility Gas Risks, CP-613

23. Functional Replacement Cost, CP-608

24. Household Personal Property, CP-24

25. Income Coverage from Dependent Locations - Separate Limits, CP-67

26. Income Coverage from Dependent Locations, CP-68

27. Increased Restoration Period - Ordinance or Law, CP-148

28. Limited Fungus and Related Perils Coverage, CP-0640

29. Loss Payable Options, CP-132

30. Manufactured Stock Valuation, CP-133

31. Market Price Valuation - Distilled Spirits, CP-135

32. Market Price Valuation – Stock, CP-134

33. Market Price Valuation – Wines, CP-136

34. Market Value, CP-609

35. Mine Subsidence Coverage, FO-158

36. Non-certified Act of Terrorism Exclusion, CL-0630

37. Optional Property Coverage, CP-23

38. Ordinance or Law Extension - Increased Cost of Construction, CP-138

39. Ordinary Payroll Exclusion, CP-140

40. Ordinary Payroll Limitation, CP-141

41. Outdoor Signs, CP-605

42. Peak Season Increase, CP-144

43. Perils Exclusion, CP-145

44. Pollutant Clean Up and Removal Coverage, CP-123

45. Power, Heat, and Refrigeration Exclusion, CP-153

46. Premium Payments, CP-155

47. Property Excluded, CP-157

48. Protective Devices, CP-614

49. Radioactive Contamination - Broad Coverage, CP-91

50. Radioactive Contamination - Limited Coverage Report Values, CP-160

51. Resident Agent Countersignature, CP-162

52. Seasonal Leases, CP-73

53. Specific Insurance, CP-164

54. Spoilage Coverage, CP-601

55. Sprinkler Leakage Earthquake Extension, CP-165

56. Storage or Repairs Valuation, CP-167

57. Terrorism Exclusions, CL-2630

58. Theft Exclusion, CP-189

59. Trees, Shrubs, and Plants, CP-610

60. Tuition Coverage, CP-75

61. Utility Interruption - Property Damage, CP-94

62. Utility Interruption - Time Element, CP-95

63. Vacancy or Unoccupancy Permit, CP-170.

64. War and Terrorism Exclusions, CL-0468

65. War, Military Action, and Terrorism Exclusion, CL-0469

66. Water Damage - Backup of Sewers and Drains, CP-607

Chapter 11

E-Issues under the Commercial Property Policy

Intangible Property

"We are heading at blinding speed into a completely new world built on a foundation of information and communication technology. Change—driven by technology and put in motion across society—will be the biggest risk of all to manage." That provocative prediction was penned in 1998 and by Scott K. Lange, former risk manager for Microsoft, for *E-Risk, Liabilities in a Wired World*, published by the National Underwriter Company when the issues of electronic and intangible property were under development.

Today a business's only property may be intangible—its customer records, services, accounts, trademarks, brands, patents, and copyrights. Such assets are often of far greater importance than the traditional tangible assets disclosed on balance sheets. Intangible property is the fuel of e-commerce. The National Underwriter Co. book *Cyber Liability and Insurance: Managing the Risks of Intangible Assets* contains what is referred to as a "Substantially Incomplete List of Intangible Assets" that shows how broad the area of intangible assets has grown in the modern era. Borrowed from there and reproduced here, intangible assets nonexclusively include:

1.   Marketing Assets

   •   Trademarks and service marks

- Trade names and brand names

- Logotypes

- Colors

2. Technology Assets

- Patents and patent applications

- Technical documentation (e.g., laboratory notebooks, technical know-how)

3. Artistic Assets

- Maps

- Literary works and copyrights

- Musical compositions

- Photographs

4. Data Processing Assets

- Software and software copyrights

- Databases

5. Engineering Assets

- Industrial designs

- Engineering drawings, schematics, and blue prints.

- Technical know-how and trade secrets

6. Customer-Related Assets

- Customer relationships, contracts, and lists

- Open purchase orders

7. Contractual Assets

- License and franchise agreements

- Operating license

8. Human Capital Assets

- Trained workforce and wages

- Union and other employment contracts

9. Location-Related Assets

- Easements and mineral exploitation rights

- Water and air rights

10. Online-Related Assets

- Domain names and Web site design

- Linkages

The commercial property policy was developed and evolved as a vehicle by which tangible property—buildings and structures, business personal property, property of others on the insured's premises—is protected. Thus, there have been some conflicts in scope of coverage, resulting in the revamping of standard policies. For example, the building and personal property form has been revised to specifically include electronic data in the property not covered section of the form. (See Chapter 1.)

Because of the growing importance of intangible assets and the challenges of cyber-security, protecting this type of property has become a major challenge facing agents, insurers, and risk managers. The traditional insurance mechanism for protecting tangible property must be reevaluated in light of the e-business world.

Insuring Intangible Assets

This country's founding fathers recognized the right of individuals and companies to protect their intellectual property. Article I, Section 8 of the Constitution says: "Congress shall have power to promote the progress of science and useful arts, by securing for limited times to authors and inventors the exclusive right to their respective writings and discoveries."

In order to properly protect these assets, they must be adequately and fully described for the insurer. Insurers have developed specialized applications for e-property.

One problem faced by insurers is how to value such assets. Traditional property can be appraised and a value set. Such property and the things that happen to it usually can be seen. But in cyber-liability instead of physically appraising a building, insurers must grapple with the following questions:

- What is the value of a concept?

- What is the value of research and development?

- What is the value of a name?

- What is the value of customer service?

- What is the value of advertising?

- What is the value of speed to market?

- What is the value of a reputation?

A simple example will suffice. What happens when an employee's laptop computer is stolen, as has happened at banks, universities, and even within the federal government? The company did not lose just the value of the physical laptop. Of much more value is the data stored on the laptop. And how is it quantified? Is it the cost to recreate the data or the cost of the physical components? The building and personal property form has been revised in various ways described in this work, for example see the treatment of electronic data in that form's property covered section in Chapter 1.

Some courts have decided that in view of the language in current policies, damage to data is not damage to tangible property and thus not covered. In *Seagate Technology, Inc., v. St. Paul Fire & Marine Ins. Co.*, 11 F. Supp.2d 1150 (N.D. Cal. 1998), a manufacturer of hardware lost the battle in court when trying to prove that defective hard drives had caused ensuing damage to tangible property. The basic holding is that the typical property insurance policy responds only to actual physical damage to a company's hardware or equipment. The forms have been clarified with this intent, as is discussed in the property not covered portion of Chapter 1 and the coverage extensions and additional coverage material in Chapter 2.

Hardly remembered by many in the IT world now, the problem known as Y2K became a nonevent on January 1, 2000. But, up until that time there was much concern on the part of businesses and their insurers. Much time, effort, pain, and press were given to the specter of the Y2K dilemma— would many computer systems cease to function as their programming was based on a 20th century calendar?—as it was expected to touch every industry, company, office, and home that utilized any aspect of technology. Everything from NASA systems to coffeepot timers were anticipated to malfunction.

The Meaning of *Property*

The building and personal property coverage form promises to pay for "direct physical loss or damage to covered property at the premises described in the Declarations caused by or resulting from any Covered Cause of Loss." In the traditional sense, property has always meant tangible property. However, the interpretation of the word *property* was challenged in court as the importance of electronic data rose. The interpretation of the word *property* has implications both for direct damage policies and business income policies. A business income policy requires damage to property at the described premises before coverage applies. If data is not property there is no insured business income loss.

In one case, *American Guarantee & Liability Ins. Co. v. Ingram Micro, Inc.*, 2000 U.S. Dist. LEXIS 7299 (D. Ariz. April 18, 2000) the judge termed such use of the word property as "archaic." In that case, Ingram Micro lost data when its computers were shut down due to a power outage. Because the only property damaged was the data, the insurer denied payment for any direct loss and for any business interruption loss. The insurer claimed that the only thing lost was data. In addition to his description of the policy interpretation as archaic, the judge also said, "At a time when computer technology dominates our professional as well as personal lives, the Court must side with Ingram's broader definition of physical damage."

The problem is that the standard property policy protects against a range of standard perils. In this new world, insureds face not only direct damage to their property, but interruption of their services. Such losses may involve a hacker getting into a company's records or Web site. Email may be stolen; access to the Web site may be severely limited. All of this costs the insured money, but these are not the exposures contemplated in the historical actuarial evolution of property rates. The answer has been to revise the building and personal property coverage form to limit electronic data and the cost to restore or recreate it, but the industry has also responded with a number of specialty and nonstandard coverage forms.

E-Property Policies

As a response to the issues surrounding e-property, insurers have developed policies to protect it. Generally, these policies fall into one of the following three categories:

- Third-party liability

- Prosecution or abatement

- First-party liability/loss

Because it is not within the purview of this book to examine third-party issues, this discussion is limited to the first-party issues surrounding e-property (see *Cyber Liability and Insurance: Managing the Risks of Intangible Assets*, published by The National Underwriter Company, for more information). Specialty coverage is available, but it is generally limited and subject to strict underwriting requirements. Such a policy pays the insured for the value of its intellectual property when a patent is stolen or a trade secret is misappropriated.

Many patents are issued each year to small businesses. Often these businesses have few, if any assets and not much cash. How can they protect their patents? One type of insurance policy is aimed at these small businesses. It provides money for *offensive litigation* once the policyholder discovers its patent has been infringed. The policyholder must document the infringement to the insurer. When the insurer is satisfied that infringement has taken place, it provides the policyholder with money to finance its litigation against the infringer. Knowing that the patent holder has access to resources to finance litigation, the infringer may be more cooperative in reaching a settlement.

The standard building and personal property coverage form has been revised to exclude electronic data under the property not covered section but provides a limited additional coverage for electronic data loss, including viruses and hacker attacks. There are also several excess and surplus lines carriers who write first-party coverage for e-assets. These policies protect against damage from the following:

1. Unauthorized access to a company's Web site;

2. Insertion of unauthorized code (a virus) into a company's system;

3. Denial of service (for example, the flooding of a site with thousands of email messages, making it difficult or impossible for the company to use the site); and

4. Denial of access (in this scenario, the wrong doer redirects traffic away from the insured's Web site, thus causing the loss of business).

In order to collect, the policies typically say that the act must be malicious. If the attacker cannot be caught, malice cannot be shown.

The last issue to examine is valuation. What these policies protect is the insured's revenue stream from his operations. As with business income policies, they settle based on actual loss sustained. Under these forms, the insured estimates business income losses and insures accordingly. The problem is in the adjustment of claims. The insured will not realize what the settlement is until the claim has been adjusted.

In many businesses the Web site and other e-operations do not earn a profit. In that case, the net loss on the Web site operation may offset any potential recovery under a business income form. Because there are no physical items to rebuild after a Web site attack, the typical site is down for only a few hours or days. Thus, the amount of income lost may appear small.

A careful review of policy language is needed when selecting coverage and a carrier to provide that coverage. Most agents will likely choose two or, perhaps, three carriers to use, so the initial choice is critical. Despite the fact that many carriers were initially reluctant to formally design products for this market, the insurers that offer coverage tend to change their forms frequently. Additional coverage to address a special exposure may be available by endorsement or through manuscript wording.

Chapter 12

Miscellaneous Commercial Property Coverage Issues

Since the introduction of the first edition of this work some commercial property coverage areas have arisen that were not the issues they have become. Primarily are the development of various terrorism endorsements following the terrorist attacks of September 11, 2001, and the subsequently enacted federal Terrorism Risk Insurance Act of 2002 (TRIA) and the Terrorism Risk Insurance Program Reauthorization Act of 2007, which extends the Terrorism Risk Insurance Act through December 31, 2014; and the hurricane seasons of 2004 and 2005 with their attendant coverage questions and disputes following hurricane, flooding, and windstorm damage and conventional insurance policies' response.

ISO Interline Terrorism Endorsements

Following the property losses due to the terrorist attacks of September 11, 2001, there was a need to clarify the insurance industry role in coverage for catastrophic damage caused by terrorist acts and the responsibility of the government. In compliance with the Terrorism Risk Insurance Extension Act (TRIA) Insurance Services Office (ISO) issued a number of endorsements for use with the commercial property policy that exclude or provide limited coverage for terrorist acts. TRIA was originally enacted in 2002. The Terrorism Risk Insurance Extension Act was enacted in 2005, followed by the Terrorism Risk Insurance Program Reauthorization Act of 2007.

The 2005 extension revised the 2002 act's definition of *insurer deductible* to include provisions for the years 2006 and 2007. The extension also excluded commercial auto, burglary and theft, surety, and farm owners multiperil insurance from its definition of *property and casualty insurance*. A new program trigger was also added, stating that for any certified act occurring after March 31, 2006, federal compensation will be paid only if resulting aggregate industry losses exceed $50 million in 2006 and $100 million in 2007.

The federal share of compensation was 90 percent of the insured losses exceeding the insurer deductible in 2006; 85 percent in 2007. The insurance marketplace aggregate retention amount for purposes of recouping the federal share was $25 billion for 2006 and $27.5 billion for 2007.

The 2007 extension changed the definition of *certified act of terrorism* to include acts executed by domestic terrorists. The deductible was fixed at 20 percent multiplied by the direct earned premium for the preceding calendar year. The federal share was also fixed at 85 percent.

The introduction to the Terrorism supplement to the ISO Commercial Lines Manual (CLM) explains the federal Terrorism Risk Insurance Act of 2002 and its effect on and coverage response from the insurance industry:

- The Terrorism Risk Insurance Act (TRIA) establishes a program within the Department of the Treasury in which the Federal Government will share the risk of loss from terrorist attacks with the insurance industry. Federal participation will be triggered when the Secretary of the Treasury certifies an act of terrorism, in concurrence with the Secretary of State and the Attorney General of the United States, to be an act of terrorism committed by an individual(s) acting on behalf of any foreign interest, provided the terrorist act results in aggregate losses in excess of an amount stated in the Act. With respect to insured losses resulting from a certified act of terrorism, the Federal Government will reimburse individual insurers for a percentage of losses (as stated in the Act) in excess of the insurer's retention, which is based on a specified percentage of the insurer's earned premium for the year preceding the loss. Insured losses covered by the program are capped at $100 billion per year unless subsequent action of Congress changes that amount; this provision serves to limit insurers' liability for losses. All insurers providing commercial property insurance are required to participate in the program to the extent of offering and making available coverage for certified acts of terrorism in accordance with the terms and conditions of coverage which apply to other perils.

- For all new and renewal business, an insurer must make available to insureds coverage for losses caused by certified acts of terrorism. The insurer must disclose to the policyholder the premium for losses covered and the federal share of compensation for such losses under the program at the time of offer, purchase and renewal of the policy.

To accomplish this, Insurance Services Office (ISO) has developed a number of interline endorsements (meaning they apply across various lines of coverage). These endorsements are used with up to a dozen coverage parts, including the following:

- Boiler and Machinery

- Commercial Crime Coverage Form

- Commercial Crime Policy

- Commercial Inland Marine

- Commercial Property Coverage Part

- Employee Theft and Forgery Policy

- Farm Coverage Part

- Government Crime Coverage Form

- Government Crime Policy

- Kidnap/ransom and extortion coverage form

- Kidnap/Ransom and Extortion Policy

- Standard Property Policy

With the passage of the 2002 TRIA and its extensions in 2005 and 2007, ISO has developed and filed many terrorism-related endorsements. Some of the endorsements exclude or limit terrorism coverage, some provide disclosures as required by TRIA, and some are conditional on TRIA being terminated or replaced with provisions that do not require insurers to make terrorism coverage available (with certain conditions).

The following is a list of the current terrorism endorsements (as of this book's printing) provided by ISO:

- Exclusion of Terrorism, IL 00 30 01 06

- Exclusion of Terrorism Involving Nuclear, Biological or Chemical Terrorism, IL 00 31 01 06

- Limitation of Coverage for Terrorism -- Sub-Limit on Annual Aggregate Basis, IL 00 32 01 06

- Exclusion of Terrorism (with Limited Exception) and Exclusion of War and Military Action, IL 09 37 01 02

- Exclusion of War, Military Action and Terrorism, IL 09 38 01 02

- Exclusion of Terrorism (with Limited Exception) and Exclusion of War and Military Action, IL 09 40 01 02

- Exclusion of War, Military Action and Terrorism, IL 09 41 01 02

- Coverage for Certified Acts of Terrorism; Cap on Losses, IL 09 50 11 02

- Removal of Exclusion of Acts of Terrorism; Cap on Certain Losses, IL 09 51 11 02

- Cap on Losses from Certified Acts of Terrorism, IL 09 52 03 08

- Exclusion of Certified Acts of Terrorism, IL 09 53 01 08

- Limited Exclusion of Acts of Terrorism (Other Than Certified Acts of Terrorism); Cap on Losses from Certified Acts OF Terrorism; Coverage for Certain Fire Losses, IL 09 54 11 02

- Exclusion of Acts of Biological or Chemical Terrorism; Cap on Losses From Certified Acts of Terrorism; Coverage for Certain Fire Losses, IL 09 55 11 02

- Exclusion of Certified Acts and Other Acts of Terrorism; Coverage for Certain Fire Losses, IL 09 56 11 02

- Exclusion of Certified Acts of Terrorism and Biological or Chemical Acts of Terrorism; Coverage for Certain Fire Losses, IL 09 57 11 02

- Exclusion of Certified Acts of Terrorism, IL 09 58 11 02

- Limited Exclusion of Acts of Terrorism (Other Than Certified Acts of Terrorism); Cap on Losses from Certified Acts of Terrorism, IL 09 59 11 02

- Exclusion of Acts of Biological or Chemical Terrorism; Cap on Losses from Certified Acts of Terrorism, IL 09 60 11 02

- Exclusion of Certified Acts and Other Acts of Terrorism, IL 09 61 11 02

- Exclusion of Certified Acts of Terrorism and Biological or Chemical Acts of Terrorism, IL 09 62 11 02

- Exclusion of Certified Acts of Terrorism; Coverage for Certain Fire Losses, IL 09 68 11 02

- Limited Exclusion of Acts of Terrorism (Other Than Certified Acts of Terrorism); Cap on Losses from Certified Acts of Terrorism; Coverage for Certain Fire Losses, IL 09 69 11 02

- Exclusion of Acts of Biological or Chemical Terrorism; Cap on Losses from Certified Acts of Terrorism; Coverage for Certain Fire Losses, IL 09 70 11 02

- Exclusion of Certified Acts and Other Acts of Terrorism; Coverage for Certain Fire Losses, IL 09 71 11 02

- Exclusion of Certified Acts of Terrorism and Biological or Chemical Acts of Terrorism; Coverage for Certain Fire Losses, IL 09 72 11 02

- Disclosure Pursuant to Terrorism Risk Insurance Act, IL 09 85 01 08

- Exclusion of Certified Acts of Terrorism Involving Nuclear, Biological or Chemical Terrorism; Cap on Covered Certified Acts Losses, IL 09 86 03 08

- Limitation of Coverage for Certified Acts of Terrorism (Sub-Limit on Annual Aggregate Basis), IL 09 87 03 08

- Exclusion of Certified Acts and Other Acts of Terrorism Involving Nuclear, Biological or Chemical Terrorism; Cap on Covered Certified Acts Losses, IL 09 91 12 03

- Limitation of Coverage for Certified Acts and Other Acts of Terrorism (Sub-Limit on Annual Aggregate Basis), IL 09 92 12 03

- Conditional Exclusion of Terrorism (Relating to Disposition of Federal Terrorism Risk Insurance Act), IL 09 95 01 07

- Conditional Exclusion of Terrorism Involving Nuclear, Biological or Chemical Terrorism (Relating to Disposition of Federal Terrorism Risk Insurance Act), IL 09 96 01 07

- Conditional Limitation of Coverage for Terrorism - Sub-Limit on Annual Aggregate Basis (Relating to Disposition of Federal Terrorism Risk Insurance Act), IL 09 97 01 07

- Disclosure of Premium through End of Year for Certified Acts of Terrorism Coverage (Pursuant to Terrorism Risk Insurance Act), IL 09 98 01 07

- Disclosure of Premium and Estimated Premium for Certified Acts of Terrorism Coverage (Pursuant to Terrorism Risk Insurance Act), IL 09 99 01 07

The ISO rules outline the process by which a terrorism exclusion may be added to policies that may not terminate until after TRIA's expiration, if at all. At that point, the broad exclusion of damage by acts of terrorism may be employed.

Catastrophic Weather Loss Claims Issues

Windstorm can be handled efficiently by private for-profit insurance companies. When windstorm causes damage not all exposed units covered by an insurer are damaged or damaged to a total extent. Flood, on the other hand, affects all exposed units in the afflicted area to total or almost total loss. This has not been the province of private insurers. Actuarially there is no way to insure the flood exposure and remain profitable or solvent. The

federal National Flood Insurance Program was developed to respond to catastrophic flood exposures in recognition that flood insurance is more in the
manner of a social insurance program and not a private enterprise coverage
area. Details about flood coverage and access to the NFIP are contained in
The FC&S, published by The National Underwriter Company.

The terrible hurricane season of 2004 struck Florida with no fewer
than four major-class storms, and the 2005 season with its triple-whammy
of hurricanes Katrina, Rita, and Wilma, caused unprecedented storm and
flooding damage throughout huge areas of the Gulf Coast, including mas-
sive damage in New Orleans.

These storms posed coverage issues previously not raised, or certainly
not so widely and prominently. Many of these questions reached the staff
of *The FC&S*. Several of these issues are presented in this section.

Wind, Water, and Wind-Driven Water

The issue that created the most controversy following Hurricane
Katrina and the subsequent breeching of the levy system allowing most
of New Orleans to flood is the interplay of the windstorm peril (covered)
and the water peril (excluded). The water damage exclusion is frequently
referred to as the flood exclusion. The questions are: does the windstorm
peril include coverage for subsequent flooding and is the water damage
exclusion validly applied to water damage that occurs subsequent to a
windstorm?

The CP 10 30's water exclusion reads:

1. We will not pay for loss or damage caused directly or indirectly
    by any of the following. Such loss or damage is excluded regard-
    less of any other cause or event that contributes concurrently or
    in any sequence to the loss.

    G. Water

        (1) Flood, surface water, waves, tides, tidal waves,
             overflow of any body of water, or their spray, all
             whether driven by wind or not;

        (2) Mudslide or mudflow;

(3) Water that backs up or overflows from a sewer, drain or sump;

(4) Water under the ground surface pressing on, or flowing or seeping through:

    (a) Foundations, walls, floors or paved surfaces;

    (b) Basements, whether paved or not; or

    (c) Doors, windows or other openings.

        But if Water, as described in g.(1) through g.(4) above, results in fire, explosion or sprinkler leakage, we will pay for the loss or damage caused by that fire, explosion or sprinkler leakage.

The Water Exclusion endorsement, CP 10 32 08 08, adds tsunamis and storm surge to G. (1) and adds "or is otherwise discharged from" before "sewer, drain or sump" in G. (2). "Sump pump or related equipment" are also inserted at the end of that section. The endorsement contains an additional category: "Waterborne material carried or otherwise moved by any of the water referred to in Paragraph 1., 3., or 4., or material carried or otherwise moved by mudslide or mudflow."

The exclusion is broad reaching based on the actuarial recognition that flood and certain other types of water damage are beyond reach of traditional private insurance; this is why the National Flood Insurance Program (NFIP) exists. But, it can be expensive and its need undervalued. Many people do not purchase flood coverage.

The argument of proponents for invalidating the water exclusion in cases arising from the 2004 and 2005 storms was both political and an issue of proximate cause. According to one theory, the wind caused the New Orleans levy system to become overextended, and, without the hurricane, there would have been no damage. Even though the stakes are much higher, the issue is the same as other consequential damage (spoilage following power outage) discussed in Chapter 1. Where there is direct wind damage, of course, that part of any loss is covered.

The first part of the exclusion seemingly encompasses all of the proximate causation issues that litigation around the windstorm versus flood damage disputes involve—tides, waves, overflows, spray, "all whether driven by wind or not." To get at specifically catastrophic (and really unin-surable) losses, ISO inserted this phrase at the end of the exclusions sec-tion: "Exclusions B.1.a. through B.1.h. apply whether or not the loss event results in widespread damage or affects a substantial area."

Although complex litigation was initiated, some Katrina homeowners cases indicate that the water exclusion will be held valid as long as insur-ers carefully assess what is covered wind damage and what is excluded as legitimate flood loss.

In *Buente vs. Allstate Ins. Co.*, No. 1:05 CV 712 LTS JMR, 2006 WL 980784 (S.D. Miss. April 12, 2006), a home was seriously damaged dur-ing Hurricane Katrina and subsequent flooding. The homeowners claimed damage by windstorm, wind-driven rain, and rising waters caused by wind and wind-driven rain. The insurer denied coverage, saying that all damage was excluded—flood includes surface water, driven by wind or not, on ground regardless of source. The insured's argument was that the water exclusion is ambiguous, as storm surge is not addressed.

The trial court upheld the exclusion; the water doing the damage was tidal water and therefore fits the policy flood definition. In a subsequent action with the same insureds on the same facts, Allstate moved to dismiss. The court ruled that the exclusions of water and flood would not neces-sarily bar recovery for storm surges. Damage from wind and rain is cov-ered regardless of later water causing additional damage that is excluded. However, again the court found that the exclusions for water damage and flood are valid. The importance of the decision is that the water or flood exclusion in property damage policies is valid, but coverage forensics will be necessary to determine what part of the loss is appropriately covered as windstorm damage and which part is legitimately excluded as flood.

Wind Percentage Deductible

The Windstorm or Hail Percentage Deductible endorsement, CP 03 21 06 95, is often used in underwriting commercial property risks in windstorm prone areas. It provides a 1, 2, or 5 percent deductible for covered damage by windstorm or hail. During the hurricane seasons of 2004 and 2005, it created some coverage confusion and disputes. The form was updated in 2007, so policy language may vary. The following scenarios illustrate this provision and its application.

Windstorm Deductible—How Applied?

The insured has a 2 percent windstorm deductible. If a hurricane struck and caused a tree to fall on the insured building, would the resulting damage to the building be subject to the 2 percent windstorm deductible or the regular policy deductible?

The 2 percent deductible would apply, although there is nothing specifically in the policy or in the windstorm percentage deductible endorsement stating this. The reasoning is that the efficient proximate cause of the tree's falling on the building is the force of the wind. The insured could point to the named peril of falling objects, but in this instance all the provisions should be given their full meaning; that is, the coverage for windstorm, the coverage for falling objects, and the deductible.

In *Roach-Strayhan-Holland Post No. 20 American Legion Club v. Continental Ins. Co.*, 112 So. 2d 680, (La. 1959), the court said, "In the absence of a definition or limitation on the subject, a 'windstorm' must be taken to be a wind of sufficient violence to be capable of damaging insured property either by impact of its own force or by projecting some object against the property, and in order to recover on a windstorm insurance policy, not otherwise limited or defined, it is sufficient to show that wind was the proximate or efficient cause of loss or damage notwithstanding other factors that contributed to loss." If this is true in order to collect on a windstorm policy, then by inference it is logical to apply the deductible to all loss proximately caused by the storm. This makes sense. Otherwise insureds could find themselves subject to two deductibles— one for the loss caused by the falling object (the tree), and another to loss caused by the force of the wind ripping off siding and part of the roof.

The following coverage scenario provides an illustration of how the percentage wind deductible is applied in a situation where the insured has premises in different locations covered under a blanket limit, all damaged by the same hurricane or windstorm.

Percent Deductible Application under Commercial Property Policy

The insured property was a strip mall consisting of several buildings in Florida. In 2004, both Hurricanes Charley and Frances damaged three of the buildings. The insured had a blanket limit on the policy for buildings. There was a 2 percent wind deductible and the company adjuster took a separate deductible on each building. The adjuster added that the deductible should be

2 percent of the total amount of insurance. On the other hand, the insured's broker believes it should be 2 percent of the amount of the damage. How many deductibles should apply, and is the percentage deductible calculated based on the total amount of the loss or the total value of the buildings?

The ISO Windstorm or Hail Percent Deductible endorsement, CP 03 21 06 95, states that "a deductible is calculated separately for, and applies separately to…each building, if two or more buildings sustain loss or damage." (The 2007 form states, "Each building that sustains damage.")Thus, in this instance, a separate deductible should be taken for each building. To further complicate matters, Charley and Frances would be viewed as separate events, and new deductibles would apply for damage caused by Frances, the second hurricane to strike.

The endorsement also provides instructions for calculating the percentage deductible. For blanket insurance, an amount equal to 2 percent (or whatever percentage is selected) of the value of the property, as reported on the most recent Statement or Report of Values, that has sustained loss or damage is deducted.

The endorsement provides an example of two buildings, each with a value of $500,000, that sustain losses. The first building sustains $40,000 in damage; the second sustains $20,000 in damage. Two percent of the first building's value of $500,000 ($10,000) is subtracted from the amount of the loss—the amount payable for the first building is $30,000. Another deductible equal to 2 percent of the second building's value of $500,000 is applied to its damage—$10,000 is subtracted from the $20,000 loss to yield an amount payable of $10,000. The most the insurer will pay is $40,000 after the application of the 2 percent wind deductible to those losses.

Under the standard ISO endorsement, it is clear that a deductible applies to each building damaged and is calculated based on the value of the building, not on the amount of the damage. This point was also made in *General Star Indemnity Company v. West Florida Village Inn, In.,* 874 So.2d 26 (Ct. App. Fla. 2004), where the court stated that the deductible of 2 percent meant 2 percent of the policy limit.

Application of Blanket Condo Policy with Wind Deductible

Situation: Blanket condo policy with wind deductible of 3% per building. Loss figures are:

Wind damage to building	$809,282
Code upgrade	78,495
Total loss	$887,777
Dollar amount of 3% deductible	$ 43,263

There is a $10,000 sub-limit for code upgrade, so $68,495 of the code loss would not be insured damage. There is no other question of coverage and no coinsurance problem.

Form is ISO CP 00 17 04 02. ISO windstorm/hail percentage deductible endorsement CP 03 21 06 95 is attached.

The endorsement does state in the deductible application section that the insurer will deduct an amount equal to the percentage deductible of the limit(s) of insurance applicable *to the property that has sustained loss or damage* (not covered loss or damage). However, the endorsement also states that the insurer will pay the amount of loss or damage in excess of the deductible.

The $10,000 of code upgrade is "additional insurance." The policy generally excludes code upgrade but reintroduces coverage subject to the sub-limit as an "additional insurance."

Question:

Should the amount of uninsured code upgrade ($68,495) be applied to reduce the amount of the applicable deductible?

Answer

The insured cannot recover more than the limit that is insured for code upgrade. Therefore, the loss should be adjusted and the deductible applied to the $809,282 property damage for a settlement of $765,999 ($809,282 - $43,263 = $765,999). The $10,000 sublimit for code upgrade is then paid in addition to the property damage settlement for a total amount paid of $775,999.

Expense to Restore or Repair Undamaged Condo Units

In the wake of Hurricane Katrina and subsequent flooding, damage to condo units raised some interesting coverage questions, such as in the following scenario.

Is Condominium Gutting Excluded as an Act or Decision? (

Several customers of an insurance company were insured on standard condominium unit-owners policies and resided in a large condominium complex. The condo building suffered hurricane damage; however, not all units sustained physical damage. None of our insureds' units were damaged. Because some of the damaged units were found to contain mold, the condo association made the decision to gut all units to prevent any further spread. The insureds looked to their carrier to cover these costs.

Assuming that the units in question did not sustain direct physical damage from wind or water, the standard condominium policy does not provide coverage in the situation described.

The policy excludes loss to property caused by *acts or decisions of any organization*. The condo association is the *organization*; the *decision* was to gut the property and the *act* was the actual gutting. Therefore, there is no coverage.

However, in the course of the gutting, if an ensuing loss occurred—such as collapse because of faulty methods in renovation or fire from an improperly disconnected gas line—that loss would be covered unless otherwise excluded.

Chinese Drywall

As reported in *The FC&S Bulletins*, an interesting side issue that arose from the hurricanes of 2005 is the matter of loss for use of inferior building supplies, especially drywall, utilized in effecting repairs. At the time, supplies of drywall were running low. The country had been through a housing boom and the destruction caused by hurricanes Katrina and Rita left ready construction materials in short supply. As a result, the construction industry turned to supplies of drywall made in China to supplement their limited supplies. Drywall manufactured by different companies is not identical, and problems now exist presumably from the Chinese drywall used during the supply shortage.

Tests of some Chinese drywall has shown that it gives off a rotten egg odor from volatile sulfur compounds when exposed to heat and moisture. In the presence of moisture these vapors create a corrosive environment. The average humidity in Florida is over 50 percent year round, which could account for why Florida is the leader in drywall complaints. The scope of this issue is still being determined. The Gypsum Association states that 300 million square feet of Chinese drywall was imported in 2006-07. A construction consultant estimates that between 2006 and the first two months of 2007 enough drywall was imported to produce at least 50,000 homes of 2,000 square feet each.

There are many coverage issues that may develop. Claims may fall under homeowners, commercial liability, or commercial property policies. Homeowners have already started filing claims with their carriers against their homeowners policies and carriers have already denied coverage. For reference, see *Baker v. American Home Assurance Company* Middle District of Florida, No. 09-cv-188-FtM-99DNF f. The homeowner sued on the basis that the gas from the drywall interfered with the use and enjoyment of the property.

If the insured property is a commercial structure, the commercial property causes of loss form needs to be reviewed. The special causes of loss form contains a standard pollution exclusion with an exception granting coverage if the pollution is caused by or results in a specified cause of loss. Specified causes of loss are fire; lightning; explosion; wind or hail; smoke; aircraft or vehicles; riot or civil commotion; vandalism; leakage from fire-extinguishing equipment; sinkhole collapse; volcanic action; falling objects; weight of ice, snow, or sleet; and water damage. There is no cause of loss for vapors emitted from drywall. Another applicable exclusion is hidden or latent defect. The chemicals in the drywall that are causing the problem vapors are not visible, and they are an integral part of the product. Therefore, they are a latent defect; the drywall itself is defective. There is no coverage provided on this policy form.

Emerging "Green" Coverage Issues

This burgeoning interest in environmentally friendly and green construction and technology presents new issues for the insurance industry. Coverages may need to change in order to provide proper coverage for green construction. Debris may need to be disposed of in a specific way, and construction/repair may be more costly than standard construction. Traditional policy language may leave gaps in coverage. Vegetative roofs are a prime example of this. Current policies do not discuss plants as part of the roof structure. Plants are generally considered as part of the landscape and coverage for them is limited. However that limited amount will not provide coverage for the plants on the roof. The question then becomes are plants on the roof considered building materials, or are they considered to be just plants? It makes a tremendous difference in coverage for the insured.

Other issues include workmanship of new technology. A contractor who has just started working with solar panels may have an increase in faulty workmanship or construction defect claims due to the learning curve of working with a new material. In such situations it then becomes important if the contractor has a professional green certification or not, and if the granting of various certifications accurately indicates the contractor's level of expertise. While proponents may say that the technology provides sturdier, energy efficient and environmentally friendly structures, the inherent underwriting risks have changed substantially. Time required to rebuild a structure may be significantly increased, and supplies and experienced labor may be even harder to obtain after a natural disaster than regular supplies, and therefore, even more expensive. As with any new technology, unanticipated issues may arise later as green materials age. Those unexpected issues may become substantial coverage gaps.

Underinsurance is another concern. If the property owner replaces or upgrades equipment with green materials that cost more to replace, the property is at risk of being underinsured unless steps are taken to ensure the property is insured to value.

Specimen Forms

ISO Forms

Form Name	Form No.	Page
Building and Personal Property Coverage Form	CP 00 10 06 07	309
Condominium Association Coverage Form	CP 00 17 06 07	325
Condominium Commercial Unit-Owners Coverage Form	CP 00 18 06 07	339
Builders Risk Coverage Form	CP 00 20 06 07	351
Business Income (and Extra Expense) Coverage Form	CP 00 30 06 07	359
Legal Liability Coverage Form	CP 00 40 06 07	369
Leasehold Interest Coverage Form	CP 00 60 06 95	373
Mortgageholders Errors and Omissions Coverage Form	CP 00 70 06 07	377
Tobacco Sales Warehouses Coverage Form	CP 00 80 06 07	389
Commercial Property Conditions	CP 00 90 07 88	395
Causes of Loss — Basic Form	CP 10 10 06 07	397
Causes of Loss — Broad Form	CP 10 20 06 07	403
Causes of Loss — Special Form	CP 10 30 06 07	411
Common Policy Conditions	IL 00 17 11 98	421

BUILDING AND PERSONAL PROPERTY COVERAGE FORM

Various provisions in this policy restrict coverage. Read the entire policy carefully to determine rights, duties and what is and is not covered.

Throughout this policy the words "you" and "your" refer to the Named Insured shown in the Declarations. The words "we", "us" and "our" refer to the Company providing this insurance.

Other words and phrases that appear in quotation marks have special meaning. Refer to Section **H.**, Definitions.

A. Coverage

We will pay for direct physical loss of or damage to Covered Property at the premises described in the Declarations caused by or resulting from any Covered Cause of Loss.

1. Covered Property

Covered Property, as used in this Coverage Part, means the type of property described in this section, **A.1.**, and limited in **A.2.**, Property Not Covered, if a Limit of Insurance is shown in the Declarations for that type of property.

a. Building, meaning the building or structure described in the Declarations, including:

(1) Completed additions;

(2) Fixtures, including outdoor fixtures;

(3) Permanently installed:

   (a) Machinery and

   (b) Equipment;

(4) Personal property owned by you that is used to maintain or service the building or structure or its premises, including:

   (a) Fire-extinguishing equipment;

   (b) Outdoor furniture;

   (c) Floor coverings; and

   (d) Appliances used for refrigerating, ventilating, cooking, dishwashing or laundering;

(5) If not covered by other insurance:

   (a) Additions under construction, alterations and repairs to the building or structure;

   (b) Materials, equipment, supplies and temporary structures, on or within 100 feet of the described premises, used for making additions, alterations or repairs to the building or structure.

b. Your Business Personal Property located in or on the building described in the Declarations or in the open (or in a vehicle) within 100 feet of the described premises, consisting of the following unless otherwise specified in the Declarations or on the Your Business Personal Property – Separation Of Coverage form:

(1) Furniture and fixtures;

(2) Machinery and equipment;

(3) "Stock";

(4) All other personal property owned by you and used in your business;

(5) Labor, materials or services furnished or arranged by you on personal property of others;

(6) Your use interest as tenant in improvements and betterments. Improvements and betterments are fixtures, alterations, installations or additions:

   (a) Made a part of the building or structure you occupy but do not own; and

   (b) You acquired or made at your expense but cannot legally remove;

(7) Leased personal property for which you have a contractual responsibility to insure, unless otherwise provided for under Personal Property Of Others.

c. **Personal Property Of Others** that is:

(1) In your care, custody or control; and

(2) Located in or on the building described in the Declarations or in the open (or in a vehicle) within 100 feet of the described premises.

However, our payment for loss of or damage to personal property of others will only be for the account of the owner of the property.

2. **Property Not Covered**

Covered Property does not include:

a. Accounts, bills, currency, food stamps or other evidences of debt, money, notes or securities. Lottery tickets held for sale are not securities;

b. Animals, unless owned by others and boarded by you, or if owned by you, only as "stock" while inside of buildings;

c. Automobiles held for sale;

d. Bridges, roadways, walks, patios or other paved surfaces;

e. Contraband, or property in the course of illegal transportation or trade;

f. The cost of excavations, grading, backfilling or filling;

g. Foundations of buildings, structures, machinery or boilers if their foundations are below:

(1) The lowest basement floor; or

(2) The surface of the ground, if there is no basement;

h. Land (including land on which the property is located), water, growing crops or lawns;

i. Personal property while airborne or waterborne;

j. Bulkheads, pilings, piers, wharves or docks;

k. Property that is covered under another coverage form of this or any other policy in which it is more specifically described, except for the excess of the amount due (whether you can collect on it or not) from that other insurance;

l. Retaining walls that are not part of a building;

m. Underground pipes, flues or drains;

n. Electronic data, except as provided under the Additional Coverage, Electronic Data. Electronic data means information, facts or computer programs stored as or on, created or used on, or transmitted to or from computer software (including systems and applications software), on hard or floppy disks, CD-ROMs, tapes, drives, cells, data processing devices or any other repositories of computer software which are used with electronically controlled equipment. The term computer programs, referred to in the foregoing description of electronic data, means a set of related electronic instructions which direct the operations and functions of a computer or device connected to it, which enable the computer or device to receive, process, store, retrieve or send data. This paragraph, **n.**, does not apply to your "stock" of prepackaged software;

o. The cost to replace or restore the information on valuable papers and records, including those which exist as electronic data. Valuable papers and records include but are not limited to proprietary information, books of account, deeds, manuscripts, abstracts, drawings and card index systems. Refer to the Coverage Extension for Valuable Papers And Records (Other Than Electronic Data) for limited coverage for valuable papers and records other than those which exist as electronic data;

p. Vehicles or self-propelled machines (including aircraft or watercraft) that:

(1) Are licensed for use on public roads; or

(2) Are operated principally away from the described premises.

This paragraph does not apply to:

(a) Vehicles or self-propelled machines or autos you manufacture, process or warehouse;

(b) Vehicles or self-propelled machines, other than autos, you hold for sale;

(c) Rowboats or canoes out of water at the described premises; or

(d) Trailers, but only to the extent provided for in the Coverage Extension for Non-owned Detached Trailers;

       CP 00 10 06 07   ☐

q. The following property while outside of buildings:

(1) Grain, hay, straw or other crops;

(2) Fences, radio or television antennas (including satellite dishes) and their lead-in wiring, masts or towers, trees, shrubs or plants (other than "stock" of trees, shrubs or plants), all except as provided in the Coverage Extensions.

3. Covered Causes Of Loss

See applicable Causes Of Loss Form as shown in the Declarations.

4. Additional Coverages

a. Debris Removal

(1) Subject to Paragraphs **(3)** and **(4)**, we will pay your expense to remove debris of Covered Property caused by or resulting from a Covered Cause of Loss that occurs during the policy period. The expenses will be paid only if they are reported to us in writing within 180 days of the date of direct physical loss or damage.

(2) Debris Removal does not apply to costs to:

(a) Extract "pollutants" from land or water; or

(b) Remove, restore or replace polluted land or water.

(3) Subject to the exceptions in Paragraph **(4)**, the following provisions apply:

(a) The most we will pay for the total of direct physical loss or damage plus debris removal expense is the Limit of Insurance applicable to the Covered Property that has sustained loss or damage.

(b) Subject to **(a)** above, the amount we will pay for debris removal expense is limited to 25% of the sum of the deductible plus the amount that we pay for direct physical loss or damage to the Covered Property that has sustained loss or damage.

(4) We will pay up to an additional $10,000 for debris removal expense, for each location, in any one occurrence of physical loss or damage to Covered Property, if one or both of the following circumstances apply:

(a) The total of the actual debris removal expense plus the amount we pay for direct physical loss or damage exceeds the Limit of Insurance on the Covered Property that has sustained loss or damage.

(b) The actual debris removal expense exceeds 25% of the sum of the deductible plus the amount that we pay for direct physical loss or damage to the Covered Property that has sustained loss or damage.

Therefore, if **(4)(a)** and/or **(4)(b)** apply, our total payment for direct physical loss or damage and debris removal expense may reach but will never exceed the Limit of Insurance on the Covered Property that has sustained loss or damage, plus $10,000.

(5) Examples

The following examples assume that there is no Coinsurance penalty.

EXAMPLE #1

Limit of Insurance:	$ 90,000
Amount of Deductible:	$ 500
Amount of Loss:	$ 50,000
Amount of Loss Payable:	$ 49,500
	($50,000 – $500)
Debris Removal Expense:	$ 10,000
Debris Removal Expense Payable:	$ 10,000
($10,000 is 20% of $50,000.)	

The debris removal expense is less than 25% of the sum of the loss payable plus the deductible. The sum of the loss payable and the debris removal expense ($49,500 + $10,000 = $59,500) is less than the Limit of Insurance. Therefore the full amount of debris removal expense is payable in accordance with the terms of Paragraph **(3)**.

EXAMPLE #2

Limit of Insurance:	$ 90,000
Amount of Deductible:	$ 500
Amount of Loss:	$ 80,000
Amount of Loss Payable:	$ 79,500
	($80,000 – $500)
Debris Removal Expense:	$ 30,000
Debris Removal Expense Payable	
Basic Amount:	$ 10,500
Additional Amount:	$ 10,000

The basic amount payable for debris removal expense under the terms of Paragraph **(3)** is calculated as follows: $80,000 ($79,500 + $500) x .25 = $20,000; capped at $10,500. The cap applies because the sum of the loss payable ($79,500) and the basic amount payable for debris removal expense ($10,500) cannot exceed the Limit of Insurance ($90,000).

The additional amount payable for debris removal expense is provided in accordance with the terms of Paragraph **(4),** because the debris removal expense ($30,000) exceeds 25% of the loss payable plus the deductible ($30,000 is 37.5% of $80,000), and because the sum of the loss payable and debris removal expense ($79,500 + $30,000 = $109,500) would exceed the Limit of Insurance ($90,000). The additional amount of covered debris removal expense is $10,000, the maximum payable under Paragraph **(4).** Thus the total payable for debris removal expense in this example is $20,500; $9,500 of the debris removal expense is not covered.

b. Preservation Of Property

If it is necessary to move Covered Property from the described premises to preserve it from loss or damage by a Covered Cause of Loss, we will pay for any direct physical loss or damage to that property:

(1) While it is being moved or while temporarily stored at another location; and

(2) Only if the loss or damage occurs within 30 days after the property is first moved.

c. Fire Department Service Charge

When the fire department is called to save or protect Covered Property from a Covered Cause of Loss, we will pay up to $1,000, unless a higher limit is shown in the Declarations, for your liability for fire department service charges:

(1) Assumed by contract or agreement prior to loss; or

(2) Required by local ordinance.

No Deductible applies to this Additional Coverage.

d. Pollutant Clean-up And Removal

We will pay your expense to extract "pollutants" from land or water at the described premises if the discharge, dispersal, seepage, migration, release or escape of the "pollutants" is caused by or results from a Covered Cause of Loss that occurs during the policy period. The expenses will be paid only if they are reported to us in writing within 180 days of the date on which the Covered Cause of Loss occurs.

This Additional Coverage does not apply to costs to test for, monitor or assess the existence, concentration or effects of "pollutants". But we will pay for testing which is performed in the course of extracting the "pollutants" from the land or water.

The most we will pay under this Additional Coverage for each described premises is $10,000 for the sum of all covered expenses arising out of Covered Causes of Loss occurring during each separate 12-month period of this policy.

e. Increased Cost Of Construction

(1) This Additional Coverage applies only to buildings to which the Replacement Cost Optional Coverage applies.

(2) In the event of damage by a Covered Cause of Loss to a building that is Covered Property, we will pay the increased costs incurred to comply with enforcement of an ordinance or law in the course of repair, rebuilding or replacement of damaged parts of that property, subject to the limitations stated in **e.(3)** through **e.(9)** of this Additional Coverage.

(3) The ordinance or law referred to in **e.(2)** of this Additional Coverage is an ordinance or law that regulates the construction or repair of buildings or establishes zoning or land use requirements at the described premises, and is in force at the time of loss.

CP 00 10 06 07

(4) Under this Additional Coverage, we will not pay any costs due to an ordinance or law that:

(a) You were required to comply with before the loss, even when the building was undamaged; and

(b) You failed to comply with.

(5) Under this Additional Coverage, we will not pay for:

(a) The enforcement of any ordinance or law which requires demolition, repair, replacement, reconstruction, remodeling or remediation of property due to contamination by "pollutants" or due to the presence, growth, proliferation, spread or any activity of "fungus", wet or dry rot or bacteria; or

(b) Any costs associated with the enforcement of an ordinance or law which requires any insured or others to test for, monitor, clean up, remove, contain, treat, detoxify or neutralize, or in any way respond to, or assess the effects of "pollutants", "fungus", wet or dry rot or bacteria.

(6) The most we will pay under this Additional Coverage, for each described building insured under this Coverage Form, is $10,000 or 5% of the Limit of Insurance applicable to that building, whichever is less. If a damaged building is covered under a blanket Limit of Insurance which applies to more than one building or item of property, then the most we will pay under this Additional Coverage, for that damaged building, is the lesser of: $10,000 or 5% times the value of the damaged building as of the time of loss times the applicable Coinsurance percentage.

The amount payable under this Additional Coverage is additional insurance.

(7) With respect to this Additional Coverage:

(a) We will not pay for the Increased Cost of Construction:

(i) Until the property is actually repaired or replaced, at the same or another premises; and

(ii) Unless the repairs or replacement are made as soon as reasonably possible after the loss or damage, not to exceed two years. We may extend this period in writing during the two years.

(b) If the building is repaired or replaced at the same premises, or if you elect to rebuild at another premises, the most we will pay for the Increased Cost of Construction, subject to the provisions of **e.(6)** of this Additional Coverage, is the increased cost of construction at the same premises.

(c) If the ordinance or law requires relocation to another premises, the most we will pay for the Increased Cost of Construction, subject to the provisions of **e.(6)** of this Additional Coverage, is the increased cost of construction at the new premises.

(8) This Additional Coverage is not subject to the terms of the Ordinance Or Law Exclusion, to the extent that such Exclusion would conflict with the provisions of this Additional Coverage.

(9) The costs addressed in the Loss Payment and Valuation Conditions, and the Replacement Cost Optional Coverage, in this Coverage Form, do not include the increased cost attributable to enforcement of an ordinance or law. The amount payable under this Additional Coverage, as stated in **e.(6)** of this Additional Coverage, is not subject to such limitation.

f. Electronic Data

(1) Under this Additional Coverage, electronic data has the meaning described under Property Not Covered, Electronic Data.

(2) Subject to the provisions of this Additional Coverage, we will pay for the cost to replace or restore electronic data which has been destroyed or corrupted by a Covered Cause of Loss. To the extent that electronic data is not replaced or restored, the loss will be valued at the cost of replacement of the media on which the electronic data was stored, with blank media of substantially identical type.

(3) The Covered Causes of Loss applicable to Your Business Personal Property apply to this Additional Coverage, Electronic Data, subject to the following:

(a) If the Causes Of Loss – Special Form applies, coverage under this Additional Coverage, Electronic Data, is limited to the "specified causes of loss" as defined in that form, and Collapse as set forth in that form.

(b) If the Causes Of Loss – Broad Form applies, coverage under this Additional Coverage, Electronic Data, includes Collapse as set forth in that form.

(c) If the Causes Of Loss Form is endorsed to add a Covered Cause of Loss, the additional Covered Cause of Loss does not apply to the coverage provided under this Additional Coverage, Electronic Data.

(d) The Covered Causes of Loss include a virus, harmful code or similar instruction introduced into or enacted on a computer system (including electronic data) or a network to which it is connected, designed to damage or destroy any part of the system or disrupt its normal operation. But there is no coverage for loss or damage caused by or resulting from manipulation of a computer system (including electronic data) by any employee, including a temporary or leased employee, or by an entity retained by you or for you to inspect, design, install, modify, maintain, repair or replace that system.

(4) The most we will pay under this Additional Coverage, Electronic Data, is $2,500 for all loss or damage sustained in any one policy year, regardless of the number of occurrences of loss or damage or the number of premises, locations or computer systems involved. If loss payment on the first occurrence does not exhaust this amount, then the balance is available for subsequent loss or damage sustained in but not after that policy year. With respect to an occurrence which begins in one policy year and continues or results in additional loss or damage in a subsequent policy year(s), all loss or damage is deemed to be sustained in the policy year in which the occurrence began.

5. **Coverage Extensions**

Except as otherwise provided, the following Extensions apply to property located in or on the building described in the Declarations or in the open (or in a vehicle) within 100 feet of the described premises.

If a Coinsurance percentage of 80% or more, or a Value Reporting period symbol, is shown in the Declarations, you may extend the insurance provided by this Coverage Part as follows:

a. **Newly Acquired Or Constructed Property**

(1) **Buildings**

If this policy covers Building, you may extend that insurance to apply to:

(a) Your new buildings while being built on the described premises; and

(b) Buildings you acquire at locations, other than the described premises, intended for:

(i) Similar use as the building described in the Declarations; or

(ii) Use as a warehouse.

The most we will pay for loss or damage under this Extension is $250,000 at each building.

(2) **Your Business Personal Property**

(a) If this policy covers Your Business Personal Property, you may extend that insurance to apply to:

(i) Business personal property, including such property that you newly acquire, at any location you acquire other than at fairs, trade shows or exhibitions;

(ii) Business personal property, including such property that you newly acquire, located at your newly constructed or acquired buildings at the location described in the Declarations; or

(iii) Business personal property that you newly acquire, located at the described premises.

The most we will pay for loss or damage under this Extension is $100,000 at each building.

(b) This Extension does not apply to:

(i) Personal property of others that is temporarily in your possession in the course of installing or performing work on such property; or

(ii) Personal property of others that is temporarily in your possession in the course of your manufacturing or wholesaling activities.

(3) Period Of Coverage

With respect to insurance on or at each newly acquired or constructed property, coverage will end when any of the following first occurs:

(a) This policy expires;

(b) 30 days expire after you acquire the property or begin construction of that part of the building that would qualify as covered property; or

(c) You report values to us.

We will charge you additional premium for values reported from the date you acquire the property or begin construction of that part of the building that would qualify as covered property.

b. Personal Effects And Property Of Others

You may extend the insurance that applies to Your Business Personal Property to apply to:

(1) Personal effects owned by you, your officers, your partners or members, your managers or your employees. This Extension does not apply to loss or damage by theft.

(2) Personal property of others in your care, custody or control.

The most we will pay for loss or damage under this Extension is $2,500 at each described premises. Our payment for loss of or damage to personal property of others will only be for the account of the owner of the property.

c. Valuable Papers And Records (Other Than Electronic Data)

(1) You may extend the insurance that applies to Your Business Personal Property to apply to the cost to replace or restore the lost information on valuable papers and records for which duplicates do not exist. But this Extension does not apply to valuable papers and records which exist as electronic data. Electronic data has the meaning described under Property Not Covered, Electronic Data.

(2) If the Causes Of Loss – Special Form applies, coverage under this Extension is limited to the "specified causes of loss" as defined in that form, and Collapse as set forth in that form.

(3) If the Causes Of Loss – Broad Form applies, coverage under this Extension includes Collapse as set forth in that form.

(4) Under this Extension, the most we will pay to replace or restore the lost information is $2,500 at each described premises, unless a higher limit is shown in the Declarations. Such amount is additional insurance. We will also pay for the cost of blank material for reproducing the records (whether or not duplicates exist), and (when there is a duplicate) for the cost of labor to transcribe or copy the records. The costs of blank material and labor are subject to the applicable Limit of Insurance on Your Business Personal Property and therefore coverage of such costs is not additional insurance.

d. Property Off-premises

(1) You may extend the insurance provided by this Coverage Form to apply to your Covered Property while it is away from the described premises, if it is:

(a) Temporarily at a location you do not own, lease or operate;

(b) In storage at a location you lease, provided the lease was executed after the beginning of the current policy term; or

(c) At any fair, trade show or exhibition.

(2) This Extension does not apply to property:

(a) In or on a vehicle; or

(b) In the care, custody or control of your salespersons, unless the property is in such care, custody or control at a fair, trade show or exhibition.

(3) The most we will pay for loss or damage under this Extension is $10,000.

e. Outdoor Property

You may extend the insurance provided by this Coverage Form to apply to your outdoor fences, radio and television antennas (including satellite dishes), trees, shrubs and plants (other than "stock" of trees, shrubs or plants), including debris removal expense, caused by or resulting from any of the following causes of loss if they are Covered Causes of Loss:

(1) Fire;

(2) Lightning;

(3) Explosion;

(4) Riot or Civil Commotion; or

(5) Aircraft.

The most we will pay for loss or damage under this Extension is $1,000, but not more than $250 for any one tree, shrub or plant. These limits apply to any one occurrence, regardless of the types or number of items lost or damaged in that occurrence.

f. Non-owned Detached Trailers

(1) You may extend the insurance that applies to Your Business Personal Property to apply to loss or damage to trailers that you do not own, provided that:

(a) The trailer is used in your business;

(b) The trailer is in your care, custody or control at the premises described in the Declarations; and

(c) You have a contractual responsibility to pay for loss or damage to the trailer.

(2) We will not pay for any loss or damage that occurs:

(a) While the trailer is attached to any motor vehicle or motorized conveyance, whether or not the motor vehicle or motorized conveyance is in motion;

(b) During hitching or unhitching operations, or when a trailer becomes accidentally unhitched from a motor vehicle or motorized conveyance.

(3) The most we will pay for loss or damage under this Extension is $5,000, unless a higher limit is shown in the Declarations.

(4) This insurance is excess over the amount due (whether you can collect on it or not) from any other insurance covering such property.

Each of these Extensions is additional insurance unless otherwise indicated. The Additional Condition, Coinsurance, does not apply to these Extensions.

B. Exclusions And Limitations

See applicable Causes Of Loss Form as shown in the Declarations.

C. Limits Of Insurance

The most we will pay for loss or damage in any one occurrence is the applicable Limit of Insurance shown in the Declarations.

The most we will pay for loss or damage to outdoor signs, whether or not the sign is attached to a building, is $2,500 per sign in any one occurrence.

The amounts of insurance stated in the following Additional Coverages apply in accordance with the terms of such coverages and are separate from the Limit(s) of Insurance shown in the Declarations for any other coverage:

1. Fire Department Service Charge;

2. Pollutant Clean-up And Removal;

3. Increased Cost Of Construction; and

4. Electronic Data.

Payments under the Preservation Of Property Additional Coverage will not increase the applicable Limit of Insurance.

D. Deductible

In any one occurrence of loss or damage (hereinafter referred to as loss), we will first reduce the amount of loss if required by the Coinsurance Condition or the Agreed Value Optional Coverage. If the adjusted amount of loss is less than or equal to the Deductible, we will not pay for that loss. If the adjusted amount of loss exceeds the Deductible, we will then subtract the Deductible from the adjusted amount of loss, and will pay the resulting amount or the Limit of Insurance, whichever is less.

When the occurrence involves loss to more than one item of Covered Property and separate Limits of Insurance apply, the losses will not be combined in determining application of the Deductible. But the Deductible will be applied only once per occurrence.

EXAMPLE #1

(This example assumes there is no Coinsurance penalty.)

Deductible:	$ 250
Limit of Insurance – Building #1:	$ 60,000
Limit of Insurance – Building #2:	$ 80,000
Loss to Building #1:	$ 60,100
Loss to Building #2:	$ 90,000

The amount of loss to Building #1 ($60,100) is less than the sum ($60,250) of the Limit of Insurance applicable to Building #1 plus the Deductible.

The Deductible will be subtracted from the amount of loss in calculating the loss payable for Building #1:

```
  $ 60,100
–     250
  $ 59,850 Loss Payable – Building #1
```

The Deductible applies once per occurrence and therefore is not subtracted in determining the amount of loss payable for Building #2. Loss payable for Building #2 is the Limit of Insurance of $80,000.

Total amount of loss payable:

$59,850 + $80,000 = $139,850

EXAMPLE #2

(This example, too, assumes there is no Coinsurance penalty.)

The Deductible and Limits of Insurance are the same as those in Example #1.

Loss to Building #1:	$ 70,000
(Exceeds Limit of Insurance plus Deductible)	
Loss to Building #2:	$ 90,000
(Exceeds Limit of Insurance plus Deductible)	
Loss Payable – Building #1:	$ 60,000
(Limit of Insurance)	
Loss Payable – Building #2:	$ 80,000
(Limit of Insurance)	
Total amount of loss payable:	$ 140,000

E. Loss Conditions

The following conditions apply in addition to the Common Policy Conditions and the Commercial Property Conditions.

1. Abandonment

There can be no abandonment of any property to us.

2. Appraisal

If we and you disagree on the value of the property or the amount of loss, either may make written demand for an appraisal of the loss. In this event, each party will select a competent and impartial appraiser. The two appraisers will select an umpire. If they cannot agree, either may request that selection be made by a judge of a court having jurisdiction. The appraisers will state separately the value of the property and amount of loss. If they fail to agree, they will submit their differences to the umpire. A decision agreed to by any two will be binding. Each party will:

a. Pay its chosen appraiser; and

b. Bear the other expenses of the appraisal and umpire equally.

If there is an appraisal, we will still retain our right to deny the claim.

3. Duties In The Event Of Loss Or Damage

a. You must see that the following are done in the event of loss or damage to Covered Property:

(1) Notify the police if a law may have been broken.

(2) Give us prompt notice of the loss or damage. Include a description of the property involved.

(3) As soon as possible, give us a description of how, when and where the loss or damage occurred.

(4) Take all reasonable steps to protect the Covered Property from further damage, and keep a record of your expenses necessary to protect the Covered Property, for consideration in the settlement of the claim. This will not increase the Limit of Insurance. However, we will not pay for any subsequent loss or damage resulting from a cause of loss that is not a Covered Cause of Loss. Also, if feasible, set the damaged property aside and in the best possible order for examination.

(5) At our request, give us complete inventories of the damaged and undamaged property. Include quantities, costs, values and amount of loss claimed.

(6) As often as may be reasonably required, permit us to inspect the property proving the loss or damage and examine your books and records.

Also permit us to take samples of damaged and undamaged property for inspection, testing and analysis, and permit us to make copies from your books and records.

(7) Send us a signed, sworn proof of loss containing the information we request to investigate the claim. You must do this within 60 days after our request. We will supply you with the necessary forms.

(8) Cooperate with us in the investigation or settlement of the claim.

b. We may examine any insured under oath, while not in the presence of any other insured and at such times as may be reasonably required, about any matter relating to this insurance or the claim, including an insured's books and records. In the event of an examination, an insured's answers must be signed.

4. Loss Payment

a. In the event of loss or damage covered by this Coverage Form, at our option, we will either:

(1) Pay the value of lost or damaged property;

(2) Pay the cost of repairing or replacing the lost or damaged property, subject to **b.** below;

(3) Take all or any part of the property at an agreed or appraised value; or

(4) Repair, rebuild or replace the property with other property of like kind and quality, subject to **b.** below.

We will determine the value of lost or damaged property, or the cost of its repair or replacement, in accordance with the applicable terms of the Valuation Condition in this Coverage Form or any applicable provision which amends or supersedes the Valuation Condition.

b. The cost to repair, rebuild or replace does not include the increased cost attributable to enforcement of any ordinance or law regulating the construction, use or repair of any property.

c. We will give notice of our intentions within 30 days after we receive the sworn proof of loss.

d. We will not pay you more than your financial interest in the Covered Property.

e. We may adjust losses with the owners of lost or damaged property if other than you. If we pay the owners, such payments will satisfy your claims against us for the owners' property. We will not pay the owners more than their financial interest in the Covered Property.

f. We may elect to defend you against suits arising from claims of owners of property. We will do this at our expense.

g. We will pay for covered loss or damage within 30 days after we receive the sworn proof of loss, if you have complied with all of the terms of this Coverage Part and:

(1) We have reached agreement with you on the amount of loss; or

(2) An appraisal award has been made.

h. A party wall is a wall that separates and is common to adjoining buildings that are owned by different parties. In settling covered losses involving a party wall, we will pay a proportion of the loss to the party wall based on your interest in the wall in proportion to the interest of the owner of the adjoining building. However, if you elect to repair or replace your building and the owner of the adjoining building elects not to repair or replace that building, we will pay you the full value of the loss to the party wall, subject to all applicable policy provisions including Limits of Insurance, the Valuation and Coinsurance Conditions and all other provisions of this Loss Payment Condition. Our payment under the provisions of this paragraph does not alter any right of subrogation we may have against any entity, including the owner or insurer of the adjoining building, and does not alter the terms of the Transfer Of Rights Of Recovery Against Others To Us Condition in this policy.

5. Recovered Property

If either you or we recover any property after loss settlement, that party must give the other prompt notice. At your option, the property will be returned to you. You must then return to us the amount we paid to you for the property. We will pay recovery expenses and the expenses to repair the recovered property, subject to the Limit of Insurance.

6. Vacancy

a. Description Of Terms

(1) As used in this Vacancy Condition, the term building and the term vacant have the meanings set forth in **(1)(a)** and **(1)(b)** below:

(a) When this policy is issued to a tenant, and with respect to that tenant's interest in Covered Property, building means the unit or suite rented or leased to the tenant. Such building is vacant when it does not contain enough business personal property to conduct customary operations.

(b) When this policy is issued to the owner or general lessee of a building, building means the entire building. Such building is vacant unless at least 31% of its total square footage is:

(i) Rented to a lessee or sub-lessee and used by the lessee or sub-lessee to conduct its customary operations; and/or

(ii) Used by the building owner to conduct customary operations.

(2) Buildings under construction or renovation are not considered vacant.

b. Vacancy Provisions

If the building where loss or damage occurs has been vacant for more than 60 consecutive days before that loss or damage occurs:

(1) We will not pay for any loss or damage caused by any of the following even if they are Covered Causes of Loss:

(a) Vandalism;

(b) Sprinkler leakage, unless you have protected the system against freezing;

(c) Building glass breakage;

(d) Water damage;

(e) Theft; or

(f) Attempted theft.

(2) With respect to Covered Causes of Loss other than those listed in **b.(1)(a)** through **b.(1)(f)** above, we will reduce the amount we would otherwise pay for the loss or damage by 15%.

7. Valuation

We will determine the value of Covered Property in the event of loss or damage as follows:

a. At actual cash value as of the time of loss or damage, except as provided in **b.**, **c.**, **d.** and **e.** below.

b. If the Limit of Insurance for Building satisfies the Additional Condition, Coinsurance, and the cost to repair or replace the damaged building property is $2,500 or less, we will pay the cost of building repairs or replacement.

The cost of building repairs or replacement does not include the increased cost attributable to enforcement of any ordinance or law regulating the construction, use or repair of any property.

However, the following property will be valued at the actual cash value even when attached to the building:

(1) Awnings or floor coverings;

(2) Appliances for refrigerating, ventilating, cooking, dishwashing or laundering; or

(3) Outdoor equipment or furniture.

c. "Stock" you have sold but not delivered at the selling price less discounts and expenses you otherwise would have had.

d. Glass at the cost of replacement with safety-glazing material if required by law.

e. Tenants' Improvements and Betterments at:

(1) Actual cash value of the lost or damaged property if you make repairs promptly.

(2) A proportion of your original cost if you do not make repairs promptly. We will determine the proportionate value as follows:

(a) Multiply the original cost by the number of days from the loss or damage to the expiration of the lease; and

(b) Divide the amount determined in **(a)** above by the number of days from the installation of improvements to the expiration of the lease.

If your lease contains a renewal option, the expiration of the renewal option period will replace the expiration of the lease in this procedure.

(3) Nothing if others pay for repairs or replacement.

F. Additional Conditions

The following conditions apply in addition to the Common Policy Conditions and the Commercial Property Conditions.

1. Coinsurance

If a Coinsurance percentage is shown in the Declarations, the following condition applies.

a. We will not pay the full amount of any loss if the value of Covered Property at the time of loss times the Coinsurance percentage shown for it in the Declarations is greater than the Limit of Insurance for the property.

Instead, we will determine the most we will pay using the following steps:

(1) Multiply the value of Covered Property at the time of loss by the Coinsurance percentage;

(2) Divide the Limit of Insurance of the property by the figure determined in Step **(1)**;

(3) Multiply the total amount of loss, before the application of any deductible, by the figure determined in Step **(2)**; and

(4) Subtract the deductible from the figure determined in Step **(3)**.

We will pay the amount determined in Step **(4)** or the limit of insurance, whichever is less. For the remainder, you will either have to rely on other insurance or absorb the loss yourself.

EXAMPLE #1 (UNDERINSURANCE)

When:		
	The value of the property is:	$ 250,000
	The Coinsurance percentage for it is:	80%
	The Limit of Insurance for it is:	$ 100,000
	The Deductible is:	$ 250
	The amount of loss is:	$ 40,000

Step **(1)**: $250,000 x 80% = $200,000

(the minimum amount of insurance to meet your Coinsurance requirements)

Step **(2)**: $100,000 ÷ $200,000 = .50

Step **(3)**: $40,000 x .50 = $20,000

Step **(4)**: $20,000 – $250 = $19,750

We will pay no more than $19,750. The remaining $20,250 is not covered.

EXAMPLE #2 (ADEQUATE INSURANCE)

When: The value of the property is: $ 250,000

The Coinsurance percentage
for it is: 80%

The Limit of Insurance for it is: $ 200,000

The Deductible is: $ 250

The amount of loss is: $ 40,000

The minimum amount of insurance to meet your Co-insurance requirement is $200,000 ($250,000 x 80%). Therefore, the Limit of Insurance in this example is adequate and no penalty applies. We will pay no more than $39,750 ($40,000 amount of loss minus the deductible of $250).

    b. If one Limit of Insurance applies to two or more separate items, this condition will apply to the total of all property to which the limit applies.

EXAMPLE #3

When: The value of the property is:

Building at Location #1: $ 75,000

Building at Location #2: $ 100,000

Personal Property
at Location #2: $ 75,000

        $ 250,000

The Coinsurance percentage
for it is: 90%

The Limit of Insurance for
Buildings and Personal Property
at Locations #1 and #2 is: $ 180,000

The Deductible is: $ 1,000

The amount of loss is:

Building at Location #2: $ 30,000

Personal Property
at Location #2: $ 20,000

        $ 50,000

Step **(1):** $250,000 x 90% = $225,000

(the minimum amount of insurance to meet your Coinsurance requirements and to avoid the penalty shown below)

Step **(2):** $180,000 ÷ $225,000 = .80

Step **(3):** $50,000 x .80 = $40,000

Step **(4):** $40,000 − $1,000 = $39,000

We will pay no more than $39,000. The remaining $11,000 is not covered.

2. Mortgageholders

    a. The term mortgageholder includes trustee.

    b. We will pay for covered loss of or damage to buildings or structures to each mortgageholder shown in the Declarations in their order of precedence, as interests may appear.

    c. The mortgageholder has the right to receive loss payment even if the mortgageholder has started foreclosure or similar action on the building or structure.

    d. If we deny your claim because of your acts or because you have failed to comply with the terms of this Coverage Part, the mortgageholder will still have the right to receive loss payment if the mortgageholder:

        (1) Pays any premium due under this Coverage Part at our request if you have failed to do so;

        (2) Submits a signed, sworn proof of loss within 60 days after receiving notice from us of your failure to do so; and

        (3) Has notified us of any change in ownership, occupancy or substantial change in risk known to the mortgageholder.

    All of the terms of this Coverage Part will then apply directly to the mortgageholder.

    e. If we pay the mortgageholder for any loss or damage and deny payment to you because of your acts or because you have failed to comply with the terms of this Coverage Part:

        (1) The mortgageholder's rights under the mortgage will be transferred to us to the extent of the amount we pay; and

        (2) The mortgageholder's right to recover the full amount of the mortgageholder's claim will not be impaired.

    At our option, we may pay to the mortgageholder the whole principal on the mortgage plus any accrued interest. In this event, your mortgage and note will be transferred to us and you will pay your remaining mortgage debt to us.

    f. If we cancel this policy, we will give written notice to the mortgageholder at least:

        (1) 10 days before the effective date of cancellation if we cancel for your non-payment of premium; or

        (2) 30 days before the effective date of cancellation if we cancel for any other reason.

g. If we elect not to renew this policy, we will give written notice to the mortgageholder at least 10 days before the expiration date of this policy.

G. Optional Coverages

If shown as applicable in the Declarations, the following Optional Coverages apply separately to each item.

1. Agreed Value

a. The Additional Condition, Coinsurance, does not apply to Covered Property to which this Optional Coverage applies. We will pay no more for loss of or damage to that property than the proportion that the Limit of Insurance under this Coverage Part for the property bears to the Agreed Value shown for it in the Declarations.

b. If the expiration date for this Optional Coverage shown in the Declarations is not extended, the Additional Condition, Coinsurance, is reinstated and this Optional Coverage expires.

c. The terms of this Optional Coverage apply only to loss or damage that occurs:

(1) On or after the effective date of this Optional Coverage; and

(2) Before the Agreed Value expiration date shown in the Declarations or the policy expiration date, whichever occurs first.

2. Inflation Guard

a. The Limit of Insurance for property to which this Optional Coverage applied will automatically increase by the annual percentage shown in the Declarations.

b. The amount of increase will be:

(1) The Limit of Insurance that applied on the most recent of the policy inception date, the policy anniversary date, or any other policy change amending the Limit of Insurance, times

(2) The percentage of annual increase shown in the Declarations, expressed as a decimal (example: 8% is .08), times

(3) The number of days since the beginning of the current policy year or the effective date of the most recent policy change amending the Limit of Insurance, divided by 365.

EXAMPLE

If: The applicable Limit of Insurance is: $ 100,000

The annual percentage increase is: 8%

The number of days since the beginning of the policy year (or last policy change) is: 146

The amount of increase is: $100,000 x .08 x 146 ÷ 365 = $ 3,200

3. Replacement Cost

a. Replacement Cost (without deduction for depreciation) replaces Actual Cash Value in the Valuation Loss Condition of this Coverage Form.

b. This Optional Coverage does not apply to:

(1) Personal property of others;

(2) Contents of a residence;

(3) Works of art, antiques or rare articles, including etchings, pictures, statuary, marbles, bronzes, porcelains and bric-a-brac; or

(4) "Stock", unless the Including "Stock" option is shown in the Declarations.

Under the terms of this Replacement Cost Optional Coverage, tenants' improvements and betterments are not considered to be the personal property of others.

c. You may make a claim for loss or damage covered by this insurance on an actual cash value basis instead of on a replacement cost basis. In the event you elect to have loss or damage settled on an actual cash value basis, you may still make a claim for the additional coverage this Optional Coverage provides if you notify us of your intent to do so within 180 days after the loss or damage.

d. We will not pay on a replacement cost basis for any loss or damage:

(1) Until the lost or damaged property is actually repaired or replaced; and

(2) Unless the repairs or replacement are made as soon as reasonably possible after the loss or damage.

 □

With respect to tenants' improvements and betterments, the following also apply:

(3) If the conditions in **d.(1)** and **d.(2)** above are not met, the value of tenants' improvements and betterments will be determined as a proportion of your original cost, as set forth in the Valuation Loss Condition of this Coverage Form; and

(4) We will not pay for loss or damage to tenants' improvements and betterments if others pay for repairs or replacement.

e. We will not pay more for loss or damage on a replacement cost basis than the least of **(1)**, **(2)** or **(3)**, subject to **f.** below:

(1) The Limit of Insurance applicable to the lost or damaged property;

(2) The cost to replace the lost or damaged property with other property:

(a) Of comparable material and quality; and

(b) Used for the same purpose; or

(3) The amount actually spent that is necessary to repair or replace the lost or damaged property.

If a building is rebuilt at a new premises, the cost described in **e.(2)** above is limited to the cost which would have been incurred if the building had been rebuilt at the original premises.

f. The cost of repair or replacement does not include the increased cost attributable to enforcement of any ordinance or law regulating the construction, use or repair of any property.

4. Extension Of Replacement Cost To Personal Property Of Others

a. If the Replacement Cost Optional Coverage is shown as applicable in the Declarations, then this Extension may also be shown as applicable. If the Declarations show this Extension as applicable, then Paragraph **3.b.(1)** of the Replacement Cost Optional Coverage is deleted and all other provisions of the Replacement Cost Optional Coverage apply to replacement cost on personal property of others.

b. With respect to replacement cost on the personal property of others, the following limitation applies:

If an item(s) of personal property of others is subject to a written contract which governs your liability for loss or damage to that item(s), then valuation of that item(s) will be based on the amount for which you are liable under such contract, but not to exceed the lesser of the replacement cost of the property or the applicable Limit of Insurance.

H. Definitions

1. "Fungus" means any type or form of fungus, including mold or mildew, and any mycotoxins, spores, scents or by-products produced or released by fungi.

2. "Pollutants" means any solid, liquid, gaseous or thermal irritant or contaminant, including smoke, vapor, soot, fumes, acids, alkalis, chemicals and waste. Waste includes materials to be recycled, reconditioned or reclaimed.

3. "Stock" means merchandise held in storage or for sale, raw materials and in-process or finished goods, including supplies used in their packing or shipping.

COMMERCIAL PROPERTY
CP 00 17 06 07

CONDOMINIUM ASSOCIATION COVERAGE FORM

Various provisions in this policy restrict coverage. Read the entire policy carefully to determine rights, duties and what is and is not covered.

Throughout this policy the words "you" and "your" refer to the Named Insured shown in the Declarations. The words "we", "us" and "our" refer to the Company providing this insurance.

Other words and phrases that appear in quotation marks have special meaning. Refer to Section **H.**, Definitions.

A. Coverage

We will pay for direct physical loss of or damage to Covered Property at the premises described in the Declarations caused by or resulting from any Covered Cause of Loss.

1. Covered Property

Covered Property, as used in this Coverage Part, means the type of property described in this section, **A.1.**, and limited in **A.2.**, Property Not Covered, if a Limit of Insurance is shown in the Declarations for that type of property.

a. Building, meaning the building or structure described in the Declarations, including:

(1) Completed additions;

(2) Fixtures, outside of individual units, including outdoor fixtures;

(3) Permanently installed:

(a) Machinery; and

(b) Equipment;

(4) Personal property owned by you that is used to maintain or service the building or structure or its premises, including:

(a) Fire-extinguishing equipment;

(b) Outdoor furniture;

(c) Floor coverings; and

(d) Appliances used for refrigerating, ventilating, cooking, dishwashing or laundering that are not contained within individual units;

(5) If not covered by other insurance:

(a) Additions under construction, alterations and repairs to the building or structure;

(b) Materials, equipment, supplies, and temporary structures, on or within 100 feet of the described premises, used for making additions, alterations or repairs to the building or structure; and

(6) Any of the following types of property contained within a unit, regardless of ownership, if your Condominium Association Agreement requires you to insure it:

(a) Fixtures, improvements and alterations that are a part of the building or structure; and

(b) Appliances, such as those used for refrigerating, ventilating, cooking, dishwashing, laundering, security or housekeeping.

But Building does not include personal property owned by, used by or in the care, custody or control of a unit-owner except for personal property listed in Paragraph **A.1.a.(6)** above.

b. Your Business Personal Property located in or on the building described in the Declarations or in the open (or in a vehicle) within 100 feet of the described premises, consisting of the following:

(1) Personal property owned by you or owned indivisibly by all unit-owners;

(2) Your interest in the labor, materials or services furnished or arranged by you on personal property of others;

(3) Leased personal property for which you have a contractual responsibility to insure, unless otherwise provided for under Personal Property Of Others.

But Your Business Personal Property does not include personal property owned only by a unit-owner.

c. Personal Property Of Others that is:

(1) In your care, custody or control; and

(2) Located in or on the building described in the Declarations or in the open (or in a vehicle) within 100 feet of the described premises.

However, our payment for loss of or damage to personal property of others will only be for the account of the owner of the property.

2. Property Not Covered

Covered Property does not include:

a. Accounts, bills, currency, food stamps or other evidences of debt, money, notes or securities. Lottery tickets held for sale are not securities;

b. Animals, unless owned by others and boarded by you;

c. Automobiles held for sale;

d. Bridges, roadways, walks, patios or other paved surfaces;

e. Contraband, or property in the course of illegal transportation or trade;

f. The cost of excavations, grading, backfilling or filling;

g. Foundations of buildings, structures, machinery or boilers if their foundations are below:

(1) The lowest basement floor; or

(2) The surface of the ground if there is no basement;

h. Land (including land on which the property is located), water, growing crops or lawns;

i. Personal property while airborne or waterborne;

j. Bulkheads, pilings, piers, wharves or docks;

k. Property that is covered under this or any other policy in which it is more specifically described, except for the excess of the amount due (whether you can collect on it or not) from that other insurance;

l. Retaining walls that are not part of a building;

m. Underground pipes, flues or drains;

n. Electronic data, except as provided under the Additional Coverage, Electronic Data. Electronic data means information, facts or computer programs stored as or on, created or used on, or transmitted to or from computer software (including systems and applications software), on hard or floppy disks, CD-ROMs, tapes, drives, cells, data processing devices or any other repositories of computer software which are used with electronically controlled equipment. The term computer programs, referred to in the foregoing description of electronic data, means a set of related electronic instructions which direct the operations and functions of a computer or device connected to it, which enable the computer or device to receive, process, store, retrieve or send data;

o. The cost to replace or restore the information on valuable papers and records, including those which exist as electronic data. Valuable papers and records include but are not limited to proprietary information, books of account, deeds, manuscripts, abstracts, drawings and card index systems. Refer to the Coverage Extension for Valuable Papers And Records (Other Than Electronic Data) for limited coverage for valuable papers and records other than those which exist as electronic data;

p. Vehicles or self-propelled machines (including aircraft or watercraft) that:

(1) Are licensed for use on public roads; or

(2) Are operated principally away from the described premises.

This paragraph does not apply to:

(a) Vehicles or self-propelled machines or autos you manufacture or warehouse;

(b) Vehicles or self-propelled machines, other than autos, you hold for sale;

(c) Rowboats or canoes out of water at the described premises; or

(d) Trailers, but only to the extent provided for in the Coverage Extension for Non-owned Detached Trailers;

q. The following property while outside of buildings:

(1) Grain, hay, straw or other crops; or

(2) Fences, radio or television antennas (including satellite dishes) and their lead-in wiring, masts or towers, trees, shrubs, or plants (other than "stock" of trees, shrubs or plants), all except as provided in the Coverage Extensions.

3. **Covered Causes Of Loss**

See applicable Causes Of Loss Form as shown in the Declarations.

4. **Additional Coverages**

a. **Debris Removal**

(1) Subject to Paragraphs (3) and (4), we will pay your expense to remove debris of Covered Property caused by or resulting from a Covered Cause of Loss that occurs during the policy period. The expenses will be paid only if they are reported to us in writing within 180 days of the date of direct physical loss or damage.

(2) Debris Removal does not apply to costs to:

(a) Extract "pollutants" from land or water; or

(b) Remove, restore or replace polluted land or water.

(3) Subject to the exceptions in Paragraph (4), the following provisions apply:

(a) The most we will pay for the total of direct physical loss or damage plus debris removal expense is the Limit of Insurance applicable to the Covered Property that has sustained loss or damage.

(b) Subject to (a) above, the amount we will pay for debris removal expense is limited to 25% of the sum of the deductible plus the amount that we pay for direct physical loss or damage to the Covered Property that has sustained loss or damage.

(4) We will pay up to an additional $10,000 for debris removal expense, for each location, in any one occurrence of physical loss or damage to Covered Property, if one or both of the following circumstances apply:

(a) The total of the actual debris removal expense plus the amount we pay for direct physical loss or damage exceeds the Limit of Insurance on the Covered Property that has sustained loss or damage.

(b) The actual debris removal expense exceeds 25% of the sum of the deductible plus the amount that we pay for direct physical loss or damage to the Covered Property that has sustained loss or damage.

Therefore, if (4)(a) and/or (4)(b) apply, our total payment for direct physical loss or damage and debris removal expense may reach but will never exceed the Limit of Insurance on the Covered Property that has sustained loss or damage, plus $10,000.

(5) **Examples**

The following examples assume that there is no Coinsurance penalty.

EXAMPLE #1

Limit of Insurance:	$ 90,000
Amount of Deductible:	$ 500
Amount of Loss:	$ 50,000
Amount of Loss Payable:	$ 49,500
	($50,000 – $500)
Debris Removal Expense:	$ 10,000
Debris Removal Expense Payable:	$ 10,000

($10,000 is 20% of $50,000.)

The debris removal expense is less than 25% of the sum of the loss payable plus the deductible. The sum of the loss payable and the debris removal expense ($49,500 + $10,000 = $59,500) is less than the Limit of Insurance. Therefore, the full amount of debris removal expense is payable in accordance with the terms of Paragraph (3).

EXAMPLE #2

Limit of Insurance:	$ 90,000
Amount of Deductible:	$ 500
Amount of Loss:	$ 80,000
Amount of Loss Payable:	$ 79,500
	($80,000 – $500)
Debris Removal Expense:	$ 30,000
Debris Removal Expense Payable	
Basic Amount:	$ 10,500
Additional Amount:	$ 10,000

The basic amount payable for debris removal expense under the terms of Paragraph **(3)** is calculated as follows: $80,000 ($79,500 + $500) x .25 = $20,000; capped at $10,500. The cap applies because the sum of the loss payable ($79,500) and the basic amount payable for debris removal expense ($10,500) cannot exceed the Limit of Insurance ($90,000).

The additional amount payable for debris removal expense is provided in accordance with the terms of Paragraph **(4)**, because the debris removal expense ($30,000) exceeds 25% of the loss payable plus the deductible ($30,000 is 37.5% of $80,000), and because the sum of the loss payable and debris removal expense ($79,500 + $30,000 = $109,500) would exceed the Limit of Insurance ($90,000). The additional amount of covered debris removal expense is $10,000, the maximum payable under Paragraph **(4)**. Thus the total payable for debris removal expense in this example is $20,500; $9,500 of the debris removal expense is not covered.

b. Preservation Of Property

If it is necessary for you to move Covered Property from the described premises to preserve it from loss or damage by a Covered Cause of Loss, we will pay for any direct physical loss or damage to that property:

(1) While it is being moved or while temporarily stored at another location; and

(2) Only if the loss or damage occurs within 30 days after the property is first moved.

c. Fire Department Service Charge

When the fire department is called to save or protect Covered Property from a Covered Cause of Loss, we will pay up to $1,000, unless a higher limit is shown in the Declarations, for your liability for fire department service charges:

(1) Assumed by contract or agreement prior to loss; or

(2) Required by local ordinance.

No Deductible applies to this Additional Coverage.

d. Pollutant Clean-up And Removal

We will pay your expense to extract "pollutants" from land or water at the described premises if the discharge, dispersal, seepage, migration, release or escape of the "pollutants" is caused by or results from a Covered Cause of Loss that occurs during the policy period. The expenses will be paid only if they are reported to us in writing within 180 days of the date on which the Covered Cause of Loss occurs.

This Additional Coverage does not apply to costs to test for, monitor or assess the existence, concentration or effects of "pollutants". But we will pay for testing which is performed in the course of extracting the "pollutants" from the land or water.

The most we will pay under this Additional Coverage for each described premises is $10,000 for the sum of all covered expenses arising out of Covered Causes of Loss occurring during each separate 12-month period of this policy.

e. Increased Cost Of Construction

(1) This Additional Coverage applies only to buildings to which the Replacement Cost Optional Coverage applies.

(2) In the event of damage by a Covered Cause of Loss to a building that is Covered Property, we will pay the increased costs incurred to comply with enforcement of an ordinance or law in the course of repair, rebuilding or replacement of damaged parts of that property, subject to the limitations stated in **e.(3)** through **e.(9)** of this Additional Coverage.

(3) The ordinance or law referred to in **e.(2)** of this Additional Coverage is an ordinance or law that regulates the construction or repair of buildings or establishes zoning or land use requirements at the described premises, and is in force at the time of loss.

(4) Under this Additional Coverage, we will not pay any costs due to an ordinance or law that:

(a) You were required to comply with before the loss, even when the building was undamaged; and

(b) You failed to comply with.

© ISO Properties, Inc., 2007

(5) Under this Additional Coverage, we will not pay for:

(a) The enforcement of any ordinance or law which requires demolition, repair, replacement, reconstruction, remodeling or remediation of property due to contamination by "pollutants" or due to the presence, growth, proliferation, spread or any activity of "fungus", wet or dry rot or bacteria; or

(b) Any costs associated with the enforcement of an ordinance or law which requires any insured or others to test for, monitor, clean up, remove, contain, treat, detoxify or neutralize, or in any way respond to, or assess the effects of "pollutants", "fungus", wet or dry rot or bacteria.

(6) The most we will pay under this Additional Coverage, for each described building insured under this Coverage Form, is $10,000 or 5% of the Limit of Insurance applicable to that building, whichever is less. If a damaged building is covered under a blanket Limit of Insurance which applies to more than one building or item of property, then the most we will pay under this Additional Coverage, for that damaged building, is the lesser of: $10,000 or 5% times the value of the damaged building as of the time of loss times the applicable Coinsurance percentage.

The amount payable under this Additional Coverage is additional insurance.

(7) With respect to this Additional Coverage:

(a) We will not pay for the Increased Cost of Construction:

(i) Until the property is actually repaired or replaced, at the same or another premises; and

(ii) Unless the repairs or replacement are made as soon as reasonably possible after the loss or damage, not to exceed two years. We may extend this period in writing during the two years.

(b) If the building is repaired or replaced at the same premises, or if you elect to rebuild at another premises, the most we will pay for the Increased Cost of Construction, subject to the provisions of **e.(6)** of this Additional Coverage, is the increased cost of construction at the same premises.

(c) If the ordinance or law requires relocation to another premises, the most we will pay for the Increased Cost of Construction, subject to the provisions of **e.(6)** of this Additional Coverage, is the increased cost of construction at the new premises.

(8) This Additional Coverage is not subject to the terms of the Ordinance Or Law Exclusion, to the extent that such Exclusion would conflict with the provisions of this Additional Coverage.

(9) The costs addressed in the Loss Payment and Valuation Conditions, and the Replacement Cost Optional Coverage, in this Coverage Form, do not include the increased cost attributable to enforcement of an ordinance or law. The amount payable under this Additional Coverage, as stated in **e.(6)** of this Additional Coverage, is not subject to such limitation.

f. Electronic Data

(1) Under this Additional Coverage, electronic data has the meaning described under Property Not Covered, Electronic Data.

(2) Subject to the provisions of this Additional Coverage, we will pay for the cost to replace or restore electronic data which has been destroyed or corrupted by a Covered Cause of Loss. To the extent that electronic data is not replaced or restored, the loss will be valued at the cost of replacement of the media on which the electronic data was stored, with blank media of substantially identical type.

(3) The Covered Causes of Loss applicable to Your Business Personal Property apply to this Additional Coverage, Electronic Data, subject to the following:

(a) If the Causes Of Loss – Special Form applies, coverage under this Additional Coverage, Electronic Data, is limited to the "specified causes of loss" as defined in that form, and Collapse as set forth in that form.

(b) If the Causes Of Loss – Broad Form applies, coverage under this Additional Coverage, Electronic Data, includes Collapse as set forth in that form.

(c) If the Causes Of Loss Form is endorsed to add a Covered Cause of Loss, the additional Covered Cause of Loss does not apply to the coverage provided under this Additional Coverage, Electronic Data.

(d) The Covered Causes of Loss include a virus, harmful code or similar instruction introduced into or enacted on a computer system (including electronic data) or a network to which it is connected, designed to damage or destroy any part of the system or disrupt its normal operation. But there is no coverage for loss or damage caused by or resulting from manipulation of a computer system (including electronic data) by any employee, including a temporary or leased employee, or by an entity retained by you or for you to inspect, design, install, modify, maintain, repair or replace that system.

(4) The most we will pay under this Additional Coverage, Electronic Data, is $2,500 for all loss or damage sustained in any one policy year, regardless of the number of occurrences of loss or damage or the number of premises, locations or computer systems involved. If loss payment on the first occurrence does not exhaust this amount, then the balance is available for subsequent loss or damage sustained in but not after that policy year. With respect to an occurrence which begins in one policy year and continues or results in additional loss or damage in a subsequent policy year(s), all loss or damage is deemed to be sustained in the policy year in which the occurrence began.

5. Coverage Extensions

Except as otherwise provided, the following Extensions apply to property located in or on the building described in the Declarations or in the open (or in a vehicle) within 100 feet of the described premises.

If a Coinsurance percentage of 80% or more is shown in the Declarations, you may extend the insurance provided by this Coverage Part as follows:

a. Newly Acquired Or Constructed Property

(1) Buildings

You may extend the insurance that applies to Building to apply to:

(a) Your new buildings while being built on the described premises; and

(b) Buildings you acquire at locations, other than the described premises, intended for:

(i) Similar use as the building described in the Declarations; or

(ii) Use as a warehouse.

The most we will pay for loss or damage under this Extension is $250,000 at each building.

(2) Your Business Personal Property

(a) If this policy covers Your Business Personal Property, you may extend that insurance to apply to:

(i) Business personal property, including such property that you newly acquire, at any location you acquire other than at fairs, trade shows or exhibitions;

(ii) Business personal property, including such property that you newly acquire, located at your newly constructed or acquired buildings at the location described in the Declarations; or

(iii) Business personal property that you newly acquire, located at the described premises.

The most we will pay for loss or damage under this Extension is $100,000 at each building.

(b) This Extension does not apply to:

(i) Personal property of others that is temporarily in your possession in the course of installing or performing work on such property; or

(ii) Personal property of others that is temporarily in your possession in the course of your manufacturing or wholesaling activities.

(3) Period Of Coverage

With respect to insurance on or at each newly acquired or constructed property, coverage will end when any of the following first occurs:

(a) This policy expires;

(b) 30 days expire after you acquire the property or begin construction of that part of the building that would qualify as covered property; or

(c) You report values to us.

We will charge you additional premium for values reported from the date you acquire the property or begin construction of that part of the building that would qualify as covered property.

b. Personal Effects And Property Of Others

You may extend the insurance that applies to Your Business Personal Property to apply to:

(1) Personal effects owned by you, your officers, your partners or members, your managers or your employees. This Extension does not apply to loss or damage by theft.

(2) Personal property of others in your care, custody or control.

The most we will pay for loss or damage under this Extension is $2,500 at each described premises. Our payment for loss of or damage to personal property of others will only be for the account of the owner of the property.

c. Valuable Papers And Records (Other Than Electronic Data)

(1) You may extend the insurance that applies to Your Business Personal Property to apply to the cost to replace or restore the lost information on valuable papers and records for which duplicates do not exist. But this Extension does not apply to valuable papers and records which exist as electronic data. Electronic data has the meaning described under Property Not Covered, Electronic Data.

(2) If the Causes Of Loss – Special Form applies, coverage under this Extension is limited to the "specified causes of loss" as defined in that form, and Collapse as set forth in that form.

(3) If the Causes Of Loss – Broad Form applies, coverage under this Extension includes Collapse as set forth in that form.

(4) Under this Extension, the most we will pay to replace or restore the lost information is $2,500 at each described premises, unless a higher limit is shown in the Declarations. Such amount is additional insurance. We will also pay for the cost of blank material for reproducing the records (whether or not duplicates exist), and (when there is a duplicate) for the cost of labor to transcribe or copy the records. The costs of blank material and labor are subject to the applicable Limit of Insurance on Your Business Personal Property and therefore coverage of such costs is not additional insurance.

d. Property Off-premises

(1) You may extend the insurance provided by this Coverage Form to apply to your Covered Property while it is away from the described premises, if it is:

(a) Temporarily at a location you do not own, lease or operate;

(b) In storage at a location you lease, provided the lease was executed after the beginning of the current policy term; or

(c) At any fair, trade show or exhibition.

(2) This Extension does not apply to property:

(a) In or on a vehicle; or

(b) In the care, custody or control of your salespersons, unless the property is in such care, custody or control at a fair, trade show or exhibition.

(3) The most we will pay for loss or damage under this Extension is $10,000.

e. Outdoor Property

You may extend the insurance provided by this Coverage Form to apply to your outdoor fences, radio and television antennas (including satellite dishes), trees, shrubs and plants (other than "stock" of trees, shrubs or plants), including debris removal expense, caused by or resulting from any of the following causes of loss if they are Covered Causes of Loss:

(1) Fire;

(2) Lightning;

(3) Explosion;

(4) Riot or Civil Commotion; or

(5) Aircraft.

The most we will pay for loss or damage under this Extension is $1,000, but not more than $250 for any one tree, shrub or plant. These limits apply to any one occurrence, regardless of the types or number of items lost or damaged in that occurrence.

f. Non-owned Detached Trailers

(1) You may extend the insurance that applies to Your Business Personal Property to apply to loss or damage to trailers that you do not own, provided that:

(a) The trailer is used in your business;

(b) The trailer is in your care, custody or control at the premises described in the Declarations; and

(c) You have a contractual responsibility to pay for loss or damage to the trailer.

(2) We will not pay for any loss or damage that occurs:

(a) While the trailer is attached to any motor vehicle or motorized conveyance, whether or not the motor vehicle or motorized conveyance is in motion;

(b) During hitching or unhitching operations, or when a trailer becomes accidentally unhitched from a motor vehicle or motorized conveyance.

(3) The most we will pay for loss or damage under this Extension is $5,000, unless a higher limit is shown in the Declarations.

(4) This insurance is excess over the amount due (whether you can collect on it or not) from any other insurance covering such property.

Each of these Extensions is additional insurance unless otherwise indicated. The Additional Condition, Coinsurance, does not apply to these Extensions.

B. Exclusions And Limitations

See applicable Causes Of Loss Form as shown in the Declarations.

C. Limits Of Insurance

The most we will pay for loss or damage in any one occurrence is the applicable Limit of Insurance shown in the Declarations.

The most we will pay for loss or damage to outdoor signs, whether or not the sign is attached to a building, is $2,500 per sign in any one occurrence.

The amounts of insurance stated in the following Additional Coverages apply in accordance with the terms of such coverages and are separate from the Limit(s) of Insurance shown in the Declarations for any other coverage:

1. Fire Department Service Charge;

2. Pollutant Clean-up And Removal;

3. Increased Cost Of Construction; and

4. Electronic Data.

Payments under the Preservation Of Property Additional Coverage will not increase the applicable Limit of Insurance.

D. Deductible

In any one occurrence of loss or damage (hereinafter referred to as loss), we will first reduce the amount of loss if required by the Coinsurance Condition or the Agreed Value Optional Coverage. If the adjusted amount of loss is less than or equal to the Deductible, we will not pay for that loss. If the adjusted amount of loss exceeds the Deductible, we will then subtract the Deductible from the adjusted amount of loss, and will pay the resulting amount or the Limit of Insurance, whichever is less.

When the occurrence involves loss to more than one item of Covered Property and separate Limits of Insurance apply, the losses will not be combined in determining application of the Deductible. But the Deductible will be applied only once per occurrence.

EXAMPLE #1

(This example assumes there is no Coinsurance penalty.)

Deductible:	$	250
Limit of Insurance – Building #1:	$	60,000
Limit of Insurance – Building #2:	$	80,000
Loss to Building #1:	$	60,100
Loss to Building #2:	$	90,000

The amount of loss to Building #1 ($60,100) is less than the sum ($60,250) of the Limit of Insurance applicable to Building #1 plus the Deductible.

The Deductible will be subtracted from the amount of loss in calculating the loss payable for Building #1:

$ 60,100
– 250

$ 59,850   Loss Payable – Building #1

The Deductible applies once per occurrence and therefore is not subtracted in determining the amount of loss payable for Building #2. Loss payable for Building #2 is the Limit of Insurance of $80,000.

Total amount of loss payable:

$59,850 + $80,000 = $139,850

EXAMPLE #2

(This example, too, assumes there is no Coinsurance penalty.)

The Deductible and Limits of Insurance are the same as those in Example #1.

Loss to Building #1:	$	70,000
(Exceeds Limit of Insurance plus Deductible)		
Loss to Building #2:	$	90,000
(Exceeds Limit of Insurance plus Deductible)		
Loss Payable – Building #1:	$	60,000
(Limit of Insurance)		
Loss Payable – Building #2:	$	80,000
(Limit of Insurance)		
Total amount of loss payable:	$	140,000

E. Loss Conditions

The following conditions apply in addition to the Common Policy Conditions and the Commercial Property Conditions.

1. Abandonment

There can be no abandonment of any property to us.

2. Appraisal

If we and you disagree on the value of the property or the amount of loss, either may make written demand for an appraisal of the loss. In this event, each party will select a competent and impartial appraiser. The two appraisers will select an umpire. If they cannot agree, either may request that selection be made by a judge of a court having jurisdiction. The appraisers will state separately the value of the property and amount of loss. If they fail to agree, they will submit their differences to the umpire. A decision agreed to by any two will be binding. Each party will:

a. Pay its chosen appraiser; and

b. Bear the other expenses of the appraisal and umpire equally.

If there is an appraisal, we will still retain our right to deny the claim.

3. Duties In The Event Of Loss Or Damage

a. You must see that the following are done in the event of loss or damage to Covered Property:

(1) Notify the police if a law may have been broken.

(2) Give us prompt notice of the loss or damage. Include a description of the property involved.

(3) As soon as possible, give us a description of how, when and where the loss or damage occurred.

(4) Take all reasonable steps to protect the Covered Property from further damage, and keep a record of your expenses necessary to protect the Covered Property, for consideration in the settlement of the claim. This will not increase the Limit of Insurance. However, we will not pay for any subsequent loss or damage resulting from a cause of loss that is not a Covered Cause of Loss. Also, if feasible, set the damaged property aside and in the best possible order for examination.

(5) At our request, give us complete inventories of the damaged and undamaged property. Include quantities, costs, values and amount of loss claimed.

(6) As often as may be reasonably required, permit us to inspect the property proving the loss or damage and examine your books and records.

Also permit us to take samples of damaged and undamaged property for inspection, testing and analysis, and permit us to make copies from your books and records.

(7) Send us a signed, sworn proof of loss containing the information we request to investigate the claim. You must do this within 60 days after our request. We will supply you with the necessary forms.

(8) Cooperate with us in the investigation or settlement of the claim.

b. We may examine any insured under oath, while not in the presence of any other insured and at such times as may be reasonably required, about any matter relating to this insurance or the claim, including an insured's books and records. In the event of an examination, an insured's answers must be signed.

4. **Loss Payment**

a. In the event of loss or damage covered by this Coverage Form, at our option, we will either:

(1) Pay the value of lost or damaged property;

(2) Pay the cost of repairing or replacing the lost or damaged property, subject to **b.** below;

(3) Take all or any part of the property at an agreed or appraised value; or

(4) Repair, rebuild or replace the property with other property of like kind and quality, subject to **b.** below.

We will determine the value of lost or damaged property, or the cost of its repair or replacement, in accordance with the applicable terms of the Valuation Condition in this Coverage Form or any applicable provision which amends or supersedes the Valuation Condition.

b. The cost to repair, rebuild or replace does not include the increased cost attributable to enforcement of any ordinance or law regulating the construction, use or repair of any property.

c. We will give notice of our intentions within 30 days after we receive the sworn proof of loss.

d. We will not pay you more than your financial interest in the Covered Property.

e. We may adjust losses with the owners of lost or damaged property if other than you. If we pay the owners, such payments will satisfy your claims against us for the owners' property. We will not pay the owners more than their financial interest in the Covered Property.

f. We may elect to defend you against suits arising from claims of owners of property. We will do this at our expense.

g. We will pay for covered loss or damage to Covered Property within 30 days after we receive the sworn proof of loss, if you have complied with all of the terms of this Coverage Part and:

(1) We have reached agreement with you on the amount of loss; or

(2) An appraisal award has been made.

If you name an insurance trustee, we will adjust losses with you, but we will pay the insurance trustee. If we pay the trustee, the payments will satisfy your claims against us.

h. A party wall is a wall that separates and is common to adjoining buildings that are owned by different parties. In settling covered losses involving a party wall, we will pay a proportion of the loss to the party wall based on your interest in the wall in proportion to the interest of the owner of the adjoining building. However, if you elect to repair or replace your building and the owner of the adjoining building elects not to repair or replace that building, we will pay you the full value of the loss to the party wall, subject to all applicable policy provisions including Limits of Insurance, the Valuation and Coinsurance Conditions and all other provisions of this Loss Payment Condition. Our payment under the provisions of this paragraph does not alter any right of subrogation we may have against any entity, including the owner or insurer of the adjoining building, and does not alter the terms of the Transfer Of Rights Of Recovery Against Others To Us Condition in this policy.

         CP 00 17 06 07   □

5. Recovered Property

If either you or we recover any property after loss settlement, that party must give the other prompt notice. At your option, the property will be returned to you. You must then return to us the amount we paid to you for the property. We will pay recovery expenses and the expenses to repair the recovered property, subject to the Limit of Insurance.

6. Unit-owner's Insurance

A unit-owner may have other insurance covering the same property as this insurance. This insurance is intended to be primary, and not to contribute with such other insurance.

7. Vacancy

a. Description Of Terms

(1) As used in this Vacancy Condition, the term building and the term vacant have the meanings set forth in **(1)(a)** and **(1)(b)** below:

(a) When this policy is issued to a tenant, and with respect to that tenant's interest in Covered Property, building means the unit or suite rented or leased to the tenant. Such building is vacant when it does not contain enough business personal property to conduct customary operations.

(b) When this policy is issued to the owner or general lessee of a building, building means the entire building. Such building is vacant unless at least 31% of its total square footage is:

(i) Rented to a lessee or sub-lessee and used by the lessee or sub-lessee to conduct its customary operations; and/or

(ii) Used by the building owner to conduct customary operations.

(2) Buildings under construction or renovation are not considered vacant.

b. Vacancy Provisions

If the building where loss or damage occurs has been vacant for more than 60 consecutive days before that loss or damage occurs:

(1) We will not pay for any loss or damage caused by any of the following even if they are Covered Causes of Loss:

(a) Vandalism;

(b) Sprinkler leakage, unless you have protected the system against freezing;

(c) Building glass breakage;

(d) Water damage;

(e) Theft; or

(f) Attempted theft.

(2) With respect to Covered Causes of Loss other than those listed in **b.(1)(a)** through **b.(1)(f)** above, we will reduce the amount we would otherwise pay for the loss or damage by 15%.

8. Valuation

We will determine the value of Covered Property in the event of loss or damage as follows:

a. At actual cash value as of the time of loss or damage, except as provided in **b.** and **c.** below.

b. If the Limit of Insurance for Building satisfies the Additional Condition, Coinsurance, and the cost to repair or replace the damaged building property is $2,500 or less, we will pay the cost of building repairs or replacement.

The cost of building repairs or replacement does not include the increased cost attributable to enforcement of any ordinance or law regulating the construction, use or repair of any property. However, the following property will be valued at the actual cash value even when attached to the building:

(1) Awnings or floor coverings;

(2) Appliances for refrigerating, ventilating, cooking, dishwashing or laundering; or

(3) Outdoor equipment or furniture.

c. Glass at the cost of replacement with safety-glazing material if required by law.

9. Waiver Of Rights Of Recovery

We waive our rights to recover payment from any unit-owner of the condominium that is shown in the Declarations.

F. Additional Conditions

The following conditions apply in addition to the Common Policy Conditions and the Commercial Property Conditions.

1. Coinsurance

If a Coinsurance percentage is shown in the Declarations, the following condition applies.

a. We will not pay the full amount of any loss if the value of Covered Property at the time of loss times the Coinsurance percentage shown for it in the Declarations is greater than the Limit of Insurance for the property.

Instead, we will determine the most we will pay using the following steps:

(1) Multiply the value of Covered Property at the time of loss by the Coinsurance percentage;

(2) Divide the Limit of Insurance of the property by the figure determined in Step (1);

(3) Multiply the total amount of loss, before the application of any deductible, by the figure determined in Step (2); and

(4) Subtract the deductible from the figure determined in Step (3).

We will pay the amount determined in Step (4) or the Limit of Insurance, whichever is less. For the remainder, you will either have to rely on other insurance or absorb the loss yourself.

EXAMPLE #1 (UNDERINSURANCE)

When: The value of the property is: $ 250,000

The Coinsurance percentage for it is: 80%

The Limit of Insurance for it is: $ 100,000

The Deductible is: $ 250

The amount of loss is: $ 40,000

Step (1): $250,000 x 80% = $200,000

(the minimum amount of insurance to meet your Coinsurance requirements)

Step (2): $100,000 ÷ $200,000 = .50

Step (3): $40,000 x .50 = $20,000

Step (4): $20,000 – $250 = $19,750

We will pay no more than $19,750. The remaining $20,250 is not covered.

EXAMPLE #2 (ADEQUATE INSURANCE)

When: The value of the property is: $ 250,000

The Coinsurance percentage for it is: 80%

The Limit of Insurance for it is: $ 200,000

The Deductible is: $ 250

The amount of loss is: $ 40,000

The minimum amount of insurance to meet your Co-insurance requirement is $200,000 ($250,000 x 80%). Therefore, the Limit of Insurance in this example is adequate and no penalty applies. We will pay no more than $39,750 ($40,000 amount of loss minus the deductible of $250).

b. If one Limit of Insurance applies to two or more separate items, this condition will apply to the total of all property to which the limit applies.

EXAMPLE #3

When: The value of the property is:

Building at Location #1: $ 75,000

Building at Location #2: $ 100,000

Personal Property at Location #2: $ 75,000

$ 250,000

The Coinsurance percentage for it is: 90%

The Limit of Insurance for Buildings and Personal Property at Locations #1 and #2 is: $ 180,000

The Deductible is: $ 1,000

The amount of loss is:

Building at Location #2: $ 30,000

Personal Property at Location #2: $ 20,000

$ 50,000

Step (1): $250,000 x 90% = $225,000

(the minimum amount of insurance to meet your Coinsurance requirements and to avoid the penalty shown below)

Step (2): $180,000 ÷ $225,000 = .80

Step (3): $50,000 x .80 = $40,000

Step (4): $40,000 – $1,000 = $39,000

We will pay no more than $39,000. The remaining $11,000 is not covered.

2. Mortgageholders

a. The term mortgageholder includes trustee.

b. We will pay for covered loss of or damage to buildings or structures to each mortgageholder shown in the Declarations in their order of precedence, as interests may appear.

c. The mortgageholder has the right to receive loss payment even if the mortgageholder has started foreclosure or similar action on the building or structure.

d. If we deny your claim because of your acts or because you have failed to comply with the terms of this Coverage Part, the mortgageholder will still have the right to receive loss payment if the mortgageholder:

(1) Pays any premium due under this Coverage Part at our request if you have failed to do so;

(2) Submits a signed, sworn proof of loss within 60 days after receiving notice from us of your failure to do so; and

(3) Has notified us of any change in ownership, occupancy or substantial change in risk known to the mortgageholder.

All of the terms of this Coverage Part will then apply directly to the mortgageholder.

e. If we pay the mortgageholder for any loss or damage and deny payment to you because of your acts or because you have failed to comply with the terms of this Coverage Part:

(1) The mortgageholder's rights under the mortgage will be transferred to us to the extent of the amount we pay; and

(2) The mortgageholder's right to recover the full amount of the mortgageholder's claim will not be impaired.

At our option, we may pay to the mortgageholder the whole principal on the mortgage plus any accrued interest. In this event, your mortgage and note will be transferred to us and you will pay your remaining mortgage debt to us.

f. If we cancel this policy, we will give written notice to the mortgageholder at least:

(1) 10 days before the effective date of cancellation if we cancel for your nonpayment of premium; or

(2) 30 days before the effective date of cancellation if we cancel for any other reason.

g. If we elect not to renew this policy, we will give written notice to the mortgageholder at least 10 days before the expiration date of this policy.

G. Optional Coverages

If shown as applicable in the Declarations, the following Optional Coverages apply separately to each item.

1. Agreed Value

a. The Additional Condition, Coinsurance, does not apply to Covered Property to which this Optional Coverage applies. We will pay no more for loss of or damage to that property than the proportion that the Limit of Insurance under this Coverage Part for the property bears to the Agreed Value shown for it in the Declarations.

b. If the expiration date for this Optional Coverage shown in the Declarations is not extended, the Additional Condition, Coinsurance, is reinstated and this Optional Coverage expires.

c. The terms of this Optional Coverage apply only to loss or damage that occurs:

(1) On or after the effective date of this Optional Coverage; and

(2) Before the Agreed Value expiration date shown in the Declarations or the policy expiration date, whichever occurs first.

2. Inflation Guard

a. The Limit of Insurance for property to which this Optional Coverage applies will automatically increase by the annual percentage shown in the Declarations.

b. The amount of increase will be:

(1) The Limit of Insurance that applied on the most recent of the policy inception date, the policy anniversary date, or any other policy change amending the Limit of Insurance, times

(2) The percentage of annual increase shown in the Declarations, expressed as a decimal (example: 8% is .08), times

(3) The number of days since the beginning of the current policy year or the effective date of the most recent policy change amending the Limit of Insurance, divided by 365.

EXAMPLE

If: The applicable Limit of Insurance is: $ 100,000

The annual percentage increase is: 8%

The number of days since the beginning of the policy year (or last policy change) is: 146

The amount of increase is: $100,000 x .08 x 146 ÷ 365 = $ 3,200

3. Replacement Cost

a. Replacement Cost (without deduction for depreciation) replaces Actual Cash Value in the Loss Condition, Valuation, of this Coverage Form.

b. This Optional Coverage does not apply to:

(1) Personal property of others;

(2) Contents of a residence; or

(3) Works of art, antiques or rare articles, including etchings, pictures, statuary, marbles, bronzes, porcelains and bric-a-brac.

Under the terms of this Replacement Cost Optional Coverage, personal property owned indivisibly by all unit-owners, and the property covered under Paragraph **A.1.a.(6)** of this Coverage Form, are not considered to be the personal property of others.

c. You may make a claim for loss or damage covered by this insurance on an actual cash value basis instead of on a replacement cost basis. In the event you elect to have loss or damage settled on an actual cash value basis, you may still make a claim for the additional coverage this Optional Coverage provides if you notify us of your intent to do so within 180 days after the loss or damage.

d. We will not pay on a replacement cost basis for any loss or damage:

(1) Until the lost or damaged property is actually repaired or replaced; and

(2) Unless the repairs or replacement are made as soon as reasonably possible after the loss or damage.

e. We will not pay more for loss or damage on a replacement cost basis than the least of (1), (2) or (3), subject to f. below:

(1) The Limit of Insurance applicable to the lost or damaged property;

(2) The cost to replace the lost or damaged property with other property:

(a) Of comparable material and quality; and

(b) Used for the same purpose; or

(3) The amount actually spent that is necessary to repair or replace the lost or damaged property.

If a building is rebuilt at a new premises, the cost described in **e.(2)** above is limited to the cost which would have been incurred if the building had been rebuilt at the original premises.

f. The cost of repair or replacement does not include the increased cost attributable to enforcement of any ordinance or law regulating the construction, use or repair of any property.

4. Extension Of Replacement Cost To Personal Property Of Others

a. If the Replacement Cost Optional Coverage is shown as applicable in the Declarations, then this Extension may also be shown as applicable. If the Declarations show this Extension as applicable, then Paragraph **3.b.(1)** of the Replacement Cost Optional Coverage is deleted and all other provisions of the Replacement Cost Optional Coverage apply to replacement cost on personal property of others.

b. With respect to replacement cost on the personal property of others, the following limitation applies:

If an item(s) of personal property of others is subject to a written contract which governs your liability for loss or damage to that item(s), then valuation of that item(s) will be based on the amount for which you are liable under such contract, but not to exceed the lesser of the replacement cost of the property or the applicable Limit of Insurance.

H. Definitions

1. "Fungus" means any type or form of fungus, including mold or mildew, and any mycotoxins, spores, scents or by-products produced or released by fungi.

2. "Pollutants" means any solid, liquid, gaseous or thermal irritant or contaminant, including smoke, vapor, soot, fumes, acids, alkalis, chemicals and waste. Waste includes materials to be recycled, reconditioned or reclaimed.

 CP 00 17 06 07

COMMERCIAL PROPERTY
CP 00 18 06 07

CONDOMINIUM COMMERCIAL UNIT-OWNERS COVERAGE FORM

Various provisions in this policy restrict coverage. Read the entire policy carefully to determine rights, duties and what is and is not covered.

Throughout this policy the words "you" and "your" refer to the Named Insured shown in the Declarations. The words "we", "us" and "our" refer to the Company providing this insurance.

Other words and phrases that appear in quotation marks have special meaning. Refer to Section **H.**, Definitions.

A. Coverage

We will pay for direct physical loss of or damage to Covered Property at the premises described in the Declarations caused by or resulting from any Covered Cause of Loss.

1. Covered Property

Covered Property, as used in this Coverage Part, means the type of property described in this section, **A.1.**, and limited in **A.2.**, Property Not Covered, if a Limit of Insurance is shown in the Declarations for that type of property.

a. Your Business Personal Property located in or on the building described in the Declarations or in the open (or in a vehicle) within 100 feet of the described premises, consisting of the following unless otherwise specified in the Declarations or on the Your Business Personal Property – Separation Of Coverage form:

(1) Furniture;

(2) Fixtures, improvements and alterations making up part of the building and owned by you;

(3) Machinery and equipment;

(4) "Stock";

(5) All other personal property owned by you and used in your business;

(6) Labor, materials or services furnished or arranged by you on personal property of others;

(7) Leased personal property for which you have a contractual responsibility to insure, unless otherwise provided for under Personal Property Of Others.

b. Personal Property Of Others that is:

(1) In your care, custody or control; and

(2) Located in or on the building described in the Declarations or in the open (or in a vehicle) within 100 feet of the described premises.

However, our payment for loss of or damage to personal property of others will only be for the account of the owner of the property.

2. Property Not Covered

Covered Property does not include:

a. Accounts, bills, currency, food stamps or other evidences of debt, money, notes or securities. Lottery tickets held for sale are not securities;

b. Animals, unless owned by others and boarded by you, or if owned by you, only as "stock" while inside of buildings;

c. Automobiles held for sale;

d. Contraband, or property in the course of illegal transportation or trade;

e. Water, growing crops or lawns;

f. Personal property while airborne or waterborne;

g. Property that is covered under another coverage form of this or any other policy in which it is more specifically described, except for the excess of the amount due (whether you can collect on it or not) from that other insurance;

h. Electronic data, except as provided under the Additional Coverage, Electronic Data. Electronic data means information, facts or computer programs stored as or on, created or used on, or transmitted to or from computer software (including systems and applications software), on hard or floppy disks, CD-ROMs, tapes, drives, cells, data processing devices or any other repositories of computer software which are used with electronically controlled equipment. The term computer programs, referred to in the foregoing description of electronic data, means a set of related electronic instructions which direct the operations and functions of a computer or device connected to it, which enable the computer or device to receive, process, store, retrieve or send data. This paragraph, **h.**, does not apply to your "stock" of prepackaged software;

i. The cost to replace or restore the information on valuable papers and records, including those which exist as electronic data. Valuable papers and records include but are not limited to proprietary information, books of account, deeds, manuscripts, abstracts, drawings and card index systems. Refer to the Coverage Extension for Valuable Papers And Records (Other Than Electronic Data) for limited coverage for valuable papers and records other than those which exist as electronic data;

j. Vehicles or self-propelled machines (including aircraft or watercraft) that:

    (1) Are licensed for use on public roads; or

    (2) Are operated principally away from the described premises.

    This paragraph does not apply to:

    (a) Vehicles or self-propelled machines or autos you manufacture, process or warehouse;

    (b) Vehicles or self-propelled machines, other than autos, you hold for sale;

    (c) Rowboats or canoes out of water at the described premises; or

    (d) Trailers, but only to the extent provided for in the Coverage Extension for Non-owned Detached Trailers;

k. The following property while outside of buildings:

    (1) Grain, hay, straw or other crops; or

(2) Fences, radio or television antennas (including satellite dishes) and their lead-in wiring, masts or towers, trees, shrubs, or plants (other than "stock" of trees, shrubs or plants), all except as provided in the Coverage Extensions;

l. Any of the following types of property contained within a unit, regardless of ownership, if your Condominium Association Agreement requires the Association to insure it:

    (1) Fixtures, improvements and alterations that are a part of the building; and

    (2) Appliances, such as those used for refrigerating, ventilating, cooking, dishwashing, laundering, security or housekeeping.

3. Covered Causes Of Loss

See applicable Causes Of Loss Form as shown in the Declarations.

4. Additional Coverages

a. Debris Removal

    (1) Subject to Paragraphs **(3)** and **(4)**, we will pay your expense to remove debris of Covered Property caused by or resulting from a Covered Cause of Loss that occurs during the policy period. The expenses will be paid only if they are reported to us in writing within 180 days of the date of direct physical loss or damage.

    (2) Debris Removal does not apply to costs to:

    (a) Extract "pollutants" from land or water; or

    (b) Remove, restore or replace polluted land or water.

    (3) Subject to the exceptions in Paragraph **(4)**, the following provisions apply:

    (a) The most we will pay for the total of direct physical loss or damage plus debris removal expense is the Limit of Insurance applicable to the Covered Property that has sustained loss or damage.

    (b) Subject to **(a)** above, the amount we will pay for debris removal expense is limited to 25% of the sum of the deductible plus the amount that we pay for direct physical loss or damage to the Covered Property that has sustained loss or damage.

 ☐

(4) We will pay up to an additional $10,000 for debris removal expense, for each location, in any one occurrence of physical loss or damage to Covered Property, if one or both of the following circumstances apply:

(a) The total of the actual debris removal expense plus the amount we pay for direct physical loss or damage exceeds the Limit of Insurance on the Covered Property that has sustained loss or damage.

(b) The actual debris removal expense exceeds 25% of the sum of the deductible plus the amount that we pay for direct physical loss or damage to the Covered Property that has sustained loss or damage.

Therefore, if **(4)(a)** and/or **(4)(b)** apply, our total payment for direct physical loss or damage and debris removal expense may reach but will never exceed the Limit of Insurance on the Covered Property that has sustained loss or damage, plus $10,000.

(5) Examples

The following examples assume that there is no Coinsurance penalty.

EXAMPLE #1

Limit of Insurance:	$ 90,000
Amount of Deductible:	$ 500
Amount of Loss:	$ 50,000
Amount of Loss Payable:	$ 49,500
	($50,000 − $500)
Debris Removal Expense:	$ 10,000
Debris Removal Expense Payable:	$ 10,000

($10,000 is 20% of $50,000.)

The debris removal expense is less than 25% of the sum of the loss payable plus the deductible. The sum of the loss payable and the debris removal expense ($49,500 + $10,000 = $59,500) is less than the Limit of Insurance. Therefore the full amount of debris removal expense is payable in accordance with the terms of Paragraph **(3)**.

EXAMPLE #2

Limit of Insurance:	$ 90,000
Amount of Deductible:	$ 500
Amount of Loss:	$ 80,000
Amount of Loss Payable:	$ 79,500
	($80,000 − $500)
Debris Removal Expense:	$ 30,000
Debris Removal Expense Payable	
Basic Amount:	$ 10,500
Additional Amount:	$ 10,000

The basic amount payable for debris removal expense under the terms of Paragraph **(3)** is calculated as follows: $80,000 ($79,500 + $500) x .25 = $20,000; capped at $10,500. The cap applies because the sum of the loss payable ($79,500) and the basic amount payable for debris removal expense ($10,500) cannot exceed the Limit of Insurance ($90,000).

The additional amount payable for debris removal expense is provided in accordance with the terms of Paragraph **(4)**, because the debris removal expense ($30,000) exceeds 25% of the loss payable plus the deductible ($30,000 is 37.5% of $80,000), and because the sum of the loss payable and debris removal expense ($79,500 + $30,000 = $109,500) would exceed the Limit of Insurance ($90,000). The additional amount of covered debris removal expense is $10,000, the maximum payable under Paragraph **(4)**. Thus the total payable for debris removal expense in this example is $20,500; $9,500 of the debris removal expense is not covered.

b. Preservation Of Property

If it is necessary to move Covered Property from the described premises to preserve it from loss or damage by a Covered Cause of Loss, we will pay for any direct physical loss or damage to that property:

(1) While it is being moved or while temporarily stored at another location; and

(2) Only if the loss or damage occurs within 30 days after the property is first moved.

c. Fire Department Service Charge

When the fire department is called to save or protect Covered Property from a Covered Cause of Loss, we will pay up to $1,000, unless a higher limit is shown in the Declarations, for your liability for fire department service charges:

(1) Assumed by contract or agreement prior to loss; or

(2) Required by local ordinance.

No Deductible applies to this Additional Coverage.

d. Pollutant Clean-up And Removal

We will pay your expense to extract "pollutants" from land or water at the described premises if the discharge, dispersal, seepage, migration, release or escape of the "pollutants" is caused by or results from a Covered Cause of Loss that occurs during the policy period. The expenses will be paid only if they are reported to us in writing within 180 days of the date on which the Covered Cause of Loss occurs.

This Additional Coverage does not apply to costs to test for, monitor or assess the existence, concentration or effects of "pollutants". But we will pay for testing which is performed in the course of extracting the "pollutants" from the land or water.

The most we will pay under this Additional Coverage for each described premises is $10,000 for the sum of all covered expenses arising out of Covered Causes of Loss occurring during each separate 12-month period of this policy.

e. Electronic Data

(1) Under this Additional Coverage, electronic data has the meaning described under Property Not Covered, Electronic Data.

(2) Subject to the provisions of this Additional Coverage, we will pay for the cost to replace or restore electronic data which has been destroyed or corrupted by a Covered Cause of Loss. To the extent that electronic data is not replaced or restored, the loss will be valued at the cost of replacement of the media on which the electronic data was stored, with blank media of substantially identical type.

(3) The Covered Causes of Loss applicable to Your Business Personal Property apply to this Additional Coverage, Electronic Data, subject to the following:

(a) If the Causes Of Loss – Special Form applies, coverage under this Additional Coverage, Electronic Data, is limited to the "specified causes of loss" as defined in that form, and Collapse as set forth in that form.

(b) If the Causes Of Loss – Broad Form applies, coverage under this Additional Coverage, Electronic Data, includes Collapse as set forth in that form.

(c) If the Causes Of Loss Form is endorsed to add a Covered Cause of Loss, the additional Covered Cause of Loss does not apply to the coverage provided under this Additional Coverage, Electronic Data.

(d) The Covered Causes of Loss include a virus, harmful code or similar instruction introduced into or enacted on a computer system (including electronic data) or a network to which it is connected, designed to damage or destroy any part of the system or disrupt its normal operation. But there is no coverage for loss or damage caused by or resulting from manipulation of a computer system (including electronic data) by any employee, including a temporary or leased employee, or by an entity retained by you or for you to inspect, design, install, modify, maintain, repair or replace that system.

(4) The most we will pay under this Additional Coverage, Electronic Data, is $2,500 for all loss or damage sustained in any one policy year, regardless of the number of occurrences of loss or damage or the number of premises, locations or computer systems involved. If loss payment on the first occurrence does not exhaust this amount, then the balance is available for subsequent loss or damage sustained in but not after that policy year. With respect to an occurrence which begins in one policy year and continues or results in additional loss or damage in a subsequent policy year(s), all loss or damage is deemed to be sustained in the policy year in which the occurrence began.

© ISO Properties, Inc., 2007   **CP 00 18 06 07**   ☐

5. Coverage Extensions

Except as otherwise provided, the following Extensions apply to property located in or on the building described in the Declarations or in the open (or in a vehicle) within 100 feet of the described premises.

If a Coinsurance percentage of 80% or more, or a Value Reporting period symbol, is shown in the Declarations, you may extend the insurance provided by this Coverage Part as follows:

a. Newly Acquired Property

(1) You may extend the insurance that applies to Your Business Personal Property to apply to:

  (a) Business personal property, including such property that you newly acquire, at any location you acquire other than at fairs, trade shows or exhibitions;

  (b) Business personal property, including such property that you newly acquire, located at your newly constructed or acquired buildings at the location described in the Declarations; or

  (c) Business personal property that you newly acquire, located at the described premises.

The most we will pay for loss or damage under this Extension is $100,000 at each building.

(2) This Extension does not apply to:

  (a) Personal property of others that is temporarily in your possession in the course of installing or performing work on such property; or

  (b) Personal property of others that is temporarily in your possession in the course of your manufacturing or wholesaling activities.

(3) Insurance under this Extension for each newly acquired property will end when any of the following first occurs:

  (a) This policy expires;

  (b) 30 days expire after you acquire the property; or

  (c) You report values to us.

We will charge you additional premium for values reported from the date you acquire the property.

b. Personal Effects And Property Of Others

You may extend the insurance that applies to Your Business Personal Property to apply to:

(1) Personal effects owned by you, your officers, your partners or members, your managers or your employees. This extension does not apply to loss or damage by theft.

(2) Personal property of others, in your care, custody or control.

The most we will pay for loss or damage under this Extension is $2,500 at each described premises. Our payment for loss of or damage to personal property of others will only be for the account of the owner of the property.

c. Valuable Papers And Records (Other Than Electronic Data)

(1) You may extend the insurance that applies to Your Business Personal Property to apply to the cost to replace or restore the lost information on valuable papers and records for which duplicates do not exist. But this Extension does not apply to valuable papers and records which exist as electronic data. Electronic data has the meaning described under Property Not Covered, Electronic Data.

(2) If the Causes Of Loss – Special Form applies, coverage under this Extension is limited to the "specified causes of loss" as defined in that form, and Collapse as set forth in that form.

(3) If the Causes Of Loss – Broad Form applies, coverage under this Extension includes Collapse as set forth in that form.

(4) Under this Extension, the most we will pay to replace or restore the lost information is $2,500 at each described premises, unless a higher limit is shown in the Declarations. Such amount is additional insurance. We will also pay for the cost of blank material for reproducing the records (whether or not duplicates exist), and (when there is a duplicate) for the cost of labor to transcribe or copy the records. The costs of blank material and labor are subject to the applicable Limit of Insurance on Your Business Personal Property and therefore coverage of such costs is not additional insurance.

d. Property Off-premises

(1) You may extend the insurance that applies to Your Business Personal Property, to apply to your business personal property while it is away from the described premises, if it is:

(a) Temporarily at a location you do not own, lease or operate;

(b) In storage at a location you lease, provided the lease was executed after the beginning of the current policy term; or

(c) At any fair, trade show or exhibition.

(2) This Extension does not apply to property:

(a) In or on a vehicle; or

(b) In the care, custody or control of your salespersons, unless the property is in such care, custody or control at a fair, trade show or exhibition.

3) The most we will pay for loss or damage under this Extension is $10,000.

e. Outdoor Property

You may extend the insurance that applies to Your Business Personal Property to apply to your outdoor fences, radio and television antennas (including satellite dishes), trees, shrubs and plants (other than "stock" of trees, shrubs or plants), including debris removal expense, caused by or resulting from any of the following causes of loss if they are Covered Causes of Loss:

(1) Fire;

(2) Lightning;

(3) Explosion;

(4) Riot or Civil Commotion; or

(5) Aircraft.

The most we will pay for loss or damage under this Extension is $1,000, but not more than $250 for any one tree, shrub or plant. These limits apply to any one occurrence, regardless of the types or number of items lost or damaged in that occurrence.

f. Non-owned Detached Trailers

(1) You may extend the insurance that applies to Your Business Personal Property to apply to loss or damage to trailers that you do not own, provided that:

(a) The trailer is used in your business;

(b) The trailer is in your care, custody or control at the premises described in the Declarations; and

(c) You have a contractual responsibility to pay for loss or damage to the trailer.

(2) We will not pay for any loss or damage that occurs:

(a) While the trailer is attached to any motor vehicle or motorized conveyance, whether or not the motor vehicle or motorized conveyance is in motion;

(b) During hitching or unhitching operations, or when a trailer becomes accidentally unhitched from a motor vehicle or motorized conveyance.

(3) The most we will pay for loss or damage under this Extension is $5,000, unless a higher limit is shown in the Declarations.

(4) This insurance is excess over the amount due (whether you can collect on it or not) from any other insurance covering such property.

Each of these Extensions is additional insurance unless otherwise indicated. The Additional Condition, Coinsurance, does not apply to these Extensions.

B. Exclusions And Limitations

See applicable Causes Of Loss Form as shown in the Declarations.

C. Limits Of Insurance

The most we will pay for loss or damage in any one occurrence is the applicable Limit of Insurance shown in the Declarations.

The most we will pay for loss or damage to outdoor signs, whether or not the sign is attached to a building, is $2,500 per sign in any one occurrence.

The amounts of insurance stated in the following Additional Coverages apply in accordance with the terms of such coverages and are separate from the Limit(s) of Insurance shown in the Declarations for any other coverage:

1. Fire Department Service Charge;

2. Pollutant Clean-up And Removal; and

3. Electronic Data.

Payments under the Preservation Of Property Additional Coverage will not increase the applicable Limit of Insurance.

© ISO Properties, Inc., 2007 CP 00 18 06 07

D. Deductible

In any one occurrence of loss or damage (hereinafter referred to as loss), we will first reduce the amount of loss if required by the Coinsurance Condition or the Agreed Value Optional Coverage. If the adjusted amount of loss is less than or equal to the Deductible, we will not pay for that loss. If the adjusted amount of loss exceeds the Deductible, we will then subtract the Deductible from the adjusted amount of loss, and will pay the resulting amount or the Limit of Insurance, whichever is less.

When the occurrence involves loss to more than one item of Covered Property and separate Limits of Insurance apply, the losses will not be combined in determining application of the Deductible. But the Deductible will be applied only once per occurrence.

EXAMPLE #1

(This example assumes there is no Coinsurance penalty.)

Deductible:	$ 250
Limit of Insurance – Building #1:	$ 60,000
Limit of Insurance – Building #2:	$ 80,000
Loss to Building #1:	$ 60,100
Loss to Building #2:	$ 90,000

The amount of loss to Building #1 ($60,100) is less than the sum ($60,250) of the Limit of Insurance applicable to Building #1 plus the Deductible.

The Deductible will be subtracted from the amount of loss in calculating the loss payable for Building #1:

$ 60,100
– 250
$ 59,850   Loss Payable – Building #1

The Deductible applies once per occurrence and therefore is not subtracted in determining the amount of loss payable for Building #2. Loss payable for Building #2 is the Limit of Insurance of $80,000.

Total amount of loss payable:

$59,850 + $80,000 = $139,850

EXAMPLE #2

(This example, too, assumes there is no Coinsurance penalty.)

The Deductible and Limits of Insurance are the same as those in Example #1.

Loss to Building #1:	$ 70,000
(Exceeds Limit of Insurance plus Deductible)	
Loss to Building #2:	$ 90,000
(Exceeds Limit of Insurance plus Deductible)	
Loss Payable – Building #1:	$ 60,000
(Limit of Insurance)	
Loss Payable – Building #2:	$ 80,000
(Limit of Insurance)	
Total amount of loss payable:	$ 140,000

E. Loss Conditions

The following conditions apply in addition to the Common Policy Conditions and the Commercial Property Conditions.

1. Abandonment

There can be no abandonment of any property to us.

2. Appraisal

If we and you disagree on the value of the property or the amount of loss, either may make written demand for an appraisal of the loss. In this event, each party will select a competent and impartial appraiser. The two appraisers will select an umpire. If they cannot agree, either may request that selection be made by a judge of a court having jurisdiction. The appraisers will state separately the value of the property and amount of loss. If they fail to agree, they will submit their differences to the umpire. A decision agreed to by any two will be binding. Each party will:

a. Pay its chosen appraiser; and

b. Bear the other expenses of the appraisal and umpire equally.

If there is an appraisal, we will still retain our right to deny the claim.

3. Condominium Association Insurance

The Condominium Association may have other insurance covering the same property as this insurance. This insurance is intended to be excess, and not to contribute with that other insurance.

4. Duties In The Event Of Loss Or Damage

a. You must see that the following are done in the event of loss or damage to Covered Property:

(1) Notify the police if a law may have been broken.

(2) Give us prompt notice of the loss or damage. Include a description of the property involved.

(3) As soon as possible, give us a description of how, when and where the loss or damage occurred.

(4) Take all reasonable steps to protect the Covered Property from further damage, and keep a record of your expenses necessary to protect the Covered Property, for consideration in the settlement of the claim. This will not increase the Limit of Insurance. However, we will not pay for any subsequent loss or damage resulting from a cause of loss that is not a Covered Cause of Loss. Also, if feasible, set the damaged property aside and in the best possible order for examination.

(5) At our request, give us complete inventories of the damaged and undamaged property. Include quantities, costs, values and amount of loss claimed.

(6) As often as may be reasonably required, permit us to inspect the property proving the loss or damage and examine your books and records.

Also permit us to take samples of damaged and undamaged property for inspection, testing and analysis, and permit us to make copies from your books and records.

(7) Send us a signed, sworn proof of loss containing the information we request to investigate the claim. You must do this within 60 days after our request. We will supply you with the necessary forms.

(8) Cooperate with us in the investigation or settlement of the claim.

b. We may examine any insured under oath, while not in the presence of any other insured and at such times as may be reasonably required, about any matter relating to this insurance or the claim, including an insured's books and records. In the event of an examination, an insured's answers must be signed.

5. Loss Payment

a. In the event of loss or damage covered by this Coverage Form, at our option, we will either:

(1) Pay the value of lost or damaged property;

(2) Pay the cost of repairing or replacing the lost or damaged property, subject to **b.** below;

(3) Take all or any part of the property at an agreed or appraised value; or

(4) Repair, rebuild or replace the property with other property of like kind and quality, subject to **b.** below.

We will determine the value of lost or damaged property, or the cost of its repair or replacement, in accordance with the applicable terms of the Valuation Condition in this Coverage Form or any applicable provision which amends or supersedes the Valuation Condition.

b. The cost to repair, rebuild or replace does not include the increased cost attributable to enforcement of any ordinance or law regulating the construction, use or repair of any property.

c. We will give notice of our intentions within 30 days after we receive the sworn proof of loss.

d. We will not pay you more than your financial interest in the Covered Property.

e. We may adjust losses with the owners of lost or damaged property if other than you. If we pay the owners, such payments will satisfy your claims against us for the owners' property. We will not pay the owners more than their financial interest in the Covered Property.

f. We may elect to defend you against suits arising from claims of owners of property. We will do this at our expense.

         CP 00 18 06 07   ☐

g. We will pay for covered loss or damage within 30 days after we receive the sworn proof of loss, if you have complied with all of the terms of this Coverage Part and:

(1) We have reached agreement with you on the amount of loss; or

(2) An appraisal award has been made.

6. Recovered Property

If either you or we recover any property after loss settlement, that party must give the other prompt notice. At your option, the property will be returned to you. You must then return to us the amount we paid to you for the property. We will pay recovery expenses to repair the recovered property, subject to the Limit of Insurance.

7. Vacancy

a. Description Of Terms

(1) As used in this Vacancy Condition, the term building and the term vacant have the meanings set forth in **(1)(a)** and **(1)(b)** below:

(a) When this policy is issued to a tenant, and with respect to that tenant's interest in Covered Property, building means the unit or suite rented or leased to the tenant. Such building is vacant when it does not contain enough business personal property to conduct customary operations.

(b) When this policy is issued to the owner or general lessee of a building, building means the entire building. Such building is vacant unless at least 31% of its total square footage is:

(i) Rented to a lessee or sub-lessee and used by the lessee or sub-lessee to conduct its customary operations; and/or

(ii) Used by the building owner to conduct customary operations.

(2) Buildings under construction or renovation are not considered vacant.

b. Vacancy Provisions

If the building where loss or damage occurs has been vacant for more than 60 consecutive days before that loss or damage occurs:

(1) We will not pay for any loss or damage caused by any of the following even if they are Covered Causes of Loss:

(a) Vandalism;

(b) Sprinkler leakage, unless you have protected the system against freezing;

(c) Building glass breakage;

(d) Water damage;

(e) Theft; or

(f) Attempted theft.

(2) With respect to Covered Causes of Loss other than those listed in **b.(1)(a)** through **b.(1)(f)** above, we will reduce the amount we would otherwise pay for the loss or damage by 15%.

8. Valuation

We will determine the value of Covered Property in the event of loss or damage as follows:

a. At actual cash value as of the time of loss or damage, except as provided in **b.** and **c.** below.

b. "Stock" you have sold but not delivered at the selling price less discounts and expenses you otherwise would have had.

c. Glass at the cost of replacement with safety-glazing material if required by law.

F. Additional Condition

COINSURANCE

If a Coinsurance percentage is shown in the Declarations, the following condition applies in addition to the Common Policy Conditions and the Commercial Property Conditions.

a. We will not pay the full amount of any loss if the value of Covered Property at the time of loss times the Coinsurance percentage shown for it in the Declarations is greater than the Limit of Insurance for the property.

Instead, we will determine the most we will pay using the following steps:

(1) Multiply the value of Covered Property at the time of loss by the Coinsurance percentage;

(2) Divide the Limit of Insurance of the property by the figure determined in Step **(1)**;

(3) Multiply the total amount of loss, before the application of any deductible, by the figure determined in Step **(2)**; and

(4) Subtract the deductible from the figure determined in Step **(3)**.

We will pay the amount determined in Step **(4)** or the limit of insurance, whichever is less. For the remainder, you will either have to rely on other insurance or absorb the loss yourself.

EXAMPLE #1 (UNDERINSURANCE)

When:	The value of the property is:	$ 250,000
	The Coinsurance percentage for it is:	80%
	The Limit of Insurance for it is:	$ 100,000
	The Deductible is:	$ 250
	The amount of loss is:	$ 40,000

Step (1): $250,000 x 80% = $200,000

(the minimum amount of insurance to meet your Coinsurance requirements)

Step (2): $100,000 ÷ $200,000 = .50

Step (3): $40,000 x .50 = $20,000

Step (4): $20,000 – $250 = $19,750

We will pay no more than $19,750. The remaining $20,250 is not covered.

EXAMPLE #2 (ADEQUATE INSURANCE)

When:	The value of the property is:	$ 250,000
	The Coinsurance percentage for it is:	80%
	The Limit of Insurance for it is:	$ 200,000
	The Deductible is:	$ 250
	The amount of loss is:	$ 40,000

The minimum amount of insurance to meet your Co-insurance requirement is $200,000 ($250,000 x 80%). Therefore, the Limit of Insurance in this Example is adequate and no penalty applies. We will pay no more than $39,750 ($40,000 amount of loss minus the deductible of $250).

b. If one Limit of Insurance applies to two or more separate items, this condition will apply to the total of all property to which the limit applies.

EXAMPLE #3

When:	The value of the property is:	
	Personal Property at Location #1:	$ 175,000
	Personal Property at Location #2:	$ 75,000
		$ 250,000
	The Coinsurance percentage for it is:	90%
	The Limit of Insurance for Personal Property at Locations #1 and #2 is:	$ 180,000
	The Deductible is:	$ 1,000
	The amount of loss is:	
	Personal Property at Location #1:	$ 30,000
	Personal Property at Location #2:	$ 20,000
		$ 50,000

Step (1): $250,000 x 90% = $225,000

(the minimum amount of insurance to meet your Coinsurance requirements and to avoid the penalty shown below)

Step (2): $180,000 ÷ $225,000 = .80

Step (3): $50,000 x .80 = $40,000

Step (4): $40,000 – $1,000 = $39,000

We will pay no more than $39,000. The remaining $11,000 is not covered.

G. Optional Coverages

If shown as applicable in the Declarations, the following Optional Coverages apply separately to each item:

1. Agreed Value

a. The Additional Condition, Coinsurance, does not apply to Covered Property to which this Optional Coverage applies. We will pay no more for loss of or damage to that property than the proportion that the Limit of Insurance under this Coverage Part for the property bears to the Agreed Value shown for it in the Declarations.

b. If the expiration date for this Optional Coverage shown in the Declarations is not extended, the Additional Condition, Coinsurance, is reinstated and this Optional Coverage expires.

       CP 00 18 06 07   □

c. The terms of this Optional Coverage apply only to loss or damage that occurs:

(1) On or after the effective date of this Optional Coverage; and

(2) Before the Agreed Value expiration date shown in the Declarations or the policy expiration date, whichever occurs first.

2. Inflation Guard

a. The Limit of Insurance for property to which this Optional Coverage applies will automatically increase by the annual percentage shown in the Declarations.

b. The amount of increase will be:

(1) The Limit of Insurance that applied on the most recent of the policy inception date, the policy anniversary date, or any other policy change amending the Limit of Insurance, times

(2) The percentage of annual increase shown in the Declarations, expressed as a decimal (example: 8% is .08), times

(3) The number of days since the beginning of the current policy year or the effective date of the most recent policy change amending the Limit of Insurance, divided by 365.

EXAMPLE

If: The applicable Limit of Insurance is: $ 100,000

The annual percentage increase is: 8%

The number of days since the beginning of the policy year (or last policy change) is: 146

The amount of increase is: $100,000 x .08 x 146 ÷ 365 = $ 3,200

3. Replacement Cost

a. Replacement Cost (without deduction for depreciation) replaces Actual Cash Value in the Loss Condition, Valuation, of this Coverage Form.

b. This Optional Coverage does not apply to:

(1) Personal property of others;

(2) Contents of a residence;

(3) Works of art, antiques or rare articles, including etchings, pictures, statuary, marbles, bronzes, porcelains and bric-a-brac; or

(4) "Stock", unless the Including "Stock" option is shown in the Declarations.

c. You may make a claim for loss or damage covered by this insurance on an actual cash value basis instead of on a replacement cost basis. In the event you elect to have loss or damage settled on an actual cash value basis, you may still make a claim for the additional coverage this Optional Coverage provides if you notify us of your intent to do so within 180 days after the loss or damage.

d. We will not pay on a replacement cost basis for any loss or damage:

(1) Until the lost or damaged property is actually repaired or replaced; and

(2) Unless the repairs or replacement are made as soon as reasonably possible after the loss or damage.

e. We will not pay more for loss or damage on a replacement cost basis than the least of **(1)**, **(2)** or **(3)**, subject to **f.** below:

(1) The Limit of Insurance applicable to the lost or damaged property;

(2) The cost to replace the lost or damaged property with other property:

(a) Of comparable material and quality; and

(b) Used for the same purpose; or

(3) The amount actually spent that is necessary to repair or replace the lost or damaged property.

If a building is rebuilt at a new premises, the cost described in **e.(2)** above is limited to the cost which would have been incurred if the building had been rebuilt at the original premises.

f. The cost of repair or replacement does not include the increased cost attributable to enforcement of any ordinance or law regulating the construction, use or repair of any property.

4. Extension Of Replacement Cost To Personal Property Of Others

a. If the Replacement Cost Optional Coverage is shown as applicable in the Declarations, then this Extension may also be shown as applicable. If the Declarations show this Extension as applicable, then Paragraph **3.b.(1)** of the Replacement Cost Optional Coverage is deleted and all other provisions of the Replacement Cost Optional Coverage apply to replacement cost on personal property of others.

b. With respect to replacement cost on the personal property of others, the following limitation applies:

If an item(s) of personal property of others is subject to a written contract which governs your liability for loss or damage to that item(s), then valuation of that item(s) will be based on the amount for which you are liable under such contract, but not to exceed the lesser of the replacement cost of the property or the applicable Limit of Insurance.

H. Definitions

1. "Pollutants" means any solid, liquid, gaseous or thermal irritant or contaminant, including smoke, vapor, soot, fumes, acids, alkalis, chemicals and waste. Waste includes materials to be recycled, reconditioned or reclaimed.

2. "Stock" means merchandise held in storage or for sale, raw materials and in-process or finished goods, including supplies used in their packing or shipping.

BUILDERS RISK COVERAGE FORM

Various provisions in this policy restrict coverage. Read the entire policy carefully to determine rights, duties and what is and is not covered.

Throughout this policy the words "you" and "your" refer to the Named Insured shown in the Declarations. The words "we", "us" and "our" refer to the Company providing this insurance.

Other words and phrases that appear in quotation marks have special meaning. Refer to Section **G.,** Definitions.

A. Coverage

We will pay for direct physical loss of or damage to Covered Property at the premises described in the Declarations caused by or resulting from any Covered Cause of Loss.

1. Covered Property

Covered Property, as used in this Coverage Part, means the type of property described in this section, **A.1.,** and limited in **A.2.,** Property Not Covered, if a Limit of Insurance is shown in the Declarations for that type of property.

Building Under Construction, meaning the building or structure described in the Declarations while in the course of construction, including:

a. Foundations;

b. The following property:

(1) Fixtures and machinery;

(2) Equipment used to service the building; and

(3) Your building materials and supplies used for construction;

provided such property is intended to be permanently located in or on the building or structure described in the Declarations or within 100 feet of its premises;

c. If not covered by other insurance, temporary structures built or assembled on site, including cribbing, scaffolding and construction forms.

2. Property Not Covered

Covered Property does not include:

a. Land (including land on which the property is located) or water;

b. The following property when outside of buildings:

(1) Lawns, trees, shrubs or plants;

(2) Radio or television antennas (including satellite dishes) and their lead-in wiring, masts or towers; or

(3) Signs (other than signs attached to buildings).

3. Covered Causes Of Loss

See applicable Causes Of Loss Form as shown in the Declarations.

4. Additional Coverages

a. Debris Removal

(1) Subject to Paragraphs **(3)** and **(4)**, we will pay your expense to remove debris of Covered Property caused by or resulting from a Covered Cause of Loss that occurs during the policy period. The expenses will be paid only if they are reported to us in writing within 180 days of the date of direct physical loss or damage.

(2) Debris Removal does not apply to costs to:

(a) Extract "pollutants" from land or water; or

(b) Remove, restore or replace polluted land or water.

(3) Subject to the exceptions in Paragraph **(4)**, the following provisions apply:

(a) The most we will pay for the total of direct physical loss or damage plus debris removal expense is the Limit of Insurance applicable to the Covered Property that has sustained loss or damage.

(b) Subject to **(a)** above, the amount we will pay for debris removal expense is limited to 25% of the sum of the deductible plus the amount that we pay for direct physical loss or damage to the Covered Property that has sustained loss or damage.

(4) We will pay up to an additional $10,000 for debris removal expense, for each location, in any one occurrence of physical loss or damage to Covered Property, if one or both of the following circumstances apply:

(a) The total of the actual debris removal expense plus the amount we pay for direct physical loss or damage exceeds the Limit of Insurance on the Covered Property that has sustained loss or damage.

(b) The actual debris removal expense exceeds 25% of the sum of the deductible plus the amount that we pay for direct physical loss or damage to the Covered Property that has sustained loss or damage.

Therefore, if **(4)(a)** and/or **(4)(b)** apply, our total payment for direct physical loss or damage and debris removal expense may reach but will never exceed the Limit of Insurance on the Covered Property that has sustained loss or damage, plus $10,000.

(5) Examples

The following examples assume that there is no Coinsurance penalty.

EXAMPLE #1

Limit of Insurance:	$ 90,000
Amount of Deductible:	$ 500
Amount of Loss:	$ 50,000
Amount of Loss Payable:	$ 49,500
	($50,000 – $500)
Debris Removal Expense:	$ 10,000
Debris Removal Expense Payable:	$ 10,000

($10,000 is 20% of $50,000.)

The debris removal expense is less than 25% of the sum of the loss payable plus the deductible. The sum of the loss payable and the debris removal expense ($49,500 + $10,000 = $59,500) is less than the Limit of Insurance. Therefore, the full amount of debris removal expense is payable in accordance with the terms of Paragraph **(3)**.

EXAMPLE #2

Limit of Insurance:	$ 90,000
Amount of Deductible:	$ 500
Amount of Loss:	$ 80,000
Amount of Loss Payable:	$ 79,500
	($80,000 – $500)
Debris Removal Expense:	$ 30,000
Debris Removal Expense Payable	
Basic Amount:	$ 10,500
Additional Amount:	$ 10,000

The basic amount payable for debris removal expense under the terms of Paragraph **(3)** is calculated as follows: $80,000 ($79,500 + $500) x .25 = $20,000; capped at $10,500. The cap applies because the sum of the loss payable ($79,500) and the basic amount payable for debris removal expense ($10,500) cannot exceed the Limit of Insurance ($90,000).

The additional amount payable for debris removal expense is provided in accordance with the terms of Paragraph **(4),** because the debris removal expense ($30,000) exceeds 25% of the loss payable plus the deductible ($30,000 is 37.5% of $80,000), and because the sum of the loss payable and debris removal expense ($79,500 + $30,000 = $109,500) would exceed the Limit of Insurance ($90,000). The additional amount of covered debris removal expense is $10,000, the maximum payable under Paragraph **(4).** Thus the total payable for debris removal expense in this example is $20,500; $9,500 of the debris removal expense is not covered.

b. Preservation Of Property

If it is necessary to move Covered Property from the described premises to preserve it from loss or damage by a Covered Cause of Loss, we will pay for any direct physical loss or damage to that property:

(1) While it is being moved or while temporarily stored at another location; and

(2) Only if the loss or damage occurs within 30 days after the property is first moved.

       CP 00 20 06 07   ☐

c. Fire Department Service Charge

When the fire department is called to save or protect Covered Property from a Covered Cause of Loss, we will pay up to $1,000, unless a higher limit is shown in the Declarations, for your liability for fire department service charges:

(1) Assumed by contract or agreement prior to loss; or

(2) Required by local ordinance.

No Deductible applies to this Additional Coverage.

d. Pollutant Clean-up And Removal

We will pay your expense to extract "pollutants" from land or water at the described premises if the discharge, dispersal, seepage, migration, release or escape of the "pollutants" is caused by or results from a Covered Cause of Loss that occurs during the policy period. The expenses will be paid only if they are reported to us in writing within 180 days of the date on which the Covered Cause of Loss occurs.

This Additional Coverage does not apply to costs to test for, monitor or assess the existence, concentration or effects of "pollutants". But we will pay for testing which is performed in the course of extracting the "pollutants" from the land or water.

The most we will pay under this Additional Coverage for each described premises is $10,000 for the sum of all covered expenses arising out of Covered Causes of Loss occurring during each separate 12-month period of this policy.

5. Coverage Extensions

a. Building Materials And Supplies Of Others

(1) You may extend the insurance provided by this Coverage Form to apply to building materials and supplies that are:

(a) Owned by others;

(b) In your care, custody or control;

(c) Located in or on the building described in the Declarations, or within 100 feet of its premises; and

(d) Intended to become a permanent part of the building.

(2) The most we will pay for loss or damage under this Extension is $5,000 at each described premises, unless a higher Limit of Insurance is specified in the Declarations. Our payment for loss of or damage to property of others will only be for the account of the owner of the property.

b. Sod, Trees, Shrubs And Plants

You may extend the insurance provided by this Coverage Form to apply to loss or damage to sod, trees, shrubs and plants outside of buildings on the described premises, if the loss or damage is caused by or results from any of the following causes of loss:

(1) Fire;

(2) Lightning;

(3) Explosion;

(4) Riot or Civil Commotion; or

(5) Aircraft.

The most we will pay for loss or damage under this Extension is $1,000, but not more than $250 for any one tree, shrub or plant. These limits apply to any one occurrence, regardless of the types or number of items lost or damaged in that occurrence.

B. Exclusions And Limitations

See applicable Causes Of Loss Form as shown in the Declarations.

C. Limits Of Insurance

The most we will pay for loss or damage in any one occurrence is the applicable Limit of Insurance shown in the Declarations.

The most we will pay for loss or damage to outdoor signs attached to buildings is $2,500 per sign in any one occurrence.

The limits applicable to the Coverage Extensions and the Fire Department Service Charge and Pollutant Clean-up And Removal Additional Coverages are in addition to the Limits of Insurance.

Payments under the Preservation Of Property Additional Coverage will not increase the applicable Limit of Insurance.

D. Deductible

In any one occurrence of loss or damage (hereinafter referred to as loss), we will first reduce the amount of loss if required by the Additional Condition – Need For Adequate Insurance. If the adjusted amount of loss is less than or equal to the Deductible, we will not pay for that loss. If the adjusted amount of loss exceeds the Deductible, we will then subtract the Deductible from the adjusted amount of loss, and will pay the resulting amount or the Limit of Insurance, whichever is less.

When the occurrence involves loss to more than one item of Covered Property and separate Limits of Insurance apply, the losses will not be combined in determining application of the Deductible. But the Deductible will be applied only once per occurrence.

EXAMPLE #1

(This example assumes there is no penalty for under-insurance.)

Deductible:	$ 1,000
Limit of Insurance – Building #1:	$ 60,000
Limit of Insurance – Building #2:	$ 80,000
Loss to Building #1:	$ 60,100
Loss to Building #2:	$ 90,000

The amount of loss to Building #1 ($60,100) is less than the sum ($61,000) of the Limit of Insurance applicable to Building #1 plus the Deductible.

The Deductible will be subtracted from the amount of loss in calculating the loss payable for Building #1:

$ 60,100
– 1,000
$ 59,100   Loss Payable – Building #1

The Deductible applies once per occurrence and therefore is not subtracted in determining the amount of loss payable for Building #2. Loss payable for Building #2 is the Limit of Insurance of $80,000.

Total amount of loss payable: $59,100 + $80,000 = $139,100.

EXAMPLE #2

(This example, too, assumes there is no penalty for underinsurance.)

The Deductible and Limits of Insurance are the same as those in Example #1.

Loss to Building #1:	$ 70,000
(Exceeds Limit of Insurance plus Deductible)	
Loss to Building #2:	$ 90,000
(Exceeds Limit of Insurance plus Deductible)	
Loss Payable – Building #1:	$ 60,000
(Limit of Insurance)	
Loss Payable – Building #2:	$ 80,000
(Limit of Insurance)	
Total amount of loss payable:	$ 140,000

E. Loss Conditions

The following conditions apply in addition to the Common Policy Conditions and the Commercial Property Conditions.

1. Abandonment

There can be no abandonment of any property to us.

2. Appraisal

If we and you disagree on the value of the property or the amount of loss, either may make written demand for an appraisal of the loss. In this event, each party will select a competent and impartial appraiser. The two appraisers will select an umpire. If they cannot agree, either may request that selection be made by a judge of a court having jurisdiction. The appraisers will state separately the value of the property and amount of loss. If they fail to agree, they will submit their differences to the umpire. A decision agreed to by any two will be binding. Each party will:

a. Pay its chosen appraiser; and

b. Bear the other expenses of the appraisal and umpire equally.

If there is an appraisal, we will still retain our right to deny the claim.

CP 00 20 06 07   ☐

3. Duties In The Event Of Loss Or Damage

a. You must see that the following are done in the event of loss or damage to Covered Property:

(1) Notify the police if a law may have been broken.

(2) Give us prompt notice of the loss or damage. Include a description of the property involved.

(3) As soon as possible, give us a description of how, when and where the loss or damage occurred.

(4) Take all reasonable steps to protect the Covered Property from further damage, and keep a record of your expenses necessary to protect the Covered Property, for consideration in the settlement of the claim. This will not increase the Limit of Insurance. However, we will not pay for any subsequent loss or damage resulting from a cause of loss that is not a Covered Cause of Loss. Also, if feasible, set the damaged property aside and in the best possible order for examination.

(5) At our request, give us complete inventories of the damaged and undamaged property. Include quantities, costs, values and amount of loss claimed.

(6) As often as may be reasonably required, permit us to inspect the property proving the loss or damage and examine your books and records.

Also permit us to take samples of damaged and undamaged property for inspection, testing and analysis, and permit us to make copies from your books and records.

(7) Send us a signed, sworn proof of loss containing the information we request to investigate the claim. You must do this within 60 days after our request. We will supply you with the necessary forms.

(8) Cooperate with us in the investigation or settlement of the claim.

b. We may examine any insured under oath, while not in the presence of any other insured and at such times as may be reasonably required, about any matter relating to this insurance or the claim, including an insured's books and records. In the event of an examination, an insured's answers must be signed.

4. Loss Payment

a. In the event of loss or damage covered by this Coverage Form, at our option, we will either:

(1) Pay the value of lost or damaged property;

(2) Pay the cost of repairing or replacing the lost or damaged property, subject to **b.** below;

(3) Take all or any part of the property at an agreed or appraised value; or

(4) Repair, rebuild or replace the property with other property of like kind and quality, subject to **b.** below.

We will determine the value of lost or damaged property, or the cost of its repair or replacement, in accordance with the applicable terms of the Valuation Condition in this Coverage Form or any applicable provision which amends or supersedes the Valuation Condition.

b. The cost to repair, rebuild or replace does not include the increased cost attributable to enforcement of any ordinance or law regulating the construction, use or repair of any property.

c. We will give notice of our intentions within 30 days after we receive the sworn proof of loss.

d. We will not pay you more than your financial interest in the Covered Property.

e. We may adjust losses with the owners of lost or damaged property if other than you. If we pay the owners, such payments will satisfy your claims against us for the owners' property. We will not pay the owners more than their financial interest in the Covered Property.

f. We may elect to defend you against suits arising from claims of owners of property. We will do this at our expense.

g. We will pay for covered loss or damage within 30 days after we receive the sworn proof of loss, if you have complied with all of the terms of this Coverage Part and:

(1) We have reached agreement with you on the amount of loss; or

(2) An appraisal award has been made.

h. A party wall is a wall that separates and is common to adjoining buildings that are owned by different parties. In settling covered losses involving a party wall, we will pay a proportion of the loss to the party wall based on your interest in the wall in proportion to the interest of the owner of the adjoining building. However, if you elect to repair or replace your building and the owner of the adjoining building elects not to repair or replace that building, we will pay you the full value of the loss to the party wall, subject to all applicable policy provisions including Limits of Insurance, the Valuation and Coinsurance Conditions and all other provisions of this Loss Payment Condition. Our payment under the provisions of this paragraph does not alter any right of subrogation we may have against any entity, including the owner or insurer of the adjoining building, and does not alter the terms of the Transfer Of Rights Of Recovery Against Others To Us Condition in this policy.

5. Recovered Property

If either you or we recover any property after loss settlement, that party must give the other prompt notice. At your option, the property will be returned to you. You must then return to us the amount we paid to you for the property. We will pay recovery expenses and the expenses to repair the recovered property, subject to the Limit of Insurance.

6. Valuation

We will determine the value of Covered Property at actual cash value as of the time of loss or damage.

F. Additional Conditions

The following conditions apply in addition to the Common Policy Conditions and the Commercial Property Conditions.

1. Mortgageholders

a. The term mortgageholder includes trustee.

b. We will pay for covered loss of or damage to buildings or structures to each mortgageholder shown in the Declarations in their order of precedence, as interests may appear.

c. The mortgageholder has the right to receive loss payment even if the mortgageholder has started foreclosure or similar action on the building or structure.

d. If we deny your claim because of your acts or because you have failed to comply with the terms of this Coverage Part, the mortgageholder will still have the right to receive loss payment if the mortgageholder:

(1) Pays any premium due under this Coverage Part at our request if you have failed to do so;

(2) Submits a signed, sworn proof of loss within 60 days after receiving notice from us of your failure to do so; and

(3) Has notified us of any change in ownership, occupancy or substantial change in risk known to the mortgageholder.

All of the terms of this Coverage Part will then apply directly to the mortgageholder.

e. If we pay the mortgageholder for any loss or damage and deny payment to you because of your acts or because you have failed to comply with the terms of this Coverage Part:

(1) The mortgageholder's rights under the mortgage will be transferred to us to the extent of the amount we pay; and

(2) The mortgageholder's right to recover the full amount of the mortgageholder's claim will not be impaired.

At our option, we may pay to the mortgageholder the whole principal on the mortgage plus any accrued interest. In this event, your mortgage and note will be transferred to us and you will pay your remaining mortgage debt to us.

f. If we cancel this policy, we will give written notice to the mortgageholder at least:

(1) 10 days before the effective date of cancellation if we cancel for your nonpayment of premium; or

(2) 30 days before the effective date of cancellation if we cancel for any other reason.

g. If we elect not to renew this policy, we will give written notice to the mortgageholder at least 10 days before the expiration date of this policy.

2. Need For Adequate Insurance

We will not pay a greater share of any loss than the proportion that the Limit of Insurance bears to the value on the date of completion of the building described in the Declarations.

     CP 00 20 06 07   ◻

EXAMPLE #1 (UNDERINSURANCE)

When: The value of the building on
the date of completion is: $ 200,000

The Limit of Insurance for it is: $ 100,000

The Deductible is: $ 500

The amount of loss is: $ 80,000

Step **(1):** $100,000 ÷ $200,000 = .50

Step **(2):** $ 80,000 x .50 = $40,000

Step **(3):** $ 40,000 – $500 = $39,500

We will pay no more than $39,500. The remaining $40,500 is not covered.

EXAMPLE #2 (ADEQUATE INSURANCE)

When: The value of the building on
the date of completion is: $ 200,000

The Limit of Insurance for it is: $ 200,000

The Deductible is: $ 1,000

The amount of loss is: $ 80,000

The Limit of Insurance in this example is adequate and therefore no penalty applies. We will pay no more than $79,000 ($80,000 amount of loss minus the deductible of $1,000).

3. **Restriction Of Additional Coverage – Collapse**

If the Causes Of Loss – Broad Form is applicable to this Coverage Form, Paragraph **C.2.f.** of the Additional Coverage – Collapse does not apply to this Coverage Form.

If the Causes Of Loss – Special Form is applicable to this Coverage Form, Paragraphs **D.2.c.** and **D.2.d.** of the Additional Coverage – Collapse do not apply to this Coverage Form.

4. **When Coverage Ceases**

The insurance provided by this Coverage Form will end when one of the following first occurs:

a. This policy expires or is cancelled;

b. The property is accepted by the purchaser;

c. Your interest in the property ceases;

d. You abandon the construction with no intention to complete it;

e. Unless we specify otherwise in writing:

(1) 90 days after construction is complete; or

(2) 60 days after any building described in the Declarations is:

(a) Occupied in whole or in part; or

(b) Put to its intended use.

G. **Definitions**

"Pollutants" means any solid, liquid, gaseous or thermal irritant or contaminant, including smoke, vapor, soot, fumes, acids, alkalis, chemicals and waste. Waste includes materials to be recycled, reconditioned or reclaimed.

BUSINESS INCOME (AND EXTRA EXPENSE) COVERAGE FORM

Various provisions in this policy restrict coverage. Read the entire policy carefully to determine rights, duties and what is and is not covered.

Throughout this policy the words "you" and "your" refer to the Named Insured shown in the Declarations. The words "we", "us" and "our" refer to the Company providing this insurance.

Other words and phrases that appear in quotation marks have special meaning. Refer to Section **F.**, Definitions.

A. Coverage

1. Business Income

Business Income means the:

a. Net Income (Net Profit or Loss before income taxes) that would have been earned or incurred; and

b. Continuing normal operating expenses incurred, including payroll.

For manufacturing risks, Net Income includes the net sales value of production.

Coverage is provided as described and limited below for one or more of the following options for which a Limit of Insurance is shown in the Declarations:

(1) Business Income Including "Rental Value".

(2) Business Income Other Than "Rental Value".

(3) "Rental Value".

If option **(1)** above is selected, the term Business Income will include "Rental Value". If option **(3)** above is selected, the term Business Income will mean "Rental Value" only.

If Limits of Insurance are shown under more than one of the above options, the provisions of this Coverage Part apply separately to each.

We will pay for the actual loss of Business Income you sustain due to the necessary "suspension" of your "operations" during the "period of restoration". The "suspension" must be caused by direct physical loss of or damage to property at premises which are described in the Declarations and for which a Business Income Limit of Insurance is shown in the Declarations. The loss or damage must be caused by or result from a Covered Cause of Loss. With respect to loss of or damage to personal property in the open or personal property in a vehicle, the described premises include the area within 100 feet of the site at which the described premises are located.

With respect to the requirements set forth in the preceding paragraph, if you occupy only part of the site at which the described premises are located, your premises means:

(a) The portion of the building which you rent, lease or occupy; and

(b) Any area within the building or on the site at which the described premises are located, if that area services, or is used to gain access to, the described premises.

2. Extra Expense

a. Extra Expense Coverage is provided at the premises described in the Declarations only if the Declarations show that Business Income Coverage applies at that premises.

b. Extra Expense means necessary expenses you incur during the "period of restoration" that you would not have incurred if there had been no direct physical loss or damage to property caused by or resulting from a Covered Cause of Loss.

We will pay Extra Expense (other than the expense to repair or replace property) to:

(1) Avoid or minimize the "suspension" of business and to continue operations at the described premises or at replacement premises or temporary locations, including relocation expenses and costs to equip and operate the replacement location or temporary location.

(2) Minimize the "suspension" of business if you cannot continue "operations".

We will also pay Extra Expense to repair or replace property, but only to the extent it reduces the amount of loss that otherwise would have been payable under this Coverage Form.

3. Covered Causes Of Loss, Exclusions And Limitations

See applicable Causes Of Loss Form as shown in the Declarations.

4. Additional Limitation – Interruption Of Computer Operations

a. Coverage for Business Income does not apply when a "suspension" of "operations" is caused by destruction or corruption of electronic data, or any loss or damage to electronic data, except as provided under the Additional Coverage – Interruption Of Computer Operations.

b. Coverage for Extra Expense does not apply when action is taken to avoid or minimize a "suspension" of "operations" caused by destruction or corruption of electronic data, or any loss or damage to electronic data, except as provided under the Additional Coverage – Interruption Of Computer Operations.

c. Electronic data means information, facts or computer programs stored as or on, created or used on, or transmitted to or from computer software (including systems and applications software), on hard or floppy disks, CD-ROMs, tapes, drives, cells, data processing devices or any other repositories of computer software which are used with electronically controlled equipment. The term computer programs, referred to in the foregoing description of electronic data, means a set of related electronic instructions which direct the operations and functions of a computer or device connected to it, which enable the computer or device to receive, process, store, retrieve or send data.

5. Additional Coverages

a. **Civil Authority**

In this Additional Coverage – Civil Authority, the described premises are premises to which this Coverage Form applies, as shown in the Declarations.

When a Covered Cause of Loss causes damage to property other than property at the described premises, we will pay for the actual loss of Business Income you sustain and necessary Extra Expense caused by action of civil authority that prohibits access to the described premises, provided that both of the following apply:

(1) Access to the area immediately surrounding the damaged property is prohibited by civil authority as a result of the damage, and the described premises are within that area but are not more than one mile from the damaged property; and

(2) The action of civil authority is taken in response to dangerous physical conditions resulting from the damage or continuation of the Covered Cause of Loss that caused the damage, or the action is taken to enable a civil authority to have unimpeded access to the damaged property.

Civil Authority Coverage for Business Income will begin 72 hours after the time of the first action of civil authority that prohibits access to the described premises and will apply for a period of up to four consecutive weeks from the date on which such coverage began.

Civil Authority Coverage for Extra Expense will begin immediately after the time of the first action of civil authority that prohibits access to the described premises and will end:

(1) Four consecutive weeks after the date of that action; or

(2) When your Civil Authority Coverage for Business Income ends;

whichever is later.

b. **Alterations And New Buildings**

We will pay for the actual loss of Business Income you sustain and necessary Extra Expense you incur due to direct physical loss or damage at the described premises caused by or resulting from any Covered Cause of Loss to:

(1) New buildings or structures, whether complete or under construction;

(2) Alterations or additions to existing buildings or structures; and

(3) Machinery, equipment, supplies or building materials located on or within 100 feet of the described premises and:

(a) Used in the construction, alterations or additions; or

(b) Incidental to the occupancy of new buildings.

If such direct physical loss or damage delays the start of "operations", the "period of restoration" for Business Income Coverage will begin on the date "operations" would have begun if the direct physical loss or damage had not occurred.

c. Extended Business Income

(1) Business Income Other Than "Rental Value"

If the necessary "suspension" of your "operations" produces a Business Income loss payable under this policy, we will pay for the actual loss of Business Income you incur during the period that:

(a) Begins on the date property (except "finished stock") is actually repaired, rebuilt or replaced and "operations" are resumed; and

(b) Ends on the earlier of:

(i) The date you could restore your "operations", with reasonable speed, to the level which would generate the business income amount that would have existed if no direct physical loss or damage had occurred; or

(ii) 30 consecutive days after the date determined in **(1)(a)** above.

However, Extended Business Income does not apply to loss of Business Income incurred as a result of unfavorable business conditions caused by the impact of the Covered Cause of Loss in the area where the described premises are located.

Loss of Business Income must be caused by direct physical loss or damage at the described premises caused by or resulting from any Covered Cause of Loss.

(2) "Rental Value"

If the necessary "suspension" of your "operations" produces a "Rental Value" loss payable under this policy, we will pay for the actual loss of "Rental Value" you incur during the period that:

(a) Begins on the date property is actually repaired, rebuilt or replaced and tenantability is restored; and

(b) Ends on the earlier of:

(i) The date you could restore tenant occupancy, with reasonable speed, to the level which would generate the "Rental Value" that would have existed if no direct physical loss or damage had occurred; or

(ii) 30 consecutive days after the date determined in **(2)(a)** above.

However, Extended Business Income does not apply to loss of "Rental Value" incurred as a result of unfavorable business conditions caused by the impact of the Covered Cause of Loss in the area where the described premises are located.

Loss of "Rental Value" must be caused by direct physical loss or damage at the described premises caused by or resulting from any Covered Cause of Loss.

d. Interruption Of Computer Operations

(1) Under this Additional Coverage, electronic data has the meaning described under Additional Limitation – Interruption Of Computer Operations.

(2) Subject to all provisions of this Additional Coverage, you may extend the insurance that applies to Business Income and Extra Expense to apply to a "suspension" of "operations" caused by an interruption in computer operations due to destruction or corruption of electronic data due to a Covered Cause of Loss.

(3) With respect to the coverage provided under this Additional Coverage, the Covered Causes of Loss are subject to the following:

(a) If the Causes Of Loss – Special Form applies, coverage under this Additional Coverage – Interruption Of Computer Operations is limited to the "specified causes of loss" as defined in that form, and Collapse as set forth in that form.

(b) If the Causes Of Loss – Broad Form applies, coverage under this Additional Coverage – Interruption Of Computer Operations includes Collapse as set forth in that form.

(c) If the Causes Of Loss Form is endorsed to add a Covered Cause of Loss, the additional Covered Cause of Loss does not apply to the coverage provided under this Additional Coverage – Interruption Of Computer Operations.

(d) The Covered Causes of Loss include a virus, harmful code or similar instruction introduced into or enacted on a computer system (including electronic data) or a network to which it is connected, designed to damage or destroy any part of the system or disrupt its normal operation. But there is no coverage for an interruption related to manipulation of a computer system (including electronic data) by any employee, including a temporary or leased employee, or by an entity retained by you or for you to inspect, design, install, maintain, repair or replace that system.

(4) The most we will pay under this Additional Coverage – Interruption of Computer Operations is $2,500 for all loss sustained and expense incurred in any one policy year, regardless of the number of interruptions or the number of premises, locations or computer systems involved. If loss payment relating to the first interruption does not exhaust this amount, then the balance is available for loss or expense sustained or incurred as a result of subsequent interruptions in that policy year. A balance remaining at the end of a policy year does not increase the amount of insurance in the next policy year. With respect to any interruption which begins in one policy year and continues or results in additional loss or expense in a subsequent policy year(s), all loss and expense is deemed to be sustained or incurred in the policy year in which the interruption began.

(5) This Additional Coverage – Interruption in Computer Operations does not apply to loss sustained or expense incurred after the end of the "period of restoration", even if the amount of insurance stated in **(4)** above has not been exhausted.

6. Coverage Extension

If a Coinsurance percentage of 50% or more is shown in the Declarations, you may extend the insurance provided by this Coverage Part as follows:

NEWLY ACQUIRED LOCATIONS

a. You may extend your Business Income and Extra Expense Coverages to apply to property at any location you acquire other than fairs or exhibitions.

b. The most we will pay under this Extension, for the sum of Business Income loss and Extra Expense incurred, is $100,000 at each location.

     CP 00 30 06 07   □

c. Insurance under this Extension for each newly acquired location will end when any of the following first occurs:

(1) This policy expires;

(2) 30 days expire after you acquire or begin to construct the property; or

(3) You report values to us.

We will charge you additional premium for values reported from the date you acquire the property.

The Additional Condition, Coinsurance, does not apply to this Extension.

B. Limits Of Insurance

The most we will pay for loss in any one occurrence is the applicable Limit of Insurance shown in the Declarations.

Payments under the following coverages will not increase the applicable Limit of Insurance:

1. Alterations And New Buildings;

2. Civil Authority;

3. Extra Expense; or

4. Extended Business Income.

The amounts of insurance stated in the Interruption Of Computer Operations Additional Coverage and the Newly Acquired Locations Coverage Extension apply in accordance with the terms of those coverages and are separate from the Limit(s) of Insurance shown in the Declarations for any other coverage.

C. Loss Conditions

The following conditions apply in addition to the Common Policy Conditions and the Commercial Property Conditions.

1. Appraisal

If we and you disagree on the amount of Net Income and operating expense or the amount of loss, either may make written demand for an appraisal of the loss. In this event, each party will select a competent and impartial appraiser.

The two appraisers will select an umpire. If they cannot agree, either may request that selection be made by a judge of a court having jurisdiction. The appraisers will state separately the amount of Net Income and operating expense or amount of loss. If they fail to agree, they will submit their differences to the umpire. A decision agreed to by any two will be binding. Each party will:

a. Pay its chosen appraiser; and

b. Bear the other expenses of the appraisal and umpire equally.

If there is an appraisal, we will still retain our right to deny the claim.

2. Duties In The Event Of Loss

a. You must see that the following are done in the event of loss:

(1) Notify the police if a law may have been broken.

(2) Give us prompt notice of the direct physical loss or damage. Include a description of the property involved.

(3) As soon as possible, give us a description of how, when, and where the direct physical loss or damage occurred.

(4) Take all reasonable steps to protect the Covered Property from further damage, and keep a record of your expenses necessary to protect the Covered Property, for consideration in the settlement of the claim. This will not increase the Limit of Insurance. However, we will not pay for any subsequent loss or damage resulting from a cause of loss that is not a Covered Cause of Loss. Also, if feasible, set the damaged property aside and in the best possible order for examination.

(5) As often as may be reasonably required, permit us to inspect the property proving the loss or damage and examine your books and records.

Also permit us to take samples of damaged and undamaged property for inspection, testing and analysis, and permit us to make copies from your books and records.

(6) Send us a signed, sworn proof of loss containing the information we request to investigate the claim. You must do this within 60 days after our request. We will supply you with the necessary forms.

(7) Cooperate with us in the investigation or settlement of the claim.

(8) If you intend to continue your business, you must resume all or part of your "operations" as quickly as possible.

b. We may examine any insured under oath, while not in the presence of any other insured and at such times as may be reasonably required, about any matter relating to this insurance or the claim, including an insured's books and records. In the event of an examination, an insured's answers must be signed.

3. Loss Determination

a. The amount of Business Income loss will be determined based on:

(1) The Net Income of the business before the direct physical loss or damage occurred;

(2) The likely Net Income of the business if no physical loss or damage had occurred, but not including any Net Income that would likely have been earned as a result of an increase in the volume of business due to favorable business conditions caused by the impact of the Covered Cause of Loss on customers or on other businesses;

(3) The operating expenses, including payroll expenses, necessary to resume "operations" with the same quality of service that existed just before the direct physical loss or damage; and

(4) Other relevant sources of information, including:

(a) Your financial records and accounting procedures;

(b) Bills, invoices and other vouchers; and

(c) Deeds, liens or contracts.

b. The amount of Extra Expense will be determined based on:

(1) All expenses that exceed the normal operating expenses that would have been incurred by "operations" during the "period of restoration" if no direct physical loss or damage had occurred. We will deduct from the total of such expenses:

(a) The salvage value that remains of any property bought for temporary use during the "period of restoration", once "operations" are resumed; and

(b) Any Extra Expense that is paid for by other insurance, except for insurance that is written subject to the same plan, terms, conditions and provisions as this insurance; and

(2) Necessary expenses that reduce the Business Income loss that otherwise would have been incurred.

c. Resumption Of Operations

We will reduce the amount of your:

(1) Business Income loss, other than Extra Expense, to the extent you can resume your "operations", in whole or in part, by using damaged or undamaged property (including merchandise or stock) at the described premises or elsewhere.

(2) Extra Expense loss to the extent you can return "operations" to normal and discontinue such Extra Expense.

d. If you do not resume "operations", or do not resume "operations" as quickly as possible, we will pay based on the length of time it would have taken to resume "operations" as quickly as possible.

4. Loss Payment

We will pay for covered loss within 30 days after we receive the sworn proof of loss, if you have complied with all of the terms of this Coverage Part and:

a. We have reached agreement with you on the amount of loss; or

b. An appraisal award has been made.

D. Additional Condition

COINSURANCE

If a Coinsurance percentage is shown in the Declarations, the following condition applies in addition to the Common Policy Conditions and the Commercial Property Conditions.

We will not pay the full amount of any Business Income loss if the Limit of Insurance for Business Income is less than:

1. The Coinsurance percentage shown for Business Income in the Declarations; times

2. The sum of:

a. The Net Income (Net Profit or Loss before income taxes), and

b. Operating expenses, including payroll expenses,

that would have been earned or incurred (had no loss occurred) by your "operations" at the described premises for the 12 months following the inception, or last previous anniversary date, of this policy (whichever is later).

 CP 00 30 06 07   □

Instead, we will determine the most we will pay using the following steps:

Step **(1)**: Multiply the Net Income and operating expense for the 12 months following the inception, or last previous anniversary date, of this policy by the Coinsurance percentage;

Step **(2)**: Divide the Limit of Insurance for the described premises by the figure determined in Step **(1)**; and

Step **(3)**: Multiply the total amount of loss by the figure determined in Step **(2)**.

We will pay the amount determined in Step **(3)** or the limit of insurance, whichever is less. For the remainder, you will either have to rely on other insurance or absorb the loss yourself.

In determining operating expenses for the purpose of applying the Coinsurance condition, the following expenses, if applicable, shall be deducted from the total of all operating expenses:

    (1) Prepaid freight – outgoing;

    (2) Returns and allowances;

    (3) Discounts;

    (4) Bad debts;

    (5) Collection expenses;

    (6) Cost of raw stock and factory supplies consumed (including transportation charges);

    (7) Cost of merchandise sold (including transportation charges);

    (8) Cost of other supplies consumed (including transportation charges);

    (9) Cost of services purchased from outsiders (not employees) to resell, that do not continue under contract;

    (10) Power, heat and refrigeration expenses that do not continue under contract (if Form **CP 15 11** is attached);

    (11) All ordinary payroll expenses or the amount of payroll expense excluded (if Form **CP 15 10** is attached); and

    (12) Special deductions for mining properties (royalties unless specifically included in coverage; actual depletion commonly known as unit or cost depletion – not percentage depletion; welfare and retirement fund charges based on tonnage; hired trucks).

EXAMPLE #1 (UNDERINSURANCE)

When: The Net Income and operating expenses for the 12 months following the inception, or last previous anniversary date, of this policy at the described premises would have been: $ 400,000

    The Coinsurance percentage is: 50%

    The Limit of Insurance is: $ 150,000

    The amount of loss is: $ 80,000

Step **(1)**: $400,000 x 50% = $200,000

    (the minimum amount of insurance to meet your Coinsurance requirements)

Step **(2)**: $150,000 ÷ $200,000 = .75

Step **(3)**: $80,000 x .75 = $60,000

We will pay no more than $60,000. The remaining $20,000 is not covered.

EXAMPLE #2 (ADEQUATE INSURANCE)

When: The Net Income and operating expenses for the 12 months following the inception, or last previous anniversary date, of this policy at the described premises would have been: $ 400,000

    The Coinsurance percentage is: 50%

    The Limit of Insurance is: $ 200,000

    The amount of loss is: $ 80,000

The minimum amount of insurance to meet your Coinsurance requirement is $200,000 ($400,000 x 50%). Therefore, the Limit of Insurance in this example is adequate and no penalty applies. We will pay no more than $80,000 (amount of loss).

This condition does not apply to Extra Expense Coverage.

E. Optional Coverages

If shown as applicable in the Declarations, the following Optional Coverages apply separately to each item.

    1. Maximum Period Of Indemnity

        a. The Additional Condition, Coinsurance, does not apply to this Coverage Form at the described premises to which this Optional Coverage applies.

b. The most we will pay for the total of Business Income loss and Extra Expense is the lesser of:

(1) The amount of loss sustained and expenses incurred during the 120 days immediately following the beginning of the "period of restoration"; or

(2) The Limit of Insurance shown in the Declarations.

2. Monthly Limit Of Indemnity

a. The Additional Condition, Coinsurance, does not apply to this Coverage Form at the described premises to which this Optional Coverage applies.

b. The most we will pay for loss of Business Income in each period of 30 consecutive days after the beginning of the "period of restoration" is:

(1) The Limit of Insurance, multiplied by

(2) The fraction shown in the Declarations for this Optional Coverage.

EXAMPLE

When:	The Limit of Insurance is:	$ 120,000
	The fraction shown in the Declarations for this Optional Coverage is:	1/4
	The most we will pay for loss in each period of 30 consecutive days is:	$ 30,000
	($120,000 x 1/4 = $30,000)	
	If, in this example, the actual amount of loss is:	
	Days 1–30:	$ 40,000
	Days 31–60:	$ 20,000
	Days 61–90:	$ 30,000
		$ 90,000
	We will pay:	
	Days 1–30:	$ 30,000
	Days 31–60:	$ 20,000
	Days 61–90:	$ 30,000
		$ 80,000

The remaining $10,000 is not covered.

3. Business Income Agreed Value

a. To activate this Optional Coverage:

(1) A Business Income Report/Work Sheet must be submitted to us and must show financial data for your "operations":

(a) During the 12 months prior to the date of the Work Sheet; and

(b) Estimated for the 12 months immediately following the inception of this Optional Coverage.

(2) The Declarations must indicate that the Business Income Agreed Value Optional Coverage applies, and an Agreed Value must be shown in the Declarations. The Agreed Value should be at least equal to:

(a) The Coinsurance percentage shown in the Declarations; multiplied by

(b) The amount of Net Income and operating expenses for the following 12 months you report on the Work Sheet.

b. The Additional Condition, Coinsurance, is suspended until:

(1) 12 months after the effective date of this Optional Coverage; or

(2) The expiration date of this policy;

whichever occurs first.

c. We will reinstate the Additional Condition, Coinsurance, automatically if you do not submit a new Work Sheet and Agreed Value:

(1) Within 12 months of the effective date of this Optional Coverage; or

(2) When you request a change in your Business Income Limit of Insurance.

d. If the Business Income Limit of Insurance is less than the Agreed Value, we will not pay more of any loss than the amount of loss multiplied by:

(1) The Business Income Limit of Insurance; divided by

(2) The Agreed Value.

 CP 00 30 06 07   □

EXAMPLE

When: The Limit of Insurance is: $ 100,000

The Agreed Value is: $ 200,000

The amount of loss is: $ 80,000

Step (1): $100,000 ÷ $200,000 = .50

Step (2): .50 x $80,000 = $40,000

We will pay $40,000. The remaining $40,000 is not covered.

4. Extended Period Of Indemnity

Under Paragraph **A.5.c., Extended Business Income,** the number 30 in Subparagraphs **(1)(b)** and **(2)(b)** is replaced by the number shown in the Declarations for this Optional Coverage.

F. Definitions

1. "Finished stock" means stock you have manufactured.

   "Finished stock" also includes whiskey and alcoholic products being aged, unless there is a Coinsurance percentage shown for Business Income in the Declarations.

   "Finished stock" does not include stock you have manufactured that is held for sale on the premises of any retail outlet insured under this Coverage Part.

2. "Operations" means:

   a. Your business activities occurring at the described premises; and

   b. The tenantability of the described premises, if coverage for Business Income Including "Rental Value" or "Rental Value" applies.

3. "Period of restoration" means the period of time that:

   a. Begins:

      (1) 72 hours after the time of direct physical loss or damage for Business Income Coverage; or

      (2) Immediately after the time of direct physical loss or damage for Extra Expense Coverage;

      caused by or resulting from any Covered Cause of Loss at the described premises; and

   b. Ends on the earlier of:

      (1) The date when the property at the described premises should be repaired, rebuilt or replaced with reasonable speed and similar quality; or

      (2) The date when business is resumed at a new permanent location.

"Period of restoration" does not include any increased period required due to the enforcement of any ordinance or law that:

   (1) Regulates the construction, use or repair, or requires the tearing down, of any property; or

   (2) Requires any insured or others to test for, monitor, clean up, remove, contain, treat, detoxify or neutralize, or in any way respond to, or assess the effects of "pollutants".

The expiration date of this policy will not cut short the "period of restoration".

4. "Pollutants" means any solid, liquid, gaseous or thermal irritant or contaminant, including smoke, vapor, soot, fumes, acids, alkalis, chemicals and waste. Waste includes materials to be recycled, reconditioned or reclaimed.

5. "Rental Value" means Business Income that consists of:

   a. Net Income (Net Profit or Loss before income taxes) that would have been earned or incurred as rental income from tenant occupancy of the premises described in the Declarations as furnished and equipped by you, including fair rental value of any portion of the described premises which is occupied by you; and

   b. Continuing normal operating expenses incurred in connection with that premises, including:

      (1) Payroll; and

      (2) The amount of charges which are the legal obligation of the tenant(s) but would otherwise be your obligations.

6. "Suspension" means:

   a. The slowdown or cessation of your business activities; or

   b. That a part or all of the described premises is rendered untenantable, if coverage for Business Income Including "Rental Value" or "Rental Value" applies.

COMMERCIAL PROPERTY
CP 00 40 06 07

LEGAL LIABILITY COVERAGE FORM

Various provisions in this policy restrict coverage. Read the entire policy carefully to determine rights, duties and what is and is not covered.

Throughout this policy the words "you" and "your" refer to the Named Insured shown in the Declarations. The words "we", "us" and "our" refer to the Company providing this insurance.

Other words and phrases that appear in quotation marks have special meaning. Refer to Section **F.** – Definitions.

A. Coverage

We will pay those sums that you become legally obligated to pay as damages because of direct physical loss or damage, including loss of use, to Covered Property caused by accident and arising out of any Covered Cause of Loss. We will have the right and duty to defend any "suit" seeking those damages. However, we have no duty to defend you against a "suit" seeking damages for direct physical loss or damage to which this insurance does not apply. We may investigate and settle any claim or "suit" at our discretion. But:

(1) The amount we will pay for damages is limited as described in Section **C.** Limits Of Insurance; and

(2) Our right and duty to defend end when we have used up the Limit of Insurance in the payment of judgments or settlements.

1. Covered Property And Limitations

Covered Property, as used in this Coverage Form, means tangible property of others in your care, custody or control that is described in the Declarations or on the Legal Liability Coverage Schedule.

Covered Property does not include electronic data. Electronic data means information, facts or computer programs stored as or on, created or used on, or transmitted to or from computer software (including systems and applications software), on hard or floppy disks, CD-ROMs, tapes, drives, cells, data processing devices or any other repositories of computer software which are used with electronically controlled equipment. The term computer programs, referred to in the foregoing description of electronic data, means a set of related electronic instructions which direct the operations and functions of a computer or device connected to it, which enable the computer or device to receive, process, store, retrieve or send data.

2. Covered Causes Of Loss

See applicable Causes of Loss Form as shown in the Declarations.

3. Additional Coverage

SUPPLEMENTARY PAYMENTS

We will pay, with respect to any claim or any "suit" against you we defend:

a. All expenses we incur.

b. The cost of bonds to release attachments, but only for bond amounts within our Limit of Insurance. We do not have to furnish these bonds.

c. All reasonable expenses incurred by you at our request, including actual loss of earnings up to $250 a day because of time off from work.

d. All costs taxed against you in the "suit".

e. Prejudgment interest awarded against you on that part of the judgment we pay. If we make an offer to pay the Limit of Insurance, we will not pay any prejudgment interest based on that period of time after the offer.

f. All interest on the full amount of any judgment that accrues after entry of the judgment and before we have paid, offered to pay, or deposited in court the part of the judgment that is within our Limit of Insurance.

These payments will not reduce the applicable Limit of Insurance.

4. Coverage Extensions

a. Additional Insureds

If the Named Insured shown in the Declarations is a partnership, limited liability company or corporation, throughout this Coverage Form, the words "you" and "your" include:

(1) Partners, members, executive officers, trustees, directors and stockholders of such partnership, limited liability company or corporation, but only with respect to their duties as such; and

(2) Managers of a limited liability company, but only with respect to their duties as such.

b. Newly Acquired Organizations

Throughout this Coverage Form, the words "you" and "your" also include any organization (other than a partnership, joint venture or limited liability company) you newly acquire or form and over which you maintain ownership or majority interest if there is no other similar insurance available to that organization.

This Coverage Extension ends:

(1) 90 days after you acquire or form the organization; or

(2) At the end of the policy period shown in the Declarations;

whichever is earlier.

This Extension does not apply to direct physical loss or damage that occurred before you acquired or formed the organization.

c. Newly Acquired Property

(1) You may extend the insurance that applies to Covered Property, as used in this Coverage Form, to apply to your liability for tangible property of others that comes under your care, custody or control after the beginning of the current policy period. This Extension is subject to the following:

(a) All terms and Conditions of this Coverage Form.

(b) Buildings must be intended for:

(i) Similar use as the building described in the Declarations or on the Legal Liability Coverage

The most we will pay as the result of any one accident for loss or damage to buildings covered under this Extension is $250,000 at each building.

(c) Personal property must be at a location:

(i) That you own; or

(ii) That is or comes under your care, custody or control;

other than at fairs or exhibitions.

The most we will pay as the result of any one accident for loss or damage to personal property covered under this Extension is $100,000 at each building.

(2) Insurance under this Extension for each item of property of others will end when any of the following first occurs:

(a) This policy expires;

(b) 30 days expire after the property has come under your care, custody or control; or

(c) You report values to us.

We will charge you additional premium for values reported from the date the property comes under your care, custody or control.

This Extension does not apply to direct physical loss or damage that occurred before the property came under your care, custody or control.

B. Exclusions And Limitations

See applicable Causes of Loss Form as shown in the Declarations.

C. Limits Of Insurance

The most we will pay in damages as the result of any one accident is the applicable Limit of Insurance shown on the Legal Liability Coverage Schedule, or in the Declarations.

Payments under the Additional Coverage and the Newly Acquired Property Coverage Extension are in addition to the Limits of Insurance.

The existence of one or more:

1. Additional Insureds, or

2. Newly Acquired Organizations,

does not increase the Limit of Insurance.

© ISO Properties, Inc., 2007 CP 00 40 06 07 ☐

D. Loss Conditions

The following conditions apply in addition to the Commercial Property Conditions:

1. **Duties In The Event Of Accident, Claim Or Suit**

   a. You must see to it that we are notified promptly of any accident that may result in a claim. Notice should include:

      (1) How, when and where the accident took place; and

      (2) The names and addresses of any witnesses.

      Notice of an accident is not notice of a claim.

   b. If a claim is made or "suit" is brought against you, you must see to it that we receive prompt written notice of the claim or "suit".

   c. You must:

      (1) Immediately send us copies of any demands, notices, summonses or legal papers received in connection with the claim or "suit";

      (2) Authorize us to obtain records and other information;

      (3) Cooperate with us in the investigation, settlement or defense of the claim or "suit"; and

      (4) Assist us, upon our request, in the enforcement of any right against any person or organization that may be liable to you because of damage to which this insurance may also apply.

   d. You will not, except at your own cost, voluntarily make a payment, assume any obligation, or incur any expense without our consent.

2. **Legal Action Against Us**

   No person or organization has a right under this Coverage Form:

   a. To join us as a party or otherwise bring us into a "suit" asking for damages from you; or

   b. To sue us on this Coverage Form unless all of its terms have been fully complied with.

A person or organization may sue us to recover on an agreed settlement or on a final judgment against you obtained after an actual trial; but we will not be liable for damages that are not payable under the terms of this Coverage Form or that are in excess of the Limit of Insurance. An agreed settlement means a settlement and release of liability signed by us, you and the claimant or the claimant's legal representative.

3. **Other Insurance**

   You may have other insurance covering the same loss as the insurance under this Coverage Form. If you do, we will pay our share of the covered loss. Our share is the proportion that the Limit of Insurance under this Coverage Form covering such loss bears to the Limits of Insurance of all insurance covering the loss.

4. **Transfer Of Rights Of Recovery Against Others To Us**

   If you have rights to recover all or part of any payment we have made under this Coverage Form, those rights are transferred to us. You must do nothing after loss to impair them. At our request, you will bring "suit" or transfer those rights to us and help us enforce them.

E. Additional Conditions

The following conditions apply in addition to the Common Policy Conditions.

1. **Amendment Of Commercial Property Conditions**

   None of the Commercial Property Conditions apply to this Coverage Form, except:

   a. Condition **A.**, Concealment, Misrepresentation Or Fraud;

   b. Condition **C.**, Insurance Under Two Or More Coverages; and

   c. Condition **E.**, Liberalization.

2. **Bankruptcy**

   Bankruptcy or insolvency of you or your estate will not relieve us of our obligations under this Coverage Form.

3. **Policy Period, Coverage Territory**

Under this Coverage Form:

a. We will pay for loss or damage caused by an accident that occurs:

(1) During the policy period shown in the Declarations; and

(2) Within the coverage territory.

b. The coverage territory is:

(1) The United States of America;

(2) Puerto Rico; and

(3) Canada.

4. **Separation Of Insureds**

The insurance under this Coverage Form applies separately to you and each additional insured, except with respect to the Limits of Insurance.

F. **Definition**

"Suit" includes an arbitration proceeding to which you must submit or submit with our consent.

 CP 00 40 06 07 ☐

COMMERCIAL PROPERTY
CP 00 60 06 95

LEASEHOLD INTEREST COVERAGE FORM

Throughout this policy the words "you" and "your" refer to the Named Insured shown in the Declarations. The words "we", "us" and "our" refer to the Company providing this insurance.

Other words and phrases that appear in quotation marks have special meaning. Refer to SECTION **F.** – DEFINITIONS.

A. COVERAGE

We will pay for loss of Covered Leasehold Interest you sustain due to the cancellation of your lease. The cancellation must result from direct physical loss of or damage to property at the premises described in the Declarations caused by or resulting from any Covered Cause of Loss.

1. Covered Leasehold Interest

Covered Leasehold Interest means the following for which an amount of "net leasehold interest" at inception is shown in the Leasehold Interest Coverage Schedule:

a. **Tenants' Lease Interest,** meaning the difference between the:

(1) Rent you pay at the described premises; and

(2) Rental value of the described premises that you lease.

b. **Bonus Payments,** meaning the unamortized portion of a cash bonus that will not be refunded to you. A cash bonus is money you paid to acquire your lease. It does not include:

(1) Rent, whether or not prepaid; or

(2) Security.

c. **Improvements and Betterments,** meaning the unamortized portion of payments made by you for improvements and betterments. It does not include the value of improvements and betterments recoverable under any other insurance, but only to the extent of such other insurance.

Improvements and betterments are fixtures, alterations, installations or additions:

(1) Made a part of the building or structure you occupy but do not own; and

(2) You acquired or made at your expense but cannot legally remove.

d. **Prepaid Rent,** meaning the unamortized portion of any amount of advance rent you paid that will not be refunded to you. This does not include the customary rent due at:

(1) The beginning of each month; or

(2) Any other rental period.

2. Covered Causes Of Loss

See applicable Causes of Loss Form as shown in the Declarations.

B. EXCLUSIONS AND LIMITATIONS

See applicable Causes of Loss Form as shown in the Declarations.

C. LIMITS OF INSURANCE

1. Applicable to Tenants' Lease Interest

a. The most we will pay for loss because of the cancellation of any one lease is your "net leasehold interest" at the time of loss.

But, if your lease is cancelled and your landlord lets you continue to use your premises under a new lease or other arrangement, the most we will pay for loss because of the cancellation of any one lease is the lesser of:

(1) The difference between the rent you now pay and the rent you will pay under the new lease or other arrangement; or

(2) Your "net leasehold interest" at the time of loss.

b. Your "net leasehold interest" decreases automatically each month. The amount of "net leasehold interest" at any time is your "gross leasehold interest" times the leasehold interest factor for the remaining months of your lease. A proportionate share applies for any period of time less than a month.

Refer to the end of this form for a table of leasehold interest factors.

2. Applicable to Bonus Payments, Improvements and Betterments and Prepaid Rent

a. The most we will pay for loss because of the cancellation of any one lease is your "net leasehold interest" at the time of loss.

But, if your lease is cancelled and your landlord lets you continue to use your premises under a new lease or other arrangement, the most we will pay for loss because of the cancellation of any one lease is the lesser of:

(1) The loss sustained by you; or

(2) Your "net leasehold interest" at the time of loss.

b. Your "net leasehold interest" decreases automatically each month. The amount of each decrease is your "monthly leasehold interest". A proportionate share applies for any period of time less than a month.

D. LOSS CONDITIONS

The following conditions apply in addition to the Common Policy Conditions and the Commercial Property Conditions.

1. Appraisal

If we and you disagree on the amount of loss, either may make written demand for an appraisal. In this event, each party will select a competent and impartial appraiser. The two appraisers will select an umpire. If they cannot agree, either may request that selection be made by a judge of a court having jurisdiction. The appraisers will state the amount of loss. If they fail to agree, they will submit their differences to the umpire. A decision agreed to by any two will be binding. Each party will:

a. Pay its chosen appraiser; and

b. Bear the other expenses of the appraisal and umpire equally.

If there is an appraisal, we will still retain our right to deny the claim.

2. Duties In The Event Of Loss Of Covered Leasehold Interest

a. You must see that the following are done in the event of loss of Covered Leasehold Interest:

(1) Notify the police if a law may have been broken.

(2) Give us prompt notice of the direct physical loss or damage. Include a description of the property involved.

(3) As soon as possible, give us a description of how, when and where the direct physical loss or damage occurred.

(4) Take all reasonable steps to protect the property at the described premises from further damage by a Covered Cause of Loss. However, we will not pay for any subsequent loss or damage resulting from a cause of loss that is not a Covered Cause of Loss. Also, if feasible, set the damaged property aside and in the best possible order for examination.

(5) As often as may be reasonably required, permit us to inspect the property proving the loss or damage and examine your books and records.

Also permit us to take samples of damaged and undamaged property for inspection, testing and analysis, and permit us to make copies from your books and records.

(6) Send us a signed, sworn proof of loss containing the information we request to investigate the claim. You must do this within 60 days after our request. We will supply you with the necessary forms.

(7) Cooperate with us in the investigation or settlement of the claim.

b. We may examine any insured under oath, while not in the presence of any other insured and at such times as may be reasonably required, about any matter relating to this insurance or the claim, including an insured's books and records. In the event of an examination, an insured's answers must be signed.

 CP 00 60 06 95 □

3. Loss Payment

We will pay for covered loss within 30 days after we receive the sworn proof of loss, if:

a. You have complied with all of the terms of this Coverage Part; and

b.(1) We have reached agreement with you on the amount of loss; or

(2) An appraisal award has been made.

4. Vacancy

a. Description of Terms

(1) As used in this Vacancy Condition, with respect to the tenant's interest in Covered Property, building means the unit or suite rented or leased to the tenant. Such building is vacant when it does not contain enough business personal property to conduct customary operations.

(2) Buildings under construction or renovation are not considered vacant.

b. Vacancy Provisions – Subleased Premises

The following provisions apply if the building where direct physical loss or damage occurs has been vacant for more than 60 consecutive days before that loss or damage occurs, provided you have entered into an agreement to sublease the described premises as of the time of loss or damage:

(1) We will not pay for any loss or damage caused by any of the following even if they are Covered Causes of Loss:

(a) Vandalism;

(b) Sprinkler leakage, unless you have protected the system against freezing;

(c) Building glass breakage;

(d) Water damage;

(e) Theft; or

(f) Attempted theft.

(2) With respect to a Covered Cause of Loss not listed in **(1)(a)** through **(1)(f)** above, we will reduce the amount we would otherwise pay for the loss or damage by 15%.

c. If you have not entered into an agreement to sublease the described premises as of the time of loss or damage, we will not pay for any loss of Covered Leasehold Interest.

E. ADDITIONAL CONDITION

The following condition replaces the Cancellation Common Policy Condition:

CANCELLATION

1. The first Named Insured shown in the Declarations may cancel this policy by mailing or delivering to us advance notice of cancellation.

2. We may cancel this policy by mailing or delivering to the first Named Insured written notice of cancellation at least:

a. 10 days before the effective date of cancellation if we cancel for nonpayment of premium; or

b. 30 days before the effective date of cancellation if we cancel for any other reason.

3. We will mail or deliver our notice to the first Named Insured's last mailing address known to us.

4. Notice of cancellation will state the effective date of cancellation. The policy will end on that date.

5. If this policy is cancelled, we will send the first Named Insured any premium refund due. The cancellation will be effective even if we have not made or offered a refund.

6. If this coverage is cancelled, we will calculate the earned premium by:

a. Computing the average of the "net leasehold interest" at the:

(1) Inception date, and

(2) Cancellation date,

of this coverage.

b. Multiplying the rate for the period of coverage by the average "net leasehold interest".

c. If we cancel, we will send you a premium refund based on the difference between the:

(1) Premium you originally paid us; and

(2) Proportion of the premium calculated by multiplying the amount in paragraph **a.** times the rate for the period of coverage for the expired term of the policy.

d. If you cancel, your refund may be less than the refund calculated in paragraph **c.**

7. If notice is mailed, proof of mailing will be sufficient proof of notice.

F. DEFINITIONS

1. **"Gross Leasehold Interest"** means the difference between the:

   a. Monthly rental value of the premises you lease; and

   b. Actual monthly rent you pay including taxes, insurance, janitorial or other service that you pay for as part of the rent.

   This amount is not changed:

   (1) Whether you occupy all or part of the premises; or

   (2) If you sublet the premises.

   Example:

Rental value of your leased premises	$5,000
Monthly rent including taxes, insurance, janitorial or other service that you pay for as part of the rent	−4,000
"Gross Leasehold Interest"	$1,000

2. **"Monthly Leasehold Interest"** means the monthly portion of covered Bonus Payments, Improvements and Betterments and Prepaid Rent. To find your "monthly leasehold interest", divide your original costs of Bonus Payments, Improvements and Betterments or Prepaid Rent by the number of months left in your lease at the time of the expenditure.

   Example:

Original cost of Bonus Payment	$12,000
With 24 months left in the lease at time of Bonus Payment	÷ 24
"Monthly Leasehold Interest"	$500

3. **"Net Leasehold Interest":**

   a. Applicable to Tenants' Lease Interest.

   "Net Leasehold Interest" means the present value of your "gross leasehold interest" for each remaining month of the term of the lease at the rate of interest shown in the Leasehold Interest Coverage Schedule.

   The "net leasehold interest" is the amount that, placed at the rate of interest shown in the Leasehold Interest Coverage Schedule, would be equivalent to your receiving the "Gross Leasehold Interest" for each separate month of the unexpired term of the lease.

   To find your "net leasehold interest" at any time, multiply your "gross leasehold interest" by the leasehold interest factor found in the table of leasehold interest factors attached to this form.

   Example:

   (20 months left in lease, 10% effective annual rate of interest)

"Gross Leasehold Interest"	$ 1,000
Leasehold Interest Factor	× 18.419
"Net Leasehold Interest"	$18,419

   b. Applicable to Bonus Payments, Improvements and Betterments or Prepaid Rent.

   "Net Leasehold Interest" means the unamortized amount shown in the Schedule. Your "net leasehold interest" at any time is your "monthly leasehold interest" times the number of months left in your lease.

   Example:

"Monthly Leasehold Interest"	$ 500
With 10 months left in lease	× 10
"Net Leasehold Interest"	$5,000

COMMERCIAL PROPERTY
CP 00 70 06 07

MORTGAGEHOLDERS ERRORS AND OMISSIONS COVERAGE FORM

Various provisions in this policy restrict coverage. Read the entire policy carefully to determine rights, duties and what is and is not covered.

Throughout this policy the words "you" and "your" refer to the Named Insured shown in the Declarations. The words "we", "us" and "our" refer to the Company providing this insurance.

Other words and phrases that appear in quotation marks have special meaning. Refer to Section I., Definitions, in this Coverage Form.

A. Coverage

1. Coverage A – Mortgageholder's Interest

We will pay for loss to your "mortgageholder's interest" in Covered Property due to error or accidental omission, by you or your representative, in the operation of your customary procedure in requiring, procuring and maintaining "valid insurance" payable to you as mortgageholder against the Covered Causes of Loss.

a. Covered Property

Covered Property means:

(1) Real property; and

(2) Personal property secured in connection with that real property.

It includes such property:

(a) During and after your foreclosure; and

(b) Sold under an agreement in which you retain title, such as a conditional sales agreement.

b. Property Not Covered

Covered Property does not include:

(1) Accounts, bills, currency, deeds, food stamps or other evidences of debt, money, notes or securities. Lottery tickets held for sale are not securities;

(2) Land (including land on which the property is located), water, growing crops or lawns; or

(3) Electronic data, meaning information, facts or computer programs stored as or on, created or used on, or transmitted to or from computer software (including systems and applications software), on hard or floppy disks, CD-ROMs, tapes, drives, cells, data processing devices or any other repositories of computer software which are used with electronically controlled equipment. The term computer programs, referred to in the foregoing description of electronic data, means a set of related electronic instructions which direct the operations and functions of a computer or device connected to it, which enable the computer or device to receive, process, store, retrieve or send data.

c. Covered Causes Of Loss

The Covered Causes of Loss are those causes of loss against which you customarily require mortgagors to provide insurance policies that protect your "mortgageholder's interest". They do not include:

(1) Causes of Loss excluded under Section B., Exclusions; or

(2) Losses insured under mortgage guarantee insurance policies or programs, or title, life, health or accident insurance policies.

© ISO Properties, Inc., 2007

d. Coverage Extension – Mortgages Serviced For Others

We will cover loss arising from mortgages owned by others and serviced by you as if you owned the "mortgageholder's interest" in them. All such mortgages must be serviced under a written contract. We will make loss payment payable jointly to you and the mortgage owner.

2. Coverage B – Property Owned Or Held In Trust

We will pay for direct physical loss of or damage to Covered Property caused by or resulting from any Covered Cause of Loss; provided the loss is not otherwise insured due to error or accidental omission, by you or your representative, in the operation of your customary procedure in procuring and maintaining "valid insurance" payable to you as owner or trustee of the Covered Property.

a. Covered Property

Covered Property means real and personal property:

(1) You own; or

(2) In which you have a fiduciary interest as trustee or otherwise.

b. Property Not Covered

Covered Property does not include:

(1) Accounts, bills, currency, deeds, food stamps or other evidences of debt, money, notes or securities. Lottery tickets held for sale are not securities;

(2) Land (including land on which the property is located), water, growing crops or lawns; or

(3) Electronic data, meaning information, facts or computer programs stored as or on, created or used on, or transmitted to or from computer software (including systems and applications software), on hard or floppy disks, CD-ROMs, tapes, drives, cells, data processing devices or any other repositories of computer software which are used with electronically controlled equipment. The term computer programs, referred to in the foregoing description of electronic data, means a set of related electronic instructions which direct the operations and functions of a computer or device connected to it, which enable the computer or device to receive, process, store, retrieve or send data.

c. Covered Causes Of Loss

The Covered Causes of Loss are:

(1) Fire.

(2) Lightning.

(3) Explosion, including the explosion of gases or fuel within the furnace of any fired vessel or within the flues or passages through which the gases of combustion pass. This cause of loss does not include loss or damage by:

(a) Rupture, bursting or operation of pressure-relief devices; or

(b) Rupture or bursting due to expansion or swelling of the contents of any building or structure, caused by or resulting from water.

(4) Windstorm or Hail, but not including:

(a) Frost or cold weather;

(b) Ice (other than hail), snow or sleet, whether driven by wind or not; or

(c) Loss or damage to the interior of any building or structure, or the property inside the building or structure, caused by rain, snow, sand or dust, whether driven by wind or not, unless the building or structure first sustains wind or hail damage to its roof or walls through which the rain, snow, sand or dust enters.

(5) Smoke causing sudden and accidental loss or damage. This cause of loss does not include smoke from agricultural smudging or industrial operations.

(6) Aircraft or Vehicles, meaning only physical contact of an aircraft, a spacecraft, a self-propelled missile, a vehicle or an object thrown up by a vehicle with the property or with the building or structure containing the property. This cause of loss includes loss or damage by objects falling from aircraft.

We will not pay for loss or damage caused by or resulting from vehicles you own or operate.

(7) Riot or Civil Commotion, including:

(a) Acts of striking employees while occupying the premises; and

(b) Looting occurring at the time and place of a riot or civil commotion.

(8) Sinkhole Collapse, meaning loss or damage caused by the sudden sinking or collapse of land into underground empty spaces created by the action of water on limestone or dolomite. This cause of loss does not include:

(a) The cost of filling sinkholes; or

(b) Sinking or collapse of land into man-made underground cavities.

(9) Volcanic Action, meaning direct loss or damage resulting from the eruption of a volcano when the loss or damage is caused by:

(a) Airborne volcanic blast or airborne shock waves;

(b) Ash, dust or particulate matter; or

(c) Lava flow.

All volcanic eruptions that occur within any 168-hour period will constitute a single occurrence.

This cause of loss does not include the cost to remove ash, dust or particulate matter that does not cause direct physical loss or damage to the property.

3. Coverage C – Mortgageholder's Liability

We will pay those sums that you become legally obligated to pay as damages due to error or accidental omission in the operation of your customary procedure in processing and maintaining "valid insurance" against the Covered Causes of Loss for the benefit of the mortgagor in amounts, and under conditions, customarily accepted by the mortgagor. We will have the right and duty to defend any "suit" seeking those damages. However, we have no duty to defend you against a "suit" seeking damages to which this insurance does not apply. We may investigate and settle any claim or "suit" at our discretion. But:

(1) The amount we will pay for damages is limited as described in Section **C.**, Limits Of Insurance; and

(2) Our right and duty to defend end when we have used up the Limit of Insurance in the payment of judgments or settlements.

The damages payable under this Coverage Form must arise out of your capacity as a mortgageholder, mortgage fiduciary or mortgage servicing agency.

a. Covered Causes Of Loss

The Covered Causes of Loss are those risks and causes of loss against which the mortgagor customarily obtains insurance policies.

They do not include:

(1) Causes of loss excluded under Section **B.**, Exclusions; or

(2) Losses insured under mortgage guarantee insurance policies or programs, or title, life, health or accident insurance policies.

b. Additional Coverage – Supplementary Payments

We will pay, with respect to any claim or any "suit" against you we defend:

(1) All expenses we incur.

(2) The cost of bonds to release attachments, but only for bond amounts within our Limit of Insurance. We do not have to furnish these bonds.

(3) All reasonable expenses incurred by you at our request, including actual loss of earnings up to $250 a day because of time off from work.

(4) All costs taxed against you in the "suit".

(5) Prejudgment interest awarded against you on that part of the judgment we pay. If we make an offer to pay the Limit of Insurance, we will not pay any prejudgment interest based on that period of time after the offer.

(6) All interest on the full amount of any judgment that accrues after entry of the judgment and before we have paid, offered to pay, or deposited in court the part of the judgment that is within our Limit of Insurance.

These payments will not reduce the applicable Limit of Insurance.

c. **Coverage Extensions**

(1) **Additional Insureds**

If the Named Insured shown in the Declarations is a partnership, limited liability company or corporation, under Coverage **C** – Mortgageholder's Liability, the words "you" and "your" are extended to include:

(a) Your partners, members, executive officers, trustees, directors and stockholders of such partnership, limited liability company or corporation, but only with respect to their duties as such; and

(b) Managers of a limited liability company, but only with respect to their duties as such.

The existence of one or more Additional Insureds does not increase the Limit of Insurance.

(2) **Newly Acquired Organizations**

Under Coverage **C** – Mortgageholder's Liability, the words "you" and "your" also include any organization (other than a partnership, joint venture or limited liability company) that you acquire or form and over which you maintain ownership or majority interest if there is no other similar insurance available to that organization.

This Coverage Extension ends:

(a) 90 days after you acquire or form the organization; or

(b) At the end of the policy period shown in the Declarations;

whichever is earlier.

This Extension does not apply to errors or accidental omissions that occurred before you acquired or formed the organization.

4. **Coverage D – Real Estate Tax Liability**

We will pay for damages for which you are legally liable due to error or accidental omission in paying real estate taxes, as agreed, on behalf of the mortgagor.

B. **Exclusions**

The following exclusions apply to Coverages **A, B, C** and **D**.

1. We will not pay for loss or damage caused directly or indirectly by any of the following. Such loss or damage is excluded regardless of any other cause or event that contributes concurrently or in any sequence to the loss.

a. **Ordinance Or Law**

The enforcement of any ordinance or law:

(1) Regulating the construction, use or repair of any property; or

(2) Requiring the tearing down of any property, including the cost of removing its debris.

This exclusion, Ordinance Or Law, applies whether the loss results from:

(a) An ordinance or law that is enforced even if the property has not been damaged; or

(b) The increased costs incurred to comply with an ordinance or law in the course of construction, repair, renovation, remodeling or demolition of property, or removal of its debris, following a physical loss to that property.

b. **Earth Movement**

(1) Earthquake, including any earth sinking, rising or shifting related to such event;

(2) Landslide, including any earth sinking, rising or shifting related to such event;

(3) Mine subsidence, meaning subsidence of a man-made mine, whether or not mining activity has ceased;

(4) Earth sinking (other than sinkhole collapse), rising or shifting including soil conditions which cause settling, cracking or other disarrangement of foundations or other parts of realty. Soil conditions include contraction, expansion, freezing, thawing, erosion, improperly compacted soil and the action of water under the ground surface.

But if Earth Movement, as described in **b.(1)** through **b.(4)** above, results in fire or explosion, we will pay for the loss or damage caused by that fire or explosion.

(5) Volcanic eruption, explosion or effusion. But if volcanic eruption, explosion or effusion results in fire or Volcanic Action, we will pay for the loss or damage caused by that fire or Volcanic Action.

c. **Governmental Action**

Seizure or destruction of property by order of governmental authority.

© ISO Properties, Inc., 2007   ☐

But we will pay for loss or damage caused by or resulting from acts of destruction ordered by governmental authority and taken at the time of a fire to prevent its spread, if the fire would be covered by this Coverage Part.

d. Nuclear Hazard

Nuclear reaction or radiation, or radioactive contamination, however caused.

But if nuclear reaction or radiation, or radioactive contamination, results in fire, we will pay for the loss or damage caused by that fire.

e. Utility Services

The failure of power, communication, water or other utility service supplied to the described premises, however caused, if the failure:

(1) Originates away from the described premises; or

(2) Originates at the described premises, but only if such failure involves equipment used to supply the utility service to the described premises from a source away from the described premises.

Failure of any utility service includes lack of sufficient capacity and reduction in supply.

Loss or damage caused by a surge of power is also excluded, if the surge would not have occurred but for an event causing a failure of power.

But if the failure or surge of power, or the failure of communication, water or other utility service, results in a Covered Cause of Loss, we will pay for the loss or damage caused by that Covered Cause of Loss.

Communication services include but are not limited to service relating to Internet access or access to any electronic, cellular or satellite network.

f. War And Military Action

(1) War, including undeclared or civil war;

(2) Warlike action by a military force, including action in hindering or defending against an actual or expected attack, by any government, sovereign or other authority using military personnel or other agents; or

(3) Insurrection, rebellion, revolution, usurped power, or action taken by governmental authority in hindering or defending against any of these.

g. Water

(1) Flood, surface water, waves, tides, tidal waves, overflow of any body of water, or their spray, all whether driven by wind or not;

(2) Mudslide or mudflow;

(3) Water that backs up or overflows from a sewer, drain or sump; or

(4) Water under the ground surface pressing on, or flowing or seeping through:

(a) Foundations, walls, floors or paved surfaces;

(b) Basements, whether paved or not; or

(c) Doors, windows or other openings.

But if Water, as described in **g.(1)** through **g.(4)** above, results in fire or explosion, we will pay for the loss or damage caused by that fire or explosion.

h. "Fungus", Wet Rot, Dry Rot And Bacteria

Presence, growth, proliferation, spread or any activity of "fungus", wet or dry rot or bacteria.

But if "fungus", wet or dry rot or bacteria results in a "specified cause of loss", we will pay for the loss or damage caused by that "specified cause of loss".

This exclusion does not apply:

1. When "fungus", wet or dry rot or bacteria results from fire or lightning; or

2. To the extent that coverage is provided in the Additional Coverage – Limited Coverage For "Fungus", Wet Rot, Dry Rot And Bacteria with respect to loss or damage by a cause of loss other than fire or lightning.

Exclusions **B.1.a.** through **B.1.h.** apply whether or not the loss event results in widespread damage or affects a substantial area.

2. We will not pay for loss or damage caused by or resulting from:

a. Discharge, dispersal, seepage, migration, release or escape of "pollutants". If you customarily require mortgagors to provide insurance against causes of loss on a special form basis (covering any cause of loss not excluded or limited in the policy), this exclusion does not apply if the discharge, dispersal, seepage, migration, release or escape is itself caused by any of the "specified causes of loss".

If the discharge, dispersal, seepage, migration, release or escape of "pollutants" results in a "specified cause of loss", we will pay for the loss or damage caused by that "specified cause of loss".

b. Artificially generated electrical, magnetic or electromagnetic energy that damages, disturbs, disrupts or otherwise interferes with any:

(1) Electrical or electronic wire, device, appliance, system or network; or

(2) Device, appliance, system or network utilizing cellular or satellite technology;

For the purpose of this exclusion, electrical, magnetic or electromagnetic energy includes but is not limited to:

(a) Electrical current, including arcing;

(b) Electrical charge produced or conducted by a magnetic or electromagnetic field;

(c) Pulse of electromagnetic energy; or

(d) Electromagnetic waves or microwaves.

But if fire results, we will pay for the loss or damage caused by that fire.

c. Any event that occurs more than 30 days after you know that an error or accidental omission may have occurred.

d. Your failure to obtain, maintain or properly handle the following types of insurance policies or programs:

(1) Title;

(2) Mortgage guarantee;

(3) Life; or

(4) Health or accident.

e. Neglect of an insured to use all reasonable means to save and preserve property from further damage at and after the time of loss.

3. We will not pay for loss or damage caused by or resulting from any of the following, **3.a.** through **3.d.** But if an excluded cause of loss that is listed in **3.a.** through **3.d.** results in a Covered Cause of Loss, we will pay for the loss or damage caused by that Covered Cause of Loss.

a. Collapse, including any of the following conditions of property or any part of the property:

(1) An abrupt falling down or caving in;

(2) Loss of structural integrity, including separation of parts of the property or property in danger of falling down or caving in; or

(3) Any cracking, bulging, sagging, bending, leaning; settling, shrinkage or expansion as such condition relates to **(1)** or **(2)** above.

This exclusion, **a.**, does not apply:

(a) To the extent that coverage is provided under the Additional Coverage – Collapse; or

(b) To collapse caused by one or more of the following:

(i) The "specified causes of loss";

(ii) Breakage of building glass;

(iii) Weight of rain that collects on a roof; or

(iv) Weight of people or personal property.

b. Weather conditions, if weather conditions contribute in any way with a cause or event excluded in Paragraph **1.** above to produce the loss or damage.

c. Acts or decisions, including the failure to act or decide, of any person, group, organization or governmental body.

d. Faulty, inadequate or defective:

(1) Planning, zoning, development, surveying, siting;

(2) Design, specifications, workmanship, repair, construction, renovation, remodeling, grading, compaction;

(3) Materials used in repair, construction, renovation or remodeling; or

(4) Maintenance;

of part or all of any property on or off the described premises.

 ☐

4. Additional Exclusion

The following provisions apply only to the specified property.

LOSS OR DAMAGE TO PRODUCTS

We will not pay for loss or damage to any merchandise, goods or other product caused by or resulting from error or omission by any person or entity (including those having possession under an arrangement where work or a portion of the work is outsourced) in any stage of the development, production or use of the product, including planning, testing, processing, packaging, installation, maintenance or repair. This exclusion applies to any effect that compromises the form, substance or quality of the product. But if such error or omission results in a Covered Cause of Loss, we will pay for the loss or damage caused by that Covered Cause of Loss.

C. Limits Of Insurance

The most we will pay under this Coverage Form for all loss arising from one error or accidental omission is the applicable Limit of Insurance shown in the Declarations, subject to the following additional limitations:

1. Under Coverage **A** – Mortgageholder's Interest, or Coverage **B** – Property Owned Or Held In Trust, we will not pay more than the least of:

   a. The amount of direct physical loss or damage determined in accordance with the insurance policies that would have covered the loss or damage if no error or accidental omission occurred, less the amount of any other insurance recovery payable to you on the Covered Property;

   b. The amount that would have been paid to you under insurance policies you would customarily have procured and maintained if the error or accidental omission had not occurred; or

   c. The amount of your "mortgageholder's interest" under Coverage **A**.

2. Under Coverage **D** – Real Estate Tax Liability, we will not pay more than 15% of the Limit of Insurance shown in the Declarations as applicable to this Coverage Form, for damages due to error or accidental omission in paying real estate taxes in connection with any single mortgage.

D. Additional Coverage – Collapse

The coverage provided under this Additional Coverage – Collapse applies only to an abrupt collapse as described and limited in **D.1.** through **D.6.**

1. For the purpose of this Additional Coverage – Collapse, abrupt collapse means an abrupt falling down or caving in of a building or any part of a building with the result that the building or part of the building cannot be occupied for its intended purpose.

2. We will pay for direct physical loss or damage to Covered Property, caused by abrupt collapse of a building or any part of a building that is insured under this Coverage Form or that contains Covered Property insured under this Coverage Form, if such collapse is caused by one or more of the following:

   a. Building decay that is hidden from view, unless the presence of such decay is known to a mortgagor prior to collapse;

   b. Insect or vermin damage that is hidden from view, unless the presence of such damage is known to a mortgagor prior to collapse;

   c. Use of defective material or methods in construction, remodeling or renovation if the abrupt collapse occurs during the course of the construction, remodeling or renovation.

   d. Use of defective material or methods in construction, remodeling or renovation if the abrupt collapse occurs after the construction, remodeling or renovation is complete, but only if the collapse is caused in part by:

      (1) A cause of loss listed in **2.a.** or **2.b.**;

      (2) One or more of the "specified causes of loss";

      (3) Breakage of building glass;

      (4) Weight of people or personal property; or

      (5) Weight of rain that collects on a roof.

3. This Additional Coverage – Collapse does **not** apply to:

   a. A building or any part of a building that is in danger of falling down or caving in:

   b. A part of a building that is standing, even if it has separated from another part of the building; or

   c. A building that is standing or any part of a building that is standing, even if it shows evidence of cracking, bulging, sagging, bending, leaning, settling, shrinkage or expansion.

4. If personal property abruptly falls down or caves in and such collapse is **not** the result of abrupt collapse of a building, we will pay for loss or damage to Covered Property caused by such collapse of personal property only if:

   a. The collapse of personal property was caused by a cause of loss listed in **2.a.** through **2.d.**; and

   b. The personal property which collapses is inside a building.

   The coverage stated in this paragraph, **4.**, does not apply to personal property if marring and/or scratching is the only damage to that personal property caused by the collapse.

5. This Additional Coverage – Collapse does not apply to personal property that has not abruptly fallen down or caved in, even if the personal property shows evidence of cracking, bulging, sagging, bending, leaning, settling, shrinkage or expansion.

6. This Additional Coverage – Collapse will not increase the Limits of Insurance provided in this Coverage Part.

7. The term Covered Cause of Loss includes the Additional Coverage – Collapse as described and limited in **D.1.** through **D.6.**

. **Additional Coverage – Limited Coverage For "Fungus", Wet Rot, Dry Rot And Bacteria**

1. The coverage described in **E.2.** only applies when the "fungus", wet or dry rot or bacteria is the result of one or more of the following causes that occurs during the policy period and only if all reasonable means were used to save and preserve the property from further damage at the time of and after that occurrence.

   a. A "specified cause of loss" other than fire or lightning; or

   b. Flood, if the Flood Coverage Endorsement applies to the affected premises.

2. We will pay for loss or damage by "fungus", wet or dry rot or bacteria. As used in this Limited Coverage, the term loss or damage means:

   a. Direct physical loss or damage to Covered Property caused by "fungus", wet or dry rot or bacteria, including the cost of removal of the "fungus", wet or dry rot or bacteria;

   b. The cost to tear out and replace any part of the building or other property as needed to gain access to the "fungus", wet or dry rot or bacteria; and

   c. The cost of testing performed after removal, repair, replacement or restoration of the damaged property is completed, provided there is a reason to believe that "fungus", wet or dry rot or bacteria are present.

3. The coverage described under **E.2.** of this Limited Coverage is limited to $15,000. Regardless of the number of claims, this limit is the most we will pay for the total of all loss or damage arising out of all occurrences of "specified causes of loss" (other than fire or lightning) and Flood which take place in a 12-month period (starting with the beginning of the present annual policy period). With respect to a particular occurrence of loss which results in "fungus", wet or dry rot or bacteria, we will not pay more than a total of $15,000 even if the "fungus", wet or dry rot or bacteria continues to be present or active, or recurs, in a later policy period.

4. The coverage provided under this Limited Coverage does not increase the applicable Limit of Insurance on any Covered Property. If a particular occurrence results in loss or damage by "fungus", wet or dry rot or bacteria, and other loss or damage, we will not pay more, for the total of all loss or damage, than the applicable Limit of Insurance on the affected Covered Property.

   If there is covered loss or damage to Covered Property, not caused by "fungus", wet or dry rot or bacteria, loss payment will not be limited by the terms of this Limited Coverage, except to the extent that "fungus", wet or dry rot or bacteria causes an increase in the loss. Any such increase in the loss will be subject to the terms of this Limited Coverage.

5. The terms of this Limited Coverage do not increase or reduce the coverage provided under the Additional Coverage – Collapse.

ADDITIONAL CONDITIONS

The following conditions apply in addition to the Common Policy Conditions.

E. Condition Applicable To Coverage A – Mortgageholder's Interest

TRANSFER OF MORTGAGE – COVERAGE A

We and all other insurance companies covering a loss, if in agreement, may pay you an amount equal to the outstanding balance on the mortgage, even if that amount is greater than the amount of loss. If so, we and the other insurance companies may demand and receive a full assignment of the mortgage, including all securities held as collateral for the debt, as interests may appear.

F. Conditions Applicable To Coverage B – Property Owned Or Held In Trust

1. **Our Options – Coverage B**

   In the event of loss or damage covered under Coverage **B**, at our option, we will either:

   a. Pay the value of lost or damaged property;

   b. Pay the cost of repairing or replacing the lost or damaged property;

   c. Take all or any part of the property at an agreed or appraised value; or

   d. Repair, rebuild or replace the property with other property of like kind and quality.

   We will give notice of our intentions within 30 days after we receive the sworn statement of loss.

   We will not pay you more than your financial interest in the Covered Property.

2. **Recovered Property – Coverage B**

   If either you or we recover any property after loss settlement, that party must give the other prompt notice. At your option, the property will be returned to you. You must then return to us the amount we paid to you for the property. We will pay recovery expenses and the expenses to repair the recovered property, subject to the Limit of Insurance.

3. **Time Period – Coverage B**

   Coverage on each item of Covered Property applies only during the period of time that:

   a. Begins on the day you acquire the property or your fiduciary interest in it begins; and

   b. Ends on the earlier of:

      (1) 90 days after the date in Paragraph **a.** above; or

      (2) The day other insurance on the property is obtained.

4. **Valuation – Coverage B**

   We will determine the value of Covered Property in the event of loss or damage at actual cash value as of the time of loss or damage.

G. Conditions Applicable To Coverage C – Mortgageholder's Liability And Coverage D – Real Estate Tax Liability

1. **Bankruptcy – Coverages C And D**

   Bankruptcy or insolvency of you or your estate will not relieve us of our obligations under Coverages **C** and **D**.

2. **Separation Of Insureds – Coverages C And D**

   The insurance under Coverages **C** and **D** applies separately to you and each additional insured, except with respect to the Limits of Insurance.

H. Conditions Applicable To All Coverages

1. **Abandonment**

   There can be no abandonment of any property to us.

2. **Appraisal – Coverages A And B Only**

   If we and you disagree on the amount of loss, either may make written demand for an appraisal of the loss. In this event, each party will select a competent and impartial appraiser. The two appraisers will select an umpire. If they cannot agree, either may request that selection be made by a judge of a court having jurisdiction. The appraisers will state separately the amount of loss. If they fail to agree, they will submit their differences to the umpire. A decision agreed to by any two will be binding. Each party will:

   a. Pay its chosen appraiser; and

   b. Bear the other expenses of the appraisal and umpire equally.

   If there is an appraisal, we will still retain our right to deny the claim.

3. **Duties In the Event Of Loss**

   a. Under Coverages **A** and **B**:

      (1) You must see that the following are done in the event of loss or damage to Covered Property:

         (a) Notify the police if a law may have been broken.

         (b) Give us prompt notice of the loss or damage once you are aware of it. Include a description of the property involved.

CP 00 70 06 07 © ISO Properties, Inc., 2007 **Page 9 of 12** ☐

(c) Take all reasonable steps to protect the Covered Property from further damage, and keep a record of your expenses necessary to protect the Covered Property, for consideration in the settlement of the claim. This will not increase the Limit of Insurance. However, we will not pay for any subsequent loss or damage resulting from a cause of loss that is not a Covered Cause of Loss. Also, if feasible, set the damaged property aside and in the best possible order for examination.

(d) At our request, give us complete inventories of the damaged and undamaged property. Include quantities, costs, values and amount of loss claimed.

(e) As often as may be reasonably required, permit us to inspect the property proving the loss or damage and examine your books and records.

Also permit us to take samples of damaged and undamaged property for inspection, testing and analysis, and permit us to make copies from your books and records.

(f) Send us a signed, sworn proof of loss containing the information we request to investigate the claim. You must do this within 60 days after our request. We will supply you with the necessary forms.

(g) Cooperate with us in the investigation or settlement of the claim.

(2) We may examine any insured under oath, while not in the presence of any other insured and at such times as may be reasonably required, about any matter relating to this insurance or the claim, including an insured's books and records. In the event of an examination, an insured's answers must be signed.

b. Under Coverages **C** and **D**:

(1) If a claim is made or "suit" is brought against you, you must see to it that we receive prompt written notice of the claim or "suit".

(2) You must:

(a) Immediately send us copies of any demands, notices, summonses or legal papers received in connection with the claim or "suit";

(b) Authorize us to obtain records and other information;

(c) Cooperate with us in the investigation, settlement or defense of the claim or "suit";

(d) Assist us, upon our request, in the enforcement of any right against any person or organization that may be liable to you because of damage to which this insurance may also apply; and

(e) If requested, give us a signed statement of facts containing the information we request to determine our rights and duties under this insurance.

(3) You will not, except at your own cost, voluntarily make a payment, assume any obligation, or incur any expense without our consent.

4. **Insurance Under Two Or More Coverages**

If two or more of this policy's coverages apply to the same loss or damage, we will not pay more than the actual amount of the loss or damage.

5. **Legal Action Against Us**

a. No one may bring a legal action against us under Coverages **A** and **B** unless:

(1) There has been full compliance with all of the terms of Coverages **A** and **B**; and

(2) The action is brought within two years after you discover the error or accidental omission.

b. No person or organization has a right under Coverages **C** and **D**:

(1) To join us as a party or otherwise bring us into a "suit" asking for damages from you; or

(2) To sue us on this Coverage Form unless all of its terms have been fully complied with.

         CP 00 70 06 07   ☐

A person or organization may sue us to recover on an agreed settlement or on a final judgment against you obtained after an actual trial; but we will not be liable for damages that are not payable under the terms of this Coverage Form or that are in excess of the Limit of Insurance. An agreed settlement means a settlement and release of liability signed by us, you and the claimant or the claimant's legal representative.

6. Liberalization

If we adopt any revision that would broaden the coverage under this Coverage Part without additional premium within 45 days prior to or during the policy period, the broadened coverage will immediately apply to this Coverage Part.

7. Loss Payment

We will pay for covered loss or damage to Covered Property within 30 days after we receive the sworn proof of loss, if you have complied with all of the terms of this Coverage Part and:

a. We have reached agreement with you on the amount of loss; or

b. An appraisal award has been made.

8. Other Insurance

a. You may have other insurance subject to the same plan, terms, conditions and provisions as the insurance under this Coverage Part. If you do, we will pay our share of the covered loss or damage. Our share is the proportion that the applicable Limit of Insurance under this Coverage Part bears to the Limits of Insurance of all insurance covering on the same basis.

b. If there is other insurance covering the same loss or damage, other than that described in **a.** above, we will pay only for the amount of covered loss or damage in excess of the amount due from that other insurance, whether you can collect on it or not. But we will not pay more than the applicable Limit of Insurance.

9. Policy Period, Coverage Territory

Under this Coverage Form:

a. These coverages only apply to:

(1) Loss or damage; or

(2) Claims or "suits" arising from an event;

that occurs during the policy period shown in the Declarations. The date of error or accidental omission does not have to be within the policy period.

b. We will pay for loss arising from errors or accidental omissions in connection with insurance policies or real estate tax payments on property located in:

(1) The United States of America (including its territories and possessions); and

(2) Puerto Rico.

10. Transfer Of Rights Of Recovery Against Others To Us

a. Under Coverages **A** and **B,** if any person or organization to or for whom we make payment under this Coverage Form has rights to recover damages from another, those rights are transferred to us to the extent of our payment. That person or organization must do everything necessary to secure our rights and must do nothing after loss to impair them. But you may waive your rights against another party in writing:

(1) Prior to a loss to your Covered Property.

(2) After a loss to your Covered Property only if, at time of loss, that party is one of the following:

(a) Someone insured by this insurance;

(b) A business firm:

(i) Owned or controlled by you; or

(ii) That owns or controls you; or

(c) Your tenant.

This will not restrict your insurance.

b. Under Coverages **C** and **D,** if you have rights to recover all or part of any payment we have made under this Coverage Form, those rights are transferred to us. You must do nothing after loss to impair them. At our request, you will bring "suit" or transfer those rights to us and help us enforce them.

11. Vacancy

We will not pay for any loss or damage if the building where loss or damage occurs, or out of which a claim or "suit" arises, has been vacant for more than 60 days before that loss or damage, or the event that gives rise to the claim or "suit".

A building is vacant unless at least 31% of its total square footage is:

a. Rented to a lessee or sub-lessee and used by the lessee or sub-lessee to conduct its customary operations; and/or

b. Used by the building owner to conduct customary operations.

12. Your Duties

You must make every reasonable effort, with respect to:

a. Coverage **A** – Mortgageholder's Interest, to require, procure and maintain "valid insurance", payable to you as mortgageholder, against the Covered Causes of Loss.

b. Coverage **B** – Property Owned Or Held In Trust, to procure and maintain "valid insurance" against the Covered Causes of Loss in amounts, and under conditions, you customarily require to protect your interest as owner, fiduciary or trustee of the Covered Property.

c. Coverage **C** – Mortgageholder's Liability, to maintain "valid insurance" against the Covered Causes of Loss in amounts, and under conditions, customarily accepted by the mortgagor, as agreed.

d. Coverage **D** – Real Estate Tax Liability, to promptly pay real estate taxes, if agreed to, on behalf of the mortgagor.

I. Definitions

1. "Fungus" means any type or form of fungus, including mold or mildew, and any mycotoxins, spores, scents or by-products produced or released by fungi.

2. "Mortgageholder's interest" means your interest, as mortgageholder, in real or personal property, including your interest in any legal fiduciary capacity.

3. "Pollutants" means any solid, liquid, gaseous or thermal irritant or contaminant, including smoke, vapor, soot, fumes, acids, alkalis, chemicals and waste. Waste includes materials to be recycled, reconditioned or reclaimed.

4. "Specified causes of loss" means the following: fire; lightning; explosion; windstorm or hail; smoke; aircraft or vehicles; riot or civil commotion; vandalism; leakage from fire-extinguishing equipment; sinkhole collapse; volcanic action; falling objects; weight of snow, ice or sleet; water damage. Water damage means accidental discharge or leakage of water or steam as the direct result of the breaking apart or cracking of any part of a system or appliance (other than a sump system including its related equipment and parts) containing water or steam.

5. "Suit" includes an arbitration proceeding to which you must submit or submit with our consent.

6. "Valid insurance" means a valid policy, or other evidence, of insurance.

CP 00 70 06 07   □

COMMERCIAL PROPERTY
CP 00 80 06 07

TOBACCO SALES WAREHOUSES COVERAGE FORM

Various provisions in this policy restrict coverage. Read the entire policy carefully to determine rights, duties and what is and is not covered.

Throughout this policy the words "you" and "your" refer to the Named Insured shown in the Declarations. The words "we", "us" and "our" refer to the Company providing this insurance.

Other words and phrases that appear in quotation marks have special meaning. Refer to Section **G.**, Definitions.

A. Coverage

We will pay for direct physical loss of or damage to Covered Property at the premises described in the Declarations caused by or resulting from any Covered Cause of Loss.

1. Covered Property

Covered Property, as used in this Coverage Part, means the following type of property for which a Limit of Insurance is shown in the Declarations:

Tobacco in Sales Warehouses, meaning leaf, loose, scrap and stem tobacco located in the building or structure described in the Declarations:

a. That belongs to others and is in your care, custody or control for auction; or

b. On your leaf account for resale.

Coverage for Tobacco in Sales Warehouses applies only between:

(1) 12:01 AM of the 15th day before the opening of the regular auction season at the described premises; and

(2) 12:01 AM of the 15th day following the official closing date of the regular auction season at the described premises.

2. Property Not Covered

Covered Property does not include:

a. Growing crops or water;

b. Tobacco that is insured under this or any other policy in which it is more specifically described, except for the excess of the amount due (whether you can collect on it or not) from that other insurance;

c. Tobacco while outside buildings or structures;

d. Tobacco while waterborne; and

e. Contraband, or property in the course of illegal transportation or trade.

3. Covered Causes Of Loss

See applicable Causes Of Loss Form as shown in the Declarations.

4. Additional Coverages

a. Debris Removal

(1) Subject to Paragraphs **(3)** and **(4)**, we will pay your expense to remove debris of Covered Property caused by or resulting from a Covered Cause of Loss that occurs during the policy period. The expenses will be paid only if they are reported to us in writing within 180 days of the date of direct physical loss or damage.

(2) Debris Removal does not apply to costs to:

(a) Extract "pollutants" from land or water; or

(b) Remove, restore, or replace polluted land or water.

(3) Subject to the exceptions in Paragraph **(4)**, the following provisions apply:

(a) The most we will pay for the total of direct physical loss or damage plus debris removal expense is the Limit of Insurance applicable to the Covered Property that has sustained loss or damage.

(b) Subject to **(a)** above, the amount we will pay for debris removal expense is limited to 25% of the sum of the deductible plus the amount that we pay for direct physical loss or damage to the Covered Property that has sustained loss or damage.

(4) We will pay up to an additional $10,000 for debris removal expense, for each location, in any one occurrence of physical loss or damage to Covered Property, if one or both of the following circumstances apply:

(a) The total of the actual debris removal expense plus the amount we pay for direct physical loss or damage exceeds the Limit of Insurance on the Covered Property that has sustained loss or damage.

(b) The actual debris removal expense exceeds 25% of the sum of the deductible plus the amount that we pay for direct physical loss or damage to the Covered Property that has sustained loss or damage.

Therefore, if **(4)(a)** and/or **(4)(b)** apply, our total payment for direct physical loss or damage and debris removal expense may reach but will never exceed the Limit of Insurance on the Covered Property that has sustained loss or damage, plus $10,000.

(5) Examples

The following examples assume that there is no Coinsurance penalty.

EXAMPLE #1

Limit of Insurance:	$ 90,000
Amount of Deductible:	$ 500
Amount of Loss:	$ 50,000
Amount of Loss Payable:	$ 49,500
	($50,000 – $500)
Debris Removal Expense:	$ 10,000
Debris Removal Expense Payable:	$ 10,000

($10,000 is 20% of $50,000.)

The debris removal expense is less than 25% of the sum of the loss payable plus the deductible. The sum of the loss payable and the debris removal expense ($49,500 + $10,000 = $59,500) is less than the Limit of Insurance. Therefore, the full amount of debris removal expense is payable in accordance with the terms of Paragraph **(3).**

EXAMPLE #2

Limit of Insurance:	$ 90,000
Amount of Deductible:	$ 500
Amount of Loss:	$ 80,000
Amount of Loss Payable:	$ 79,500
	($80,000 – $500)
Debris Removal Expense:	$ 30,000
Debris Removal Expense Payable	
Basic Amount:	$ 10,500
Additional Amount:	$ 10,000

The basic amount payable for debris removal expense under the terms of Paragraph **(3)** is calculated as follows: $80,000 ($79,500 + $500) x .25 = $20,000; capped at $10,500. The cap applies because the sum of the loss payable ($79,500) and the basic amount payable for debris removal expense ($10,500) cannot exceed the Limit of Insurance ($90,000).

The additional amount payable for debris removal expense is provided in accordance with the terms of Paragraph **(4),** because the debris removal expense ($30,000) exceeds 25% of the loss payable plus the deductible ($30,000 is 37.5% of $80,000), and because the sum of the loss payable and debris removal expense ($79,500 + $30,000 = $109,500) would exceed the Limit of Insurance ($90,000). The additional amount of covered debris removal expense is $10,000, the maximum payable under Paragraph **(4).** Thus, the total payable for debris removal expense in this example is $20,500; $9,500 of the debris removal expense is not covered.

b. Preservation Of Property

If it is necessary to move Covered Property from the described premises to preserve it from loss or damage by a Covered Cause of Loss, we will pay for any direct physical loss or damage to that property:

(1) While it is being moved or while temporarily stored at another location; and

(2) Only if the loss or damage occurs within 30 days after the property is first moved.

c. **Fire Department Service Charge**

When the fire department is called to save or protect Covered Property from a Covered Cause of Loss, we will pay up to $1,000, unless a higher limit is shown in the Declarations, for your liability for fire department service charges:

(1) Assumed by contract or agreement prior to loss; or

(2) Required by local ordinance.

No deductible applies to this Additional Coverage.

d. **Pollutant Clean-up And Removal**

We will pay your expense to extract "pollutants" from land or water at the described premises if the discharge, dispersal, seepage, migration, release or escape of the "pollutants" is caused by or results from a Covered Cause of Loss that occurs during the policy period. The expenses will be paid only if they are reported to us in writing within 180 days of the date on which the Covered Cause of Loss occurs.

This Additional Coverage does not apply to costs to test for, monitor or assess the existence, concentration or effects of "pollutants". But we will pay for testing which is performed in the course of extracting the "pollutants" from the land or water.

The most we will pay under this Additional Coverage for each described premises is $10,000 for the sum of all covered expenses arising out of Covered Causes of Loss occurring during each separate 12-month period of this policy.

5. **Coverage Extension**

PROPERTY OFF-PREMISES

You may extend the insurance provided by this Coverage Form to apply to Covered Property that is temporarily located in a building or structure you do not own, lease or operate. This Extension does not apply to Covered Property:

a. In a vehicle;

b. In the care, custody or control of your salespersons; or

c. At any fair or exhibition.

The most we will pay for loss or damage under this Extension is $10,000.

This Extension is additional insurance. The Additional Condition, Need For Full Reports, does not apply to this Extension.

B. **Exclusions And Limitations**

See applicable Causes Of Loss Form as shown in the Declarations.

C. **Limits Of Insurance**

The most we will pay for loss or damage in any one occurrence is the applicable Limit of Insurance shown in the Declarations.

The limits applicable to the Coverage Extension and the Fire Department Service Charge and Pollutant Clean-up And Removal Additional Coverages are in addition to the Limits of Insurance.

Payments under the Preservation Of Property Additional Coverage will not increase the applicable Limit of Insurance.

D. **Deductible**

In any one occurrence of loss or damage (hereinafter referred to as loss), we will first reduce the amount of loss if required by the Additional Condition – Need For Full Reports. If the adjusted amount of loss is less than or equal to the Deductible, we will not pay for that loss. If the adjusted amount of loss exceeds the Deductible, we will then subtract the Deductible from the adjusted amount of loss, and will pay the resulting amount or the Limit of Insurance, whichever is less.

E. **Loss Conditions**

The following conditions apply in addition to the Common Policy Conditions and the Commercial Property Conditions.

1. **Abandonment**

There can be no abandonment of any property to us.

2. **Appraisal**

If we and you disagree on the value of the property or the amount of loss, either may make written demand for an appraisal of the loss. In this event, each party will select a competent and impartial appraiser. The two appraisers will select an umpire. If they cannot agree, either may request that selection be made by a judge of a court having jurisdiction. The appraisers will state separately the value of the property and amount of loss. If they fail to agree, they will submit their differences to the umpire. A decision agreed to by any two will be binding. Each party will:

a. Pay its chosen appraiser; and

b. Bear the other expenses of the appraisal and umpire equally.

If there is an appraisal, we will still retain our right to deny the claim.

3. Duties In The Event Of Loss Or Damage

a. You must see that the following are done in the event of loss or damage to Covered Property:

(1) Notify the police if a law may have been broken.

(2) Give us prompt notice of the loss or damage. Include a description of the property involved.

(3) As soon as possible, give us a description of how, when and where the loss or damage occurred.

(4) Take all reasonable steps to protect the Covered Property from further damage, and keep a record of your expenses necessary to protect the Covered Property, for consideration in the settlement of the claim. This will not increase the Limit of Insurance. However, we will not pay for any subsequent loss or damage resulting from a cause of loss that is not a Covered Cause of Loss. Also, if feasible, set the damaged property aside and in the best possible order for examination.

(5) At our request, give us complete inventories of the damaged and undamaged property. Include quantities, costs, values and amount of loss claimed.

(6) As often as may be reasonably required, permit us to inspect the property proving the loss or damage and examine your books and records.

Also permit us to take samples of damaged and undamaged property for inspection, testing and analysis, and permit us to make copies from your books and records.

(7) Send us a signed, sworn proof of loss containing the information we request to investigate the claim. You must do this within 60 days after our request. We will supply you with the necessary forms.

(8) Cooperate with us in the investigation or settlement of the claim.

b. We may examine any insured under oath, while not in the presence of any other insured and at such times as may be reasonably required, about any matter relating to this insurance or the claim, including an insured's books and records. In the event of an examination, an insured's answers must be signed.

4. Loss Payment

a. In the event of loss or damage covered by this Coverage Form, at our option, we will either:

(1) Pay the value of lost or damaged property;

(2) Pay the cost of repairing or replacing the lost or damaged property, subject to **b.** below;

(3) Take all or any part of the property at an agreed or appraised value; or

(4) Repair, rebuild or replace the property with other property of like kind and quality, subject to **b.** below.

We will determine the value of lost or damaged property, or the cost of its repair or replacement, in accordance with the applicable terms of the Valuation Condition in this Coverage Form or any applicable provision which amends or supersedes the Valuation Condition.

b. The cost to repair, rebuild or replace does not include the increased cost attributable to enforcement of any ordinance or law regulating the construction, use or repair of any property.

c. We will give notice of our intentions within 30 days after we receive the sworn proof of loss.

d. We will not pay you more than your financial interest in the Covered Property.

e. We may adjust losses with the owners of lost or damaged property if other than you. If we pay the owners, such payments will satisfy your claims against us for the owners' property. We will not pay the owners more than their financial interest in the Covered Property.

f. We may elect to defend you against suits arising from claims of owners of property. We will do this at our expense.

g. We will pay for covered loss or damage within 30 days after we receive the sworn proof of loss, if you have complied with all of the terms of this Coverage Part and:

(1) We have reached agreement with you on the amount of loss; or

(2) An appraisal award has been made.

 CP 00 80 06 07   ☐

5. Recovered Property

If either you or we recover any property after loss settlement, that party must give the other prompt notice. At your option, the property will be returned to you.

You must then return to us the amount we paid to you for the property. We will pay recovery expenses and the expenses to repair the recovered property, subject to the Limit of Insurance.

6. Valuation

a. We will determine the value of Tobacco in Sales Warehouses in the event of loss or damage at the average price on sales of tobacco of like grades and types:

(1) On the day loss occurs;

(2) On the two sales days immediately prior to the day loss occurs; and

(3) On the two sales days immediately following the day loss occurs.

b. Prices will be based on sales at the tobacco sales warehouse nearest the premises where loss or damage occurs. We will determine the average price as follows:

(1) Divide the total sales by the total number of pounds; and

(2) Deduct any unearned warehouse charges, unearned auction fees and unpaid government taxes at the time of the loss.

F. Additional Conditions

The following conditions apply in addition to the Common Policy Conditions and the Commercial Property Conditions.

1. Need For Full Reports

a. We will not pay a greater proportion of loss than:

(1) The values you reported, divided by

(2) The value of the Covered Property during the last auction season,

if your last report of values before loss or damage at any location shows less than the full value of the Covered Property at that location during the last auction season.

b. For locations you acquire after the last report of values, we will not pay a greater proportion of loss than:

(1) The values you reported for all locations, divided by

(2) The value of the Covered Property at all locations during the last auction season.

2. Premium Adjustment

a. The premium charged at the inception of each policy year is an advance premium. We will determine the final premium for this insurance after the policy year or expiration, based on your reports of value.

b. Based on the difference between the advance premium and the final premium, for each policy year, we will:

(1) Charge additional premium; or

(2) Return excess premium.

3. Reports Of Value

You must file with us a report, within 30 days of the official closing of the sales auction season, showing separately for each location listed in the Declarations:

a. The total number of pounds of tobacco sold and resold during the last sales auction season; and

b. The total price paid per pound.

G. Definitions

"Pollutants" means any solid, liquid, gaseous or thermal irritant or contaminant, including smoke, vapor, soot, fumes, acids, alkalis, chemicals and waste. Waste includes materials to be recycled, reconditioned or reclaimed.

COMMERCIAL PROPERTY CONDITIONS

This Coverage Part is subject to the following conditions, the Common Policy Conditions and applicable Loss Conditions and Additional Conditions in Commercial Property Coverage Forms.

A. CONCEALMENT, MISREPRESENTATION OR FRAUD

This Coverage Part is void in any case of fraud by you as it relates to this Coverage Part at any time. It is also void if you or any other insured, at any time, intentionally conceal or misrepresent a material fact concerning:

1. This Coverage Part;

2. The Covered Property;

3. Your interest in the Covered Property; or

4. A claim under this Coverage Part.

B. CONTROL OF PROPERTY

Any act or neglect of any person other than you beyond your direction or control will not affect this insurance.

The breach of any condition of this Coverage Part at any one or more locations will not affect coverage at any location where, at the time of loss or damage, the breach of condition does not exist.

C. INSURANCE UNDER TWO OR MORE COVERAGES

If two or more of this policy's coverages apply to the same loss or damage, we will not pay more than the actual amount of the loss or damage.

D. LEGAL ACTION AGAINST US

No one may bring a legal action against us under this Coverage Part unless:

1. There has been full compliance with all of the terms of this Coverage Part; and

2. The action is brought within 2 years after the date on which the direct physical loss or damage occurred.

E. LIBERALIZATION

If we adopt any revision that would broaden the coverage under this Coverage Part without additional premium within 45 days prior to or during the policy period, the broadened coverage will immediately apply to this Coverage Part.

F. NO BENEFIT TO BAILEE

No person or organization, other than you, having custody of Covered Property will benefit from this insurance.

G. OTHER INSURANCE

1. You may have other insurance subject to the same plan, terms, conditions and provisions as the insurance under this Coverage Part. If you do, we will pay our share of the covered loss or damage. Our share is the proportion that the applicable Limit of Insurance under this Coverage Part bears to the Limits of Insurance of all insurance covering on the same basis.

2. If there is other insurance covering the same loss or damage, other than that described in 1. above, we will pay only for the amount of covered loss or damage in excess of the amount due from that other insurance, whether you can collect on it or not. But we will not pay more than the applicable Limit of Insurance.

H. POLICY PERIOD, COVERAGE TERRITORY

Under this Coverage Part:

1. We cover loss or damage commencing:

   a. During the policy period shown in the Declarations; and

   b. Within the coverage territory.

2. The coverage territory is:

   a. The United States of America (including its territories and possessions);

   b. Puerto Rico; and

   c. Canada.

I. TRANSFER OF RIGHTS OF RECOVERY AGAINST OTHERS TO US

If any person or organization to or for whom we make payment under this Coverage Part has rights to recover damages from another, those rights are transferred to us to the extent of our payment. That person or organization must do everything necessary to secure our rights and must do nothing after loss to impair them. But you may waive your rights against another party in writing:

1. Prior to a loss to your Covered Property or Covered Income.

2. After a loss to your Covered Property or Covered Income only if, at time of loss, that party is one of the following:

    a. Someone insured by this insurance;

    b. A business firm:

        (1) Owned or controlled by you; or

        (2) That owns or controls you; or

    c. Your tenant.

This will not restrict your insurance.

COMMERCIAL PROPERTY
CP 10 10 06 07

CAUSES OF LOSS – BASIC FORM

A. Covered Causes Of Loss

When Basic is shown in the Declarations, Covered Causes of Loss means the following:

1. Fire.

2. Lightning.

3. Explosion, including the explosion of gases or fuel within the furnace of any fired vessel or within the flues or passages through which the gases of combustion pass. This cause of loss does not include loss or damage by:

   a. Rupture, bursting or operation of pressure-relief devices; or

   b. Rupture or bursting due to expansion or swelling of the contents of any building or structure, caused by or resulting from water.

4. Windstorm or Hail, but not including:

   a. Frost or cold weather;

   b. Ice (other than hail), snow or sleet, whether driven by wind or not; or

   c. Loss or damage to the interior of any building or structure, or the property inside the building or structure, caused by rain, snow, sand or dust, whether driven by wind or not, unless the building or structure first sustains wind or hail damage to its roof or walls through which the rain, snow, sand or dust enters.

5. Smoke causing sudden and accidental loss or damage. This cause of loss does not include smoke from agricultural smudging or industrial operations.

6. Aircraft or Vehicles, meaning only physical contact of an aircraft, a spacecraft, a self-propelled missile, a vehicle or an object thrown up by a vehicle with the described property or with the building or structure containing the described property. This cause of loss includes loss or damage by objects falling from aircraft.

   We will not pay for loss or damage caused by or resulting from vehicles you own or which are operated in the course of your business.

7. Riot or Civil Commotion, including:

   a. Acts of striking employees while occupying the described premises; and

   b. Looting occurring at the time and place of a riot or civil commotion.

8. Vandalism, meaning willful and malicious damage to, or destruction of, the described property.

   We will not pay for loss or damage caused by or resulting from theft, except for building damage caused by the breaking in or exiting of burglars.

9. Sprinkler Leakage, meaning leakage or discharge of any substance from an Automatic Sprinkler System, including collapse of a tank that is part of the system.

   If the building or structure containing the Automatic Sprinkler System is Covered Property, we will also pay the cost to:

   a. Repair or replace damaged parts of the Automatic Sprinkler System if the damage:

      (1) Results in sprinkler leakage; or

      (2) Is directly caused by freezing.

   b. Tear out and replace any part of the building or structure to repair damage to the Automatic Sprinkler System that has resulted in sprinkler leakage.

   Automatic Sprinkler System means:

   (1) Any automatic fire-protective or extinguishing system, including connected:

      (a) Sprinklers and discharge nozzles;

      (b) Ducts, pipes, valves and fittings;

      (c) Tanks, their component parts and supports; and

      (d) Pumps and private fire protection mains.

   (2) When supplied from an automatic fire-protective system:

      (a) Non-automatic fire-protective systems; and

      (b) Hydrants, standpipes and outlets.

    □

10. Sinkhole Collapse, meaning loss or damage caused by the sudden sinking or collapse of land into underground empty spaces created by the action of water on limestone or dolomite. This cause of loss does not include:

    a. The cost of filling sinkholes; or

    b. Sinking or collapse of land into man-made underground cavities.

11. Volcanic Action, meaning direct loss or damage resulting from the eruption of a volcano when the loss or damage is caused by:

    a. Airborne volcanic blast or airborne shock waves;

    b. Ash, dust or particulate matter; or

    c. Lava flow.

    All volcanic eruptions that occur within any 168-hour period will constitute a single occurrence.

    This cause of loss does not include the cost to remove ash, dust or particulate matter that does not cause direct physical loss or damage to the described property.

B. Exclusions

1. We will not pay for loss or damage caused directly or indirectly by any of the following. Such loss or damage is excluded regardless of any other cause or event that contributes concurrently or in any sequence to the loss.

    a. **Ordinance Or Law**

        The enforcement of any ordinance or law:

        (1) Regulating the construction, use or repair of any property; or

        (2) Requiring the tearing down of any property, including the cost of removing its debris.

        This exclusion, Ordinance Or Law, applies whether the loss results from:

        (a) An ordinance or law that is enforced even if the property has not been damaged; or

        (b) The increased costs incurred to comply with an ordinance or law in the course of construction, repair, renovation, remodeling or demolition of property, or removal of its debris, following a physical loss to that property.

    b. **Earth Movement**

        (1) Earthquake, including any earth sinking, rising or shifting related to such event;

        (2) Landslide, including any earth sinking, rising or shifting related to such event;

        (3) Mine subsidence, meaning subsidence of a man-made mine, whether or not mining activity has ceased;

        (4) Earth sinking (other than sinkhole collapse), rising or shifting including soil conditions which cause settling, cracking or other disarrangement of foundations or other parts of realty. Soil conditions include contraction, expansion, freezing, thawing, erosion, improperly compacted soil and the action of water under the ground surface.

        But if Earth Movement, as described in **b.(1)** through **(4)** above, results in fire or explosion, we will pay for the loss or damage caused by that fire or explosion.

        (5) Volcanic eruption, explosion or effusion. But if volcanic eruption, explosion or effusion results in fire or Volcanic Action, we will pay for the loss or damage caused by that fire or Volcanic Action.

    c. **Governmental Action**

        Seizure or destruction of property by order of governmental authority.

        But we will pay for loss or damage caused by or resulting from acts of destruction ordered by governmental authority and taken at the time of a fire to prevent its spread, if the fire would be covered under this Coverage Part.

    d. **Nuclear Hazard**

        Nuclear reaction or radiation, or radioactive contamination, however caused.

        But if nuclear reaction or radiation, or radioactive contamination, results in fire, we will pay for the loss or damage caused by that fire.

    e. **Utility Services**

        The failure of power, communication, water or other utility service supplied to the described premises, however caused, if the failure:

        (1) Originates away from the described premises; or

        (2) Originates at the described premises, but only if such failure involves equipment used to supply the utility service to the described premises from a source away from the described premises.

        Failure of any utility service includes lack of sufficient capacity and reduction in supply.

Loss or damage caused by a surge of power is also excluded, if the surge would not have occurred but for an event causing a failure of power.

But if the failure or surge of power, or the failure of communication, water or other utility service, results in a Covered Cause of Loss, we will pay for the loss or damage caused by that Covered Cause of Loss.

Communication services include but are not limited to service relating to Internet access or access to any electronic, cellular or satellite network.

f. War And Military Action

(1) War, including undeclared or civil war;

(2) Warlike action by a military force, including action in hindering or defending against an actual or expected attack, by any government, sovereign or other authority using military personnel or other agents; or

(3) Insurrection, rebellion, revolution, usurped power, or action taken by governmental authority in hindering or defending against any of these.

g. Water

(1) Flood, surface water, waves, tides, tidal waves, overflow of any body of water, or their spray, all whether driven by wind or not;

(2) Mudslide or mudflow;

(3) Water that backs up or overflows from a sewer, drain or sump; or

(4) Water under the ground surface pressing on, or flowing or seeping through:

(a) Foundations, walls, floors or paved surfaces;

(b) Basements, whether paved or not; or

(c) Doors, windows or other openings.

But if Water, as described in **g.(1)** through **(4)** above, results in fire, explosion or sprinkler leakage, we will pay for the loss or damage caused by that fire, explosion or sprinkler leakage.

h. "Fungus", Wet Rot, Dry Rot And Bacteria

Presence, growth, proliferation, spread or any activity of "fungus", wet or dry rot or bacteria.

But if "fungus", wet or dry rot or bacteria results in a Covered Cause of Loss, we will pay for the loss or damage caused by that Covered Cause of Loss.

This exclusion does not apply:

1. When "fungus", wet or dry rot or bacteria results from fire or lightning; or

2. To the extent that coverage is provided in the Additional Coverage – Limited Coverage For "Fungus", Wet Rot, Dry Rot And Bacteria with respect to loss or damage by a cause of loss other than fire or lightning.

Exclusions **B.1.a.** through **B.1.h.** apply whether or not the loss event results in widespread damage or affects a substantial area.

2. We will not pay for loss or damage caused by or resulting from:

a. Artificially generated electrical, magnetic or electromagnetic energy that damages, disturbs, disrupts or otherwise interferes with any:

(1) Electrical or electronic wire, device, appliance, system or network; or

(2) Device, appliance, system or network utilizing cellular or satellite technology.

For the purpose of this exclusion, electrical, magnetic or electromagnetic energy includes but is not limited to:

(a) Electrical current, including arcing;

(b) Electrical charge produced or conducted by a magnetic or electromagnetic field;

(c) Pulse of electromagnetic energy; or

(d) Electromagnetic waves or microwaves.

But if fire results, we will pay for the loss or damage caused by that fire.

b. Rupture or bursting of water pipes (other than Automatic Sprinkler Systems) unless caused by a Covered Cause of Loss.

c. Leakage or discharge of water or steam from any part of a system or appliance containing water or steam (other than an Automatic Sprinkler System), unless the leakage or discharge occurs because the system or appliance was damaged by a Covered Cause of Loss. But we will not pay for loss or damage caused by or resulting from continuous or repeated seepage or leakage of water, or the presence or condensation of humidity, moisture or vapor, that occurs over a period of 14 days or more.

d. Explosion of steam boilers, steam pipes, steam engines or steam turbines owned or leased by you, or operated under your control.

But if explosion of steam boilers, steam pipes, steam engines or steam turbines results in fire or combustion explosion, we will pay for the loss or damage caused by that fire or combustion explosion.

e. Mechanical breakdown, including rupture or bursting caused by centrifugal force.

But if mechanical breakdown results in a Covered Cause of Loss, we will pay for the loss or damage caused by that Covered Cause of Loss.

f. Neglect of an insured to use all reasonable means to save and preserve property from further damage at and after the time of loss.

3. **Special Exclusions**

The following provisions apply only to the specified Coverage Forms.

a. **Business Income (And Extra Expense) Coverage Form, Business Income (Without Extra Expense) Coverage Form, Or Extra Expense Coverage Form**

We will not pay for:

(1) Any loss caused by or resulting from:

(a) Damage or destruction of "finished stock"; or

(b) The time required to reproduce "finished stock".

This exclusion does not apply to Extra Expense.

(2) Any loss caused by or resulting from direct physical loss or damage to radio or television antennas (including satellite dishes) and their lead-in wiring, masts or towers.

(3) Any increase of loss caused by or resulting from:

(a) Delay in rebuilding, repairing or replacing the property or resuming "operations", due to interference at the location of the rebuilding, repair or replacement by strikers or other persons; or

(b) Suspension, lapse or cancellation of any license, lease or contract. But if the suspension, lapse or cancellation is directly caused by the "suspension" of "operations", we will cover such loss that affects your Business Income during the "period of restoration" and any extension of the "period of restoration" in accordance with the terms of the Extended Business Income Additional Coverage and the Extended Period of Indemnity Optional Coverage or any variation of these.

(4) Any Extra Expense caused by or resulting from suspension, lapse or cancellation of any license, lease or contract beyond the "period of restoration".

(5) Any other consequential loss.

b. **Leasehold Interest Coverage Form**

(1) Paragraph **B.1.a.**, Ordinance Or Law, does not apply to insurance under this Coverage Form.

(2) We will not pay for any loss caused by:

(a) Your cancelling the lease;

(b) The suspension, lapse or cancellation of any license; or

(c) Any other consequential loss.

c. **Legal Liability Coverage Form**

(1) The following exclusions do not apply to insurance under this Coverage Form:

(a) Paragraph **B.1.a.,** Ordinance Or Law;

(b) Paragraph **B.1.c.,** Governmental Action;

(c) Paragraph **B.1.d.,** Nuclear Hazard;

(d) Paragraph **B.1.e.,** Utility Services; and

(e) Paragraph **B.1.f.,** War And Military Action.

(2) The following additional exclusions apply to insurance under this Coverage Form:

(a) **Contractual Liability**

We will not defend any claim or "suit", or pay damages that you are legally liable to pay, solely by reason of your assumption of liability in a contract or agreement. But this exclusion does not apply to a written lease agreement in which you have assumed liability for building damage resulting from an actual or attempted burglary or robbery, provided that:

(i) Your assumption of liability was executed prior to the accident; and

(ii) The building is Covered Property under this Coverage Form.

(b) **Nuclear Hazard**

We will not defend any claim or "suit", or pay any damages, loss, expense or obligation, resulting from nuclear reaction or radiation, or radioactive contamination, however caused.

C. **Additional Coverage – Limited Coverage For "Fungus", Wet Rot, Dry Rot And Bacteria**

1. The coverage described in **C.2.** and **C.6.** only applies when the "fungus", wet or dry rot or bacteria is the result of one or more of the following causes that occurs during the policy period and only if all reasonable means were used to save and preserve the property from further damage at the time of and after that occurrence.

a. A Covered Cause of Loss other than fire or lightning; or

b. Flood, if the Flood Coverage Endorsement applies to the affected premises.

2. We will pay for loss or damage by "fungus", wet or dry rot or bacteria. As used in this Limited Coverage, the term loss or damage means:

a. Direct physical loss or damage to Covered Property caused by "fungus", wet or dry rot or bacteria, including the cost of removal of the "fungus", wet or dry rot or bacteria;

b. The cost to tear out and replace any part of the building or other property as needed to gain access to the "fungus", wet or dry rot or bacteria; and

c. The cost of testing performed after removal, repair, replacement or restoration of the damaged property is completed, provided there is a reason to believe that "fungus", wet or dry rot or bacteria are present.

3. The coverage described under **C.2.** of this Limited Coverage is limited to $15,000. Regardless of the number of claims, this limit is the most we will pay for the total of all loss or damage arising out of all occurrences of Covered Causes of Loss (other than fire or lightning) and Flood which take place in a 12-month period (starting with the beginning of the present annual policy period). With respect to a particular occurrence of loss which results in "fungus", wet or dry rot or bacteria, we will not pay more than a total of $15,000 even if the "fungus", wet or dry rot or bacteria continues to be present or active, or recurs, in a later policy period.

4. The coverage provided under this Limited Coverage does not increase the applicable Limit of Insurance on any Covered Property. If a particular occurrence results in loss or damage by "fungus", wet or dry rot or bacteria, and other loss or damage, we will not pay more, for the total of all loss or damage, than the applicable Limit of Insurance on the affected Covered Property.

If there is covered loss or damage to Covered Property, not caused by "fungus", wet or dry rot or bacteria, loss payment will not be limited by the terms of this Limited Coverage, except to the extent that "fungus", wet or dry rot or bacteria causes an increase in the loss. Any such increase in the loss will be subject to the terms of this Limited Coverage.

The terms of this Limited Coverage do not increase or reduce the coverage provided under Paragraph **b.** of Covered Causes Of Loss **).**, Sprinkler Leakage.

The following, **6.a.** or **6.b.**, applies only if Business Income and/or Extra Expense Coverage applies to the described premises and only if the "suspension" of "operations" satisfies all terms and conditions of the applicable Business Income and/or Extra Expense Coverage Form.

a. If the loss which resulted in "fungus", wet or dry rot or bacteria does not in itself necessitate a "suspension" of "operations", but such "suspension" is necessary due to loss or damage to property caused by "fungus", wet or dry rot or bacteria, then our payment under Business Income and/or Extra Expense is limited to the amount of loss and/or expense sustained in a period of not more than 30 days. The days need not be consecutive.

b. If a covered "suspension" of "operations" was caused by loss or damage other than "fungus", wet or dry rot or bacteria but remediation of "fungus", wet or dry rot or bacteria prolongs the "period of restoration", we will pay for loss and/or expense sustained during the delay (regardless of when such a delay occurs during the "period of restoration"), but such coverage is limited to 30 days. The days need not be consecutive.

D. Limitation

We will pay for loss of animals only if they are killed or their destruction is made necessary.

E. Definitions

"Fungus" means any type or form of fungus, including mold or mildew, and any mycotoxins, spores, scents or by-products produced or released by fungi.

CAUSES OF LOSS – BROAD FORM

A. Covered Causes Of Loss

When Broad is shown in the Declarations, Covered Causes of Loss means the following:

1. Fire.

2. Lightning.

3. Explosion, including the explosion of gases or fuel within the furnace of any fired vessel or within the flues or passages through which the gases of combustion pass. This cause of loss does not include loss or damage by:

   a. Rupture, bursting or operation of pressure-relief devices; or

   b. Rupture or bursting due to expansion or swelling of the contents of any building or structure, caused by or resulting from water.

4. Windstorm or Hail, but not including:

   a. Frost or cold weather;

   b. Ice (other than hail), snow or sleet, whether driven by wind or not; or

   c. Loss or damage to the interior of any building or structure, or the property inside the building or structure, caused by rain, snow, sand or dust, whether driven by wind or not, unless the building or structure first sustains wind or hail damage to its roof or walls through which the rain, snow, sand or dust enters.

5. Smoke causing sudden and accidental loss or damage. This cause of loss does not include smoke from agricultural smudging or industrial operations.

6. Aircraft or Vehicles, meaning only physical contact of an aircraft, a spacecraft, a self-propelled missile, a vehicle or an object thrown up by a vehicle with the described property or with the building or structure containing the described property. This cause of loss includes loss or damage by objects falling from aircraft.

We will not pay for loss or damage caused by or resulting from vehicles you own or which are operated in the course of your business.

7. Riot or Civil Commotion, including:

   a. Acts of striking employees while occupying the described premises; and

   b. Looting occurring at the time and place of a riot or civil commotion.

8. Vandalism, meaning willful and malicious damage to, or destruction of, the described property.

We will not pay for loss or damage caused by or resulting from theft, except for building damage caused by the breaking in or exiting of burglars.

9. Sprinkler Leakage, meaning leakage or discharge of any substance from an Automatic Sprinkler System, including collapse of a tank that is part of the system.

If the building or structure containing the Automatic Sprinkler System is Covered Property, we will also pay the cost to:

   a. Repair or replace damaged parts of the Automatic Sprinkler System if the damage:

     (1) Results in sprinkler leakage; or

     (2) Is directly caused by freezing.

   b. Tear out and replace any part of the building or structure to repair damage to the Automatic Sprinkler System that has resulted in sprinkler leakage.

Automatic Sprinkler System means:

   (1) Any automatic fire-protective or extinguishing system, including connected:

     (a) Sprinklers and discharge nozzles;

     (b) Ducts, pipes, valves and fittings;

     (c) Tanks, their component parts and supports; and

     (d) Pumps and private fire protection mains.

   (2) When supplied from an automatic fire-protective system:

     (a) Non-automatic fire-protective systems; and

     (b) Hydrants, standpipes and outlets.

10. Sinkhole Collapse, meaning loss or damage caused by the sudden sinking or collapse of land into underground empty spaces created by the action of water on limestone or dolomite. This cause of loss does not include:

   a. The cost of filling sinkholes; or

   b. Sinking or collapse of land into man-made underground cavities.

11. Volcanic Action, meaning direct loss or damage resulting from the eruption of a volcano when the loss or damage is caused by:

   a. Airborne volcanic blast or airborne shock waves;

   b. Ash, dust or particulate matter; or

   c. Lava flow.

All volcanic eruptions that occur within any 168-hour period will constitute a single occurrence.

This cause of loss does not include the cost to remove ash, dust or particulate matter that does not cause direct physical loss or damage to the described property.

12. Falling Objects

But we will not pay for loss or damage to:

   a. Personal property in the open; or

   b. The interior of a building or structure, or property inside a building or structure, unless the roof or an outside wall of the building or structure is first damaged by a falling object.

13. Weight Of Snow, Ice Or Sleet

But we will not pay for loss or damage to personal property outside of buildings or structures.

14. Water Damage

   a. Water Damage, meaning accidental discharge or leakage of water or steam as the direct result of the breaking apart or cracking of a plumbing, heating, air conditioning or other system or appliance, that is located on the described premises and contains water or steam.

However, Water Damage does not include:

   (1) Discharge or leakage from:

      (a) An Automatic Sprinkler System;

      (b) A sump or related equipment and parts, including overflow due to sump pump failure or excessive volume of water; or

      (c) Roof drains, gutters, downspouts or similar fixtures or equipment;

   (2) The cost to repair any defect that caused the loss or damage;

   (3) Loss or damage caused by or resulting from continuous or repeated seepage or leakage of water, or the presence or condensation of humidity, moisture or vapor, that occurs over a period of 14 days or more; or

   (4) Loss or damage caused by or resulting from freezing, unless:

      (a) You do your best to maintain heat in the building or structure; or

      (b) You drain the equipment and shut off the water supply if the heat is not maintained.

   b. If coverage applies subject to **a.** above, and the building or structure containing the system or appliance is Covered Property, we will also pay the cost to tear out and replace any part of the building or structure to repair damage to the system or appliance from which the water or steam escapes. But we will not pay the cost to repair any defect that caused the loss or damage.

B. Exclusions

   1. We will not pay for loss or damage caused directly or indirectly by any of the following. Such loss or damage is excluded regardless of any other cause or event that contributes concurrently or in any sequence to the loss.

   a. Ordinance Or Law

The enforcement of any ordinance or law:

   (1) Regulating the construction, use or repair of any property; or

   (2) Requiring the tearing down of any property including the cost of removing its debris.

This exclusion, Ordinance Or Law, applies whether the loss results from:

      (a) An ordinance or law that is enforced even if the property has not been damaged; or

      (b) The increased costs incurred to comply with an ordinance or law in the course of construction, repair, renovation, remodeling or demolition of property, or removal of its debris, following a physical loss to that property.

   b. Earth Movement

   (1) Earthquake, including any earth sinking, rising or shifting related to such event;

   (2) Landslide, including any earth sinking, rising or shifting related to such event;

   (3) Mine subsidence, meaning subsidence of a man-made mine, whether or not mining activity has ceased;

         ☐

(4) Earth sinking (other than sinkhole collapse), rising or shifting including soil conditions which cause settling, cracking or other disarrangement of foundations or other parts of realty. Soil conditions include contraction, expansion, freezing, thawing, erosion, improperly compacted soil and the action of water under the ground surface.

But if Earth Movement, as described in **b.(1)** through **(4)** above, results in fire or explosion, we will pay for the loss or damage caused by that fire or explosion.

(5) Volcanic eruption, explosion or effusion. But if volcanic eruption, explosion or effusion results in fire, building glass breakage or Volcanic Action, we will pay for the loss or damage caused by that fire, building glass breakage or Volcanic Action.

c. Governmental Action

Seizure or destruction of property by order of governmental authority.

But we will pay for loss or damage caused by or resulting from acts of destruction ordered by governmental authority and taken at the time of a fire to prevent its spread, if the fire would be covered under this Coverage Part.

d. Nuclear Hazard

Nuclear reaction or radiation, or radioactive contamination, however caused.

But if nuclear reaction or radiation, or radioactive contamination, results in fire, we will pay for the loss or damage caused by that fire.

e. Utility Services

The failure of power, communication, water or other utility service supplied to the described premises, however caused, if the failure:

(1) Originates away from the described premises; or

(2) Originates at the described premises, but only if such failure involves equipment used to supply the utility service to the described premises from a source away from the described premises.

Failure of any utility service includes lack of sufficient capacity and reduction in supply.

Loss or damage caused by a surge of power is also excluded, if the surge would not have occurred but for an event causing a failure of power.

But if the failure or surge of power, or the failure of communication, water or other utility service, results in a Covered Cause of Loss, we will pay for the loss or damage caused by that Covered Cause of Loss.

Communication services include but are not limited to service relating to Internet access or access to any electronic, cellular or satellite network.

f. War And Military Action

(1) War, including undeclared or civil war;

(2) Warlike action by a military force, including action in hindering or defending against an actual or expected attack, by any government, sovereign or other authority using military personnel or other agents; or

(3) Insurrection, rebellion, revolution, usurped power, or action taken by governmental authority in hindering or defending against any of these.

g. Water

(1) Flood, surface water, waves, tides, tidal waves, overflow of any body of water, or their spray, all whether driven by wind or not;

(2) Mudslide or mudflow;

(3) Water that backs up or overflows from a sewer, drain or sump; or

(4) Water under the ground surface pressing on, or flowing or seeping through:

(a) Foundations, walls, floors or paved surfaces;

(b) Basements, whether paved or not; or

(c) Doors, windows or other openings.

But if Water, as described in **g.(1)** through **g.(4)** above, results in fire, explosion or sprinkler leakage, we will pay for the loss or damage caused by that fire, explosion or sprinkler leakage.

h. "Fungus", Wet Rot, Dry Rot And Bacteria

Presence, growth, proliferation, spread or any activity of "fungus", wet or dry rot or bacteria.

But if "fungus", wet or dry rot or bacteria results in a Covered Cause of Loss, we will pay for the loss or damage caused by that Covered Cause of Loss.

This exclusion does not apply:

1. When "fungus", wet or dry rot or bacteria results from fire or lightning; or

2. To the extent that coverage is provided in the Additional Coverage – Limited Coverage For "Fungus", Wet Rot, Dry Rot And Bacteria with respect to loss or damage by a cause of loss other than fire or lightning.

Exclusions **B.1.a.** through **B.1.h.** apply whether or not the loss event results in widespread damage or affects a substantial area.

2. We will not pay for loss or damage caused by or resulting from:

a. Artificially generated electrical, magnetic or electromagnetic energy that damages, disturbs, disrupts or otherwise interferes with any:

   (1) Electrical or electronic wire, device, appliance, system or network; or

   (2) Device, appliance, system or network utilizing cellular or satellite technology.

   For the purpose of this exclusion, electrical, magnetic or electromagnetic energy includes but is not limited to:

   (a) Electrical current, including arcing;

   (b) Electrical charge produced or conducted by a magnetic or electromagnetic field;

   (c) Pulse of electromagnetic energy; or

   (d) Electromagnetic waves or microwaves.

   But if fire results, we will pay for the loss or damage caused by that fire.

b. Explosion of steam boilers, steam pipes, steam engines or steam turbines owned or leased by you, or operated under your control.

   But if explosion of steam boilers, steam pipes, steam engines or steam turbines results in fire or combustion explosion, we will pay for the loss or damage caused by that fire or combustion explosion.

c. Mechanical breakdown, including rupture or bursting caused by centrifugal force.

   But if mechanical breakdown results in a Covered Cause of Loss, we will pay for the loss or damage caused by that Covered Cause of Loss.

d. Neglect of an insured to use all reasonable means to save and preserve property from further damage at and after the time of loss.

3. **Special Exclusions**

The following provisions apply only to the specified Coverage Forms.

a. **Business Income (And Extra Expense) Coverage Form, Business Income (Without Extra Expense) Coverage Form, Or Extra Expense Coverage Form**

   We will not pay for:

   (1) Any loss caused by or resulting from:

      (a) Damage or destruction of "finished stock"; or

      (b) The time required to reproduce "finished stock".

      This exclusion does not apply to Extra Expense.

   (2) Any loss caused by or resulting from direct physical loss or damage to radio or television antennas (including satellite dishes) and their lead-in wiring, masts or towers.

   (3) Any increase of loss caused by or resulting from:

      (a) Delay in rebuilding, repairing or replacing the property or resuming "operations", due to interference at the location of the rebuilding, repair or replacement by strikers or other persons; or

      (b) Suspension, lapse or cancellation of any license, lease or contract. But if the suspension, lapse or cancellation is directly caused by the "suspension" of "operations", we will cover such loss that affects your Business Income during the "period of restoration" and any extension of the "period of restoration" in accordance with the terms of the Extended Business Income Additional Coverage and the Extended Period Of Indemnity Optional Coverage or any variation of these.

   (4) Any Extra Expense caused by or resulting from suspension, lapse or cancellation of any license, lease or contract beyond the "period of restoration".

   (5) Any other consequential loss.

© ISO Properties, Inc., 2007   **CP 10 20 06 07**   □

b. **Leasehold Interest Coverage Form**

(1) Paragraph **B.1.a.**, Ordinance Or Law, does not apply to insurance under this Coverage Form.

(2) We will not pay for any loss caused by:

(a) Your cancelling the lease;

(b) The suspension, lapse or cancellation of any license; or

(c) Any other consequential loss.

c. **Legal Liability Coverage Form**

(1) The following exclusions do not apply to insurance under this Coverage Form:

(a) Paragraph **B.1.a.**, Ordinance Or Law;

(b) Paragraph **B.1.c.**, Governmental Action;

(c) Paragraph **B.1.d.**, Nuclear Hazard;

(d) Paragraph **B.1.e.**, Utility Services; and

(e) Paragraph **B.1.f.**, War And Military Action.

(2) The following additional exclusions apply to insurance under this Coverage Form:

(a) **Contractual Liability**

We will not defend any claim or "suit", or pay damages that you are legally liable to pay, solely by reason of your assumption of liability in a contract or agreement. But this exclusion does not apply to a written lease agreement in which you have assumed liability for building damage resulting from an actual or attempted burglary or robbery, provided that:

(i) Your assumption of liability was executed prior to the accident; and

(ii) The building is Covered Property under this Coverage Form.

(b) **Nuclear Hazard**

We will not defend any claim or "suit", or pay any damages, loss, expense or obligation, resulting from nuclear reaction or radiation, or radioactive contamination, however caused.

C. **Additional Coverage – Collapse**

The coverage provided under this Additional Coverage – Collapse applies only to an abrupt collapse as described and limited in **C.1.** through **C.7.**

1. For the purpose of this Additional Coverage – Collapse, abrupt collapse means an abrupt falling down or caving in of a building or any part of a building with the result that the building or part of the building cannot be occupied for its intended purpose.

2. We will pay for direct physical loss or damage to Covered Property, caused by abrupt collapse of a building or any part of a building that is insured under this Coverage Form or that contains Covered Property insured under this Coverage Form, if such collapse is caused by one or more of the following:

a. Fire; lightning; explosion; windstorm or hail; smoke; aircraft or vehicles; riot or civil commotion; vandalism; leakage from fire-extinguishing equipment; sinkhole collapse; volcanic action; breakage of building glass; falling objects; weight of snow, ice or sleet; water damage, meaning accidental discharge or leakage of water or steam as the direct result of the breaking apart or cracking of a plumbing, heating, air conditioning or other system or appliance (other than a sump system including its related equipment and parts), that is located on the described premises and contains water or steam; all only as insured against in this Coverage Part;

b. Building decay that is hidden from view, unless the presence of such decay is known to an insured prior to collapse;

c. Insect or vermin damage that is hidden from view, unless the presence of such damage is known to an insured prior to collapse;

d. Weight of people or personal property;

e. Weight of rain that collects on a roof;

f. Use of defective material or methods in construction, remodeling or renovation if the abrupt collapse occurs during the course of the construction, remodeling or renovation. However, if such collapse occurs after construction, remodeling or renovation is complete and is caused in part by a cause of loss listed in **2.a.** through **2.e.**, we will pay for the loss or damage even if use of defective material or methods, in construction, remodeling or renovation, contributes to the collapse.

This Additional Coverage – Collapse does not limit the coverage otherwise provided under this Causes of Loss Form for the causes of loss listed in **2.a.**

3. This **Additional Coverage – Collapse** does **not** apply to:

   a. A building or any part of a building that is in danger of falling down or caving in;

   b. A part of a building that is standing, even if it has separated from another part of the building; or

   c. A building that is standing or any part of a building that is standing, even if it shows evidence of cracking, bulging, sagging, bending, leaning, settling, shrinkage or expansion.

4. With respect to the following property:

   a. Outdoor radio or television antennas (including satellite dishes) and their lead-in wiring, masts or towers;

   b. Awnings, gutters and downspouts;

   c. Yard fixtures;

   d. Outdoor swimming pools;

   e. Fences;

   f. Piers, wharves and docks;

   g. Beach or diving platforms or appurtenances;

   h. Retaining walls; and

   i. Walks, roadways and other paved surfaces;

   if an abrupt collapse is caused by a cause of loss listed in **2.b.** through **2.f.** we will pay for loss or damage to that property only if:

   (1) Such loss or damage is a direct result of the abrupt collapse of a building insured under this Coverage Form; and

   (2) The property is Covered Property under this Coverage Form.

5. If personal property abruptly falls down or caves in and such collapse is **not** the result of abrupt collapse of a building, we will pay for loss or damage to Covered Property caused by such collapse of personal property only if:

   a. The collapse of personal property was caused by a cause of loss listed in **2.a.** through **2.f.** above;

   b. The personal property which collapses is inside a building; and

   c. The property which collapses is not of a kind listed in **4.**, regardless of whether that kind of property is considered to be personal property or real property.

The coverage stated in this Paragraph **5.** does not apply to personal property if marring and/or scratching is the only damage to that personal property caused by the collapse.

6. This Additional Coverage – Collapse does not apply to personal property that has not abruptly fallen down or caved in, even if the personal property shows evidence of cracking, bulging, sagging, bending, leaning, settling, shrinkage or expansion.

7. This Additional Coverage – Collapse will not increase the Limits of Insurance provided in this Coverage Part.

8. The term Covered Cause of Loss includes the Additional Coverage – Collapse as described and limited in **C.1.** through **C.7.**

D. **Additional Coverage – Limited Coverage For "Fungus", Wet Rot, Dry Rot And Bacteria**

1. The coverage described in **D.2.** and **D.6.** only applies when the "fungus", wet or dry rot or bacteria is the result of one or more of the following causes that occurs during the policy period and only if all reasonable means were used to save and preserve the property from further damage at the time of and after that occurrence.

   a. A Covered Cause of Loss other than fire or lightning; or

   b. Flood, if the Flood Coverage Endorsement applies to the affected premises.

2. We will pay for loss or damage by "fungus", wet or dry rot or bacteria. As used in this Limited Coverage, the term loss or damage means:

   a. Direct physical loss or damage to Covered Property caused by "fungus", wet or dry rot or bacteria, including the cost of removal of the "fungus", wet or dry rot or bacteria;

   b. The cost to tear out and replace any part of the building or other property as needed to gain access to the "fungus", wet or dry rot or bacteria; and

   c. The cost of testing performed after removal, repair, replacement or restoration of the damaged property is completed, provided there is a reason to believe that "fungus", wet or dry rot or bacteria are present.

3. The coverage described under **D.2.** of this Limited Coverage is limited to $15,000. Regardless of the number of claims, this limit is the most we will pay for the total of all loss or damage arising out of all occurrences of Covered Causes of Loss (other than fire or lightning) and Flood which take place in a 12-month period (starting with the beginning of the present annual policy period). With respect to a particular occurrence of loss which results in "fungus", wet or dry rot or bacteria, we will not pay more than a total of $15,000 even if the "fungus", wet or dry rot or bacteria continues to be present or active, or recurs, in a later policy period.

4. The coverage provided under this Limited Coverage does not increase the applicable Limit of Insurance on any Covered Property. If a particular occurrence results in loss or damage by "fungus", wet or dry rot or bacteria, and other loss or damage, we will not pay more, for the total of all loss or damage, than the applicable Limit of Insurance on the affected Covered Property.

   If there is covered loss or damage to Covered Property, not caused by "fungus", wet or dry rot or bacteria, loss payment will not be limited by the terms of this Limited Coverage, except to the extent that "fungus", wet or dry rot or bacteria causes an increase in the loss. Any such increase in the loss will be subject to the terms of this Limited Coverage.

5. The terms of this Limited Coverage do not increase or reduce the coverage provided under Paragraph **b.** of Covered Cause Of Loss **9.**, Sprinkler Leakage, or Paragraph **b.** of Covered Causes Of Loss **14.**, Water Damage, or under the Additional Coverage – Collapse.

6. The following, **6.a.** or **6.b.**, applies only if Business Income and/or Extra Expense Coverage applies to the described premises and only if the "suspension" of "operations" satisfies all terms and conditions of the applicable Business Income and/or Extra Expense Coverage Form.

   a. If the loss which resulted in "fungus", wet or dry rot or bacteria does not in itself necessitate a "suspension" of "operations", but such "suspension" is necessary due to loss or damage to property caused by "fungus", wet or dry rot or bacteria, then our payment under Business Income and/or Extra Expense is limited to the amount of loss and/or expense sustained in a period of not more than 30 days. The days need not be consecutive.

   b. If a covered "suspension" of "operations" was caused by loss or damage other than "fungus", wet or dry rot or bacteria but remediation of "fungus", wet or dry rot or bacteria prolongs the "period of restoration", we will pay for loss and/or expense sustained during the delay (regardless of when such a delay occurs during the "period of restoration"), but such coverage is limited to 30 days. The days need not be consecutive.

E. Limitation

We will pay for loss of animals only if they are killed or their destruction is made necessary.

F. Definitions

"Fungus" means any type or form of fungus, including mold or mildew, and any mycotoxins, spores, scents or by-products produced or released by fungi.

COMMERCIAL PROPERTY
CP 10 30 06 07

CAUSES OF LOSS – SPECIAL FORM

Words and phrases that appear in quotation marks have special meaning. Refer to Section **G.**, Definitions.

A. Covered Causes Of Loss

When Special is shown in the Declarations, Covered Causes of Loss means Risks Of Direct Physical Loss unless the loss is:

1. Excluded in Section **B.**, Exclusions; or

2. Limited in Section **C.**, Limitations;

that follow.

B. Exclusions

1. We will not pay for loss or damage caused directly or indirectly by any of the following. Such loss or damage is excluded regardless of any other cause or event that contributes concurrently or in any sequence to the loss.

   a. Ordinance Or Law

   The enforcement of any ordinance or law:

   (1) Regulating the construction, use or repair of any property; or

   (2) Requiring the tearing down of any property, including the cost of removing its debris.

   This exclusion, Ordinance Or Law, applies whether the loss results from:

   (a) An ordinance or law that is enforced even if the property has not been damaged; or

   (b) The increased costs incurred to comply with an ordinance or law in the course of construction, repair, renovation, remodeling or demolition of property, or removal of its debris, following a physical loss to that property.

   b. Earth Movement

   (1) Earthquake, including any earth sinking, rising or shifting related to such event;

   (2) Landslide, including any earth sinking, rising or shifting related to such event;

   (3) Mine subsidence, meaning subsidence of a man-made mine, whether or not mining activity has ceased;

   (4) Earth sinking (other than sinkhole collapse), rising or shifting including soil conditions which cause settling, cracking or other disarrangement of foundations or other parts of realty. Soil conditions include contraction, expansion, freezing, thawing, erosion, improperly compacted soil and the action of water under the ground surface.

   But if Earth Movement, as described in **b.(1)** through **(4)** above, results in fire or explosion, we will pay for the loss or damage caused by that fire or explosion.

   (5) Volcanic eruption, explosion or effusion. But if volcanic eruption, explosion or effusion results in fire, building glass breakage or Volcanic Action, we will pay for the loss or damage caused by that fire, building glass breakage or Volcanic Action.

   Volcanic Action means direct loss or damage resulting from the eruption of a volcano when the loss or damage is caused by:

   (a) Airborne volcanic blast or airborne shock waves;

   (b) Ash, dust or particulate matter; or

   (c) Lava flow.

   All volcanic eruptions that occur within any 168-hour period will constitute a single occurrence.

   Volcanic Action does not include the cost to remove ash, dust or particulate matter that does not cause direct physical loss or damage to the described property.

   c. Governmental Action

   Seizure or destruction of property by order of governmental authority.

   But we will pay for loss or damage caused by or resulting from acts of destruction ordered by governmental authority and taken at the time of a fire to prevent its spread, if the fire would be covered under this Coverage Part.

© ISO Properties, Inc., 2007

d. Nuclear Hazard

Nuclear reaction or radiation, or radioactive contamination, however caused.

But if nuclear reaction or radiation, or radioactive contamination, results in fire, we will pay for the loss or damage caused by that fire.

e. Utility Services

The failure of power, communication, water or other utility service supplied to the described premises, however caused, if the failure:

(1) Originates away from the described premises; or

(2) Originates at the described premises, but only if such failure involves equipment used to supply the utility service to the described premises from a source away from the described premises.

Failure of any utility service includes lack of sufficient capacity and reduction in supply.

Loss or damage caused by a surge of power is also excluded, if the surge would not have occurred but for an event causing a failure of power.

But if the failure or surge of power, or the failure of communication, water or other utility service, results in a Covered Cause of Loss, we will pay for the loss or damage caused by that Covered Cause of Loss.

Communication services include but are not limited to service relating to Internet access or access to any electronic, cellular or satellite network.

f. War And Military Action

(1) War, including undeclared or civil war;

(2) Warlike action by a military force, including action in hindering or defending against an actual or expected attack, by any government, sovereign or other authority using military personnel or other agents; or

(3) Insurrection, rebellion, revolution, usurped power, or action taken by governmental authority in hindering or defending against any of these.

g. Water

(1) Flood, surface water, waves, tides, tidal waves, overflow of any body of water, or their spray, all whether driven by wind or not;

(2) Mudslide or mudflow;

(3) Water that backs up or overflows from a sewer, drain or sump; or

(4) Water under the ground surface pressing on, or flowing or seeping through:

(a) Foundations, walls, floors or paved surfaces;

(b) Basements, whether paved or not; or

(c) Doors, windows or other openings.

But if Water, as described in **g.(1)** through **g.(4)** above, results in fire, explosion or sprinkler leakage, we will pay for the loss or damage caused by that fire, explosion or sprinkler leakage.

h. "Fungus", Wet Rot, Dry Rot And Bacteria

Presence, growth, proliferation, spread or any activity of "fungus", wet or dry rot or bacteria.

But if "fungus", wet or dry rot or bacteria results in a "specified cause of loss", we will pay for the loss or damage caused by that "specified cause of loss".

This exclusion does not apply:

1. When "fungus", wet or dry rot or bacteria results from fire or lightning; or

2. To the extent that coverage is provided in the Additional Coverage – Limited Coverage For "Fungus", Wet Rot, Dry Rot And Bacteria with respect to loss or damage by a cause of loss other than fire or lightning.

Exclusions **B.1.a.** through **B.1.h.** apply whether or not the loss event results in widespread damage or affects a substantial area.

2. We will not pay for loss or damage caused by or resulting from any of the following:

a. Artificially generated electrical, magnetic or electromagnetic energy that damages, disturbs, disrupts or otherwise interferes with any:

(1) Electrical or electronic wire, device, appliance, system or network; or

(2) Device, appliance, system or network utilizing cellular or satellite technology.

         CP 10 30 06 07   □

For the purpose of this exclusion, electrical, magnetic or electromagnetic energy includes but is not limited to:

   (a) Electrical current, including arcing;

   (b) Electrical charge produced or conducted by a magnetic or electromagnetic field;

   (c) Pulse of electromagnetic energy; or

   (d) Electromagnetic waves or microwaves.

But if fire results, we will pay for the loss or damage caused by that fire.

b. Delay, loss of use or loss of market.

c. Smoke, vapor or gas from agricultural smudging or industrial operations.

d. (1) Wear and tear;

   (2) Rust or other corrosion, decay, deterioration, hidden or latent defect or any quality in property that causes it to damage or destroy itself;

   (3) Smog;

   (4) Settling, cracking, shrinking or expansion;

   (5) Nesting or infestation, or discharge or release of waste products or secretions, by insects, birds, rodents or other animals.

   (6) Mechanical breakdown, including rupture or bursting caused by centrifugal force. But if mechanical breakdown results in elevator collision, we will pay for the loss or damage caused by that elevator collision.

   (7) The following causes of loss to personal property:

      (a) Dampness or dryness of atmosphere;

      (b) Changes in or extremes of temperature; or

      (c) Marring or scratching.

But if an excluded cause of loss that is listed in **2.d.(1)** through **(7)** results in a "specified cause of loss" or building glass breakage, we will pay for the loss or damage caused by that "specified cause of loss" or building glass breakage.

e. Explosion of steam boilers, steam pipes, steam engines or steam turbines owned or leased by you, or operated under your control. But if explosion of steam boilers, steam pipes, steam engines or steam turbines results in fire or combustion explosion, we will pay for the loss or damage caused by that fire or combustion explosion. We will also pay for loss or damage caused by or resulting from the explosion of gases or fuel within the furnace of any fired vessel or within the flues or passages through which the gases of combustion pass.

f. Continuous or repeated seepage or leakage of water, or the presence or condensation of humidity, moisture or vapor, that occurs over a period of 14 days or more.

g. Water, other liquids, powder or molten material that leaks or flows from plumbing, heating, air conditioning or other equipment (except fire protective systems) caused by or resulting from freezing, unless:

   (1) You do your best to maintain heat in the building or structure; or

   (2) You drain the equipment and shut off the supply if the heat is not maintained.

h. Dishonest or criminal act by you, any of your partners, members, officers, managers, employees (including leased employees), directors, trustees, authorized representatives or anyone to whom you entrust the property for any purpose:

   (1) Acting alone or in collusion with others; or

   (2) Whether or not occurring during the hours of employment.

This exclusion does not apply to acts of destruction by your employees (including leased employees); but theft by employees (including leased employees) is not covered.

i. Voluntary parting with any property by you or anyone else to whom you have entrusted the property if induced to do so by any fraudulent scheme, trick, device or false pretense.

j. Rain, snow, ice or sleet to personal property in the open.

k. Collapse, including any of the following conditions of property or any part of the property:

(1) An abrupt falling down or caving in;

(2) Loss of structural integrity, including separation of parts of the property or property in danger of falling down or caving in; or

(3) Any cracking, bulging, sagging, bending, leaning, settling, shrinkage or expansion as such condition relates to **(1)** or **(2)** above.

But if collapse results in a Covered Cause of Loss at the described premises, we will pay for the loss or damage caused by that Covered Cause of Loss.

This exclusion, **k.**, does not apply:

(a) To the extent that coverage is provided under the Additional Coverage – Collapse; or

(b) To collapse caused by one or more of the following:

(i) The "specified causes of loss";

(ii) Breakage of building glass;

(iii) Weight of rain that collects on a roof; or

(iv) Weight of people or personal property.

l. Discharge, dispersal, seepage, migration, release or escape of "pollutants" unless the discharge, dispersal, seepage, migration, release or escape is itself caused by any of the "specified causes of loss". But if the discharge, dispersal, seepage, migration, release or escape of "pollutants" results in a "specified cause of loss", we will pay for the loss or damage caused by that "specified cause of loss".

This exclusion, **l.**, does not apply to damage to glass caused by chemicals applied to the glass.

m. Neglect of an insured to use all reasonable means to save and preserve property from further damage at and after the time of loss.

3. We will not pay for loss or damage caused by or resulting from any of the following, **3.a.** through **3.c.** But if an excluded cause of loss that is listed in **3.a.** through **3.c.** results in a Covered Cause of Loss, we will pay for the loss or damage caused by that Covered Cause of Loss.

a. Weather conditions. But this exclusion only applies if weather conditions contribute in any way with a cause or event excluded in Paragraph **1.** above to produce the loss or damage.

b. Acts or decisions, including the failure to act or decide, of any person, group, organization or governmental body.

c. Faulty, inadequate or defective:

(1) Planning, zoning, development, surveying, siting;

(2) Design, specifications, workmanship, repair, construction, renovation, remodeling, grading, compaction;

(3) Materials used in repair, construction, renovation or remodeling; or

(4) Maintenance;

of part or all of any property on or off the described premises.

4. Special Exclusions

The following provisions apply only to the specified Coverage Forms.

a. Business Income (And Extra Expense) Coverage Form, Business Income (Without Extra Expense) Coverage Form, Or Extra Expense Coverage Form

We will not pay for:

(1) Any loss caused by or resulting from:

(a) Damage or destruction of "finished stock"; or

(b) The time required to reproduce "finished stock".

This exclusion does not apply to Extra Expense.

(2) Any loss caused by or resulting from direct physical loss or damage to radio or television antennas (including satellite dishes) and their lead-in wiring, masts or towers.

(3) Any increase of loss caused by or resulting from:

(a) Delay in rebuilding, repairing or replacing the property or resuming "operations", due to interference at the location of the rebuilding, repair or replacement by strikers or other persons; or

(b) Suspension, lapse or cancellation of any license, lease or contract. But if the suspension, lapse or cancellation is directly caused by the "suspension" of "operations", we will cover such loss that affects your Business Income during the "period of restoration" and any extension of the "period of restoration" in accordance with the terms of the Extended Business Income Additional Coverage and the Extended Period Of Indemnity Optional Coverage or any variation of these.

(4) Any Extra Expense caused by or resulting from suspension, lapse or cancellation of any license, lease or contract beyond the "period of restoration".

(5) Any other consequential loss.

b. Leasehold Interest Coverage Form

(1) Paragraph **B.1.a.**, Ordinance Or Law, does not apply to insurance under this Coverage Form.

(2) We will not pay for any loss caused by:

(a) Your cancelling the lease;

(b) The suspension, lapse or cancellation of any license; or

(c) Any other consequential loss.

c. Legal Liability Coverage Form

(1) The following exclusions do not apply to insurance under this Coverage Form:

(a) Paragraph **B.1.a.**, Ordinance Or Law;

(b) Paragraph **B.1.c.**, Governmental Action;

(c) Paragraph **B.1.d.**, Nuclear Hazard;

(d) Paragraph **B.1.e.**, Utility Services; and

(e) Paragraph **B.1.f.**, War And Military Action.

(2) The following additional exclusions apply to insurance under this Coverage Form:

(a) Contractual Liability

We will not defend any claim or "suit", or pay damages that you are legally liable to pay, solely by reason of your assumption of liability in a contract or agreement. But this exclusion does not apply to a written lease agreement in which you have assumed liability for building damage resulting from an actual or attempted burglary or robbery, provided that:

(i) Your assumption of liability was executed prior to the accident; and

(ii) The building is Covered Property under this Coverage Form.

(b) Nuclear Hazard

We will not defend any claim or "suit", or pay any damages, loss, expense or obligation, resulting from nuclear reaction or radiation, or radioactive contamination, however caused.

5. Additional Exclusion

The following provisions apply only to the specified property.

LOSS OR DAMAGE TO PRODUCTS

We will not pay for loss or damage to any merchandise, goods or other product caused by or resulting from error or omission by any person or entity (including those having possession under an arrangement where work or a portion of the work is outsourced) in any stage of the development, production or use of the product, including planning, testing, processing, packaging, installation, maintenance or repair. This exclusion applies to any effect that compromises the form, substance or quality of the product. But if such error or omission results in a Covered Cause of Loss, we will pay for the loss or damage caused by that Covered Cause of Loss.

C. Limitations

The following limitations apply to all policy forms and endorsements, unless otherwise stated.

1. We will not pay for loss of or damage to property, as described and limited in this section. In addition, we will not pay for any loss that is a consequence of loss or damage as described and limited in this section.

    a. Steam boilers, steam pipes, steam engines or steam turbines caused by or resulting from any condition or event inside such equipment. But we will pay for loss of or damage to such equipment caused by or resulting from an explosion of gases or fuel within the furnace of any fired vessel or within the flues or passages through which the gases of combustion pass.

    b. Hot water boilers or other water heating equipment caused by or resulting from any condition or event inside such boilers or equipment, other than an explosion.

    c. The interior of any building or structure, or to personal property in the building or structure, caused by or resulting from rain, snow, sleet, ice, sand or dust, whether driven by wind or not, unless:

    (1) The building or structure first sustains damage by a Covered Cause of Loss to its roof or walls through which the rain, snow, sleet, ice, sand or dust enters; or

    (2) The loss or damage is caused by or results from thawing of snow, sleet or ice on the building or structure.

    d. Building materials and supplies not attached as part of the building or structure, caused by or resulting from theft.

    However, this limitation does not apply to:

    (1) Building materials and supplies held for sale by you, unless they are insured under the Builders Risk Coverage Form; or

    (2) Business Income Coverage or Extra Expense Coverage.

    e. Property that is missing, where the only evidence of the loss or damage is a shortage disclosed on taking inventory, or other instances where there is no physical evidence to show what happened to the property.

    f. Property that has been transferred to a person or to a place outside the described premises on the basis of unauthorized instructions.

2. We will not pay for loss of or damage to the following types of property unless caused by the "specified causes of loss" or building glass breakage:

    a. Animals, and then only if they are killed or their destruction is made necessary.

    b. Fragile articles such as statuary, marbles, chinaware and porcelains, if broken. This restriction does not apply to:

    (1) Glass; or

    (2) Containers of property held for sale.

    c. Builders' machinery, tools and equipment owned by you or entrusted to you, provided such property is Covered Property.

    However, this limitation does not apply:

    (1) If the property is located on or within 100 feet of the described premises, unless the premises is insured under the Builders Risk Coverage Form; or

    (2) To Business Income Coverage or to Extra Expense Coverage.

3. The special limit shown for each category, **a.** through **d.**, is the total limit for loss of or damage to all property in that category. The special limit applies to any one occurrence of theft, regardless of the types or number of articles that are lost or damaged in that occurrence. The special limits are:

    a. $2,500 for furs, fur garments and garments trimmed with fur.

    b. $2,500 for jewelry, watches, watch movements, jewels, pearls, precious and semiprecious stones, bullion, gold, silver, platinum and other precious alloys or metals. This limit does not apply to jewelry and watches worth $100 or less per item.

    c. $2,500 for patterns, dies, molds and forms.

    d. $250 for stamps, tickets, including lottery tickets held for sale, and letters of credit.

These special limits are part of, not in addition to, the Limit of Insurance applicable to the Covered Property.

This limitation, **C.3.,** does not apply to Business Income Coverage or to Extra Expense Coverage.

         CP 10 30 06 07   □

4. We will not pay the cost to repair any defect to a system or appliance from which water, other liquid, powder or molten material escapes. But we will pay the cost to repair or replace damaged parts of fire-extinguishing equipment if the damage:

    a. Results in discharge of any substance from an automatic fire protection system; or

    b. Is directly caused by freezing.

However, this limitation does not apply to Business Income Coverage or to Extra Expense Coverage.

D. Additional Coverage – Collapse

The coverage provided under this Additional Coverage – Collapse applies only to an abrupt collapse as described and limited in **D.1.** through **D.7.**

1. For the purpose of this Additional Coverage – Collapse, abrupt collapse means an abrupt falling down or caving in of a building or any part of a building with the result that the building or part of the building cannot be occupied for its intended purpose.

2. We will pay for direct physical loss or damage to Covered Property, caused by abrupt collapse of a building or any part of a building that is insured under this Coverage Form or that contains Covered Property insured under this Coverage Form, if such collapse is caused by one or more of the following:

    a. Building decay that is hidden from view, unless the presence of such decay is known to an insured prior to collapse;

    b. Insect or vermin damage that is hidden from view, unless the presence of such damage is known to an insured prior to collapse;

    c. Use of defective material or methods in construction, remodeling or renovation if the abrupt collapse occurs during the course of the construction, remodeling or renovation.

    d. Use of defective material or methods in construction, remodeling or renovation if the abrupt collapse occurs after the construction, remodeling or renovation is complete, but only if the collapse is caused in part by:

        (1) A cause of loss listed in **2.a.** or **2.b.**;

        (2) One or more of the "specified causes of loss";

        (3) Breakage of building glass;

        (4) Weight of people or personal property; or

        (5) Weight of rain that collects on a roof.

3. This **Additional Coverage – Collapse** does **not** apply to:

    a. A building or any part of a building that is in danger of falling down or caving in;

    b. A part of a building that is standing, even if it has separated from another part of the building; or

    c. A building that is standing or any part of a building that is standing, even if it shows evidence of cracking, bulging, sagging, bending, leaning, settling, shrinkage or expansion.

4. With respect to the following property:

    a. Outdoor radio or television antennas (including satellite dishes) and their lead-in wiring, masts or towers;

    b. Awnings, gutters and downspouts;

    c. Yard fixtures;

    d. Outdoor swimming pools;

    e. Fences;

    f. Piers, wharves and docks;

    g. Beach or diving platforms or appurtenances;

    h. Retaining walls; and

    i. Walks, roadways and other paved surfaces;

if an abrupt collapse is caused by a cause of loss listed in **2.a.** through **2.d.**, we will pay for loss or damage to that property only if:

    (1) Such loss or damage is a direct result of the abrupt collapse of a building insured under this Coverage Form; and

    (2) The property is Covered Property under this Coverage Form.

5. If personal property abruptly falls down or caves in and such collapse is **not** the result of abrupt collapse of a building, we will pay for loss or damage to Covered Property caused by such collapse of personal property only if:

    a. The collapse of personal property was caused by a cause of loss listed in **2.a.** through **2.d.**;

    b. The personal property which collapses is inside a building; and

    c. The property which collapses is not of a kind listed in **4.**, regardless of whether that kind of property is considered to be personal property or real property.

The coverage stated in this Paragraph **5.** does not apply to personal property if marring and/or scratching is the only damage to that personal property caused by the collapse.

6. This Additional Coverage – Collapse does not apply to personal property that has not abruptly fallen down or caved in, even if the personal property shows evidence of cracking, bulging, sagging, bending, leaning, settling, shrinkage or expansion.

7. This Additional Coverage – Collapse will not increase the Limits of Insurance provided in this Coverage Part.

8. The term Covered Cause of Loss includes the Additional Coverage – Collapse as described and limited in **D.1.** through **D.7.**

. **Additional Coverage – Limited Coverage For "Fungus", Wet Rot, Dry Rot And Bacteria**

1. The coverage described in **E.2.** and **E.6.** only applies when the "fungus", wet or dry rot or bacteria is the result of one or more of the following causes that occurs during the policy period and only if all reasonable means were used to save and preserve the property from further damage at the time of and after that occurrence.

   a. A "specified cause of loss" other than fire or lightning; or

   b. Flood, if the Flood Coverage Endorsement applies to the affected premises.

2. We will pay for loss or damage by "fungus", wet or dry rot or bacteria. As used in this Limited Coverage, the term loss or damage means:

   a. Direct physical loss or damage to Covered Property caused by "fungus", wet or dry rot or bacteria, including the cost of removal of the "fungus", wet or dry rot or bacteria;

   b. The cost to tear out and replace any part of the building or other property as needed to gain access to the "fungus", wet or dry rot or bacteria; and

   c. The cost of testing performed after removal, repair, replacement or restoration of the damaged property is completed, provided there is a reason to believe that "fungus", wet or dry rot or bacteria are present.

3. The coverage described under **E.2.** of this Limited Coverage is limited to $15,000. Regardless of the number of claims, this limit is the most we will pay for the total of all loss or damage arising out of all occurrences of "specified causes of loss" (other than fire or lightning) and Flood which take place in a 12-month period (starting with the beginning of the present annual policy period). With respect to a particular occurrence of loss which results in "fungus", wet or dry rot or bacteria, we will not pay more than a total of $15,000 even if the "fungus", wet or dry rot or bacteria continues to be present or active, or recurs, in a later policy period.

4. The coverage provided under this Limited Coverage does not increase the applicable Limit of Insurance on any Covered Property. If a particular occurrence results in loss or damage by "fungus", wet or dry rot or bacteria, and other loss or damage, we will not pay more, for the total of all loss or damage, than the applicable Limit of Insurance on the affected Covered Property.

   If there is covered loss or damage to Covered Property, not caused by "fungus", wet or dry rot or bacteria, loss payment will not be limited by the terms of this Limited Coverage, except to the extent that "fungus", wet or dry rot or bacteria causes an increase in the loss. Any such increase in the loss will be subject to the terms of this Limited Coverage.

5. The terms of this Limited Coverage do not increase or reduce the coverage provided under Paragraph **F.2.** (Water Damage, Other Liquids, Powder Or Molten Material Damage) of this Causes Of Loss Form or under the Additional Coverage – Collapse.

6. The following, **6.a.** or **6.b.**, applies only if Business Income and/or Extra Expense Coverage applies to the described premises and only if the "suspension" of "operations" satisfies all terms and conditions of the applicable Business Income and/or Extra Expense Coverage Form.

a. If the loss which resulted in "fungus", wet or dry rot or bacteria does not in itself necessitate a "suspension" of "operations", but such "suspension" is necessary due to loss or damage to property caused by "fungus", wet or dry rot or bacteria, then our payment under Business Income and/or Extra Expense is limited to the amount of loss and/or expense sustained in a period of not more than 30 days. The days need not be consecutive.

b. If a covered "suspension" of "operations" was caused by loss or damage other than "fungus", wet or dry rot or bacteria but remediation of "fungus", wet or dry rot or bacteria prolongs the "period of restoration", we will pay for loss and/or expense sustained during the delay (regardless of when such a delay occurs during the "period of restoration"), but such coverage is limited to 30 days. The days need not be consecutive.

F. Additional Coverage Extensions

1. Property In Transit

This Extension applies only to your personal property to which this form applies.

a. You may extend the insurance provided by this Coverage Part to apply to your personal property (other than property in the care, custody or control of your salespersons) in transit more than 100 feet from the described premises. Property must be in or on a motor vehicle you own, lease or operate while between points in the coverage territory.

b. Loss or damage must be caused by or result from one of the following causes of loss:

(1) Fire, lightning, explosion, windstorm or hail, riot or civil commotion, or vandalism.

(2) Vehicle collision, upset or overturn. Collision means accidental contact of your vehicle with another vehicle or object. It does not mean your vehicle's contact with the roadbed.

(3) Theft of an entire bale, case or package by forced entry into a securely locked body or compartment of the vehicle. There must be visible marks of the forced entry.

c. The most we will pay for loss or damage under this Extension is $5,000.

This Coverage Extension is additional insurance. The Additional Condition, Coinsurance, does not apply to this Extension.

2. Water Damage, Other Liquids, Powder Or Molten Material Damage

If loss or damage caused by or resulting from covered water or other liquid, powder or molten material damage loss occurs, we will also pay the cost to tear out and replace any part of the building or structure to repair damage to the system or appliance from which the water or other substance escapes. This Coverage Extension does not increase the Limit of Insurance.

3. Glass

a. We will pay for expenses incurred to put up temporary plates or board up openings if repair or replacement of damaged glass is delayed.

b. We will pay for expenses incurred to remove or replace obstructions when repairing or replacing glass that is part of a building. This does not include removing or replacing window displays.

This Coverage Extension, **F.3.**, does not increase the Limit of Insurance.

G. Definitions

1. "Fungus" means any type or form of fungus, including mold or mildew, and any mycotoxins, spores, scents or by-products produced or released by fungi.

2. "Specified causes of loss" means the following: fire; lightning; explosion; windstorm or hail; smoke; aircraft or vehicles; riot or civil commotion; vandalism; leakage from fire-extinguishing equipment; sinkhole collapse; volcanic action; falling objects; weight of snow, ice or sleet; water damage.

a. Sinkhole collapse means the sudden sinking or collapse of land into underground empty spaces created by the action of water on limestone or dolomite. This cause of loss does not include:

(1) The cost of filling sinkholes; or

(2) Sinking or collapse of land into man-made underground cavities.

b. Falling objects does not include loss or damage to:

   (1) Personal property in the open; or

   (2) The interior of a building or structure, or property inside a building or structure, unless the roof or an outside wall of the building or structure is first damaged by a falling object.

c. Water damage means accidental discharge or leakage of water or steam as the direct result of the breaking apart or cracking of a plumbing, heating, air conditioning or other system or appliance (other than a sump system including its related equipment and parts), that is located on the described premises and contains water or steam.

© ISO Properties, Inc., 2007   **CP 10 30 06 07**   ☐

COMMON POLICY CONDITIONS

All Coverage Parts included in this policy are subject to the following conditions.

A. Cancellation

1. The first Named Insured shown in the Declarations may cancel this policy by mailing or delivering to us advance written notice of cancellation.

2. We may cancel this policy by mailing or delivering to the first Named Insured written notice of cancellation at least:

   a. 10 days before the effective date of cancellation if we cancel for nonpayment of premium; or

   b. 30 days before the effective date of cancellation if we cancel for any other reason.

3. We will mail or deliver our notice to the first Named Insured's last mailing address known to us.

4. Notice of cancellation will state the effective date of cancellation. The policy period will end on that date.

5. If this policy is cancelled, we will send the first Named Insured any premium refund due. If we cancel, the refund will be pro rata. If the first Named Insured cancels, the refund may be less than pro rata. The cancellation will be effective even if we have not made or offered a refund.

6. If notice is mailed, proof of mailing will be sufficient proof of notice.

B. Changes

This policy contains all the agreements between you and us concerning the insurance afforded. The first Named Insured shown in the Declarations is authorized to make changes in the terms of this policy with our consent. This policy's terms can be amended or waived only by endorsement issued by us and made a part of this policy.

C. Examination Of Your Books And Records

We may examine and audit your books and records as they relate to this policy at any time during the policy period and up to three years afterward.

D. Inspections And Surveys

1. We have the right to:

   a. Make inspections and surveys at any time;

   b. Give you reports on the conditions we find; and

   c. Recommend changes.

2. We are not obligated to make any inspections, surveys, reports or recommendations and any such actions we do undertake relate only to insurability and the premiums to be charged. We do not make safety inspections. We do not undertake to perform the duty of any person or organization to provide for the health or safety of workers or the public. And we do not warrant that conditions:

   a. Are safe or healthful; or

   b. Comply with laws, regulations, codes or standards.

3. Paragraphs 1. and 2. of this condition apply not only to us, but also to any rating, advisory, rate service or similar organization which makes insurance inspections, surveys, reports or recommendations.

4. Paragraph 2. of this condition does not apply to any inspections, surveys, reports or recommendations we may make relative to certification, under state or municipal statutes, ordinances or regulations, of boilers, pressure vessels or elevators.

E. Premiums

The first Named Insured shown in the Declarations:

1. Is responsible for the payment of all premiums; and

2. Will be the payee for any return premiums we pay.

F. Transfer Of Your Rights And Duties Under This Policy

Your rights and duties under this policy may not be transferred without our written consent except in the case of death of an individual named insured.

If you die, your rights and duties will be transferred to your legal representative but only while acting within the scope of duties as your legal representative. Until your legal representative is appointed, anyone having proper temporary custody of your property will have your rights and duties but only with respect to that property.

Index

AAIS

    additional coverages 263, 266
    additional property excluded and limitations 276
    building and personal property coverage part 264
    covered property 264
    endorsements 278
    how much we pay 271
    loss payment 272
    other conditions 273
    other coverage parts 277
    property excluded and limitations 265
    special causes of loss form 274
    supplemental coverages 267
    valuation 270
    what must be done in case of a loss 269
Abandonment 117
Absence of Profits 179
Abrupt collapse 196
Accounting Documentation—Who Pays? 155
Acts or decisions exclusion 98
Actual cash value 122
    broad evidence rule 122
    fair market value 122
    personal property 123
    raw materials 123
    replacement cost less depreciation 122
Additional conditions 127
    coinsurance 127
    mortgageholders 127, 198
Additional conditions, builders risk 138
    collapse and removal of one cause 138
    mortgageholders 138
    need for adequate insurance 138
    when coverage ceases 139
Additional coverages 81, 157
    debris removal 35
    electronic data 35
    fire department service charge 35
    increased cost of construction 35
    pollutant cleanup and removal 35
    preservation of property 35
Additional coverage extensions, special form 104
    business personal property in transit 104
    cost to tear out system 105
    glass, temporary plates 105
Agreed value 50, 170
    building or contents 51

    coinsurance not applicable 51
    eligible property 51
    predetermined amount.. 51
    statement of values.. 51
Aircraft or vehicles 63
    physical contact with.. 63
    falling objects 63
    objects thrown up by a vehicle... 63
Airports Closed by Order of Civil Authority 159
American Association of Insurance Services (AAIS)................... 263
    building and personal property coverage part...................... 264
    commercial properties program 263
    eligibility 263
Animals...26, 102, 265, 275, 276
Application of Blanket Condo Policy with Wind Deductible.................... 302
Application of Negligent Work Exclusion.................................... 164
Application of the mechanical breakdown exclusion..................... 81
Appraisal.. 117
    method to settle differences 117
Appraisal Clause and Disinterested Appraisers 118
Appraisal of a loss 118
Artificially generated electrical, magnetic, or electromagnetic
    exclusion in named perils forms 80
    exclusion in special perils form 87
Basic causes of loss form 58
    aircraft or vehicles...58, 63
    explosion 58
    explosion, definition... 58
    explosions excluded 59
    fire 58
    friendly fire doctrine 58
    hostile fire.. 58
    lightning... 58
    riot or civil commotion 65
    sinkhole collapse 68
    smoke.. 62
    sprinkler leakage 67
    vandalism.. 66
    volcanic action... 69
    windstorm or hail 59
Beverly Hills Supper Club.. 109
Blanket coverage.. 149
Broad form causes of loss.. 69
    additional 3 perils.. 69
    additional coverage of collapse... 69
    falling objects 69
    water damage.. 71
    weight of ice, snow, or sleet.. 69
Builders' Machinery, Tools, and Equipment 103
Builders Risk.. 131
    additional conditions 138

additional coverages..136
blanket coverage option 132
building renovations...140
completed value...140
coverage extensions..136
coverage options..140
covered causes of loss 144
covered property..136
deductible 145
limits of insurance 145
loss conditions...145
property not covered 143
reporting form 140
Building coverage 10
additions and alterations...14
completed additions..12
fixtures...12
permanently installed machinery and equipment..................13
personal property used to maintain building..........................13
Building materials and supplies of others 142
application of extension 142
basic amount, $5,000..142
Business Income—Bomb Threat?...152
Business income coverage form..145
Business personal property 16
furniture and fixtures...16
labor or services of others 18
leased personal property..25
machinery and equipment 17
property used in the insured's business 18
stock...17
tenant's use interest in improvements and betterments 19
Cancellation 107, 187
Carpeting in condominiums...207
Catastrophic weather loss claims issues 296
Chinese drywall 303
Civil authority...157, 176
Coinsurance...127
and the deductible 128
principle...127
Coinsurance application in a total loss 128
Collapse...82, 96
"abrupt falling down"..82
covered causes of collapse 82
hidden decay, new provision...82
hidden insect damage, new provision 82
personal property...83
serious impairment to building 82
significant change in 2000 form..82
special form exclusion...96
what is not collapse 82

Commercial condominium unit-owners form 211
    additional coverages and coverage extension 211
    property 210
    limits and deductible 211
    loss conditions 211
    other provisions 211
Commercial property conditions 107
    concealment, misrepresentation, or fraud 110
    control of property 111
    insurance under two or more coverages 112
    legal action against the insurer 112
    liberalization 112
    no benefit to bailee 112
    other insurance 113
    policy period, coverage territory 113
    subrogation 113
Commercial property endorsements 221
    additional building property 221
    additional covered property 221
    additional exclusions 221
    additional insured and loss payee 222
    additional locations special coinsurance provision 222
    additional property not covered 223
    agricultural products storage 225
    alcoholic beverage tax exclusion 226
    blanket insurance – margin clause option 226
    brands and labels 227
    broken or cracked glass 227
    building glass under tenant's policy 227
    business income changes – beginning of the period of restoration 228
    business income – discretionary payroll expense 228
    business income – landlord as additional insured 229
    business income – ordinary payroll limitation or exclusion 229
    burglary and robbery protective safeguards 229
    cap on losses from certified acts of terrorism 230
    changes – electronic data 231
    changes – fungus, wet rot, dry rot and bacteria 232
    civil authority change(s) 232
    condominium commercial unit owners optional coverages 232
    contributing insurance 233
    debris removal additional insurance 233
    deductible limitation 233
    dependent properties 233
    disclosure pursuant to terrorism risk insurance act 234
    distilled spirits and wins market value 234
    earthquake and volcanic eruption 235
    earthquake inception endorsement 236
    electrical apparatus 236
    electronic commerce, e-commerce 237
    electronic data, changes 233
    flood coverage endorsement 239

functional building valuation 240
functional personal property valuation, other than stock....................242
grain properties..243
household personal property coverage..243
leased property 244
legal liability..244
loss payable provisions 244
manufacturer's consequential loss assumption 245
manufacturer's selling price, finished stock 246
market value stock..246
molten material...246
multiple deductible...246
multiple location/premium and dispersion credit application..............247
newly acquired/constructed property - increased limit.......................247
off-premises services, direct damage..247
ordinance or law coverage 248
outdoor trees, shrubs, and plants..249
outside signs 250
peak season limit of insurance 250
pier and wharf additional covered causes of loss 251
pollutant cleanup and removal additional aggregate limit...................251
protective safeguards..252
radio or TV antennas..253
radioactive contamination 253
report of values..254
spoilage coverage 254
sprinkler leakage exclusion...255
sprinkler leakage - earthquake extension...256
storage or repairs limited liability..256
tentative rates...256
terrorism endorsements 257
theft exclusion 257
utility services 257
vacancy changes...257
vacancy permit 258
value reporting form...258
vandalism exclusion 259
water exclusion...259
watercraft exclusion 260
windstorm or hail direct damage...260
windstorm or hail exclusion...261
windstorm or hail percentage deductible 260
your business personal property - separation of coverage...................261
Common policy conditions..107
cancellation..107
changes 108
examination of your books and records...108
inspections and surveys...108
premiums 109
transfer of rights and duties...109
Completed additions 12

Concealment, misrepresentation, or fraud.. 116
    "any other insured" 117
    definition of "void" 116
    material facts 116
    use of building... 116
Concurrent causation exclusions 97
    acts or decisions 98
    inadequate planning, design, etc. 98
    legal doctrine... 97
    weather conditions... 98
Condominium associations form 206
    business personal property.. 208
    "if the agreement requires"... 207
    covered property, six classes... 207
    other provisions 209
Consequential loss 8
Construction types 6
Continuous or repeated seepage of water.. 93
Contributing insurance.. 4
Control of property 111
    protection from the acts of others 111
Coverage extensions 35, 43, 163
    newly acquired or constructed property.. 43
    nonowned detached trailers... 43
    outdoor property.. 43
    personal effects and property of others... 43
    property off-premises 43
    valuable papers and records, cost of research... 43
Coverage extensions, builders risk 136
    building supplies and materials of others... 136
    trees, shrubs, and plants 137
Coverage options, builders risk 140
    builders risk reporting form 140
    building materials of others.. 142
    building renovations... 142
    collapse during construction 141
    separate or subcontractors interest 141
    theft of building materials, etc. 141
Coverage part.. 3
Covered cuases of loss.. 153
Covered property 9
    building.. 9
    business personal property 9
    property of others 9
Covered property, builders risk policy 134
    building materials and supplies.. 134
    building under construction.. 134
    fixtures and machinery... 134
    meaning of "construction" 134
    no coverage for business personal property... 135
    no coverage for property of others... 135

temporary structures 135
Damage by police action 85
Debris removal 37
   additional amount 37, 38
   example 37, 38
   newer, longer definition 37
   no requirement to repair or replace 38
   pollutants 37
   top limit 37
Debris removal coverage and coinsurance provision 37
Debris removal–volunteer expense 38
Defined terms 12
Direct loss or damage 8
Discharge of pollutants 96, 97
   new exception to the exclusion 96
Dishonest or criminal acts exclusion 94
   coverage for destruction by employee 94
   court decisions 94
   limited liability companies 94
Duties of the insured in the event of a loss 119
   eight duties 119-120
   examination under oath 120
"E-Issues" under the CP policy 283
   current policy language 283
   insuring intangible assets 285
   meaning of property 287
   e-property policies 288
Earth movement exclusion 74
   naturally occurring phenomena 74
Electronic data 31, 42, 157, 214
Equipment damaged by a covered peril–spoilage loss consequential 9
Excavation of broken water pipe covered? 28
Exclusions - named peril forms 72
   artificially generated current 80
   concurrent causation 81
   earth movement 74
   governmental action 75
   mechanical breakdown 80
   nuclear hazard 76
   ordinance or law 73
   steam boiler explosion 59
   utility services 76
   war and military action 77
   water 78
Expense to reduce loss 162
Exposure 5
Extended business income 161
Extended loss after operations resume 148, 153
Extended period of indemnity 171
Extension of replacement cost to personal property of others 59
Extra expense coverage form 152

Falling objects...69
    property covered..69
    property not covered 69
Finished stock 155
Fire department service charge...39
    difference from homeowners policy 39
Fire department service charge covered? 39
Firewalls..5
Flood 179
Foundations as property not covered...29
Friendly fire doctrine 58
Fungus, wet rot, dry rot, and bacteria.......................................79, 83, 197, 202
Governmental action exclusion 75
    example of when exclusion applies 75
    example of when exclusion does not apply 75
Green coverage issues..304
Gunshot as explosion..59
Heavy construction and the earth movement exclusion...................................86
Hostile fire 58
Improvements and betterments...19
    different from trade fixtures 21
    recovery for loss under the CP...21, 22
    repairs made by a landlord 22
    repairs made by a tenant-insured 22
    repairs not made 23
    repairs not made, effect of lease 25
Improvements and betterments–coverage dependent on term of lease?.......19
"In the open"..15
Inadequate planning, design, etc. exclusion 97
Increased cost of construction 40
    conditions 42
    example 42
    limit 42
    newly added coverage 42
Indirect loss..8
    spoilage..8
Inflation guard...50
building or personal property 50
example...50
Ingress and egress..178
Inspections and surveys condition..108
    Beverly Hills Supper Club 109
    not a warranty by the insurer 109
Insuring agreement 7
Interruption of computer operations..161, 175
ISO interline terrorism endorsement 291
ISO rules 3
ISO simplified business income program...149
Interstate accounts..4
Is condominuim gutting excluded as an act or decision?...............................303
Lawn tent as a fixture 12

Leasehold interest form 183
    bonus payments 184
    cancellation 185, 187
    causes of loss 185
    exclusions 185
    improvements and betterments 184
    leasehold interest factors 188
    limitations 185
    limits of insurance 186
    loss conditions 187
    schedule form CP 19 60 188
    what is insured 183
Leasehold interest–terms in a lease 185
Legal liability coverage form 211
    additional conditions 212, 219
    amount of insurance 213
    coverage 214
    coverage extensions 215
    ineligible additional insureds 215
    loss conditions 218
    newly acquired property 216
    perils and exclusions 216
    property of others 216
    rules 216
Liberalization condition 219
    example of 219
Limitations under the special form 100
    boilers or water heating equipment 100
    building interiors 100
    building materials 101
    missing property 101
    personal property in a building 100
    steam boilers, pipes, engines, or turbines 100
    transferred property 102
Limited property to specified causes of loss 102
    animals 102
    coverage for specified perils only 102
    fragile articles 102
    owned builders equipment or tools 102
    photographic lenses 103
    valuable papers and records 103
Limits of insurance, builders risk 137
    sublimit on outdoor signs 137
Limits of insurance and deductible 114
    application of deductible 115
    coverage extensions, addition to the limit 114
    preservation of property, within the limit 114
Loss conditions 117
    abandonment and appraisal 117
    duties in the event of a loss 119
    loss payment 121

recovered property...124
vacancy...124
Loss conditions, leasehold interest form 187
   clauses removed 188
   similar to CP policy...188
Loss during foreclosure 191
Loss payment...121
   four options 121
   property of others 121
Losses that happen over a period of time................................88
   animals...88
   coverage for resulting losses 88
   nesting or infestation...88
   settling, cracking, shrinking, or expansion 88
   specified causes of loss 89
   wear and tear, etc...88
   wear and tear, example..89
   wear and tear, purpose of..90
May the exclusion of excavation costs be applied to debris removal?........27
Marble slab as fragile article 103
Maximum period of indemnity...169
Meaning of locations you "own, lease, or operate" 48
Mechanical breakdown exclusion..91
   example of coverage...92
   special form exclusion...92
Mechanical breakdown exclusion and concurrent causation 92
Mercantile or nonmanufacturing risk 146
Missing property–no physical evidence 102
Modular office system as fixture..16
Monthly limit of indemnity 169
Mortgageholders 128
   denial of claim to insured...128
   rights and duties 129
Mortgageholders E&O form..189
   additional conditions 189
   collapse..192
   conditions applicable to all forms 189
   coverage agreements 190
   coverage A - mortgageholder's interest............................190
   coverage B - property owned or held in trust 191
   coverage C - mortgageholder's liability............................192
   coverage D - real estate tax liability 193
   definitions..202
   exclusions 205
   limits of insurance..216
Mortgageholder's E&O - coverage A 190
   causes of loss...190
   covered property..190
   error in obtaining or maintaining insurance.....................190
   property not covered 190
Mortgageholder's E&O - coverage B 191

    limited perils..191
    property owned or held in trust..191
    time limit on coverage..192
Mortgageholder's E&O - coverage C..192
    needed when purchasing own coverage...192
Mortgageholder's E&O - coverage D...193
    real estate tax liability..193
Mortgageholders E&O form, conditions...199
    abandonment...199
    appraisal...199
    duties in the event of loss..199
    insurance under two or more coverages...200
    legal action against the insurer...200
    liberalization..201
    loss payment..201
    other insurance..201
    policy period, territory...201
    transfer of rights of recovery...201
    vacancy...202
    your duties...202
Mortgageholders interest..202
Multiple policies...4
Named perils causes of loss..57
    basic form...58
    broad form..69
Necessary suspension...150
Need for builders risk on renovations to existing buildings....................142
Neglect..97
Newly acquired location...44
Newly acquired or constructed property...44
    business personal property...45
    conditions...45
    limit...45
    time period..45
Nonfunctioning water tower as covered property....................................11
Nonowned detached trailers...49
    limit...50
    reason for new coverage...50
    requirements for coverage..50
Nuclear exclusion..86
Occupancy..5
Open perils exclusions..87
    animals..88
    artificially generated electric current...87
    better covered elsewhere..87
    collapse...90
    continuous or repeated seepage of water...93
    delay, loss of use or market...88
    dishonest or criminal acts...94
    discharge of pollutants...96
    historically uninsurable events...87

    losses that happen over a period of time..88
    mechanical breakdown...90
    neglect 97
    rain, snow, ice or sleet and property in the open................................94
    smoke, vapor, smudging 88
    steam boiler explosion...100
    trick or device...95
    underwriting policy 87
    water, other liquids, powder, molten material 94
Optional coverages 35, 50, 169
    agreed value...50
    extension of replacement cost to personal property of others 50
    inflation guard 51
    replacement cost..52
Ordinance or law exclusion 74
    example of when applied 74
    limited additional coverage 74
Other coverage forms 183
    leasehold interest...183
    mortgageholders E&O..189
    tobacco in sales warehouses..203
    commercial condominium unit-owners..210
    condominium associations 206
    legal liability..211
Other exposures 178
Other insurance condition...118
    example of..119
Other relevant provisions of the CP policy 114
    limits of insurance and deductible 114
Outdoor property..49
    limit 49
    restores coverage 49
Outdoor sprinkler system as underground pipes? 30
Party walls... 122, 138
Period of restoration 151
Permanently installed..13
Personal property of others..25
    account of the owner 26
    coverage extension 35
    need for bailees coverage 46
    personal effects..46
Policy term...3
Pollutant cleanup and removal 40
    annual aggregate amount..40
    costs not covered 40
Pollutant defined...206
Pollution cleanup 40
Premises, meaning of...15
Preservation of property 38
    any direct physical loss 38
Property in transit 105

Property not covered..26
    accounts, bills, etc. 26
    airborne personal property 29
    animals...26
    autos held for sale..27
    bridges, roadways, etc. 27
    bulkheads...29
    contraband 27
    cost of excavations, etc. 27
    cost to replace or restore 31
    electronic data 31
    fences...33
    foundations 28
    grain, hay, etc. 33
    growing crops 29
    land 29
    plants 34
    radio or TV antennas..33
    retaining walls 30
    research costs...31
    satellite dishes 33
    shrubs...33
    specifically described property..30
    trees 30
    underground pipes 30
    vehicles..32
    water 29
    waterborne personal property...30
Property off-premises 48
    limit 48
    stock...48
    where covered 48
Protection 5
Protection class codes..6
    definitions
Reimbursement for expenses to prevent further loss 70
Remodeling as "vandalism" 66
Repeated seepage or leakage 93
Replacement by substitution–commercial property 53
Replacement cost..52
    amount payable 52
    claim procedure 52
    eligible property 52
    ineligible property 52
    "on the same premises"...52
    tenants improvements and betterments 53
Replacement cost–new location 55
Replacement cost–reconditioned property 54
Restaurant closed due to robbery 162
Riot or civil commotion..65
    "Black's Law Dictionary" definition 65

common definition 65
court decisions 65
looting 65
striking employees 65
Schedule form CP 19 60, leasehold interest 188
Separate and subcontractors interest 141
Settling, cracking, shrinking, or expansion 88
decisions favoring insured and insurer 89
Sinkhole collapse 68
cost of filling in 68
definition 68
Sinkhole collapse under CP form 68
Smoke 62
definition of 62
excluded causes 63
product of combustion 62
vapors as smoke 62
Sod, trees, shrubs, and plants 137
Special covered causes of loss 85
additional coverage extensions 104
"all risks", use of 85
assumption of coverage 86
difference from named perils 85
exclusions 87, 88
limitations 100
losses that happen over a period of time 88
open perils exclusions 87
similarities to named perils forms 86
special theft limits 103
Special exclusions 99
Sprinkler leakage 67
automatic sprinkler system 67
cost to repair system 68
cost to tear out and replace structure 68
exclusion endorsement 68
vacancy - no coverage 68
Steam boiler explosion 93
named peril forms exclusion 85
special form exclusion 93
Steam boilers–condition or event inside 100
Structure, defined 11
Subrogation condition 112
waiver of 112
Tarp blown off – damage to roof? 61
Terrorism 291
Terrorism Risk Insurance Act (TRIA) 291
Terrorism Risk Insurance Extension Act 292
Theft 103
special limits 103
Tobacco in sales warehouses 203
additional conditions 205

additional coverages 204
coverage extension 205
covered property 203
deductible 205
definitions 205
exclusions and limitations 205
loss conditions 205
policy term 207
reports by insured 207
Transfer of rights and duties 113
death of the named insured 113
Trick or device exclusion 95
Underwriting 5
Utility services exclusion 76
applies regardless of cause of outage 76
lightning strike off-premises 76
resulting damage 76
Vacancy 124
definition of 124
exemptions 124
handling of losses in vacant building 125
no coverage for sprinkler leakage 125
no coverage for vandalism 125
Valuable papers and records, cost of research 47
limit 47
Valuation 125
exceptions to ACV 125, 126
glass 125
losses under $2,500 125
stock 126
tenants improvements and betterments 126
Valuation and selling price 127
Value of the building on the completion date 133
Valuing business personal property 123
Vandalism
definition 66
exclusion endorsement 72
glass coverage 67
vacancy 67
Virus 43
Volcanic action 69
Voluntary parting with property 95
War exclusion 77
court cases 77
genuine warlike act 78
Water damage 71, 89
Water damage and boarded-up windows 101
Water damage–costs to repair leak even if building is undamaged 72
Water exclusion 78
Water, other liquids, powder, molten material 94
accidental discharge 71

     cost of tearing out and replacing structure..71
     hydrostatic water pressure...79
     narrowing of coverage in 2000 form 72
     repeated leakage 71
     sprinkler system...71, 79
     surface water 78
     sump pump overflow..78
Wear and tear exclusion–damage to shower stall 90
Weather conditions exclusion..98
Weight of ice, snow, or sleet...69
     gutters and downspouts...70
Wind, water and wind-driven water...297
Windstorm or hail...59
     damage to building's interior..60
     direct loss from windstorm, court decisions 59
     frost or cold weather not covered...59
     not included as..59
     percentage deductible..299
     property in poor condition...60
     removal of peril via endorsement...62